Yours for the Revolution

Edited by John Graham

"YOURS FOR THE REVO- LUTION"

The *Appeal to Reason,*

1895–1922

University of Nebraska Press: Lincoln and London

The paper in this book meets the minimum
requirements of American National Standard
for Information Sciences – Permanence of Paper
for Printed Library Materials, ANSI Z39.48-1984

Library of Congress Cataloging in Publication Data

"Yours for the revolution": the Appeal to reason,
1895-1922 / edited by John Graham.

p. cm.

Includes index.

ISBN 0-8032-2111-8. – ISBN 0-8032-7028-3 (pbk.)

1. Appeal to reason (Kansas City, Mo.) – History.
2. American newspapers – History. 3. Press, Communist – United States – History. 4. Press, Socialist –
United States – History. 5. Communism – United
States – History. 6. Socialism – United States – History. I. Graham, John, 1940- . II. Appeal to reason
(Kansas City, Mo.).

HX1.Y66 1990 89-35721 CIP

335.5'05 – dc20

Publication of this book was assisted
by a grant from
The Andrew W. Mellon Foundation.

Who built the seven gates of Thebes?
The books are filled with the names of kings.
Was it kings who hauled the craggy blocks of stone . . .
In the evening when the Chinese wall was finished
Where did the masons go?

Bertolt Brecht

We die with the dying:
See, they depart, and we go with them.
We are born with the dead:
See, they return, and bring us with them. . . .
A people without history
Is not redeemed from time, for history is a pattern
Of timeless moments. . . .
History is now. . . .

T. S. Eliot

In Memoriam: J. A. Wayland, 1854–1912

Contents

Preface

"I received a letter the other day," Jack London wrote in 1905. "It was from a man in Arizona. It began, 'Dear Comrade.' It ended, 'Yours for the revolution.' I replied to the letter, and my letter began, 'Dear Comrade.' It ended, 'Yours for the Revolution.' In the United States there are 400,000 men, of men and women nearly 1,000,000, who begin their letters 'Dear Comrade,' and end them 'Yours for the Revolution.'" Although now almost erased from our collective memory by a national history that has selectively focused on the American character, war, party politics, ideas, and great men to the virtual exclusion of "faceless," "inarticulate" working people and insurgent radicals, those same Americans, native born and immigrant alike, created a revolutionary socialist movement as the twentieth century began. By revolution they meant a fundamental economic, political, and cultural change in the social reality brought about by American capitalism's newly developed industrial and financial order. The electoral agent in the movement for radical change was the Socialist party; its method was to be democratic victory at the polls. However, American socialism was composed of much more than the party itself. The activist counter-institution that propelled the movement, the socialist newspaper that more than any other reveals the movement's life and aspirations, its victories and defeats, its politics, consciousness, and culture was the *Appeal to Reason*.

The industrial transformation of the United States profoundly altered America's landscape and social relations. An agricultural, rural republic immediately following the Civil War, America and its centers of power became predominantly urban by 1900; the population greatly increased and became ethnically enriched as millions of new immigrants entered the country; and an economic elite developed that derived its power from its ownership of banks and credit, mills, railroads, mines, and the massive factories that increasingly became the principal form of production. Monopolies and trusts arose to prevent competition between sometimes opposing interests within the business elite, and the newly powerful corporation, directly as well as indirectly through its influence in federal and state governments, became the instrument to plan and order the nation's economic and political life. The state, in its varied executive, legislative, and judicial capacities, adapted to legitimize American capital's growing dominance, and it adapted as well to oppose insurgent challenges from popular reform and radical movements. Corporate interest was transformed into the national interest in the process, and economic power was translated into political and ideological authority.

No significant sphere of activity was left unaffected by these dramatic alterations in the structure and relations of American life. Agriculturally, as production for local consumption changed to production for national and international consumption, farmers found themselves subordinated to powerful railroads and commodity exchanges over which they had no control. Crop liens and tenant farming increased each decade; deserted farmhouses and unpaid mortgages outnumbered the families who remained in many rural areas; and thousands of migrants wandered a country still resonant with the promise of democratic access to the land or turned to the cities in search of work. In the cities themselves, laborers found that the nature and the meaning of work had changed as face-to-face relations between employer and employee were replaced by routinized division of labor in an instrumentalized factory environment. The exercise of craft and skill, which for generations had given satisfaction and dignity to labor, was everywhere under threat or disappearing. Mechanized assembly-line work supplanted semi-autonomous control over time and the task at hand. The traditional meaning of time itself fractured as it came to be governed by the factory whistle and the speed of automated machinery. Factory discipline and the values of capitalist production—regularity, time-saving thrift, and "industriousness"—became increasingly replicated not only in community institutions and culture but in the texture of family life as well. Everywhere, it seemed, time-honored values and patterns of life were being restructured or destroyed by the expanding market economy.

For many Americans, the sweeping changes in the conditions of life created an awareness of class relations. In the span of a single post–Civil War generation, the 1890 U.S. Census reports, one percent of the population took for itself more of the national wealth than the remaining citizens owned, and the bulk of the population faced daily struggles for economic survival. In a country with both revolutionary and longstanding Christian traditions of social justice, a country in which the recognition that one class of people could not justly be subordinated to another

class was still a reverberating legacy from the Civil War, a significant proportion of Americans took promises of economic as well as political liberty seriously. Millions of citizens did not, in short, passively acquiesce to corporate capitalism's operative denial of egalitarian ideals and opportunities. Those Americans were not the ignored and invisible subjects of our standard history texts, nor were they mere economic beings who were blindly, voicelessly pushed about by vast economic forces they could neither understand nor affect. Instead, resourceful, sometimes rebellious Americans interacted inventively with their varied circumstances and affirmatively made their own history. Throughout the latter years of the nineteenth century, working people refused to become alienated factory operatives and instead organized labor unions; landless tenants and migrants refused to become degraded instruments of a landlord's profit and organized insurgent agricultural movements. As the twentieth century began, the inheritor of many of those democratic strivings was the Socialist party. The principal expression of the socialist movement, the newspaper that introduced socialism into the public discourse, was the *Appeal to Reason*.

No American newspaper has had the character, impact, and indignant fervor of the *Appeal*. Founded by J. A. Wayland and published after 1897 in Girard, Kansas, edited by Wayland and Fred Warren during its most influential years, no left paper in America has mobilized insurgent sentiment as successfully as the *Appeal* or matched its paid circulation and vast readership. During political campaigns and crises, single-issue printings reached as high as 4,100,000 copies —a world record, the paper's staff like to comment, that broke totals the *Appeal* had itself earlier established. If there were working conditions or a strike to publicize in West Virginia, Colorado, or California, the *Appeal* was there; if Milwaukee, Wisconsin, and Schenectady, New York, voted the Socialist ticket, *Appeal* correspondents reported the victories; if states were without their own socialist papers, the *Appeal* printed individual state editions; if capitalist muck needed to be raked in Chicago, Fred Warren suggested a novel about the meatpacking industry to

Upton Sinclair, sent him an advance to write it, and then serialized *The Jungle* in the *Appeal*. The *Appeal* had a profound effect on America during its nearly thirty years of publication.

The *Appeal*'s fundamental purpose was twofold: "to war against oppression and vast wrongs, dispelling the tears, the blood, the woe of Capitalism," and to imbue Americans with actively egalitarian, nonexploitative values. If voters could be made to understand that capitalism functioned by denying workers the full product of their labor, that socialism would permit a just distribution of the nation's wealth and opportunities and create the conditions for human freedom to flourish, capitalism and its political superstructure could be voted out of existence. As a mass-circulation newspaper during a period when the printed word had much greater power than presently, the *Appeal* battled effectively against American capital's growing control over national consciousness. The only radical newspaper distributed in many areas of the United States, the *Appeal* brought non-capitalist news and culture to millions of Americans.

The *Appeal* irregularly maintained a woman's column, published Karl Marx, Friedrich Engels, John Ruskin, William Morris, Edward Bellamy, Charlotte Perkins Gilman, Jack London, William Dean Howells, Kate Richards O'Hare, Eugene Debs, Tom Paine (an earlier propagandist for "common sense" and "an appeal to reason"), as well as the poems and personal reports of literally thousands of less well-known and now unremembered Americans. The editorial policy of "Tell the *Appeal*" meant that substantial parts of many issues of the paper were written by citizens widely dispersed throughout the United States. Much more than simply a newspaper, the *Appeal* was a participatory counterinstitution that actively represented the socialist movement. The *Appeal* sent out its own socialist propaganda vans and organizers, sponsored study clubs, socialist schools, and speaking tours. Prior to World War I, the paper's staff coordinated an *Appeal* Army of 80,000 agitators who sold subscriptions to the *Appeal*, dropped extra copies at union halls and train stations, wrote newspaper editors and congresspeople to protest or support impending legislation, and participated in national and local political struggles. "The *Appeal* is yours for the revolution," J. A. Wayland wrote to the socialist movement. In turn, the men and women who composed that movement fought for the *Appeal* as their own.

Although never an official vehicle for the Socialist party, the *Appeal* was nevertheless dependent on its fate. When Socialists and other elements of the domestic left opposed America's participation in World War I, the opportunity to suppress American radicalism arose. Accusing the left of lack of patriotism and of impeding the war effort, corporate capitalism and federal and state governments crushed radical movements with a ferocity never seen before or since in America. By 1921, anarchists were either jailed or deported; some five thousand men and women had been arrested in a single federal sweep; the Industrial Workers of the World was shattered and its leaders murdered, imprisoned, or exiled; and the Socialist party, its leadership also in prison and its energy focused on defensive battles, was destroyed for generations as a vital force in American life. The *Appeal* was federally censored during World War I, temporarily compelled to support the American war effort, and then, its vitality broken, it dissolved in 1922.

Ten years earlier, as the January 5, 1912, issue of the *Appeal to Reason* was being made up, Charles L. Phifer, a columnist and associate editor of the paper, paused in the commotion of his work to reflect on the *Appeal*. As usual, thousands of letters from readers had been sent to the paper's office in Girard that week telling of injustice, of suffering, of privations borne and resisted in dignity and self-respect. A small number of those letters had been set in type, but even those few had to be cut for lack of space. Watching them disappear, Phifer wrote, made him "fill up." Phifer had worked for thirty-two years in city and country newspaper offices, ever since he had escaped from the woolen mills as a boy to become a printer's apprentice, but he had never seen a paper like the *Appeal*. "The *Appeal* is not as good as it ought to be," he wrote.

It is crude—I know it. It isn't "literary" or pretty. But it touches souls every week. Sometimes I stand in awe of the fact, sensing the deeper and unexpressed forces and feelings of a nation, of a world, surge upon me, calling for outlet; and if I thought I did justice to it I should realize I was inadequate for the position. I like literature; I like art; but sometimes I think the Appeal, *harsh and ugly as it is, partial as it is and must be, is, after all, the truest literature of the day, tracing the richest art of the soul, and that future bibliographs will go through its files to catch the spirit of an awakening people speaking in broken sentences through it.*

The *Appeal to Reason* is all of that, and now, decades after it ceased publication, it can be more than a monument to an awakened, emancipatory impulse from our national history. "Every image of the past that is not recognized by the present as one of its own concerns threatens to disappear irretrievably," Walter Benjamin writes. It is in this sense, which is not an idle matter of antiquarian knowledge or of our looking backward nostalgically at a ghost walking the streets of forgotten towns, that the *Appeal* can enter our contemporary world to speak directly to us in its own words. Upon its entrance, the idea of the past as "long ago" is transformed by the joining of past and present into what is always the current situation. Then we are no longer permitted to merely observe the *Appeal* and the awakening community of people whose lives and voices it expressed. Instead, they appear, in their own images, to question with us our claims to progress, to probe our strivings and our passivity, to judge the freedom and the possibilities of our present way of life.

ONE

The *Appeal to Reason*

"Gee, I ain't seen a paper in three weeks."

"I like to read the paper, too," said Mac. "I like to know what's goin' on in the world."

"A lot of lies most of it . . . all owned by the interests."

"Hearst's on the side of the people."

"I don't trust him any more'n the rest of 'em."

"Ever read *The Appeal to Reason*?"

"Say, are you a Socialist?"[1]—John Dos Passos, *The 42nd Parallel*

Mac was a socialist and so were millions of other Americans during the first two decades of the twentieth century. Now nearly hidden by a selectively written national history, the *Appeal to Reason* was more closely identified with the socialist movement than any other paper. Published from 1895 to 1922, the *Appeal* preceded the formation of the Socialist party in 1901 and, more than any other socialist institution, gave ongoing life, power, and a sense of community to insurgent radicals. No paper more effectively articulated and politicized American dissent than the *Appeal*, nor did any other paper, regardless of its politics, circulate as widely throughout the United States. Cheap even at the turn of the century at fifty cents a year, twenty-five cents for clubs of four or more subscribers, the weekly *Appeal* cost ten cents for a three-month trial subscription. Published after 1897 in Gir-

ard, Kansas, the *Appeal* reached a paid circulation of over 760,000 in 1913, a figure that not only dwarfed the circulation of all but a few popular periodicals at the time, but one that remains a record among left publications in America. The *Appeal* succeeded at a time when there was a real option to capitalism in America, a time when people spoke of the cooperative commonwealth and the coming nation with hope, expectation, and meaning. Week after week, year after year, the *Appeal to Reason* was the single most influential expression of the socialist demand for a just, egalitarian world.

The story of the *Appeal* begins with its founder, Julius Augustus Wayland. The "One Hoss Editor" was born in Versailles, Indiana, on April 26, 1854, the youngest of seven children. Four months afterward a cholera epidemic took the lives of his father and four brothers and sisters and left the surviving family members to contend unevenly with poverty. Wayland spent less than two years in school (later, remembering when he started writing for his first paper, he said that he "did not know a noun from a verb"), and at sixteen was hired as a printer's apprentice at the *Versailles Gazette*. Wayland learned press work and typesetting, moved on to neighboring newspapers, worked as a tramp printer until 1872, and then returned to Indiana and bought the *Gazette* with an-

Masthead of the *Coming Nation* during Fred D. Warren's editorship in Rich Hill, Missouri, September 26, 1903. Courtesy University of Colorado Historical Collections.

18,236

New Subs since July 1st on Van 3. Boost it to 25,000. The Van is needed at the Front.

COMING

FRED D. WARREN, Editor.
E. N. RICHARDSON, Ass't Editor.

No. 499

This paper is sent to no one after expiration of subscription.

Rich H

EXTRA

PROGRESS can have no end.

FREEDOM is not a purchasable thing.

NEVER lie to yourself. It doesn't pay, and you're sure to get caught at it.

THE most abject slave on earth is the man who is a slave to his prejudices.

THE boss's profit is the difference between what you earn and

IF you watch the daily press you will notice that the number of women going to Paris in search of the latest thing in gowns and bonnets are about equal to the number who commit suicide because of poverty—poverty due, not because there is not enough wealth produced but because under the crazy capitalistic "divide up" system under which we live there is too much.

I MET a republican politician the other day who assured me he had been reading up on Socialism and was convinced we were right. "As soon as you get a little stronger I'll be with you," said this wily politician. And herein lies the danger

ator Spooner u away in a recent he advocated a president and lo gressmen. Let s selves that the c to get off the ba without a strugg

A FRIEND w the working peo leader." That the matter with they have submi too long alread year out they ha against their ow their bosses or t workers must g leadership idea

other printer. Eighteen months later, Wayland became its sole owner and made the paper a success. After marrying Etta Bevan in 1877, he edited a series of partisan newspapers (at the time, newspapers were commonly funded by political parties), and temporarily obtained a local postmastership from President Rutherford Hayes's administration. A radical Republican newspaperman, Wayland and his editorial politics made enemies. Once a mob "roped him round the neck and talked lynching"; another time he faced down a sheriff who had already killed several men.[2]

In 1882 Wayland moved to Pueblo, Colorado, a booming industrial and mining center before the national depression of the early and mid–1890s, and with two associates began a small newspaper. When it failed, he put on his printer's apron again and established Wayland's One-Hoss Print Shop, an identification he would retain long after the *Appeal to Reason*'s sophisticated printing facilities were the equal of all but a few of the largest metropolitan dailies. It was also in Pueblo that Wayland developed a talent for

real estate speculation. After buying a building to house his printing operation, he was offered two thousand dollars more than his purchase price and he took it. Wayland extended the simple process to other property and, when he left Colorado in 1893, had amassed some eighty thousand dollars in gold and government bonds. Wayland's profits proved to be an easy way to support his growing family and, ultimately, to begin his socialist newspapers.

Wayland discovered socialism in Pueblo. In 1890, he recalled later, "I incidently fell into conversation about some strikes on the railroads, with William Bradford, an English shoemaker, who gave me a pamphlet to read on the subject, from the economic or Socialist viewpoint."

To be brief, he "landed" me good and hard. He carefully nursed me into reading Carlyle, Ruskin, Gronlund and other works, and I realized for the first time that I was an ignoramus. I got interested and read rapidly.

I saw a new light and found what I never knew ex-

THE NATION

PUBLISHED EVERY SATURDAY. 50c. PER YEAR.
IN CLUBS OF FOUR, AND OVER, 25c PER YEAR.

Saturday, September 26, 1903   Entered June 14, 1901, as second-class matter P.O.Rich Hill,Mo.,act of congress, March 3,1879   **Tenth Year**

e it
hich
for
con-
em-
oing
kers

Vhat
rong
t is
day,
led"
and
vote
r by
The
this
h be

To Spend $100,000
To Defeat Carey !

You will remember reading in the Coming Nation of March 21st, the Washington tele-gram announcing the fight which the National Republican Committee had inaugurated against our Massachusetts comrades. The republicans, assisted by the democrats, have made good their word, so far as arrogant wealth can dam the irresistable tide of progress.
Here is a letter from Comrade Fred E. Irish, assistant state secretary of Massachusetts:

BOSTON, MASS., Sept. 19th, 1903.

---

isted. I closed up my real estate business and devoted my whole energies to the work of trying to get my neighbors to grasp the truths I had learned.[3]

Laurence Gronlund's The Cooperative Commonwealth (1884), the first significant exposition of Marxian theory by an American socialist, explained labor theory of value, competition and overproduction, the futility of reformist remedies, class relations, and the nature of the state in clear, noncapitalist terms. Wayland returned to Edward Bellamy's utopian novel of a socialist future, Looking Backward (copies of which he would give time and time again to people seeking political understanding), read socialist theorist John Ruskin with admiration, and reentered political life with new knowledge and purpose. Finding that the New York–based Socialist Labor party had little or no influence in Pueblo and had allied itself there with the People's party, Wayland did likewise. He believed that the populist movement, still in its authentic form in the early 1890s, would eventually lead to socialism. "The small farmers are going to get there," Wayland wrote,

"and I want to say that the Socialist platform will be carried into effect by the same Populists."[4]

Wayland's urge to begin a socialist newspaper was growing stronger, and he sensed that economic depression was imminent. He sold his real estate and left Colorado for Greensburg, Indiana, where he published the first issue of the Coming Nation in April, 1893. Wayland doubted whether it would succeed. "My ideal then was a circulation of 10,000 a week. That sounded very large to me. I knew I had enough money to run it several years even if it did not pay."[5] Wayland and his family were ostracized in Greensburg, but the Coming Nation was successful almost immediately. In six months' time the paper had 14,000 subscribers; nine months later that figure had risen to 60,000, and the Coming Nation was the most widely circulated socialist newspaper in America.

The Coming Nation was similar in form to the earliest issues of the Appeal. The first of the paper's four pages characteristically contained Wayland's commentary and observations. Wayland had an extraordinary ability to compress complex social and eco-

"Home of the *Coming
Nation,* Greensburg, Ind.,
1893. From J. A. Wayland,
Leaves of Life, (Girard,
Kan.: *Appeal to Reason,*
1912).

Mailing room employees of
the *Appeal to Reason,* ca.
1908. Courtesy Special
Collections, Pittsburgh
State University Library.

nomic issues into evocative prose. Works by Gronlund, Bellamy, Ruskin, Thomas Carlyle, and less well known socialist essayists and poets were reprinted in the *Coming Nation,* but writings of Marx and Engels were not. Wayland, in fact, had not read them in the early 1890s. Instead, he placed the new paper directly in the mainstream of the broad Reform movement. The *Coming Nation* supported both the People's party and the Socialist Labor party. Wayland, regardless of his advocacy of socialism, was more attracted to the grass-roots power of populism than to the hierarchical Socialist Labor party controlled by Daniel DeLeon. Wayland's primary purpose was to convert readers to socialism, not engage in partisan battles which would divide the growing insurgent movement into sectarian factions and weaken its effects.

As the *Coming Nation* reached a circulation far greater than its country editor had permitted himself to hope for, Wayland planned another enterprise—a self-sufficient, socialist community. Income from the *Coming Nation* exceeded costs, and it was money he wished to return to the socialist movement. The Ruskin colony, located on 2000 acres bought by Wayland north of Tennessee City, Tennessee, established to provide "every convenience that the rich enjoy, permanent employment at wages higher than ever dreamed of by laborers, with all the advantages of good schools, free libraries, natatoriums, gymnasiums, lecture halls and pleasure grounds,"[6] represented a utopian attempt on Wayland's part to live a socialist life in a capitalist United States. The *Coming Nation* was to be the Ruskin colony's central institution. Income from the paper and job printing would be put in a common fund from which all colonists would draw their pay. Wayland was aware that previous communities had usually failed to survive in America, but he believed that socialists living in a cooperative atmosphere could make Ruskin a model of human possibility. "One practical success," he wrote, "showing that men can live and love in peace and plenty, will do more toward bringing the Brotherhood of Man than a thousand speakers."[7]

Wayland published the last issue of the *Coming*

Nation in Greensburg on July 21, 1894, moved the paper and its presses to Tennessee four days later, and discovered almost immediately that he was not a communitarian at heart. Nor was the colony's atmosphere one of utopian harmony. The rocky, wooded land Wayland's Tennessee agent had purchased was little better than forbidding. Newly constructed accommodations were rough—many no more than shanties. In addition to the disagreements predictable among some one hundred colonists, most of whom had not known each other before arriving, the problems of publishing weekly issues of the *Coming Nation* exacerbated tension. Divisive economic questions arose as well.

In Wayland's version of events, he deeded his land to the Ruskin Co-operative Association and made out a bill of sale for the *Coming Nation,* its books, and its cash on hand. Certain of Wayland's opponents in the colony, however, reported that he never gave over control of the paper. Precisely what occurred is shrouded in conflicting accounts,[8] but Wayland and his family departed from Ruskin in July, 1895, while the *Coming Nation* remained with the colonists. "As soon as I find a suitable location and create a medium for my pen," Wayland wrote in his final editorial, "you will find my little banner in the thickest of the fight for economic liberty."[9] A month later Wayland had located himself in Kansas City, Missouri. The medium for his pen was the *Appeal to Reason.*

As Wayland began publication of the *Appeal* on August 6, 1895, he was 41. His romance with communitarianism was over. A reserved man often at odds with the confident J. A. Wayland who appeared in print, the private Wayland would have preferred to publish the *Appeal* anonymously had postal laws permitted. The Wayland who appeared in print was not simply a persona, for Wayland exposed his emotional life considerably more than was customary for a turn-of-the-century American male, but the public J. A. Wayland was far different from the man who traveled under the pseudonym J. A. Wilson, who attended socialist conventions anonymously and unrecognized, and who, except in rare instances, was too embarrassed to speak from a public rostrum. Tall, thin, quiet

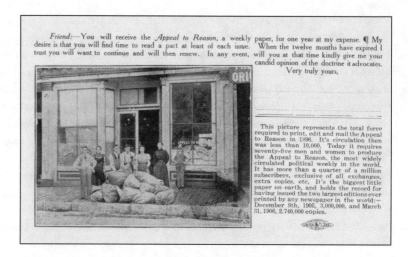

Friend:—You will receive the *Appeal to Reason*, a weekly paper, for one year at my expense. ¶ My desire is that you will find time to read a part at least of each issue. When the twelve months have expired I trust you will want to continue and will then renew. In any event, will you at that time kindly give me your candid opinion of the doctrine it advocates.

Very truly yours,

This picture represents the total force required to print, edit and mail the Appeal to Reason in 1896. It's circulation then was less than 10,000. Today it requires seventy-five men and women to produce the Appeal to Reason, the most widely circulated political weekly in the world. It has more than a quarter of a million subscribers, exclusive of all exchanges, extra copies, etc. It's the biggest little paper on earth, and holds the record for having issued the two largest editions ever printed by any newspaper in the world:— December 9th, 1905, 3,000,000, and March 31, 1906, 2,740,000 copies.

Postcard mailed to recipients of *Appeal to Reason* subscriptions in 1907. Courtesy University of Colorado Historical Collections.

in manner, his sandy hair turned gray in his forties, reticent about important areas of his personal life, Wayland put the socialist movement before fame or self-aggrandizement. Only rarely did he depart from his refusal to have his photograph taken.

Wayland knew about economic and emotional uncertainty, about poverty from his days as a child and young newspaperman, and he had as well a wife and five children dependent upon him for support. Nor was he a stranger to self-doubt and melancholy. "There have been many dark hours—days and months of them together," Wayland would write in 1906. "I have walked the floor many a night; I have walked the silent woods and lonely railroad tracks with feelings akin to suicide; the rest would be so sweet; what a relief to end it all. And then I would busy myself in work to forget the troubles and losses. I kept on."[10] Wayland kept on to end the madness of capitalism: "If every conscious Socialist will only do his share in the work of agitation, we will soon have the children out of the factories, the sweat-shops out of business, the capitalist out of existence and the people out of misery. The Cause is worth all you have."[11]

Unlike the *Coming Nation,* the *Appeal to Reason* did not quickly find a significant readership. Initially his own editor, typesetter, and business manager, Wayland first moved the *Appeal* from Missouri to Kansas City, Kansas, and then, after a several month suspension, to Girard, a small county seat of some

twenty-five hundred inhabitants in the southeast corner of Kansas. Each move was an attempt to save on expenses, but the *Appeal* was hindered more by the national political climate of the late 1890s than by excessive costs. The populist movement was dying in slow stages, the Socialist party was not yet born and, shortly after Wayland had built the *Appeal*'s circulation up to 45,000, an outbreak of patriotic frenzy arising from the Spanish-American War reduced circulation to 22,000. At one point in 1899 Wayland was a week away from suspending publication altogether. Thereafter, although circulation periodically fluctuated and during certain periods the paper was forced to accept advertising, the *Appeal* operated on its income from subscriptions.

The first years of the twentieth century were transitional ones for the *Appeal*. The 1896 elections, which brought the People's party into fusion with the Democrats and sealed populism's defeat, had led the *Appeal* into direct support of the Socialist Labor party. The paper supported Eugene V. Debs and the Social Democracy movement in the 1900 elections, and when the Socialist party formed in 1901, the *Appeal* committed itself to the new party. The paper's growth brought Wayland satisfaction—by 1900 the *Appeal* reached 100,000 subscribers—but it was a satisfaction tempered by the death of his wife from cancer in 1898. Wayland took on a significant part of the responsibility of raising his children, and he gave over certain of the paper's tasks to newly hired staffers. A new business manager, E. W. Dodge, began to adapt mainstream publishing strategies to the *Appeal*—advertising and subscription contests, for example—and by 1902 the *Appeal*'s circulation of 150,000 was the fourth highest of any weekly in America. In 1900, moreover, Fred D. Warren joined the paper.

The *Appeal* was at its strongest and most influential during Warren's editorship and association with Wayland. The Socialist party made its most dramatic gains during the Wayland-Warren years, and the *Appeal* was essential to the party's growth and effect. Far from being a psychoreligious, chiliastic movement, the evidence is clear that the great majority of Socialist party members chose their politics for objective reasons.[12] A single factor in that choice is dominant. A 1908 national survey found that 52 percent of the rank and file discovered socialism through reading; James Green's recent analysis of 495 *Appeal* subscription salespeople and agitators reveals that 74 percent converted to socialism through reading and study.[13] The *Appeal* had the largest circulation of any radical paper in the United States, and in many areas of the country it was the only radical paper available. The *Appeal* was read and passed on to friends and neighbors week after week.

Born in 1872 in Arcola, Illinois, Fred Warren had a midwestern background similar to Wayland's. Warren's father's grain business failed in the Panic of 1873, and the family moved to Rich Hill, Missouri, a small coal- and zinc-mining town. At eighteen, with his younger brother Ben, Warren began a Republican newspaper. When it succumbed in 1893 to the depression, Warren returned to job printing. After being converted to socialism by discussion and reading, Warren became publisher and editor of the socialist *Bates County Critic* in 1898. Short and slight in stature, moral and uncompromising in his outlook, superintendent of the local Methodist Sunday School, Warren abhorred social injustice. Warren came to the *Appeal* as a printer with his brother Ben and E. N. Richardson, a socialist staffer from the *Critic*, and in 1901 became managing editor. The next year a dispute occurred between Ben Warren and Charles Breckon, the *Appeal*'s labor editor, and the Warren brothers and Richardson returned to Rich Hill. There, with the Ruskin colony and the *Coming Nation* having both collapsed, they picked up the paper's subscription list and brought the *Coming Nation* back to life. Early in 1904, seeking to bring Warren back as managing editor and consolidate the *Coming Nation* with the *Appeal,* Wayland bought the *Coming Nation* for five thousand dollars and the Warren brothers and Richardson returned to Girard. Contemplating the return of his first socialist paper, it seemed to Wayland as though his child had come back after years away from home. "I feel a delight and relief that I have not felt in years," he wrote.[14]

At the *Appeal* as well as nationally, much had changed since Warren's first days in Girard. Wayland viewed the *Appeal* as the expression of the new socialist movement, and he had hired Ernest Untermann to define the paper's socialism more "scientifically." Untermann had translated Marx into English, and he not only stengthened Wayland's theoretical understanding but, as managing editor and columnist, he gave a more explicitly Marxian structure to the *Appeal*'s analysis of events as well. Additionally, the autumn before Warren returned to Girard, a strike was provoked at the paper by working conditions and by Wayland's gift of one thousand dollars to the Socialist party.

Socialists themselves, the paper's staff understood that they were not paid full value for their labor, and they knew that control of the paper ultimately rested with Wayland. Wayland was perfectly aware that his ownership of the *Appeal* was at odds with socialist principles, but after his unhappy experience with the *Coming Nation,* he was unable to devise a collective ownership structure for the *Appeal* that did not threaten his conception of the paper's purpose and future direction. The pressure from these contradictions erupted in October, 1903, when all but four of the fifty people working at the *Appeal* formed a union (until that time only the paper's printers had been unionized) and struck. Wayland agreed to the new local's demand for personnel changes and increased wages, sought to turn over the *Appeal* to the Socialist party (prevented by a clause prohibiting publication of a party newspaper), and ultimately decided against democratizing ownership of the *Appeal*. The consequences of that decision would dramatically influence the paper's course in the years to come.

Fred Warren, with advice and encouragement from Wayland, brought the *Appeal* into a twentieth century increasingly different from the 1890s. Widespread popular discontent, as well as a general sense that capitalism's new economic and political arrangements were susceptible to change, mobilized a variety of progressive forces. Both reformist and radical unions organized working people at a dramatically increased pace, and the new trusts and corporations were met with resistance and strikes. Tentatively at first, and then with an extraordinary burst of power, muckraking journalists exposed corruption and gave the press a political influence unimagined a decade before. The power of the printed word in turn-of-the-century America is difficult to overestimate: in the absence of competing media, newspapers and periodicals were the hegemonic means of understanding an America dramatically more isolated than today's. At the same time, advances in printing and press technology made mass-circulation newspapers a reality for publishers. Socialists at the *Appeal* believed their paper could become the vehicle to carry their vision of a just American commonwealth throughout the United States. Like Tom Paine's earlier appeal to reason, the *Appeal* could be made a national influence for the economic and political order to reckon with.

Wayland and Warren determined that rather than simply reporting significant news, the *Appeal* would become an activist institution representing its readers and the socialist movement. The paper would make events happen and alter the course of others. Warren simultaneously decided to build circulation—to 500,000 or even 1,000,000 copies—to give the *Appeal* a readership that would make it a radical counterinstitution with a real measure of power in America. The socialist movement needed an inexpensive, mass-circulation newspaper to legitimize and define its life, and Americans needed an alternative to cap-italist-defined news stories and commentary. The decision to chart an activist course for the *Appeal,* to engage directly in political battles, proved necessary; as the *Appeal*'s circulation and influence increased, attempts to suppress the paper were inevitable. By 1912 all of the *Appeal* editors had been indicted, some several times, and hardly a year passed without threats to the paper's existence.

The first federal attempt to suppress the *Appeal* occurred during 1901, when the U.S. Post Office sought to halt the paper's growth and agitational effect. In 1901 the *Appeal*'s circulation averaged some 150,000, many of whom were "chance purchasers." Many subscribers ordered extra copies of the *Appeal* to distribute in their neighborhoods and at public places; other readers paid subscription costs for friends or designated readers; and still others sent in extra subscription money for the *Appeal* to choose its own beneficiaries of a year of socialist commentary. "Chance copies" were crucial if the socialist movement was to reach the unconverted and expand. When Third Assistant Postmaster General Edwin C. Madden ruled that bundles of the *Appeal* could not be mailed at second-class rates (a common and inexpensive practice for all newspapers at the time), Warren succeeded in having the ruling overturned, only to be met by a new threat. Unless it could be proven within ten days' time that the *Appeal*'s subscribers had paid for their paper with their own money, the Post Office would take away the paper's second-class permit altogether. In eight days, the *Appeal* obtained sixty-eight thousand subscriber signatures, saved its permit, and learned that it could rely on its readership in an emergency. The victory established a pattern that the paper followed throughout its years of publication. The *Appeal* gave front-page publicity to its battles with federal authorities and simultaneously mobilized its readers to write their congressmen and newspapers in support of what superficially appeared to be a defenseless weekly in an out-of-the-way Kansas town. The unity between the *Appeal* and its readers was essential. The *Appeal* became a movement paper, one that socialists identified as

Third Girard home of the
Appeal to Reason and
staff, 1905. Courtesy
Special Collections,
Pittsburgh State University
Library.

Clerical staff, *Appeal to
Reason,* 1908. Courtesy
Special Collections,
Pittsburgh State University
Library.

theirs to support and save, one that articulated, fought, and won socialist battles.

As the Socialist party grew in influence, and as the circulation of the *Appeal* increased, harassment and threats of censorship increased as well. The announcement in 1903 of a one-million copy Populist edition, designed to attract ex–People's party supporters to socialism, brought a Post Office directive that the *Appeal* could mail no more extra copies than its number of subscribers, but Wayland disregarded the threat and the government chose not to press the issue. Local postmasters, at times it seemed from throughout the United States, destroyed or refused to deliver copies of the paper. In 1906, when Eugene V. Debs wrote in the *Appeal* that if Western Federation of Miners leaders Bill Haywood and Charles Moyer were sentenced to death by an Idaho court, "a million revolutionists, at least will meet [capital and the state] with guns,"[15] the paper was banned from the Canadian mails for its "seditious" character. Warren, in concert with publicity generated by the *Appeal* in Canadian reform and socialist papers, was successful in having the ban lifted. However, the U.S. Post Office soon renewed its prohibition against mailing more copies than there were subscribers when the *Appeal* published a three-million-copy Rescue Edition publicizing the Moyer-Haywood case. The paper lost circulation until thousands of protests from readers and *Appeal* publicity again succeeded in reversing the order, but the paper's commitment to the Western Federation of Miners and its leadership gave the *Appeal* an unequaled reputation as the foremost print advocate of socialist and radical labor causes.

Warren's and Wayland's redefinition of the *Appeal* led not only to a politically activist role for the paper but to investigative stories and articles written exclusively for *Appeal* readers. Newly hired writers reported on a broad range of issues: rural and metropolitan poverty, legislative and judicial corruption, labor battles, immigration, child labor, the white slave trade, even at times conditions in Mexico, Nicaragua, Honduras, and European countries. The paper grew to eight and often twelve pages containing socialist and labor stories, Wayland's commentary, socialist

parables, national news stories, political essays and excerpts from socialist classics, as well as poetry and fiction. The *Appeal* became more alive and vital than ever.

The most famous of the paper's new features was the serialized appearance of Upton Sinclair's *The Jungle*. Warren had read Sinclair's Civil War novel, *Manassas,* and late in 1904 approached Sinclair with the idea for a novel about a different group of exploited slaves, the immigrant workers in the Chicago meat packing houses. With five hundred dollars advanced by the *Appeal,* Sinclair spent seven weeks investigating and living among packing house workers, and then began a new "Uncle Tom's Cabin" about Chicago's wage slaves. The novel's effect upon the *Appeal*'s 1905 readership, two to three times greater than its 150,000 to 175,000 subscribers, made *The Jungle* a *cause célèbre* even before it appeared in book form the following year.

The Jungle was the most famous piece of literature to appear in the *Appeal,* but the best known of the new writers hired by Wayland and Warren was Eugene Victor Debs. Socialist candidate for President, Debs was more public figure than writer, but he wrote scores of articles for the *Appeal* after his arrival in Girard in January, 1907. Debs represented the Socialist party and the socialist movement nationally. His association with the *Appeal*—formally comprised of writing for the paper and speaking under its auspices on *Appeal* lecture tours, informally by his presence and participation in the Girard community of socialists— helped give the *Appeal* its public identity as the primary voice of the socialist movement.

Apart from the Socialist party itself, the *Appeal* was the most important socialist institution in America during the century's first decade. Often the *Appeal*'s presence and effects were more far-reaching than the party's. With Bill Haywood publicly associated more with the Industrial Workers of the World than with the Socialist party, Wayland, Warren, and Debs were the most famous Socialists in the United States. During non-election years particularly, the *Appeal* provided the excitement, vitality, and the continuity the socialist movement needed. Week after week, the *Appeal* was the dominant force linking the dispersed socialist community together. The only truly national socialist paper, the most widely read left periodical in American history, the *Appeal* inspired readers with its success, bold headlines, investigations, battles, and victories. Its ongoing appearance legitimized socialism in particular and radicalism in general. The *Appeal* helped create a culture of resistance that gave life and energy to the socialist movement.

To create that culture, to make the *Appeal* more than simply a newspaper, Warren and Wayland established forms through which readers could support and participate in the *Appeal*'s life as a movement institution. The paper sent out its own socialist organizers; it sponsored Study Clubs and supplied literature; and it established a widespread Agitation League with special funds to propagate socialism and send copies of the *Appeal* to school teachers, union members, state and federal legislators, as well as to newspaper editors throughout the United States. The *Appeal*'s Lecture Bureau sent Debs, Warren, Ryan Walker (the paper's political illustrator), and other socialists on speaking engagements for which the price of admission was a year's subscription to the paper. For some fifteen to twenty state Socialist party organizations without the means to print their own newspaper, the *Appeal* printed individual state editions. At a time when working people often were denied access to a local paper, the *Appeal* commonly flooded strike districts with special editions and favorable publicity. As a movement paper, moreover, the paper's columns were open to first-hand accounts by strikers. Substantial portions of many, many issues were written by American men and women who were otherwise unknown, and the paper's policy of "Tell the *Appeal*" gave its pages unusual diversity, excitement, and access to the lives of working people.

The *Appeal* also developed a Salesmen Army of agitators and propagandists who sold subscriptions to the paper and distributed extra copies at public meetings, in barbershops and union halls, on trains and street corners, on porches and doorsteps, wherever the *Appeal* could be read and socialism encountered. Like the *Appeal* itself, the Salesmen Army was

a phenomenon like nothing else in American publishing or radical history: at its high point in 1913, the Army had grown to 80,000 activists, nearly all of whom could be reached in two days' time when necessary.[16] The Army helped to build the subscription lists necessary to support the *Appeal* and its projects financially, but it was also an organized force that fought for socialism and for the paper as its expression. In election after election the number of state and local *Appeal* subscriptions corresponded directly to Socialist voting strength.

As the *Appeal* Army grew over the years, it gained its own coordinator and editor, first E. N. Richardson and then Grace Brewer, as well as its own column in the paper. Most Army members worked in their own communities selling subscriptions and distributing bundle-rate *Appeals*. Others, like Louis Klamroth, took the paper on the road where for years he supported himself by selling radical books, pamphlets, and *Appeals,* despite being "arrested twenty-nine times for street speaking, driven out of twenty-five places, prohibited from speaking in forty places, being egged twenty times, knocked down and clubbed, hose turned on him, and buckets of water thrown on him."[17] The Army distributed *Appeals* during Socialist campaigns and supported the paper year after year. When the Post Office imposed chance copy restrictions, for example, *Appeal* agitators doubled and redoubled their efforts to keep necessary subscriptions coming in. Similarly, when the anti-radical Penrose Bill proposed in 1908 to exclude periodicals from second-class mail privileges if the postmaster general so decided, the *Appeal* called on Army members to flood their congressmen with protests. After the Bill was defeated in committee, the *Appeal* reported that members of the Senate and House had been deluged with protests against the Bill from every state in the union. The *Appeal* Army acted because the *Appeal* was their paper; it represented their lives and hopes.

The *Appeal* was in healthy condition as the 1910s began. Both Socialist party membership and the paper's circulation were on the rise. Despite the short-term effects of postal edicts, the *Appeal* had steadily increased its circulation and subscription lists to

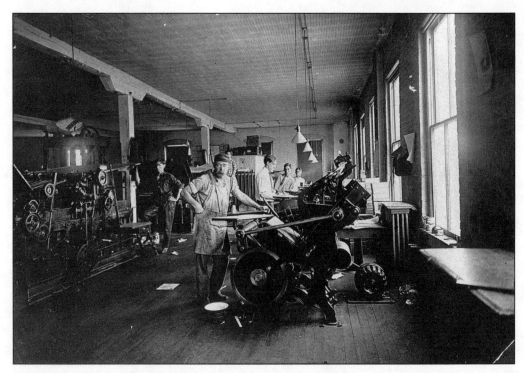

Presses of the *Appeal to Reason,* 1908. Courtesy Special Collections, Pittsburgh State University Library.

275,000 in February, 1907, 477,000 in January, 1911, and by May, 1912, over 500,000 for the first time. The paper had continuously improved its publishing capabilities, and in 1912 occupied its fourth and largest building in Girard. The *Appeal* had become Girard's largest employer. Slightly more than one hundred people (some one-third of whom were women) worked forty-seven-hour weeks under model union conditions. Wayland also believed in buying the best presses available; in emergencies the huge three-deck Goss was capable of printing and folding forty-five thousand papers an hour. The normal rate was more on the order of twenty thousand an hour, a figure that yielded some five hundred thousand papers a day, yet even that was hardly enough for the big editions totalling two million to four million copies. Looming over the activity and optimism at the *Appeal,* however, were dark clouds.

In 1907, seeking to publicize the secretive "kidnapping" and transport of Western Federation of Miners leaders from Colorado to an Idaho jail, Fred War-

ren had advertised a $1000 reward in the *Appeal* for the return to Kentucky of Republican ex-Governor William S. Taylor. Indicted for the murder of his Democratic successor in 1900, Taylor had fled to Pennsylvania and Indiana, where Republican governors conveniently refused Kentucky's official demands and one hundred thousand dollar reward for his return. Warren's attack on the politicized character of American justice succeeded only too well: Theodore Roosevelt's Attorney General, Charles J. Bonaparte, directed that Warren be indicted for sending the reward offer through the U.S. mails. Harassed for two years by federal pre-trial delays, Warren was finally found guilty and sentenced to six months at hard labor and a $1500 fine. Ultimately, the embarrassing publicity about the case generated by the *Appeal* caused President William Howard Taft to pardon Warren, but before he did so the *Appeal* mounted another attack.

Anticipating that he would spend his hard labor sentence at Leavenworth, Warren decided to muckrake the model Kansas prison. An investigation disclosed that

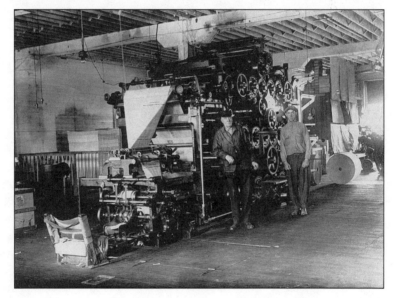

Linotype operators,
Appeal to Reason, 1915.
Courtesy Special
Collections, Pittsburgh
State University Library.

Press operators running
the May 15, 1920, issue of
the *Appeal to Reason* on
the Goss Press. Courtesy
Special Collections,
Pittsburgh State University
Library.

Leavenworth was a sinkhole of corruption, graft, sodomy, and brutality by prison officials amounting to murder. Warren, whose moral values were formed in a largely Victorian, Midwestern ethos, was outraged. He ran the stories. Federal officials, faced publicly with facts they knew, were forced to investigate; they sacked the deputy warden (whom the *Appeal* wanted charged with manslaughter and "unnatural acts"), permitted the warden to "resign," and fired a number of lesser functionaries. Regardless of the official corroboration of the *Appeal*'s charges, however, Warren, Wayland, and C. L. Phifer were indicted in November, 1911, for sending "indecent, filthy, obscene, lewd, and lascivious printed matter" through the mails. The indictment was ordered in Washington, the *Topeka Journal* reported. Federal Prosecutor Harry T. Bone "was summoned to Washington, where he discussed the Warren charges with George W. Wickersham, Attorney General. Then Bone came back to Kansas and went to work."[18] The *Appeal* editors (including Gene Debs, whom the government added to the indictment) won their case in the spring of 1912, but they were quickly reindicted by Bone on slightly reworded charges.

If legal threats were not enough, the *Appeal* was attacked from another quarter: Harrison G. Otis and his virulently procapitalist *Los Angeles Times*. For the better part of 1911, the *Appeal* had supported James B. Macnamara, his brother John, and Ortie McManigal, iron workers who had been arrested for dynamiting the *Times* building. Socialism had quickly become merged with the case when Job Harriman, Debs's running mate in 1900, became the union men's lawyer, and when the Socialist party chose Los Angeles for a mayoralty campaign and Harriman as its candidate. The *Appeal,* with no ties to the ethnically-oriented Iron Workers Union, assumed the Macnamaras were innocent and sent staff reporter George Shoaf to Los Angeles to unearth the explanation for the explosion that killed 20 employees. This time, however, the union men were guilty. They confessed four days before the mayoralty election and brought the Socialist party, to that point virtually assured of victory, down to resounding defeat. The defeat of labor and socialism in Los Angeles embol-

dened Otis and federal officials to attack the *Appeal* with new political leverage and power.

In Girard, as the *Appeal* staff once again prepared for trial, federal agents and reporters hostile to socialism roamed the streets seeking and fabricating evidence to prosecute the paper's editors for new crimes. Never in its previous battles had the *Appeal* been subjected to such pressure. The paper's offices were repeatedly broken into; once Wayland's and staff writer Algie Simons's lives were saved only because a gun misfired. Fabrication, moreover, succeeded where accuracy failed. Incredible stories were printed about arson, child-mutilation, and murder among Wayland's ancestors, thereby "proving" his inherited criminal nature. Wayland was publicly accused of seducing an orphaned girl of fourteen, taking her to Missouri where she was killed during an abortion, and he was reliably informed that Bone was preparing to prosecute him for violating the Mann Act.

For Wayland, fifty-eight years old, strains of melancholy and fatalism present in his character for as long as he could remember, the attacks finally became more than he wanted to endure. Late at night on November 10, 1912, he put the barrel of a pistol into his mouth and committed suicide. Explanations for his death varied—a disappointing vote for Debs in the election just a few days earlier, unresolved grief over the death by automobile accident of his second wife a little over a year previously, recurring cancer, a threatened indictment that would drag him, the *Appeal,* and socialism into the courts and newspapers—but how these and other factors combined will remain uncertain. With Warren as managing editor, Wayland had gradually become as much a presence as a person at the *Appeal,* and he felt a deep horror at how he was soon to be obscenely discussed and misunderstood. Wayland certainly did not fear death, and he knew when he had had enough. He had trained himself years before to sacrifice his personal life for the socialist movement, and he was willing to do it a final time. Before he died, Wayland put a note into his copy of Bellamy's *Looking Backward* and left it on the table by the bed where he would die: "The struggle under the competitive system is not worth the effort; let it pass." Wayland was defeated in November, 1912, but not until then. "Grief is for the naked lives of those who have made the world no better,"[19] Kate Richards O'Hare wrote encouragingly from St. Louis, but in Girard, and throughout the United States, socialists felt deep loss and grief.

The *Appeal* editors won their second trial on the Leavenworth case in May, 1913, eighteen months after the first indictment; Warren and the Wayland children sued periodicals for printing the libelous tales about Wayland and won as well. Wayland's death, however, brought irremediable changes to the *Appeal*. His earlier inability to institute a cooperative ownership structure for the paper meant that its ownership and control rested with the Wayland family. Whether for financial reasons or somehow to honor the memory of his father, Walter Wayland took his father's place as publisher of the *Appeal,* hired Louis Kopelin as managing editor, and apparently forced Warren from the paper. Warren officially resigned in July, 1914, but, like Debs, he left the *Appeal* the summer before. Grace Brewer, E. N. Richardson, C. L. Phifer, and many of the old staff remained for a time, but from August, 1913, the paper was Kopelin's to manage and direct. Although trained at the *Appeal* for years, Walter Wayland was without radical will or political sophistication and attended almost exclusively to business details.

The *Appeal* reached its highest circulation in 1913 (over three-quarters of a million), but within a few years subscriptions and circulation began to fall significantly. Two factors were primarily responsible: the effects of World War I and poor editorial direction. For all of Kopelin's newspaper experience (he had begun newspaper work at fourteen, served as publicity director for Wisconsin Socialist Victor Berger, and had been managing editor of the *New York Call*), his background did not equip him to understand the *Appeal*'s largely Debsian socialist audience. He was unimaginative as an editor, and his writing never had the power and vitality of Wayland's or Warren's. Nor were matters helped in 1915 when Kopelin hired Emanuel Julius, another writer with an Eastern, metropolitan background. Julius soon married Marcet Haldeman,

Girard's banking heiress and niece of Jane Addams (who suggested the married name of Haldeman-Julius), and Marcet's inherited wealth enabled her husband to buy first a third interest in the *Appeal* and finally entire ownership of the paper. A political dilettante, a man who toyed with socialism and had no convictions that seriously challenged his own self-interest, Haldeman-Julius proved to have no commitment to the socialist movement and neither understood nor valued the *Appeal*'s significance in the movement.

The domestic effects of World War I were crucial to the *Appeal*'s decline. The Great War dominated socialist and national consciousness from its outset in 1914, three years before American capitalism and the Wilson administration officially entered the conflict and used it as a pretext to crush domestic radicalism. The world war, the shift to the right of public consciousness, division in the Socialist party, the repression and delegitimization of American radicalism, the departure of old *Appeal* staffers, circulation losses, and the inability of Kopelin, Haldeman-Julius, and Walter Wayland to redirect the *Appeal* and mobilize its readers all pushed the paper into decline. Antiwar writers and activists George R. Kirkpatrick and Allan Benson (the Socialist party's presidential candidate in 1916, but a man who soon resigned from the party to support the American war effort) were hired, and initially the *Appeal* allied itself with the Socialist party's condemnation of the war as a grim, shabby battle between competing capitalist nations. However, upon America's entry into the war, the passage of the Espionage Act and the Sedition Act, the imprisonment of radicals and the censoring of antiwar periodicals, the *Appeal* adopted a patriotic, prowar position and renamed itself the *New Appeal* to accentuate its shift in political policy. Haldeman-Julius and Kopelin withdrew the paper's allegiances from the antiwar Socialist party, sought to erect an essentially liberal Social Democratic League in its place, and then, upon the conclusion of World War I, moved to oppose the war and the ensuing division of spoils at Versailles. Symbolizing that reversal was the restoration of the paper's original name, the *Appeal to Reason*. The *Ap-*

peal's readership and influence had not been built on confusion and opportunism, however, and the paper lost further force and constituency when the Socialist party was splintered by repression and the consequent divisiveness within the radical movement.

The last issue of the *Appeal to Reason* appeared on November 4, 1922, but the paper had been truly alive only sporadically during its final years of publication. It was replaced by the *Haldeman-Julius Weekly*. "By improving one's self," Haldeman-Julius wrote as the new paper's credo, "the degree of general excellence will be permanently improved. The *Haldeman-Julius Weekly,* hitherto known as the *Appeal to Reason,* will carry out a carefully wrought policy of individual self help and development through one's own efforts."[20] For socialists, the irony was inescapable. The old *Appeal*'s understanding of the impossibility of even conceiving a self apart from historical and contemporaneous relations, of the practical necessity of mobilizing a people with a shared vision of economic and social justice, of an egalitarian world that could only be brought into being by mutual effort and caring for others, had dissolved into barren self-interest.

J. A. Wayland's final words had been desolate, but he had helped to build a socialist movement, America's greatest radical paper, and he had left a legacy of insurgency and struggle. Haldeman-Julius was more an undertaker than executioner of the *Appeal*; by 1922 both the socialist movement and its dominant paper had been beaten back. However, the *Appeal*'s dissolution symbolized the end of a time that truly was alive with liberating possibilities. As historically apt as a futile belief in self-help may have been for the disillusioned American 1920s, the *Appeal*'s claims on the present, then as now, cannot be disavowed or settled that cheaply.

J. A. Wayland's editorial in the Appeal's *first issue articulated principles that would guide the paper for the next two decades.*

J. A. Wayland, One-Hoss Editor

That the phenomenal concentration of property and business under the control of monopolies known as corporations, trusts and combines, is changing the commercial aspect of the world and with it also changing the social relations, is evident to any man or woman who stops to think. But in the struggle for existence or supremacy, neither poor nor rich take the time or have any inclination to stop and think. At no time in history has combination succeeded combination, in greater and greater aggregations, like the present. The little fellow is no longer in it. That there will come a logical end of it all, that it can not go on forever, ought to startle not only the masses who are being reduced to serfdom, but also the few who are climbing the dizzy heights supported only by the duplicity of the masses, likely at any moment to throw off the burden, like a Samson. The history of the past teaches a lesson that can be ignored only at great peril. To explain in my humble way, the tendency of the times, to point out the rocks, and to inspire hope of a fairer, more orderly system, is the mission of this publication. That it will be greeted with ridicule by some is expected. There has never been a reformer in any field of thought who has not met the withering scorn and contumely of those too ignorant to understand him. But as new and better machines displace labor by millions, as combinations crush out the well-to-do class, as government by judges displaces the kind our fathers left us, there will come a time when the people will be forced by necessity, not only to listen to but to practice a different political economy than the dog-eat-dog of competition. Private monopoly is always oppressive, public monopoly always beneficent. This is the lesson.

Learn it, or perish as perished all the civilizations of the past.

August 31, 1895

Personal accounts from socialist agitators who sold subscriptions to the Appeal *(and from other readers as well) were a characteristic feature of the paper. Thousands of letters arrived weekly after the Appeal's circulation became substantial, and the paper's editorial writers were informed of local, regional, and national conditions far better than their Kansas location might otherwise suggest.*

Iconoclasts

A REAL HERO

I have been in the reform move for 17 years, a Populist up to four years ago, when I became a confirmed Socialist. I am 73 years old and blind. God bless you. I wish I could meet you; you seem like a brother to me. It takes men of your grit to move the world. I send you 12 subs. and think I can send you more later, being old and blind I can't accomplish much. Enclosed find list.

S. D. STRONG, *Lewiston, Idaho*

GIVES A HELPING HAND

I wish your paper was in the hands of every voter in the land. I have been a people's party man but I now see that it is best to go to the bottom of existing evils, and nothing short of practical socialism will do any good. From now forward I am a full-fledged Socialist; not because I am in a distressed condition, for such is not the case, as I own as fine a body of land as there is in Graves county; more than 800 acres well improved and use about 10 to 12 families per year. And that is one great reason for my faith, seeing their poverty so continually. However, they seem well pleased with their condition; they don't appear to realize that there is anything wrong.

W. A. GILLIAM, *Melber, Ky.*

A WARM STAR, IS SOUTHWORTH

The *Appeal* is the greatest of all great papers on earth. Last year I sent you 73 subs. and I now send you 88 subscribers and $2.20. Next year I shall never rest until I reach the 100 mark; besides I sell and give away lots of books. My way is this: I employ at times several men and as far as possible secure their subs, always guaranteeing satisfaction or paying them back. Also got two editors and other business men I deal with here at home to try it; they all like it, or keep renewing at least. Now, brothers, we can do all this with a little effort and you will be surprised. I call it my paper and it goes by that name (my name) here, all recognizing me as an established agent. Let us every one be an agent without pay or per cent, and you will feel rewarded in the fact and conscience of doing good. Spread the light, encourage the editor and in years to come we will be proud of the work we have done for humanity.

O. M. SOUTHWORTH, *Benton Harbor, Mich.*

ONE FRUITFUL ACT

I became a reader of the *Appeal* the other day when I first received a copy from a man who is to me unacquainted. While giving he looked at me gravely and said, "Read, think and act!" I gazed at him with astonishment and thought that is somebody who wanted me to blow up the city of Chicago with dynamite, on account of its boodle aldermen. Nevertheless, I hurried home and began to read; its contents caused me enthusiasm. Every article of the *Appeal* is a gem. I, who used to 'Rah! for Mr. Humbug, became immediately an adherent of the principles it advocates. Please allow me to express my sincere gratitude through the columns of your paper to the unknown gentleman, for he was my eye opener.

M. JOSEPHSON, *Chicago, Ill.*

A MAN YOU DON'T MEET EVERY DAY

Inclosed find list of 20 yearly subs and money order for $10. When I approach a man to get his name for the *Appeal*, I feel he is doing himself a great favor to get his name written among the "elect." I do not feel under any obligations to him for it, common sense offers no other terms for him. I believe there is more instantaneous conversion, more scale-knocking power in the *Appeal* than all else since the eyes of Saul of Tarsus were made clear-sighted.

JOHN D. HESKELL, *Abilene, Kan.*

A PESSIMIST

I have been instructed the past year by your efforts; still, I have no faith in your line of reform; in fact, I have no faith in humanity. It is not yet clear to me that it was not a mistake when a few souls, that is eight, were saved from the flood.

L. D. WILSON, *Reedtown, O.*

PLEASED WITH OUR SUCCESS

I send 10 cents in stamps for papers of the two last editions. It made my heart glad to read that the *Appeal* is booming. I studied socialism in Germany and read many books and papers, but your paper is one of the best.

KARL NEWBOLD, *Lansdale, Pa.*
February 4, 1899

The Appeal *sponsored many subscription contests during its years of publication. They illuminate part of American life and culture as well as circulation strategy.*

Number of Subscribers
52,126

The actual number of subscribers on the *Appeal*'s list, *who have paid for it themselves*, is 52,126. This does NOT include subscriptions which have been paid for by others, nor the extras sold each issue,

which number many thousand copies. Now, I figure that I can carry 25,000 more subscriptions at the present prices and have a small amount to invest for the good of the cause. I therefore propose that, as soon as the circulation, figured from THIS BASIS here stated, shall increase to 75,000 copies weekly, to give to the Socialists in the city which shall then have the most subscribers

A FIRST CLASS BRASS BAND

consisting of seventeen pieces, beautifully nickel plated, and in every way superior to those used by ordinary bands. It will be composed as follows:

Three Marceau E-b Cornets		
Four	"	B-b "
Four	"	E-b Altos
Two	"	B-b Tenors
One	"	" Baritone
"	"	" Bass
Two	"	E-b Bass

To this the *Appeal* will add a snare and bass drum of the best kind. These instruments are of the highest grade and made by Marceau, of Paris, France, and we purchase from the importing house. The city which gets this prize will have one of the best sets of instruments in the country—one that will discount eight out of ten bands in the United States. The band will be turned over to the Social Democratic branch in the city which wins it, conditioned upon its free use for the good of the cause. Now, remember, that this will be given as soon as the circulation increases to 75,000 from the figures printed in the box at the left of the head on this page. Every subscriber sent in, no difference where from, helps it nearer the goal. When the figures reach 75,000 the band will be at once given to the city having the most subscribers to the *Appeal*. We cannot tell you how different cities are standing until the contest closes, but as a matter of information will say that Chicago now stands at the head with 516 subscribers, Kansas City next with 510, San Francisco next with 501, and there are seventeen other cities having between

450 and 500 subscribers. Any town of 5000 or more population might win this band by energetic hustling.

November 25, 1899

The Appeal *regularly exchanged copies with other newspapers, and during certain periods sent copies to every newspaper editor in America. In 1899 a small fund to pay postage costs was volunteered by readers and, during 1900, Wayland reported that hundreds of thousands of columns from the* Appeal *were reprinted by newspapers throughout the United States. Not every editorial response, however, was as favorable as those that follow.*

An Account of Stewardship

JONESBORO, ARK., *Enterprise*

The *Appeal to Reason*, the organ of the Socialists, published at Girard, Kans., is a fearless and outspoken exponent of the doctrine of Socialism. It may be fighting a losing fight, in fact there may be as little hope for perfection in the social world as there is in the religious world. Yet this newspaper discusses issues in a firm, fearless and commendable way. It strikes at the very root of social evils and arraigns men who grind relentless heels upon the neck of those who earn their bread by the sweat of their brows. It strikes at corruption in high places, and "Appeals to Reason" for the dawning of God's perfect day when in all this glad land there will be neither slave nor subject, nor monarch, nor king, nor millionaire, nor mendicant. It pleads for the universal brotherhood of man; it declares the hod carrier the superior of the pampered and non producing prince. It owns neither mendicant nor master and claims by right of creation all men are equal.

This is a beautiful doctrine, this doctrine of Socialism. It believes that as long as some men have plenty and to spare that no man should be allowed to go hungry while others are overfed, none should go naked, while others' wardrobes are full of raiment, none should sleep on a bed of grass as long as there are empty beds and vacant rooms. The Socialist doctrine may be impossible to us, but no one who has read the life of the ancient Christ doubts for a moment that the creator intended mankind for a common brotherhood and He never intended that one should serve and another rule. However far off the ultimate hope of the *Appeal to Reason* may be, it is a paper full of genuine and wholesome thought and worthy of any man's careful study who seeks to know the right and do it.

Journal, MANKATO, MINN.

For some time we have been receiving the *Appeal to Reason*, the well-known Socialist paper published at Girard, Kansas. At first we were actually afraid of this paper. Our custom was to tear off wrapper, look cursory over its columns and then dump it into our well-filled waste basket and forget it entirely until the next copy would come when the same action would take place, only we would dwell longer upon the headings, and later on, read articles now and then. But we must say that we actually read every copy of that paper now and we are deeply impressed with the straight-forward arguments, live editorials and other matter bristling with the purest and best of the queen's English found on every one of the four pages of this wonderful paper of a hundred thousand circulation. Its influence is perhaps greater, more far-reaching in extent, than any other paper published in this country, and it is certainly an element in politics, for it is cutting wide swaths in the political field of every state, and through the influence, mainly, of this paper we predict that the vote given Debs and Harriman will be a surprisingly large one. There are no advertisements, the paper receiving its support through its large list of subscribers. It is a weekly published for fifty cents a year, and is certainly one of the most remarkable papers published in the world.

Exeter, N. C., *Enterprise*

The *Appeal to Reason*, this is the name of a very curious paper published down at Girard, Kansas, which has occasionally been quoted, so far as its milder paroxysms of idiocy go, in these columns. Its editor is foolish enough to believe that the human race is composed of reasoning animals, instead of hogs, each looking out for a little more than his portion of swill, and this novelty makes it a rather curious and interesting publication. It advocates socialism, a system that proposes to give to each man exactly what he earns and no more, and which of course can never prevail because it will always be opposed by the people who have brains and the people with brains have and will likely always control affairs, in the interest of themselves. However, as a freak publication, advocating the world lifting itself up by its bootstraps, it is worth sending a stamp for a sample copy.

November 24, 1900

While personal accounts published in the Appeal *often expressed grief as well as dedication, their emphasis centered on the need for social change.*

His Last Letter

Dear Comrades: After nearly forty years of hard toil and consuming anxiety, the poor house and suicide is my only choice. I have a wife and little boy in Tampa, Fla., a little boy in Texas and a daughter in Oklahoma—scattered to the four winds of the earth—will likely go to ruin for want of my advice and protection.

Just think, comrades, we used to hear talk of the poor black man sold from his children. Is it not worse for a white man? Just think, no one is secure and your dear loved ones are likely to be torn from you and left in the hands of ignorant, selfish persons.

That this beautiful, fertile nation is reeking and groaning under a huge load of ignorance, crime and misery. I've been the most willing worker for the last ten years, I've done all I could, I never tire of working and talking for Socialism. In 1899, not being able to do any better, I took a wheel-barrow load of books and papers, and pushed along the dusty roads through the scorching hot winds of Kansas. Two months in 1900, I took a one-horse cart and went to Grand Junction, Colo., and back to Oklahoma, and put over a thousand books and many papers into the hands of thinking people, convincing many that Socialism is our only salvation.

Socialism has been my only religion for ten years. I would not die if I could do any more for the good cause; but my health is gone. While I should be in my prime I can do no more for myself or for humanity. I will take a big dose of laudanum tonight and die a few weeks sooner in order to put my little hard earned money into the good cause I've worked so hard for, that would otherwise go to feed me, and also to avoid unnecessary suffering.

I can do no more, but I hope my soul will be with you. I pray and beg of you to be of good cheer and courage. "Do not fear to own the cause or blush to speak the name." If you can't talk (nearly all persons can if they will try) you can do a world of good by distributing literature.

Don't let 'em rest until such barbarous customs are completely abolished. We now have more than half the people half converted. Nearly all the people are thinking of Socialism, have got over the scare and are investigating. Our principles cannot be refuted, for Right is on our side and we are bound to succeed and the end is not far.

The above letter without signature, address or date upon it, and a postal money order for $2.50 enclosed were received at the *Appeal* office May 25. There were no instructions as to what the money was for and the name of the writer was obtained at the post office from the postal advice. The money with more was sent to the family of the deceased in Tampa, Fla., by the *Appeal*.

Alas! for the sadness and misery of this world to the many, when it should and can be an Eden for all.

June 7, 1902

The *Appeal* plant has the appearance of a great factory. Workmen in the adjoining lots building coalsheds, teamsters delivering cars of coal, machinists and masons erecting the huge boiler and setting the engine, the steam fitters putting in the steam heating plant, workmen putting additional shafting and pulleys for new printing machinery, in addition to the forty employees, make the citizens here open their eyes in amazement. The force is working extra this week, special State editions being printed for seventeen States. The orders for extra copies this issue, up to the time of closing this, the last form, is about 200,000. Of this Massachusetts orders 30,000; California, 25,000; Texas, 25,000; Indiana, 20,000; Illinois, 20,000; Ohio, 15,000; the balance being in orders of 5,000 and less. Part of the list will be a day or more later this week than usual in consequence. Whoop 'em up. Our day is coming.

October 11, 1902

Honor To Whom Honor Is Due

J. A. WAYLAND

While appreciating the spirit that prompts the many letters [of praise] that reach my desk, and which are like sunshine on a path often dark and discouraging, I do not desire to have the credit for results that justly belong to others. The *Appeal* has done the greatest work in the movement, that I feel and know, but Wayland is not the force that makes the *Appeal*. Alone I would never have been heard of and the *Appeal* would have no power. The force that has made the *Appeal* is the army of workers that have worked late and early, making all kinds of sacrifices, members of it often doing without even many of the necessaries of life that they might devote the few cents thus saved to spreading the *Appeal*, in which they have confidence. Their work is greater than mine, for they do their work without hope of recognition, without being known—doing it for that love of Truth and Right that has been behind all the greatest acts of members of the human family. My name under the head of the paper (a legal necessity or it would not be there) gives me the credit for all the work of that wonderful invisible army who are scouring the highways and byways of every section of the vast expanse of this nation. To that unnumbered, unnamed, aggregation of self-sacrificing workers is due all the power, all the results and all the honor that attaches to the *Appeal*. Without them it would long ago have died. And it has been no easy task for them in another way. Many efforts have been made to alienate them from the *Appeal*—by denouncing the *Appeal* as being a capitalistic sheet, as being a financial trick to enrich me, as being run by a dishonest trickster—all these have had the effect of alienating a few, but the mass of the workers have remained with it, and its greatness is their devotion and confidence. Instead of scattering their work they have combined it with wonderful effect. Had all efforts at teaching been combined thus the movement would have been ten years ahead of what it is, and we would today be entering upon the first acts of the Co-operative Commonwealth.

Socialism is coming in our day. It is no longer a dream of the clouds, but is coming earthward. If the *Appeal* can continue its work a few more years with the same increase of circulation it has had, its work will be done and its plant can be turned over to the Socialist public for such purpose or uses as that public may see fit to apply it to. It could no longer remain private capital. It would be the delight of my life to turn it over to the public, but so long as it must remain in private hands, no matter how many there are in the ownership, it is just as safe with me as with any other set of men.

October 25, 1902

Many populist editors, themselves a formidable force in the 1880s and 1890s, helped to bring socialism to old People's party supporters.

The *Appeal* Must Have Money to Circulate the Populist Edition

Comrades, the *Appeal* has reached a point in the development of the special Populist edition where we know that we will need money and lots of it—to circulate the *Appeal* just where it ought to go. A form letter was sent to the populist editors who are still keeping up the fight, asking them to furnish us names of populists. The responses are just beginning to come in. From Nebraska one paper offers us 20,000 and one true-hearted Kansas editor takes off his coat to copy us a list of 4,000. Do you need any further proof that this issue is not coming a moment too soon? I estimate that we will have 200,000 names with which no funds will be sent. To print this number of copies will cost

$1,000. Now comrades, on the present basis every 8-page edition of the *Appeal* is printed at a loss. I must have assistance to mail out these papers and have only three weeks in which to raise the money. The Army must help. However, this will be the most important issue of the paper in its history, and the *Appeal* to get the good works started will begin this fund with one hundred dollars.

January 3, 1903

Late in 1903, Appeal employees struck for better working conditions and for a role in determining the paper's policies and personnel. The issues raised by the strike were never fully resolved.

The *Appeal* Unionized

J. A. WAYLAND

It takes a long time to get some people to realize what a proposition means. The *Appeal* has been preaching unionism and urging the working class to organize for years, and only just now has its own employes taken its advice. The printers would not have organized here but for my urging them to do so, but I waited for the other employes to organize or not, as they saw fit. I have repeatedly written that "liberty cannot be given but must be taken," and that men and women who would not make an effort to free themselves were not fit for liberty. The employes in every factory, workshop and farm should organize a union, just as employers are organizing, and study and prepare for the day when labor shall take possession of the world and operate its industries for its own benefit. Labor will gain much by the social contact of organization—will gain lessons that it MUST know before it will ever be able to meet the cunning of capitalists and conquer them in the political and economic fields.

I hope to see every employe in Girard organized this winter, and with the organization now started there is no reason why they should not be able to dictate hours, wages and conditions of labor.

October 24, 1903

The Story of the *Appeal* strike and its Settlement

A. W. RICKER

. . . The *Appeal to Reason* is an immense part of the American Socialist movement. Its circulation is the greatest of any Socialist publication in the world. Its greatness is the product of many minds, and of much effort besides that of its founder, though the *Appeal* without Wayland, would be like the proverbial play *Hamlet* with Hamlet omitted. We have had difficulty and a strike in the office, and it has been of such a character, and such magnitude, that we feel obliged to give the party, and the army who are a part of the creators of the paper, a sufficient sketch of the matter to acquaint them with the essentials. The writer of this article came to the *Appeal* office with Comrade Untermann in December of last year. Comrade Untermann became associate editor, and scientific writer, and the writer associate editor and circulation manager. Up to that time as is well known the *Appeal* had been a propaganda paper exclusively. It had confined its field entirely to the skirmish line, and the unconverted. There is no writer on either side of the water who can measure pens with the founder of this paper in this peculiar field. It is not boasting to say that 90 per cent of the created Socialist sentiment in the nation outside of New York can have its origin so far as a periodical is concerned, traced to the *Appeal*, and still further to the caustic paragraphs of Wayland. The entry of Comrades Untermann and the writer added new fields to the *Appeal*. Untermann is a scientific writer with a reputation on both sides of the water, and the writer's previous experience with party machinery and organization work irresistibly led him to take up the work of organizing the

Appeal army into Socialist locals. The *Appeal* became both a propaganda and party paper. Its circulation began to mount. With $4,000.00 in the treasury January 1st, we made arrangements to spend $25,000.00 in 6 months in necessary improvements to equip the paper for its coming greatness, and the office for its constantly growing work. Almost immediately after the writer joined the *Appeal* staff, Comrade Wayland announced his wish to leave the plant to the movement at his death, and to take no profits from it while living. In due time announcement was made in the paper to this effect. It was then that trouble began in the office. Nearly two years ago the *Appeal* plant was organized as a corporation, with five shareholders. Two of these stockholders had long been associated with Comrade Wayland. One was W. F. Phelps, business manager, the other C. D. Bevans, a relative. The plan to cut out dividends was objectionable to both of these individuals, and from that time on the inner workings of the office have been inharmonious. In due time there came to the office and identified with the editorial work, Miss Josephine Conger, W. P. Mason, Geo. D. Brewer, Chas. L. Breckon and G. H. Lockwood. All of these comrades are staunch Socialists. The office began to be filled with the Socialist spirit, but the lack of harmony, due to the incompatible elements grew. In the meantime we were getting ready to unionize the shop, and in time succeeded, a report of which appeared in No. 412. The report did not mention the fact, however, that the organization of the union was effected against the bitter opposition of Messrs. Phelps and Bevans, but such was the case, and matters soon climaxed. The editorial staff demanded the dismissal of the above parties, and they were so objectionable to the employes in the office that by a unanimous vote they agreed to support our demand. On Friday we presented our demands to Comrade Wayland. In all matters pertaining to the organization of the office, scale of wages, etc., he cheerfully agreed, but declined to grant our demand for the discharge of the two members of the corporation. We immediately resigned, and in 20 minutes every employe of the office was paid off, had walked out of the office, and not a wheel was turning. We were on strike and six members of the staff were out arrayed in opposition to the Comrade they all loved, and were supported by every member of the union. A battle short but intense began. It was waged on one side, by those who loved the man Wayland, but were ready to battle with him on a question of principle, and by the other, by one who was cut off from all those who were his constant associates in the office, and who had to match friendship and the good of the office, against family ties, and business agreements. Right and justice won the struggle, in 30 hours. On Sunday at noon Comrade Wayland met us at his home and an agreement was reached amidst an affecting scene where there were not a few damp eyelashes, and at 2:30 in the afternoon we marched to the office 51 strong, filed by our grizzled chief, shook his hand, and gave him three rousing cheers. No happier body of people ever went to work. The dramatic hours of the struggle had welded these 51 hearts together, and the affecting termination added another—the man against whom we had struck.

The following is the proposition submitted by J. A. Wayland at the public meeting held at the Court House. Its proposals were fully concurred in by the union at its meeting on Sunday:

Girard, Kansas, Oct. 24, 1903

That the Appeal *force return to their several places as they were when they went out, with the exception of Mr. Phelps, who has resigned the position he held.*

That Jon. G. Wayland remain at cashier's desk until the secretary of the national committee of the Socialist party shall send a competent man for cashier, as my associate in management, who shall be employed as a regular co-worker, and if he shall prove incompetent that the national secretary shall appoint another. That he shall keep all accounts and that all surplus over running expenses shall be turned over to the national committee of the Socialist party. That the accounts shall be kept in the name of the Appeal to Reason, *and shall be subject to my check except where I shall give the said national appointee power to check.*

That I contend only for the right to appoint heads of the department which shall be left in arbitration to the national secretary.

That union rules shall govern the office.

That no employe shall be prejudiced for any action taken on either side of the disagreement.

J. A. Wayland

There is peace and harmony in the office. We are a unit in purpose, We are going to make the old *Appeal* sizzle with fervor. We are in here this morning working with a faith and determination that can move mountains. There is such an omnipotence to thought, that we believe you have caught something of our feelings for the mail is pouring in, as it has not for months. The *Appeal* staff sends a hearty greeting to you. The old ship has been through a storm here during the past week, but not a mast has gone overboard, nor a sail been lost. The barnacles are all washed off her hull, and she rides three feet further out of the water. The old battle-scarred captain is still on the deck surrounded by a crew that will "Never give up the ship."

November 7, 1903

To the *Appeal* Army Comrades:

I Want to Talk to You a Moment

J. A. WAYLAND

The *Appeal* has had a crisis. That was the outward expression of a conflict that waged a fearful struggle within me. When all but four of the *Appeal* force walked out I was dazed. If it had been for more wages or shorter hours I should have known how to satisfy that. But being for the removal of three stockholders and officers in the Appeal Publishing Co., who had been with it from its first issue—two being relatives, and one my own blood, it was a difficult matter for me. It tried my very soul. I felt I could not grant such a demand. I tendered the *Appeal* plant to the National Committee of the Socialist party. It was the only thing I could think of. National Secretary Mailly wired me that the constitution of the party prevented the committee from taking it. Had I considered the matter I knew that, but in my distracted condition I did not consider. I could not go on with the paper without the workers. I could not and would not employ non-union assistants, as capitalists do. I was unfortunate in not having any cool head to counsel with—one with no interest on either side of the controversy. All about me had become partisan. I felt like a mariner in a stout ship tossed at the mercy of a storm because there were none to handle the machinery that would prove efficient against the wind-tossed sea.

The secretary-treasurer resigned and yet there was no compromise. I decided to discontinue the paper and went home. I was sick. No physical pain equals mental pain. The work I had set myself to do, and had done for twelve years to the best of my ability, seemed to halt. I felt incompetent. I had passed through a number of trying times in these twelve years but had risen to the occasion. I felt that the strain and the added years had rendered me unfit.

There was a sense of relief when I felt it was all over. The long strain, the anxiety, the uncertainty. I still had a little means left. I could sell the office and live in comfort. The old hard life would pass from me. I sat down before the grate at the house with my wife and daughter. They were weeping. Perhaps I was too.

I reviewed the past years of struggle. The vision of the *Appeal* Army, with its thousands who had stood by me in every trial, passed before me. I saw poor men and poor women who had given up badly needed dimes to help the work for industrial deliverance. They confided in me. I never asked but they responded. What would they think? What would they feel? How many would sink discouraged, hopes blasted, confidence lost? Should a few be permitted to stand between? Shall I sink self, even life if need be, for those who need it? Shall I take up the burden and go on? And the wife

Appeal to Reason postcard postmarked October 24, 1912. Courtesy Gene DeGruson.

said, "The Army has been faithful to you." And I decided.

The *Appeal* force announced a public meeting at the Court House. I had just a few minutes to note down the proposition before the meeting. I asked them permission to present my acquiescence. It brought joy to them and will to the Army. In their encouragement will I get my happiness. And I take up the yoke with a lighter heart.

Pardon me for this personality. I do not like to burden you with my troubles, but you know a trouble shared is a trouble divided. I could not tell it without using the personal pronoun I often. But I have unbosomed myself to you and I feel relieved. I will let the other workers on the paper tell the story for themselves. There is nothing to conceal. I do not question their integrity. They have the same interest in the paper and the cause that I have. I am only on a salary the same as they.

The *Appeal* has paid no dividends. It never will. I shall continue to guard its interest for the benefit of the Cause. It will be stronger than ever I hope.It ought to put many thousands at the disposal of the party this year, if you will still have the faith. I have tried to merit your confidence. If you have lost confidence, I can only go on until your action renders me unable to continue. The *Appeal* is in your hands. It has no money value to me. I am here to serve you if you want—to retire and leave you the property if you wish.

I have not lost faith in you.

November 7, 1903

The Appeal's request that readers assist another newspaper is an example of the mutual support common in the socialist movement: by 1918, Gaa Paa had a weekly circulation of four thousand.

Comrade Mengshoel, publisher of the Norwegian edition of the *Appeal*, named *Gaa Paa*, desires to move the plant to Minneapolis, where he can get considerable local patronage. The *Appeal* has

given him the printing plant, and as it will require some money to move it and locate, he asks the comrades to advance him some money on subscription cards. He has not been able to make it pay expenses, except that the *Appeal* has advanced him paper and presswork without pay; but in Minneapolis there is a large Scandinavian population, and he could get much help locally that cannot be had at this distance. The paper is doing good work for the cause, and will be a power if properly located. Those of the comrades who can use subscriptions are urged to send to him for a few cards. He and his wife and son have worked very hard and are made of the right material for our cause. You can advance a dollar or two for cards that you can sell later.

August 6, 1904

Like other members of the Appeal community, Wayland performed the "insignificant" tasks necessary to build the socialist movement.

Will You Help?

J. A. WAYLAND

Last week I rode sixty-five miles, circulating *Appeals* and pamphlets about Girard. One evening after work I made twenty miles and left an *Appeal* and two pamphlets at every farm house. Don't feel too dignified to do such work; you should rather have a pride in it. I know of no method better than such work, and the most humble can do it and by it do just as effective work as the most brilliant speaker. I intend to keep this up during the entire campaign, giving fresh literature at each covering of the same roads. I do this after my day's work in the office is done. Ten thousand men doing this two or four hours a week would make a tremendous breach in capitalism this fall.

September 3, 1904

Short-Hand Talk by the "One Hoss"

This is the day of concentration and specialties. The world has no place for the jack-of-all-trades—it's the specialist—the man who knows how to do one thing better than anybody else—who occupies the center of the stage.

The *Appeal* is an agitation sheet—that and nothing more. I am an agitator. The propaganda of Socialism is my specialty. I have made a success of it, with the assistance of 25,000 other agitators, whose specialty has been the propaganda of Socialism. Following this agitation has come a party. And a party organized under the limitations and requirements of today, lends itself easily to quarrels and internal strife. It's the capitalistic instinct still struggling for mastery. I have taken no part in these quarrels. I have taken no part in party matters—other than as a member of Girard Local. I have never attended a state or national convention of the Socialist party. I am not a politician. I would be lost among the tacticians whose work it is to shape a party out of the sentiment which the *Appeal* and the *Appeal* Army have created during the past twelve years.

I have been severely criticized because the *Appeal* was not more of a party paper—because it did not ally itself with the platform Socialists or take up the cudgel on behalf of the so-called "impossiblist." Important as are party matters, there is a question of more importance: THE WORK OF CREATING THE SOCIALIST SENTIMENT OUT OF WHICH IS BEING BUILT A POLITICAL PARTY, AND WITHOUT WHICH NO PARTY COULD EXIST.

More than a decade ago I resolved to lend myself to this work to the best of my ability. The work of organization I left to others—to the rank and file—because it's not in my line. I have no desire to be other than a private in the party, counting just one. I have repeatedly refused to accept even a local or state office—and have used my influence to prevent anyone connected with the *Appeal* becoming identified in an official way with the state or national organization, in order to leave the *Appeal* unhampered in this pioneer agitation work. I am still firmly convinced that this policy will enable the *Appeal* to do greater work for Socialism than to use this huge machine to crush this faction or that. This policy has met with the hearty approval of the great majority of the men and women whose untiring efforts have been the means of building up this paper. The *Appeal* is run by the Army comrades, and their will is my will. Within the past week, however, I have received a half dozen or so letters, of which the following is a type:

Wichita, Kan., April 30, 1905
J. A. Wayland, Girard, Kans.

Dear Comrade:—In view of the slump in subscribers, I would take occasion to state that you should be cognizant of the fact that the rank and file of the Socialists are past the point where we can fight under cover, and realize the fact that "he who is not for us is against us." While I, individually, am in sympathy with the Appeal *and am doing what I can to further its cause—little enough to be sure, but something as the days roll on—I am well aware that since the Socialists demand it, that to gain and hold popularity, your (or any other) paper must help us in our fight for a clean-up in party matters. You have been kept posted no doubt by both sides as to the party's growing pains, yet you refuse to outline your standing or express through the columns of the* Appeal *your ideas or your sympathy with either one side or the other. On the one* side you are accused of being simply a "capitalistic grafter," on the other with being a "traitor." All because you will neither line up for the "bourgeois Socialists" or with the ones who demand a clean-up in the working class party. Now, if you want us to stand by the Appeal, *let the* Appeal *stand with us.* Take a tumble, Comrade, and show your colors, and if clear, as I believe you to be, we will stir things up once more for the old cause. If you are on the side of the "bourgeois" or platform Socialism, you need to expect no support from us, who agitate, preach and teach, and by the eternal will stand by, the Marxian philosophy.

Yours for the proletarian revolution.

Dr. E. W. O'Brien

Whether Comrade O'Brien has correctly analyzed the situation I leave to you. I could, had I the space, produce letters identical with his from former S. L. P. members during the early nineties. "You must support the DeLeon faction or be boycotted out of existence," said one side. On the other side the *Appeal* was threatened with annihilation. During these crises in party affairs the *Appeal* kept its face towards the enemy, and its prow headed straight for the Co-operative Commonwealth. I could have wrecked the *Appeal* and the Socialist party by taking one side or the other.

You who have supported my hands during these years are to be the judge whether the course I have taken was right or wrong.

Today we face a crisis very similar to the ones I have alluded to. The same elements of discord which divided the forces of the early Socialist Party are now at work. Shall the *Appeal* lend its aid to one faction—(and possibly the wrong one, as my judgment is no better than yours)—or shall it continue its work of tearing down the walls of capitalism? Shall it continue to be the powerful battering ram of the Social Revolution it has in the past, or shall it pass out of existence ignobly fighting well-meaning, but mayhap mistaken, comrades?

I want you to decide whether the smoke shall continue to roll from the *Appeal* stack or whether

there shall be another building in Girard "for rent."

May 13, 1905

———

The three-million-copy Trust Edition in 1905 taxed the Appeal's printing capacity to its limit, though even this figure would be exceeded in the future.

Contributions to the fund to send the Trust Edition to one million business firms in the United States: $1802.40

> 3,047,200

Is the total number of copies of the Trust Edition ordered up to and including November 16th.

No more copies of that issue can be sold, and no more contributions for sending it to business men can be accepted.

I wish to thank each one and everyone that has contributed to the success of the Trust Edition. The total results of your efforts have been not only to exceed the actual paid issue that any other paper ever got out by the stupendous excess of 2,000,000 copies, but you have practically made it impossible for any other paper to ever equal the record you have made.

Personally I feel very grateful to you, individually and collectively, for this token of your confidence. No man ever had before placed at his disposal 3,000,000 papers upon which to place ideas, with an army of Paul Reveres scattered all over a great nation, ready and willing to put them before the eyes and brains of the nation.

The World is surely ours.

Yours for Socialism,

J. A. Wayland

November 25, 1905

Full of autobiographical resonance, "A Vision of the Future" reveals the power of Wayland's convictions and the experience that produced them.

A Vision of the Future

J. A. WAYLAND

Julius Augustus Wayland, April, 1908.

When I look at the ferment of this insane social system; when I see its corruption, bribery, oppression, suicides, murders, robberies, prostitution, drunkenness and rapid concentration of wealth; when I see the masses apparently dead asleep to the meaning of their condition or to what it is tending; when I see the little business men grow weaker as the greater ones grow stronger; when I see the rulers taking to themselves more and more power while the millions gradually let slip their influence in public affairs; when I see the courts more and more becoming only tools for the rich, while the poor are helpless before the law; when I see the voters losing what little comprehension they had of the purpose of the ballot, using it merely as a means to favor some scheming, cunning, self-seeking friend with a fat place; when I see the great corporations corraling the lands in great tracts, filling the waterways with their own ships and exploiting the riches of the mines for their kingly self-aggrandizement; I say, when I look over this alleged civilization and see these things, I feel a hopelessness that makes me heartsick, and I wonder if it is worth the struggle, and if life is worth its care and if annihilation were not a joy.

Then, there is another view: I remember how I felt when I received my first impression of the social system as it is. I woke up as from a dream, and beheld the horrors about me stripped of their flimsy covering and nauseating in their nakedness. I had caught a glimpse of a higher, delightful harmoniousness; and it was so beautiful, so just, that I felt all would accept it as soon as they were told of it; that the present hateful thing could all be re-modeled in a few years; that people would flock to the New Civilization as soon as they would read or hear of it. At that time there were no papers or magazines to tell the beautiful story; no books to explain it, except a few academically written volumes on out-of-the-way shelves in public libraries—books which nobody read.

I threw myself into the work of getting the message to the people with a wild delirium of enthusiasm; I read, and talked, and wrote, and printed and circulated the printed page; I stood on the street corners and handed the passers a leaflet or pamphlet; I mailed copies to thousands of names without considering the character of the recipients; I put years of life and energy into a few months. Gradually it began to dawn on me that the job was greater than I had felt in my first enthusiasm; I had been too optimistic; it would take years of persistent, systematic work; a siege must be laid to the inertia and ignorance of the masses, attacking such as were mentally ready for the change, and others as they were gradually jolted loose from the hypnotic spell of the capitalist skinners. I had a business and newspaper training; I had owned and successfully operated some fifteen publications; I had succeeded where others had failed; I had retired from the business some years before, but now I turned to the newspaper with a new ideal; that journalistic training would enable me to print, publish and distribute the message to the people at less cost than by any other method; so I put my neck again in the yoke I had thrown away. I had a message to give and I must have the messenger.

So I went to work to create the messenger that would awaken the people, that would agitate and educate them, and, from the mass thus converted, would produce an army of helpers and honey-comb the nation with the ferment, carrying the word of hope to the farthest nooks and corners; we needed literature, and the brains of the nation would produce it, for I knew that latent genius was everywhere, needing only the suggestion to burst forth. I knew there were thousands who would respond as quickly as I to the impulse of a New Social Order.

I dreamed of a time when I could send out 10,000 copies of the paper a week—a circulation I had never aspired to for any of my previous publications. There were no fifty-cent papers in the nation at that time. I figured that I could print a fifty-cent paper with no advertising, and, with a circulation of 10,000 copies, pay the expenses. Little did I dream of the 300,000 circulation that awaited it. My paper was greeted with a welcome from the first issue, though I was unknown outside my home county. The samples I sent out brought back subscriptions by the hundreds, by the thousands; and I was swamped for lack of facilities. Such a reception naturally increased my enthusiasm. Hundreds were soliciting for the paper without any remuneration. They also demanded books and pamphlets; and they were printed and bought by the ton. And the *Appeal* Army grew and grew and grew until it numbered thousands—thirty thousands; and the vote grew and grew year by year; and other papers started,

and magazines. And then the capitalist papers and magazines began to sit up and take notice. At first they ignored; then they sneered; then they maligned—and then some of them began to discuss it. The magazines began to print things; they sought Socialist writers who had been hanging on the outer edge of want and isolation. These writers had largely been created during the sixteen years since I began to cry out in the wilderness of Mammon—practically all of them. Most of them had their attention directed to the subject by reason of the work of the *Appeal's* Invisible Army—for the Army had made the paper, as, without their unpaid efforts, it could not have had a thousand subscribers. Even the president took notice of the *Appeal's* story of *The Jungle*, by Comrade Sinclair, and the parliaments of Europe and the world awoke as it had never been awakened to the growth of the Socialist Crusade.

But do not think that this has been done without sacrifices and heart-aches. It has not all been rosy and smiling success. There have been many dark hours—days and months of them together. I have walked the floor many a night; I have walked the silent woods and lonely railroad tracks with feelings akin to suicide; the rest would be so sweet; what a relief to end it all. And then I would busy myself in work to forget the troubles and losses. I kept on. How-many times I have written to cheer you when my heart was sad and the outlook gloomy. Through it all we have worked on together, you and I, and behold the result! We have made the greatest propaganda paper the world has ever seen; a paper with greater influence today than any other publication in the world. It may not be profound and it may not be polished in grammatical construction—but then you know the world is full of people who are not polished, and we are trying to reach them. The great battles of the world have not been fought and won by polished humanity. We are of this great unpolished army, you and I, and I have no apologies to offer for either of us. We have done something which the polished fellows refused to do—done something that needed doing. And now the polished fellows are coming. Our literary comrades are getting the highest rates of all writers for their productions—and you volunteers of the *Appeal* Army have made this possible at this time.

Now we shall have more help. Papers and magazines are multiplying; our writers are multiplying; conditions are making for greater strides than we have yet made; our names may not be remembered, but the influence of the work we have done will never perish, but go on growing as the centuries fade away. The *Appeal* Army has built an imperishable monument, though it will not be penciled with the names of thousands who have given up their lives for the cause of Human Liberty.

When I turn from the ferment of fraud and crime, and look at this picture of progress, made from almost nothing to a national movement inside of sixteen years—then I know we are sure of success, that the future belongs to Socialism, and see its first faint streaks of light on the eastern horizon.

We know that the Future belongs to us!

December 8, 1906

The Bundle Brigade

The Bundle Brigade is composed of that division of the *Appeal* Army that subscribes for a bundle of five copies or more each and every week and drops them in likely places. Here are a couple of letters which show how the work is done and what the results are:

"A man dropped a sample copy of your paper inside my fence; that's why I took a notion to subscribe."—Erick Gustara, Sunnyvale, Calif.

"Enclosed find $1.75 for which send the Appeal *to the seven enclosed names. I have been a Republican all my life until eight or ten months ago, when I ran across a copy of the* Appeal to Reason, *which had been left on my front porch. I read it and subscribed for the paper and voted the straight Socialist ticket in November and intend to do so from now on."—Buell, Shelbyville, Ind.*

I don't know who it was that dropped these papers on the front porch and in the yard of these new recruits to the Socialist party; but whoever they are they performed an important service for this mighty movement. There are now 3,329 *Appeal* Army comrades who subscribe for weekly bundles, and in thousands of cities and towns and villages the work of silently making recruits is going on. Let me urge that every comrade who is not now on the bundle list add his name to it. A bundle of five each week for one year costs $1; a bundle of ten, $2; 25 copies, $5. . . .

January 5, 1907

Bully for Oklahoma

Last week we started the Oklahoma state edition of the *Appeal*. It is the same edition as this with the exception of the third page, which is given over entirely to news from Oklahoma and editorial comment on state politics by Comrade Branstetter, the State Secretary. The cost of this edition to the Oklahoma comrades is nothing, except the work of maintaining the list at 25,000. In fact, the *Appeal* pays to the state office $10 per week, thus lightening the financial burden of maintaining state headquarters.

The great value of this edition to the movement in Oklahoma lies in the fact that the State

Secretary talks to 25,000 people every week. He reaches the membership four times a month with news and announcements. It places the movement in each county in close touch with the comrades in all other counties and with the state office. It gives the Oklahoma comrades a state paper with a larger circulation than any weekly Socialist publication in the United States and a larger circulation in Oklahoma than that of any old party daily or weekly printed within its borders.

Any state in the union may have a special state edition of the *Appeal* on the same terms, and there are a dozen states that ought to have a list of 25,000 easily. Once attained it automatically maintains itself.

July 18, 1908

Letters to the Appeal sometimes reflected a certain hostility to socialism. In October, 1908. Fred Warren was under indictment in the Taylor case and preparing for trial at Fort Scott, Kansas.

Wow!
Biff!
Bang!

New York City, Oct. 12, 1908.
Fred D. Warren,
Editor Appeal to Reason,
Girard, Kans.

Sir: I have seen with great disgust your vile, filthy and ignorant publication, and it is a great surprise to me that the authorities of so progressive a section of the country as the west evidently is, allow such an ignorant jackass as you must be to call yourself an editor. The lying and malicious statements made in your paper are absolutely revolting and disgusting to any decent minded person. To be brief, your paper can only be equalled in its filthiness by your own rotten mind, and if you ever get to the city and any one gets wise to you, you will certainly be horsewhipped which is far too good for you. Myself and a good many friends to whom I have shown your infamous "spawn," would like to meet you in an eight-foot room where we would teach you better than this letter can our opinion of you. Maxmillian Feldman, Rm. 2312 Park Row Bldg. P.S. We certainly shall do all in our power to suppress the publication of your vile sheet.

I should be very glad indeed to accommodate Mr. Feldman by visiting New York, but every moment of my time from now until the election is occupied with work on the *Appeal* during the day and at night by some speaking engagement in the third Kansas district doing what I can to insure the election of Ben Wilson to congress.

I am making no dates "after the election" as I have a very pressing engagement with Uncle Sam at Fort Scott and my future movements are therefore shrouded in more or less mystery.

If Mr. Roosevelt's department of justice (?) will give the *Appeal* editor a trial we are quite confident of vindication and in that event we will be at liberty to travel about the United States, and it is more than likely that I will visit New York before the holidays. I shall notify Mr. Feldman on my arrival and give him my city address. I note Mr. Feldman takes the precaution of announcing that himself and a "good many friends" will be there to greet me in an eight-foot ring. A coward always depends on his "friends" to back him.

The *Appeal* editor's fighting weight is 117 lbs. net. It is possible that between now and the holidays I will be able to train down to the Feldman size.

October 24, 1908

Appeal to Reason editor Fred D. Warren at his desk in Girard. The Charles H. Kerr company was the primary American publisher of socialist literature during the early decades of the twentieth century. Courtesy University of Colorado Historical Collections.

Comrade Fred Warren

SOCIALIST EDITOR WHO WAS
CONVICTED AND SENTENCED
BY A FEDERAL COURT, U. S. A.

"IN conclusion, permit me to say that I am not asking the mercy or leniency of this court. I have committed no crime and there is festering in my conscience no accusation of guilt, but if my conviction and punishment will serve to rivet public attention upon the abuses which I have tried to point out, then I shall feel that I have not suffered this humiliation in vain.

"After all, this is the price of human progress. Why should I expect immunity? The courts have ever been and are to-day the bulwarks of the ruling class. Why should they not punish offenders against that class?"— *Extract from Warren's Federal Court Speech.* Paper, 10 cents

CHARLES H. KERR & COMPANY
118 W. KINZIE STREET. CHICAGO

Many accounts of the Appeal *Army appeared over the years. Wayland's description explains how essential the Army was to the paper's life and influence.*

The Wonderful Army

J. A. WAYLAND

Fifty-six thousand men and women are behind the *Appeal*. It is the greatest Army in the nation. They infest every city, town and hamlet of the land. They solicit subscriptions, sell and distribute books and pamphlets on economic topics on every highway. They work without money and without price. They not only pay their own expenses, postage and costs of money orders on what they solicit, but often pay for the subscriptions out of their own scanty purses. No other publication on earth has such an Army. No other Army has such a determination, loyalty and ability. If the *Appeal* paid each worker only $1 a year, not their postage money, it would mean $56,000 a year—a sum that would bankrupt it in a few months. That is why the *Appeal* can be printed at such a low rate; that is why it sells literature at a price that astonishes other publishers; that is why

the great building in Girard is filled with the most wonderful modern machinery and methods for supplying this tremendous demand. This is why no other paper can understand why the subs roll in by the hundreds of thousands when other papers are making frantic efforts to stem the tide of declining business. And what a power when so many work together like a well-drilled Army! It touches every part of the nation such as no other paper does, and it touches people who can THINK. And thinking people have many times the power and influence that others do. This Army is increasing rapidly. It is gathering tens of thousands a year now. We have the machinery whereby we can start a letter to each member of this Army in 48 hours from the time its need is known. This Army is the greatest force in the movement. It can be relied on to act when it is shown the reasons for action. In the coming time the members of this Army will tell the story to their children and they will repeat it to their grandchildren, just as do the grandchildren of the old-time abolitionists with their "grapevine telegraph" and "underground highways" for the helping of runaway slaves. Say, this is a great time to live, and we are the livest members of the race.

October 15, 1910

Helen Keller Writes

Wrentham, Mass., December 4, 1910:

The *Appeal to Reason*, Girard, Kan.

Dear Appeal—I enclose a check to be used for subscriptions to the *Appeal to Reason*. I am prompted to this by indignation at the unrighteous conviction of the editor, Mr. Fred Warren.

I believe that the conviction is unrighteous, although I have arrived at this conclusion with some hesitancy. For a mere woman, denied participation in government, must needs speak timidly of the mysterious mental processes of men, and especially of ermined justices. No doubt any layman would give offense who should be guilty of the indiscretion of criticising the decision of a high court. Still, the more I study Mr. Warren's case in the light of the United States constitution, which I have under my fingers, the more I am persuaded either that I do not understand, or that the judges do not. I used to honor our courts, which I was told were no respecters of persons. I was glad and proud in the thought of our noble heritage—a free law open to all children of the nation alike. But I have come not only to doubt the divine impartiality ascribed to our judiciary, but also to question whether our judges are conspicuous for simple good sense and fair dealing. We may be pardoned if we regard some of their decisions merely as human imperfection, a result of our common mortality, dependent for their seeming inequity upon our poor human prejudice and ignorance.

Are not these the facts: Several years ago three officers of the Western Federation of Miners were indicted for a murder committed in Idaho. They were in Colorado, and the governor of that state did not extradite them. They were kidnaped and brought to an Idaho prison. They applied to the supreme court for a writ of habeas corpus, on the ground that they were illegally held because they had been illegally captured. The supreme court replied: "Even if it be true that the arrest and deportation of Pettibone, Moyer and Haywood from Colorado was by fraud and connivance to which the governor of Colorado was a party, this does not make out a case of violation of the rights of the appellants under the constitution and the laws of the United States."

Some years before this event ex-Governor Taylor of Kentucky was indicted for murder, and was wanted in his state. Mr. Warren offered a reward for the capture of Mr. Taylor and his return to the Kentucky authorities. I understand that it is not an unusual thing for a citizen to aid in this manner in the apprehension of a fugitive from justice.

To what twistings, turnings and dark interpretation must the judges of the circuit court be driven in order to send Mr. Warren to prison! As I understand it, a federal law defining the kind of matter which it is a crime to mail has been stretched to cover his act. What was the act? The offer of a reward was printed on the outside of envelopes mailed from Girard by Mr. Warren. This was construed as threatening because it was an encouragement to others to kidnap a man under indictment. This the supreme court had by implication declared to be an innocent act; for in the case of Pettibone, Moyer and Haywood the accomplished act itself was held to be no infringment of the rights of a citizen.

One need not be a Socialist to realize the significance, the gravity, not of Mr. Warren's offense, but of the offense of the judges against the constitution, and against democratic rights. It is provided that "congress shall make no law . . . abridging the freedom of speech or of the press." Surely this means that we are free to print and mail any innocent matter. What Mr. Warren printed and mailed had been established by the supreme court as innocent. What beam was in the eye of the honorable judges of the supreme court? Or what mote

Appeal to Reason editors
George D. Brewer and
Eugene V. Debs, Minot,
North Dakota, October 11,
1910. Courtesy Special
Collections, Pittsburgh
State University.

was in the eye of the justices of the circuit courts? It is evident that their several decisions do not stand in the same light. It has been my duty, my life-work to study physical blindness, its causes and its prevention. I learn that our physicians are making great progress in the cure and the prevention of blindness. What surgery of politics, what antiseptic of common sense and right thinking, shall be applied to cure the blindness of our judges, and to prevent the blindness of the people, who are the court of last resort?

Faithfully yours,
Helen Keller
December 24, 1910

Hardly intimidated by criticism, the Appeal was proud of its purpose and socialist objectives.

Terrorizing by Clamor and Votes

The Appeal to Reason *is asking Socialists to contribute to a fund to send the paper to the voters of California till the election of 1912 at the rate of 50 cents. This newspaper can well afford to enter on such a campaign scheme for boosting its own circulation, and enhancing the value of its advertising. There is thrift as well as anarchy in the plans of the Socialist propagandists. However, that is not the point. The proposal is to terrorize the courts. That paper is a recognized organ of militant Socialism in the United States, and has won a position of great influence. Its action and spirit, therefore, are to be accepted as that of Socialism. If that is the case, then Socialists are committed to a program of anarchy, for terrorizing by clamor and votes is as evil in effect as terrorizing by dynamite.—Fort Worth (Texas)* Register.

The *Register* has stated the case exactly. We are after more subscribers, not only in California, but also throughout the nation. Like other papers, we live on our subscription list, but, unlike the capitalist press, we are not in the newspaper business with the sole and only object of what we can get out of it, but for the purpose of creating a political revolution.

The *Register* is also correct in its statement that we are trying to terrorize the courts. More than this. We are trying to abolish the capitalist courts entirely.

"Terrorizing by clamor and votes." That's a good phrase. We could not make one that better fits the case. We are clamoring 52 weeks in the year. Our clamor is making votes, and these same votes are terrorizing the judges. Precisely. That's the only thing that WILL terrorize them. The only thing they and the whole capitalist class fear.

The *Appeal* has been preaching political revolution for years, to the end that we may bring about a complete change in our economic system. Our objective is democratic control of the capital of the nation. By capital we mean the railroads, the mines, factories, and places where men work to earn their bread. The control of the nation's work shops will give us control of our jobs, by which we will regulate the hours of labor, the sanitary surroundings, and the measure of our compensation. From the nation's natural resources we will build ourselves houses, instead of hovels, in which to live. We will destroy disease, by abolishing the conditions that cause disease. In other words, we are aiming at a new society that will produce wealth, for use, and not for profit. It will be a worker's country, an industrial commonwealth. We expect to reach this result by means of the ballot box—the election of political officials who will take the reins of government, as mayors, sheriffs, legislators, judges, and, finally, the president of the nation. So long as they leave us the ballot, we will advocate its sole use as a means to our ends.

If they disfranchise us, then we will advocate physical force as did our forefathers—armed revolution—a general strike—the raising of mobs.

Work force in front of fourth and final Girard home of the Appeal to Reason. Courtesy Museum of Crawford County, Girard, Kansas.

Disfranchised people have the inalienable right to use any weapon within reach for the attainment of their rights and liberties. Until that time comes, and we hope it never may, any other means than the ballot box can arouse no considerable public approval in this country.

For the first time in our history, the working people are seriously learning how to use the weapons our forefathers handed them in 1776. These sturdy ancestors said then that just governments spring from the consent of the people. The only thing the working class have won through the years that have followed has been universal suffrage, which now exists for men except in a few states in the south. Soon this right will be granted to the women. The task that is ours is to teach our toiling millions how to use this weapon. We are seeking to get into the workers' heads one idea, that of a solid class-conscious vote. Once having freed the worker from the superstition of his capitalist party, we have little trouble in teaching him the lesson of Socialism. We are urging the workers to political solidarity, which, when accomplished, will give into our hands all the machinery of power—executive, judicial, legislative and military.

This is our program in California where we are concentrating our energy, because Morgan and his fellow conspirators, who represent the militant capitalist class, have chosen this state for the battle ground. There are 100,000 union members in California. Naturally, they are our first objective. Around this militant band who are now having to fight for their very existence, we will group the great body of unorganized workers, while the scattered and exploited farmers will support the wings of this army. These industrial elements make up the great majority of the voters of the state, and man to man we must reach them, rouse their slumbering intelligence, teach them the lesson of class action, and urge them on to political revolution.

These are the wealth producers of the state. It is they who do the work and bear the brunt of life. They who have the inalienable right to life, liberty and pursuit of happiness. They are the people to whom California, by right, belongs, and not the Southern Pacific railroad, the Morgans and the Guggenheims. The judges on the California benches are mere puppets of capitalism. Long have they ruled and terrorized the people. The time has come when the people are going to do some terrorizing themselves.

June 24, 1911

The Appeal *received many letters similar to this "Open Confession" from an anonymous correspondent in North Dakota. With literacy and access to education far from universal, and rural America much larger and more isolated than at present, the* Appeal *brought not only economic and political philosophy but news and culture to millions of American homes.*

An Open Confession

For a long time I have been thinking of writing the *Appeal* a confession of appreciation. I have at times helped it a little but it has done a hundred times as much for me. Though it is fifteen years ago since the *Appeal* hustler touched me up for a quarter and went his way I will never forget the incident, as that is just what made a man out of me. He got my quarter and name and it did not take him two minutes. I have often wondered who he might be. I had never read a newspaper in my life outside of some local prattle and had scarcely any education. One day I got into an argument about Socialists being free lovers and finding I did not know enough to defend them as they should be, I wrote Wayland asking for some books. He made out a list for me that cost six dollars. I bought them all and when I went to read them I found there were a lot of big words that I did not know and I got a dictionary and set to work to find out and to secure a bit of education. I wish every young man had a library like mine. When I say it has made a man out of me I mean in the sense the unknowing can not conceive.—Box 294, Kenmore, N.D.

December 30, 1911

Both Wayland and Warren were often accused of making huge profits from the Appeal and from other sources. As a rule, the accusations were easy to disprove.

Warren's Zinc Mine to be Given Away

FRED D. WARREN

A few weeks ago the American reading public was informed under big headlines in the daily press that the editor of the *Appeal to Reason* had made a big strike in the zinc mining district of Missouri and his wealth therefrom reached a figure of dizzy heights. The following paragraph is taken from the Buffalo *Express*, of June the 9th and fairly represents the majority of the stories published, doubtless for the purpose of creating distrust in the minds of those who have been supporting the *Appeal to Reason* in its work for Socialism. The *Express* says:

Fred D. Warren, the Appeal *editor, has fared pretty well. The money he got out of his small interest in the* Appeal to Reason *he put into Missouri lands. Zinc was discovered on his property and a town grew up around the zinc mines. He is said to be almost as wealthy as Wayland. He sold his zinc mines and he sold the town that grew up around the zinc mines.*

This alleged zinc mine is located in Stone County, Mo., a few miles from Galena, the county seat. I know this must be the property referred to by the metropolitan press, as it is the only bit of real estate I ever owned in the state of Missouri, excepting a six-room cottage in Rich Hill, Mo. There are forty acres in this "valuable" plot of ground, the description on the abstract reads as follows: SE1/4 NW1/4 Sec. 13, Twp. 22, R. 23. I purchased this forty-acre farm five years ago for the purpose of some day retiring to this Ozark retreat far from the haunts of federal judges and district attorneys. However, life has been too strenuous and I have been unable to realize this dream. Rumors of the discovery of the valuable deposit of zinc and lead have reached Girard in the past but I have never taken the time to make an investigation. These rumors were doubtless the foundation for the story so widely circulated of my valuable zinc mine.

Just at this time I am much more interested in the circulation of the *Appeal* than I am in any zinc and lead mine that I may happen to possess, and I have therefore decided to give the property to someone who reads these lines. It will be given to the four persons who send in the largest number of subscriptions to the *Appeal to Reason*. The plot will be divided into four ten-acre tracts. Tracts No. 1 and 2 will be given away in September. Tract No. 1 will be open to all entries. Tract No. 2 will be open to only those contestants who have never sent a club of subscribers to the *Appeal*. By making this restriction we give both our old and our new friends an opportunity to share in the wealth which the capitalist press has credited to me. . . .

August 31, 1912

Wayland's suicide on November 10, 1912, saddened friends and comrades nationwide. His death opened the way to the sale of the Appeal *and contributed to both its loss of influence and to its ultimate demise.*

Last Conversation With My Father

JON G. WAYLAND

In the last conversation I had with my father, on Tuesday after election day, at the depot, as I was returning to school, he said, after talking over the persecution at Fort Scott: "My boy, I am going to end it all; I cannot longer stand this persecution, mental oppression and misunderstanding. I have done my work living and worn myself out, and perhaps my death will further the interests of the cause."

I remonstrated with him, but to no avail. He said, "It will do no good to argue for I have made up my mind."

Not once during this talk did he exhibit any feeling of malice or hatred toward even those gov-

ernment officials who are directly responsible for the death. He felt it was all a part of the order of life and unavoidable.

As I entered the train I turned to wave my last goodbye, with the confident hope that he would feel better after a good night's sleep, and despairing mood pass away. With a heavy brow, but kindly smile which he always wore, he said, "Good bye Jon."

November 23, 1912

To a Good Soldier

KATE RICHARDS O'HARE

We shed no tears of grief; grief is for the naked lives of those who have made the world no better.

We have no idle, vain, regrets; for who are we to judge, or say that he has shirked his task or left some work undone? No eyes can count the seed that he has sown, the thoughts that he has planted in a million souls now covered deep beneath the mold of ignorance which will not spring into life until the snows have heaped upon his grave and the sun of springtime comes to reawake the sleeping world.

Sleep on, our comrade; rest your weary mind and soul; sleep sweet and deep, and if in other realms the boon is granted that we may again take up our work, you will be with us and give us of your strength, your patience and your loyalty to your fellow men. We bring no ostentatious tributes of our love, we spend not gold for flowers for your tomb, but with hearts that rejoice at your deliverance offer a comrade's tribute to lie above your breast—the red flag of human brotherhood.

November 23, 1912

Tomorrow We Fight

A. W. RICKER

Wayland was in at the beginning, when the working people heard the word of Socialism with a shudder, viewed the Socialist with suspicion, and the public treated him with ostracism. He lived long enough to see this pass and the people yield to our propaganda. He also lived long enough to feel the iron heel of privilege, and to become the mark of its hireling bloodhounds. No longer does plutocracy ignore us, and the hireling capitalist press treat us with a sneer of contempt. A million voters have spoken at the ballot box. And ninety per cent of these owe their first thought of Socialism, just as does the writer, to the *Appeal to Reason*. We have become dangerous, therefore must we be watched and persecuted. This was new to Wayland, who in all these years has never pushed his personality to the fore, but always his ideas. Persecution, personal attack, slander and abuse, weapons he himself had never used drove him to suicide.

We, who know Wayland best, fully understand that his act was one of superlative bravery—done with the same unfaltering courage, and self-sacrifice that has made him in former years always willing to efface himself for the movement's good. He effaced himself, not through fear, as his enemies will charge, but to foil the conspiracy against the paper he founded and which he loved better than his own life. He knew he was leaving it in hands incorruptible. He had long ago picked Warren as his successor and turned the paper over to him. Wayland is dead. The *Appeal* lives. Today we mourn. Tomorrow we fight.

November 23, 1912

comings, and being human, of course he had some, all classes agree that he devoted the highest and the best that was in him to the service of mankind. His theory of life may have been wrong but he was true to that theory and met death with it on his lips. He believed that the competitive system was wrong; that is, that a system which encouraged this ceaseless struggle to acquire more of the material things of life than you could properly use, when by so doing you deprived some of your fellow men of the bare necessities of life, was wrong. He believed that there were enough of the good things in this world to properly supply all if equitably divided. His fight was for such an equitable division. The more you think about that theory, the more you become convinced that the man who advocated it was not a crank nor an enemy of mankind.

Try as we may those hopeless words, "The struggle under the competitive system is not worth the effort; let it pass," will keep ringing in our ears as well as yours. They are words that burn into the soul of mankind. They are words that live long after poor Wayland is forgotten. That there is much wrong with the economic system of this country nearly all will agree and the day is not far distant when there will be a change for the better. It may come through the blood of our children or it may come through peaceful and wise legislation, but it will come. . . .

November 23, 1912

Words that Burn

FROM *Daily*, ARKANSAS CITY, ARK.

"The struggle under the competitive system is not worth the effort. Let it pass." With this final message to his fellow men J. A. Wayland, by his own hand, passed from the battle of life to the supposed peace of death. In his untimely death, the poor, the oppressed, the afflicted, lost a brother and a friend. Whatever may have been his short-

From thousands of articles written by J. A. Wayland, Fred Warren chose to reprint "Why of the 'One Hoss'" as an epigraph for his friend.

Why of the "One Hoss"

J. A. WAYLAND

Criticism and inquiries why I use the soubriquet "One Hoss" have been coming in much of late. While in Pueblo, Colo., I operated a small job printing office. I had only a few fonts of type and one little press and my competitors were well supplied with all modern conveniences. I had to make a living and I went to work to get it. I named the office the "One-Hoss Print Shop" and used it as an imprint. I never abandoned the plebeian appellation, although in four years the business grew to occupy a brick block of its own full of presses of best make. I am not ashamed of the record. I worked physically and mentally and am proud of it. After that I made thousands of dollars speculating in real estate, but that is nothing to be proud of. My critics fear the vulgarism of "one hoss" will detract. I write to the laboring classes who are not shocked at such expressions. I am one of them and proud of that. Dull as they are they are the salt of the earth and any reform that ever comes must come through them. To them I have given all that I have, all that I am and all that I may be, and by them I expect to be misunderstood. But in my own way I shall lecture them and explain to them and exhort them to better conditions. I would not give much for the culture, refinement and thoughtfulness of those who fail to understand the one hoss.

November 23, 1912

Frank Gardner's experience as an Appeal agitator was shared by many American labor organizers and socialists.

An Agitator's Experience

FRANK GARDNER

I have just been arrested, searched, released and run out of Coalwood, W. Va. I sent you a telegram a few minutes ago, but may not receive a reply before I leave Iaeger. Coalwood is a mining camp nine miles from Iaeger and owned solely by the Carter Coal company. Iaeger is a free town (no mines) on the Norfolk and Western railroad, run-

ning up Tug river. I have been a United Mine Worker for twelve years, but have not paid any dues since February, 1913, having been in the non-union fields of old Virginia since that time.

About three weeks ago I came from Old Virginia to Coalwood, W. Va., where I secured work as a coal digger, digging for 30 cents per ton pick work. I mined, shot and loaded cars for 60 cents that were six feet wide, eight and a half feet long and from two and a half to three feet deep. The gauge of the track was four feet by the rule and the seams of coal four and one-half. Powder sold for $2 per keg—Dupont thribble of powder that I have bought all over western Kentucky for $1.25. I worked fourteen nights—long enough to have my mail changed to my new address and to send a dollar for subs and get in an order for some *Appeals*. This morning I started distributing the papers to a few of the miners. About noon I was sitting in front of the company store (there being no other in the place) when Horton, the mine guard, came along with a pistol in his belt and the following conversation followed:

Horton: Here, I want to speak to you. Graham is your name, isn't it?

Graham: Yes, sir (raising up).

Horton: Have you been handling the Socialist papers around here today?

Graham: Yes, sir, the *Appeal to Reason*.

Horton: Are you a Socialist?

Graham: Yes, sir, I sure am.

Horton: How long have you been one?

Graham: About eight years.

Horton: Are you doing this work here?

Graham: What, distributing papers?

Horton: Yes, and working for Socialism.

Graham: Well, yes, I have worked for Socialism and circulated the *Appeal* everywhere I have been for the past eight years, though on my own hook, as an individual.

About this time he seized me and began to search my pockets, at the same time saying: "Let me see what you've got on you." He then took me inside the coal company's office telling me all the while that they could not have Socialists nor Socialism around there at all, and saying that he was going to call the squire. I told him in the presence of four or five men that he had no right to detain me, without a warrant. He told me not to get "rosey." Then I asked, "Am I under arrest? And what for?" He told me to never mind and stand right where I was, that he would telephone the squire and see what to have done with me. I said, "You can't do anything but pay me off."

He could not get the squire because the line was down, so he called over another line for Mr. English who I suppose was the superintendent of the mines and told him that he had a fellow there in the office that had been scattering Socialist literature and that he dug coal in No. 1 mine.

After some consultation he turned to the bookkeeper and instructed him to pay me off and ordered me to get my clothes and get out of there on the first train. I did as he suggested for I had no gun and it was lonesome there. Horton told me several times that my name would be published and that I would get no more work in this field.

FRANK GARDNER *Iaeger, W. Va.*

August 2, 1913

Louis Klamroth was the best-known member of the Appeal *Army.*

Appeal Agitator Dead

A telegram to the *Appeal* announces the death of Louis Klamroth. "The Mightiest War Horse in the *Appeal* Army." That is the title given him years ago by that other mighty war horse, J. A. Wayland. And never was a title more appropriate. Comrade Louis Klamroth was born in Cincinnati, Ohio; moved to California in 1893. Here he read *Looking Backward* and Wayland's *Coming Nation*. In 1894 he started traveling for the *Coming Nation* and later for the *Appeal*. He has traveled over seventeen states, and through British Colum-

bia. He was arrested twenty-nine times for street speaking, driven out of twenty-five places, prohibited from speaking in forty places, been egged twenty times, knocked down and clubbed, hose turned on him, and buckets of water thrown on him. But in spite of all, or rather by the aid of this peculiar encouragement, he took over 100,000 subscriptions for Socialist papers and sold over 15,000 books. He never would accept any of the premiums given away by the *Appeal* during his long years of service. He was nearly seventy years old. He made a good fight. The world is better off because of Louis Klamroth. Future generations will live in a better world because of him. May he rest in peace.

November 22, 1913

The political principles of the New Appeal, *Emanuel Halde-man-Julius's rendering of Wayland's original vision, appeared often during the spring of 1918. Created to avoid wartime censorship, both the* New Appeal *and its principles are much-trimmed versions of Wayland's and Warren's paper and socialist politics. "The* New Appeal's *Fighting Platform" is particularly significant for what it evades—the meaning and consequences of World War I.*

The *New Appeal*'s Fighting Platform

The *New Appeal* believes in the superiority of public ownership of the nation's great industries over private ownership of the industries, from the standpoint both of justice and efficiency. We believe in the extension of the principles of democracy to industry, in the creation of a real fellowship of workers collectively owning and democratically managing the commonly used machinery of life and labor. We believe in the elimination of those methods of exploitation and oppression expressed in the terms of rent, interest and profit. We believe in the establishment of service as the supreme social law, in rewarding no man except for useful labor actually performed and in guaranteeing to all such labor its full reward.

In order to make our political democracy complete, the *New Appeal* favors the immediate granting of nation-wide suffrage to women, through the adoption by Congress and the states of the Susan B. Anthony amendment to the Constitution of the United States.

As measures for safeguarding our democracy and making it more effective, the *New Appeal* regards as important the application of the initiative, referendum and recall, both in state and national politics.

That minority political parties, representing the civic and social ideals of substantial groups of citizens, may be properly recognized in the active machinery of government, the *New Appeal* advocates the adoption of the system of proportional representation in state and nation.

The *New Appeal* views as dangerous to the progress of democracy the continued exercise by the courts of the land of the usurped power to pass upon the constitutionality of laws enacted by the elected representatives of the people, and as further inimical to the workings of justice the almost unlimited power of the courts to issue injunctions; and we believe that these undemocratic powers should be taken away.

The *New Appeal* believes that those basic rights of democracy—free press, free speech and free assemblage—should be jealously guarded and should be held inviolate.

The *New Appeal* favors gradual increases in the income, corporation and inheritance tax provisions, with a view to steadily reducing excessive fortunes and curbing the power of unjust wealth and to providing large sums with which to finance the progressive socialization of industry through the government.

The *New Appeal* believes that the government should as rapidly as possible take over the tele-graphs, telephones and all the important means of transportation and communication in the nation.

The *New Appeal* commends the food control measures adopted by the administration as being steps in a right direction, and with the object of lowering the cost of living and of protecting the producer and the consumer, on the farm and in the city, we advocate government, state or municipal ownership of grain elevators, stockyards, storage warehouses and other agencies of distribution.

The *New Appeal* believes that natural resources, such as mines, quarries, oil wells, forests and water power should be made public possessions.

The *New Appeal* urges as highly important at this time the utilization of all idle cultivable land, through collective ownership or through the taxation out of the hands of private owners of all land values that do not arise legitimately out of the actual cultivation and improvement of the land.

The *New Appeal* favors a comprehensive program of war taxation that will tax war profits and idle land to the limit and thus help to remove from the shoulders of the common people a great part of the financial burdens brought by the war.

Considering the present great demand for labor created by the need for war materials and the withdrawal of hundreds of thousands of workers from the industries into the military camps, the *New Appeal* believes that the government should adopt a thorough, efficient system of organizing the labor supply of the country with a view to getting workers for all the jobs and jobs for all the workers.

The *New Appeal* favors the continuance after the war of the present government control over factories engaged in producing war munitions and that the government direct their production after the war into the channels of peace, to the producing of agricultural and manufacturing implements and machinery that will be used in building up the great wealth-producing industries of the nation on a basis of socialization.

The *New Appeal* heartily approves of the recent

bill passed by Congresss prohibiting the sale in interstate commerce of goods produced by establishments employing child labor, and believes that the prohibition of child labor should be made effective within the states.

The *New Appeal* favors all laws for the protection of the workers, such as shorter workdays, higher wages, weekly rest periods, minimum wage laws, regular inspection of workshops, factories and mines with laws for the strict enforcement of safe and sanitary conditions of labor.

The *New Appeal* believes in rational restrictions of the employment of women, that their life and health may not be endangered by employment in occupations for which they are manifestly unsuited, and we favor the remuneration of women workers on the basis of equal pay with men for equal work performed.

The *New Appeal* favors all laws protecting the right of workers, men and women, to organize, establishing the principle of collective bargaining and promoting the principles of industrial democracy.

The *New Appeal* advocates industrial insurance of the workers against unemployment, sickness, accident, etc., and the establishment of old age and maternity pensions.

The measures we have outlined as falling in line with the policy of the *New Appeal* are the more important measures that have been agitated in the field of social reform. Added to these are many other ideas and proposals, all affecting the public interest in their particular spheres, that receive the aid of the *New Appeal*. Wherever there is a struggle going on around a vital public issue, the *New Appeal* upholds the side of public good against the side of privileged greed, the side of social and political progress against the side of reaction.

The *New Appeal* invites the support of all those who believe in these principles of social, industrial and political progress.

May 25, 1918

With the Appeal's politics severely compromised and its subscription base damaged by World War I and its repressive aftermath, the paper's editors and publisher tried a variety of financial pleas in its concluding years. As Haldeman-Julius lost his belief in socialism and concentrated the Appeal's resources on publishing inexpensive books, the Appeal's force and vitality continued to decline until November, 1922, when it ceased publication altogether.

Vote for the *Appeal's* Life or Death!

Your Ballot on This Referendum Must Decide Whether Your Paper Shall Now End Its Career—We Await Your Verdict

EMANUEL HALDEMAN-JULIUS

This is the saddest moment in the history of the *Appeal*. A conference of the editors has just been held and our decision is:

LET THE READERS DECIDE THE DEATH OF THE *APPEAL*.

We are at the end of our rope. We have done everything we could possibly think of to avert this tragic happening. Three weeks ago we rushed a circular letter to the *Appeal* Army headed "Will You Let the *Appeal* Die?" Two weeks ago Upton Sinclair came to Girard and issued a page broadside announcing new plans for a greater and better *Appeal* and urging the Army to show its appreciation by putting the Grand Old Paper on a self-sustaining basis. Last week a half page of the *Appeal* headed "Will You Let the *Appeal* Suspend?" was devoted to the serious situation now confronting us.

To all these pleas, appeals and cries for help only a few have responded. We have watched every mail for a sign or an indication that the old guard is on the march—that reinforcements are coming, but so far there has been no such good sign or promising indication. We cannot understand it. We are in no mood to try to explain it. We have no time to reason or speculate. The overwhelming fact is that the *Appeal* is sinking quickly into a financial abyss. Persons struggling desperately to save themselves have no time for speculation. Only action—effective and immediate help—counts.

At the conference just held we have gone over the letters from the *Appeal* Army. We have found some praising the *Appeal* and its great work in the past and its present heroic efforts to uphold the standard of truth in these trying times. Some of these letters were accompanied by practical expressions of help in the way of pledges and subscriptions, but other letters contained advice entirely beside the point in this desperate crisis. Surely, there still must be thousands of members of the *Appeal* Army who are yet to be heard from. You must be among them. It is inconceivable that the *Appeal* after its brilliant record of a quarter of a century is to be deserted by its faithful Army in this of all times. On the other hand, we have no way of making it certain that help is on the way and that next week will bring the much desired relief from our present terrible position.

As told before, the *Appeal* has now a deficit of $15,000, with a weekly deficit of $300 to $400. That this cannot go on is evident to any sensible person. We have just about run out of our credit and our creditors will wait no longer.

· ·

If you intend to vote that the *Appeal* shall live, let your vote be accompanied by a contribution that will enable us to carry your wish into effect. Let the size of your contribution be determined by your love for the *Appeal* and the principles it upholds. Let only your financial means limit the maximum amount you will contribute. Give as much as you can afford and help save the life of the *Appeal*.

On the other hand, if you believe that a paper like The *Appeal* is no longer needed—that the people can be left to the mercies of the "Brass Check" newspapers—that labor can be entrusted

to the loving care of the exploiters—that the capitalist politicians are to enjoy our confidence—that economic conditions are in need of no improvement—then vote that the *Appeal* shall die and cast your ballot accordingly on the following referendum. We can only keep going until July 30 and we expect that you will mail your ballot—one way or the other—not later than July 30. Better mail your ballot immediately. This matter is too serious to be fooled with or delayed. Let there be no unnecessary suspense. We are ready for your verdict.

The statement is addressed to you—who read these lines—and we expect to have your answer shortly. If you do not vote at all you will be counted among those who have decreed the death of the *Appeal*. So if you do not wish us to misunderstand your position make it clear whether you wish the *Appeal* to live or die on the following referendum. This is final. We have had our last say. It is now your say. What shall it be?

LIFE FOR THE *APPEAL*?

or

DEATH FOR THE *APPEAL*?

Cast your vote on this referendum ballot:

Appeal's Referendum Ballot
Shall It Be Life or Death? Vote now!
Appeal to Reason, Girard, Kans.

Below I am casting my ballot whether the *Appeal* shall live or DIE. I am putting an "X" mark in a square accordingly.

☐ LIFE. I enclose $_____ to save the *Appeal*. This is my contribution to cover the $15,000 deficit.

☐ DEATH. I am taking the responsibility on myself to decree the death of the *Appeal to Reason*.

My name is _____

City _____

(Mail this Referendum Ballot not later than July 30)

July 15, 1922

TWO

Common Sense and
Political Philosophy

Socialism: A theory or system of social reform which contemplates a complete reconstruction of society, with a more just and equitable distribution of property and labor. In popular usage, the term is often employed to indicate any lawless, revolutionary social schemes.[1]

The wage of a horse amounts to the hay, oats, corn, stable room and pasture he consumes. If his labor would produce no more than the things consumed by him he would be an unprofitable horse. The wage of human workers amounts to the food, clothing and shelter it buys. If a man's labor would produce no more than the value of his wages he would be unprofitable to his master—the man who hires him. It is the surplus that the horse and man produce that make both profitable, and it is this surplus that working animals produce but do not consume that makes their masters wealthy. Can you get that through your cocoanut?—*Appeal to Reason*, August 31, 1907

With distortion abroad, the *Appeal* sought to explain the meaning and implications of socialism in unavoidably plain terms. For the *Appeal* as for the American Socialist party, the central elements of socialism were public, democratized ownership and control of the means of production, production for use instead of for profit, and a classless, egalitarian society in which members received full value for their intellectual and physical labor. As critical as

these fundamental elements are to an understanding of socialism, however, outside of history they are inert and consequently at odds with Marxist theory. The *Appeal*'s socialism was a systematic theory of historical and contemporary social development and, with understanding divorced from active participation in social process an impossibility, socialism was simultaneously the practice of transforming the economic and political conditions prohibiting human emancipation.

Upon finding the dynamics and relations of capitalism (production for private profit) obscured, the *Appeal* characteristically used the labor theory of value to create reader understanding. Like Marx and numerous other political economists, writers for the *Appeal* understood that the value of a product was determined by the amount of socially necessary labor required to produce it. Hardly a conclusion restricted to the left (not only David Ricardo but Adam Smith subscribed to labor theory, for example), belief in labor theory of value was widespread in the United States. "Labor is prior to and independent of capital," Abraham Lincoln wrote in 1861. "Capital is only the fruit of labor, and could never have existed if labor had not first existed."[2] Charles Schwab, president of the Bethlehem Steel Company, declared in 1916: "Nothing has any value until turned over by the hand of labor. Everything is begun by the hand of labor and is finished by the hand of labor. Labor has produced all the wealth of the world."[3] What Marx and the *Appeal* recognized in addition is that labor power, reduced to a purchasable commodity (for wages) by capitalism, is different in kind from other commodities because it is the source of surplus value.

Like labor theory, surplus value provided effective conceptual leverage. Capital, the *Appeal* explained, paid only for necessary labor, the socially determined amount necessary for working people to reproduce their energy and return to the job. Necessary labor time, however, constituted only a part of the workday. Surplus labor, production during the remainder of the day, week, or year, was appropriated in the form of surplus value by the owner of the means of production. Put another way, capitalism's wage laborers worked roughly half the week for themselves and half the week for the owner of the means of production. Mystified by capitalist ideology as the return on investment, surplus value (unpaid production) was the source of profit and capitalism's mainspring.

The concept of surplus value revealed a great deal more to *Appeal* columnists. Appropriation of surplus value explained capital accumulation and explained how the capitalist class, performing little or no productive labor, lived off the labor of the working class. Surplus value explained 1915 American distribution-of-wealth figures showing that 2 percent of the population owned 60 percent of the national wealth, while 65 percent of the population lived in or at the edge of poverty.[4] To understand surplus value was to understand the otherwise unintelligible socialist tenets of "each according to his deeds" and "abolition of the wage system." If receiving full value for the expenditure of productive labor constituted equity, no such thing as a "fair wage" could exist under capitalist conditions. In its place stood wage slavery—exploited dependence on the owner of the means of production for the means of life.

For the *Appeal*, the mode of production (capitalism, in the case of the United States) was the primary but not the exclusive determinant of social reality. Relationship to the means of production—whether one owned them or sold labor power to the owner, whether one was a Carnegie or an iron mill worker—generally determined not only economic and social condition but consciousness as well. Any modern mode of production created a complex, dominant way of life, one in which "noneconomic" institutions and spheres were themselves conditioned, directly and indirectly, by economic influences. Determined by the mode of production were specific social and political systems that served to legitimate it and, under capitalism, to perpetuate the power of the class owning the means of production. Not even comprehensible if viewed as unrelated to the mode of production, historically specific relations of production included not only social and political institutions but semi-autonomous forms of social consciousness—cultural, political, and moral values.

Neither Marx nor the *Appeal* put primary emphasis on economic consequences such as the distribution of income. Human development and human freedom were the fundamental goals of socialism and the crucial measures of how rich or how shrunken human life was under capitalism. Consequently, Andrew Carnegie's personal income in 1899—$71,428 a day, more than the income of "35,000 working slaves" averaging their $2 per day—was most compelling to the *Appeal* for what it revealed about the structure and relations of capitalism, not what it revealed about Carnegie's fortune. Susceptible to reform (through estate taxes, income taxes, or higher wages), the distribution of income could be improved without changing the structural conditions and relations of a capitalist society. Dependence on another for the means of life inevitably produced a pervasive state of bondage—economic, political, and social subordination for the working class, the human costs of victimizing their fellows for the governing class. Regardless of how ideologically disguised and hidden from awareness, better-paid slaves remain slaves, less wealthy masters remain masters.

The *Appeal*'s political alternative emerged from the socialist values implicit in its critique of capitalism, from its belief that men and women make their own history, and from political factors that made envisioning a socialist society necessary. *Appeal* writers understood Marx's argument that the ever-moving revolutionary process would so alter capitalist consciousness, relations, and institutions as to make the specifics of socialist society impossible to predict, but they were nonetheless compelled to try. Attacked by capitalist politicians and continually asked by readers what socialist life would be like, the *Appeal* offered socialist solutions to capitalist problems throughout its years of publication. Americans wanted practical answers.

In bare outline, socialists believed in democratized public ownership of the means of social production. Depending on the scope of the enterprise, ownership would be vested in national, state, or local governments, much as the U.S. Postal Service, state universities, and public schools were owned and operated at the time. Without the enormous surplus value "tax" appropriated by capitalists, personal income would not prove enormously difficult to equalize, and the necessarily less expensive goods produced under socialist conditions would be available to all. Cooperative effort and ownership would become general, but a variety of private enterprises would continue to exist if their owners chose to operate them individually. Personal property would remain personal property. Once the antisocial consequences of profit and the wastefulness of competition were removed and replaced by democratically planned production for use and human need, the semi-luxurious necessities of life could be obtained for all by the daily labor of no more than four hours of America's able-bodied citizens. All adults would choose their vocations; more or less repellent work that could not be performed by machine could (there was no consensus) be given additional monetary reward, given social honor as well, and be temporary for those engaged in it.

Since conditions of life determined consciousness, motives of cooperation and community service would replace capitalism's motives of selfishness and greed. A socialist mode of production and set of relations, humane values and institutions, political liberty irrespective of gender, dramatically increased free-

dom from economic necessity, and a pervasive spirit of human cooperation would permit men and women to discover their unalienated individual and social nature and to develop new realms of freedom. Science, art, and literature would thrive, the capacity to feel and create beauty would be expanded, and all interpersonal relationships would be enriched. The socialist state, no longer swollen and deformed by its responsibility to preserve capitalism, would decrease in size and change in kind. The costs of government would be subtracted from full value for production, but full value would be restored to the producer in the form of such social benefits as free education and medical care. The new commonwealth would serve the people, not govern them by direct and indirect force.

In addition to developing a fundamental political philosophy, American socialists formed positions on a variety of important political and social questions. Few of those policies were quite as vital as labor's position in a broad insurgent strategy. Officially, the Socialist party subscribed to a strategy directing that the struggle against capitalism was to be mounted on two fronts, one in the realm of politics (activity directed toward electoral victory at the polls) and the other at the point of production (union organizing). The first was the exclusive territory of the Socialist party, the second the province of the labor movement. On virtually no level, however, did the two-arm conception prove to be anything but flawed and divisive. Political and union activities so interpenetrated each other that ongoing conflict soon developed between the formally separate but associated realms.

Socialists were faced with the fact that trade union activity does not create revolutionary consciousness, and they were faced as well by a Samuel Gompers-led American Federation of Labor (AFL) that was hostile to socialism. Accomodationist and narrowly reformist, the AFL never challenged the structure and relations of capitalism, moreover, the AFL's orientation hindered labor solidarity by its division of workers by craft and by its rejection of unskilled workers. Socialists sought to change the AFL's craft union philosophy to industrial unionism (integrating all workers at an industry into a single union). and they tried as well through the internal influence of socialist union members to make the AFL class-conscious and socialist. Their defeat on both counts encouraged the formation of the Industrial Workers of the World (IWW), a radical union created to organize the unorganized and confront capitalism by direct action.

Founded in 1905, its first elected officers all socialists, the IWW assumed from the outset that reform could not meaningfully alter the structural nature of capitalism. Declaring that the "working class and the employing class have nothing in common," that there "can be no peace so long as hunger and want are found among millions of working people and the few, who make up the employing class, have all the good things in life,"[5] the IWW set out to paralyze the economy by a general strike, assume state power, democratize control of the means of production, and create an egalitarian society in place of capitalism.

In its most polemical form, IWW philosophy held that electoral activity was irrelevant until capitalism was deposed: "Dropping pieces of paper into a hole in a box never did achieve emancipation for the working class, and to my thinking it never will achieve it." the IWW's Father Thomas Hagarty argued.[6] Captured as much as the Socialist party by mistaken two-arm theory, the IWW provoked conflict with the Socialist party and exacerbated tensions between conservative and left-wing factions in the party itself.

Unity between the Socialist party and American labor was crucial if capitalism was to be overturned. Instead, American capitalism succeeded in limiting the growth of unionism, and it succeeded as well in making influential union leaders (such as Samuel Gompers and the United Mine Workers' John Mitchell) unwitting accomplices in union ineffectuality. Although never monolithic, American labor remained ideologically dominated by the AFL. The IWW, because of its radical politics, was destroyed as a serious threat by state repression during World War I and its aftermath. At the same time, however, adherence to the flawed two-arm theory contributed to the lack of unity between the Socialist party and labor, and most socialists (including *Appeal to Reason*

writers) insisted all the more on the primacy of electoral action when unity failed. Trapped by an inadequate strategy, they had no other option.

The Socialist party's official position on women's rights, "equal civil and political rights for men and women," was adopted as an immediate demand at the party's founding convention in 1901. Socialists campaigned for woman suffrage in every state where it was denied and, in several states, were either influential or primarily responsible for its passage. In Nevada, for example, Socialists cast 5,451 votes when suffrage passed by some 2,500 votes in 1914. Widespread socialist efforts were the more impressive when contrasted to the rejection of women's rights by the Republican and Democratic parties. Progressive though the Socialist gender policy was, however, it did not reflect internal party conflicts on "the woman question" or reveal much about the day to day realities encountered by women in the socialist movement.Socialist women, some 10 to 15 percent of the party by organizer Caroline Lowe's estimate in 1912, occasionally rose to authority both locally and at the party's national level, but those who did so were a distinct minority. Socialists of both genders were agreed on the general proposition that socialism could not be a movement for men alone, but how that recognition was to be translated into practice was never fully resolved.

Turn-of-the-century socialists struggled personally and collectively with capitalist and patriarchal social formations, but the movement was without an adequate understanding of gender, home and family, monogamy, and feminism. Nor, as Mari Jo Buhle writes, were socialists more than partially helped by orthodox materialist theory.[7] In the *Communist Manifesto,* Marx and Engels viewed patriarchy as a precapitalist relation of production: "The Bourgeoisie, wherever it has got the upper hand, has put an end to all feudal, patriarchal . . . relations."[8] The purported absence of male domination and female subordination in capitalism and its culture could provide neither a clear understanding of gender issues nor a basis for their egalitarian resolution. Additionally, uncritical materialist theory had the effect of polarizing socialists into class-centered and feminist camps.

Orthodox theory of class and gender was most forcefully presented in the *Appeal* by May Simons. "Whether an industrial worker or a home producer," Simons argued, woman's "problem has become identical with that of the laboring man, how to obtain all that she produces. . . . Civilization, the capitalist stage of it at least, has destroyed . . . division of sexes in labor." Socialism, therefore, could not be a "sex movement"—particularly not one influenced by bourgeois suffragists.[9] For Josephine Conger, however, who began conducting the *Appeal's* Woman's Department shortly after 1900, Simons's analysis was too reductionist and at odds with contemporary reality. Conger, together with other women active in the Woman's National Socialist Union (WNSU), had learned the value of separate feminist practice: "It is absolutely necessary for women to associate themselves in woman's clubs, in order to do their best work. . . ." Working exclusively in the Socialist party was impractical: "Men and women have not felt themselves equals under the capitalist system, and it is impossible for them to come together suddenly . . . and feel and act as though they were upon an absolute equality. This state of affairs is decidedly Utopian. We may reach it some day—it is one of the things we are hoping and working for—but we have not reached it THIS day."[10] Rejecting the argument that capitalism impacted men and women identically, the *Appeal* publicized the WNSU's activities and supported Conger's feminist politics. When Conger began editing and publishing the *Progressive Woman,* Wayland printed the magazine on the *Appeal* presses.

The *Appeal* reflected the normative socialist analysis that the breakup of home and family, prostitution, and a variety of other social evils were primarily attributable to capitalism. *Appeal* columnists at times idealized and sentimentalized womanhood, but the paper was hardly limited to chivalrous sexism. Wayland believed in self-determination for *both* men and women. When Socialist men, after campaigning for woman's suffrage in California, attacked newly enfranchised women for voting for capitalist candidates in 1911, Wayland was explicit in his support of "women's power over their own lives" even if "they always voted against Socialism. . . ."[11] The day to day operation of the *Appeal* generally reflected the gender values of the dominant culture (women characteristically handled subscription details while the paper's editors were predominantly men), but self-determination and egalitarian practice were not mere abstractions. When Wayland and Warren's *Appeal* published Woman's Editions, for example, the editorship, writing, and politics of the issues were turned over entirely to women. Support for women's rights continued during Haldeman-Julius's tenure as editor and owner, but that support became increasingly more programmatic in its materialist analysis. Socialist understanding of women's oppression was far in advance of capitalist gender ideology, but socialism's orthodox version, which mechanically gave class subsuming primacy over gender issues, was too imprisoned to explain or challenge the many forms of subordination faced by women in and out of the socialist movement.

Immigration proved to be a vexed problem for socialists as well. The demands of social justice seemed everywhere to collide with economic and political reality. In 1900 the percentage of immigrants in the United States stood at 13.6 percent, slightly less than the 14.7 percent tabulated by the U.S. census in both 1890 and 1910. Immigrants constituted 40 percent of the population of America's twelve largest cities at the beginning of the twentieth century; a further 20 percent of those metropolitan populations had arrived just one generation earlier.[12] Immigrants from different ethnic backgrounds and national origins— arriving with different skills at different times, settling in different areas and conditions—did not share a homogenous set of experiences, but nearly everywhere they were met with nativist and exclusionist sentiment.

Immigrants were predominantly restricted either to jobs at the bottom of the wage scale or to piece work, where no wage scale existed. Unaware of American conditions and trade unions, often unable to speak English, new immigrants were used (as were blacks) not only as scabs and strikebreakers but to prevent labor solidarity generally. Labor historian John R. Commons's experience at a large Chicago meat packing company in 1904 was representative, not exceptional: "I saw seated around the benches of the company's employment office a sturdy group of Nordics. I asked the employment agent, 'How comes it you are employing only Swedes?' He answered, 'Well you see, it is only for this week. Last week we employed Slovaks. We change about among the different nationalities and languages. It prevents them from getting together.' "[13] Predictably, the AFL and conservative unions, finding their wage scales and organizations threatened by the influx of foreign-born workers, actively cooperated with chauvinist elements of the American population to limit immigration.

Immigration and its effects divided American socialists. A substantial number of socialists was unwilling to alienate an AFL movement on record for immigration restriction. Others absorbed the chauvinism and racism of the times. Victor Berger, a conservative socialist leader from Milwaukee and member of the party's National Executive Committee, favored European immigration but was adamant in his opposition toward Asiatic immigration. If millions of "yellow men" were to be permitted entry, Berger declared, "this country is absolutely sure to become a black-and-yellow country within a few generations."[14] The response from the socialist left and its spokesman Eugene V. Debs was equally forthright: "If Socialism, international, revolutionary Socialism, does not stand staunchly, unflinchingly, and uncompromisingly for the working class and for the exploited and oppressed masses of all lands, then it stands for none and its claim is a false pretense and its profession a delusion and snare."[15] In summary, the immigration question was so complicated by prejudice and by its economic and political consequences that socialists were unable to reach a unified position on the issue.

The same winds of divisiveness swept through the *Appeal*. On the one hand, the *Appeal* recognized that society's fundamental problem lay in an economic system that legalized the theft of surplus value from all workers, immigrant as well as native-born. Ethnic hostility and exclusionist sentiment were viewed pri-

marily as capitalist relations. Since working people produced more than they were paid in return, room for all existed in America. Regardless of that analysis, however, the *Appeal* was too rarely able to free itself from racial prejudice against Chinese "coolie" laborers. The majority of the *Appeal* writers, more captives of their times than they recognized, absorbed racial prejudices from the dominant culture and found neither the opportunity nor the political will to undo their effects.

Prejudice against people of color was nearly ubiquitous in turn-of-the-century America. The Socialist party's position on black Americans was developed at its founding convention in 1901. Recognizing the multiple layers of exploitative discrimination faced by blacks (as workers, as blacks, and for some, as women), the resolution acknowledged that blacks, "because of their long training in slavery and but recent emancipation therefrom, occupy a peculiar position in the working class." "Therefore," the resolution continued, we "invite the Negro to membership and fellowship with us in the world movement for economic emanicipation by which equal liberty and opportunity shall be secured to every man, and fraternity become the order of the world."[16] It proved to be one thing to recognize racial oppression, however, and another to struggle actively against it. Individual socialists sought to make racism a critical question, but the Socialist party's institutional attitude remained confused and cautious.

Party practice regarding racial issues was contradictory. Although the National Executive Committee refused to grant a state charter to a Louisiana local in 1903 because its platform advocated the "separation of the black and white races into separate communities, each race to have charge of its own affairs," segregated socialist locals later existed in Florida and Mississippi, where black party members did not belong to locals but paid dues directly to the state secretary.[17] Debs refused to speak before segregated audiences and declared, "Of course the Negro will not be satisfied with equality with reservation. Why should he be? Would you?"[18] Conscious and unconscious racism certainly existed among socialists, but many honestly believed (as they did with gender) that issues of race were subsumed by class, that socialism could make no special appeal to a specific group. Other socialists argued that an active party commitment to racial equality would not only mean a loss of votes nationally but the utter defeat of organizing campaigns in the South. Yet other socialists, W. E. B. Du Bois and William English Walling in particular, were crucially instrumental in the founding of the NAACP. "We must treat the Negro on a plane of absolute political and social equality," Walling wrote.[19] The lack of unity meant that the Socialist party made little attempt to appeal to blacks and failed to battle consistently for interracial justice.

The *Appeal* was thrown into a different kind of confusion by racial issues. During the paper's early years, the editors wrote that socialism would solve racial inequality by segregating blacks, with full political and economic rights, in autonomous, separate but equal territories. "What will Socialism mean for the negro? It will mean a house to live in, work with the product of his labor in his own hands, and separate territory in the United States to live in, where he can work out his own destiny, undisturbed by the presence of the white man."[20] The *Appeal* relied upon autonomy, the liberating effects of socialism, and democracy to resolve the race question. Racial prejudice could only be solved by "free men," both white and black. If, in later years, black and white Americans wanted full social equality and an end to segregation, that was a matter for popular decision at the polls. In the racist atmosphere at the turn of the century (the Supreme Court's *Plessy* v. *Ferguson* decision had upheld the "separate but equal" principle in 1896), the *Appeal* saw no conflict between separate but equal segregation and the principle of justice for all.

There is no doubt whatever that the *Appeal* considered its socialist version of segregation just and progressive, but precisely how segregated status could lead to social equality, or how an islanded enclave could equally participate in a surrounding modern economy was never explained and is difficult to imagine. As the years went on, segregation disappeared from the *Appeal* and its writers became in-creasingly explicit in their belief that divisiveness around race and color was "stupid prejudice." However, even as late as 1921, Haldeman-Julius assured a questioning reader that nothing in the socialist program would produce full social association between blacks and whites: "The only equality Socialism can or will enforce will be equality of economic opportunity and political rights."[21] The later *Appeal* condemned racial oppression, but socialism became such a small part of Haldeman-Julius's beliefs after World War I that the linkage between economic, political, and social equality was invisible for him.

Socialism, both as a political philosophy and as an insurgent movement, challenged American capitalism directly during the first two decades of the twentieth century. Committed to a just, egalitarian society, socialists were certain that capitalism served only a small, powerful class and could not provide even economic welfare for the population at large. With superficial reform unable to alter capitalism's basis and relations, only revolutionary change to a nonexploitative, classless commonwealth offered an end to prehistory and to the beginnings of a truly human world. Socialists sought to create that world, and they sought to describe its kind and condition. Sometimes their vision was more clouded than they expected it would be. But their evocations were powered by a democratic, utopian impulse for collective and individual freedom without which a social movement is bankrupt. Without the idea of the future, a transformed world is an impossibility.

Survival of the Fittest

Those who think, or pretend to think, that this system is of divine origin and cannot be improved or changed, quote the phrase "survival of the fittest" as though that law of nature applied to our social order. If it were true, it applies to China or Russia or the aborigines of Africa; and no change can ever occur there because its ag'in' natur'. Survival of the fittest applies to the brute creation because they cannot make any change in their surroundings. Man can. That law, applied to society, means that where physical prowess is the condition, those best fitted, either by nature or training, will survive. Under a bad social structure the worst elements will survive. Under a just social structure the just will survive. If the human reason is not a factor in making changes desirable by his ideals, turn out all the fine horses, cattle and hogs, and see how many race horses, registered cattle and hogs will survive. If the reason of man can produce a better breed of animals by changing their conditions of life, cannot a better race of men be created by changing their conditions? Is a child raised in the vilest dens to develop the best talents needed by society? Under a robber system must not honest men be pushed to the wall? If you want honest men you must enact laws under which dishonesty can find no incentive to survive. If you want honest legislators you must first take out of private hands the great industries whose millions are used to corrupt public officials for special privileges. . . . No man, unless he has slaves under some form, can get money enough to corrupt legislators and judges. Without temptation there would be no corruption. So long as conditions are left that invite corruption, there will be injustice and the just will be despoiled. Had railroads been public property there would never have been the Credit Mobilier. Had banks been public there never would be the shameful conditions we see at Washington today. Under the present system the cunning, the crafty, the avaricious, the thief, the briber and the perjurer survive, and their opposites perish. Reverse the system, substitute private monopoly by public monopoly and you will have just the opposite effects. Which prefer you?

September 28, 1895

Appeal to Reason, April 11, 1914.

In the midst of plenty you are starving. In the midst of natural wealth and mechanical means waiting idly for the hand of Labor many of you are deprived of employment, while those to whom work is given must toil increasingly for a decreasing pittance. The more you produce the less you get. Why?

Simply because that plenty of your own creation, those machines of your own make, and nature itself, the common inheritance of men, have been appropriated by a class—the capitalistic class.

That class, which you have enriched, keeps you in poverty. That class, which you have raised to power, keeps you in subjection.

Its maladministration of affairs, public and private, is stupendous: its corruption, notorious; its despotism, intolerable.

You have given it the earth and everything on it. You are its tenants at will; its wage-slaves when at work, and mere vagrants trespassing on it when out of work.

True, you still have some political rights. You are citizens. Once a year, at the ballot box, each of you is the equal of a billionaire, and your majority would be fifty to one were you all united on election day into one grand party of emancipation.

But your masters are cunning. With their machinery of production they array you against each other—the unemployed against the employed—in the daily struggle for life. You fight; they win.

Likewise, with their political machinery they array you against each other —the so-called Democrats against the so-called Republicans—in the annual wrangle between office seekers pledged to do their bidding. You vote; they govern.

The machine-made candidates presented to your choice are carefully selected by your oppressors to legislate and administer against your class. Whichever you may thus elect is of necessity an enemy to you and a venal servant of your masters.

FELLOW WORKMEN, STRIKE FOR LIBERTY!

Strike at the polls for the Co-operative Commonwealth.

One strike there and for such an object will do you more good than a thousand strikes for a morsel of bread.

Get rid at last of the superstition that there would be no capital if there were no capitalists. For it is this absurd notion which alone keeps you in bondage; which makes each of you look beggingly to some capitalist for employment in servitude, instead of looking fraternally to each other for mutual service in co-operation.

Can you indeed believe, in this age of reason, that there would be no wealth if there were no thieves; that there would be no land, no machinery, no industry, no exchange, if there were no monopolists; and no good management, no order, no society, if there were no corrupt legislators, no venal judges, no prostitutes of any sort?

May 16, 1896

Want Blood or Work

The wage slaves of the rubber trust down in Rhode Island have been eating some of the fruits of protection to American labor. The trust "shut down" its works at Alice and Millville and the protected laborers were left to root for themselves. Meanwhile the sewer board of Woonsocket, an adjoining town, let a large contract and Italians were employed to do the work. Then the protected rubber trust slaves posted the following circular over the city in the night:

CONDITIONS OF THE UNITED STATES AT CHRISTMAS. 1895.

Appeal to Reason, December 21, 1895.

"We, the undersigned, want 500 able-bodied men to-morrow morning sharp to eject those Italians. We must have either blood or labor."

> *"WOONSOCKET LABORERS."*

That the blood of the average protected American wage-slave is getting a little thin does not admit of doubt, but these Woonsocket laborers are wrong. What they really need is good common sense, some information concerning the natural rights of man and enough manhood to demand their rights, which always means an opportunity for every one to earn food sufficient to fill him so full of good blood that he will not want to drink the blood of his brother.

The Woonsocket laborers are wholly ignorant or else unmindful of the fact that their Italian brothers, whose job or blood they are clamoring for, are in the same condition as themselves; that they too have stomachs, stomachs that are as empty as the promises of old party politicians, and that an empty stomach is the mother of that an-

cient and universally respected observation, that "self-preservation is the first law of life," and applies to all others as well as to ourselves. These Woonsocket wage-slaves, however, are very much like all other wage-slaves in their small understanding of the cause of their distress, and have come to regard their other brothers, who take turns with them at working and starving, as the real, if not their only enemy. There is little hope of better conditions for either the Woonsocket rubber trust slaves or the wage-slaves of other corporations until they can stretch their vision beyond the one whose starving condition forces him to take their jobs, and see in the background the master who is starving them all.

All this foolishness on the part of the rubber trust wage-slaves of Woonsocket, and all other wage-slaves, who club each other to death in their desperation for an opportunity to earn a slave's living, will bring no alarm to their masters. Indeed, this is what he wants them to do, and having so arranged industrial conditions that there are always more pegs than there are holes to drive them in, the master finds it amusing to see the fellows who are out fight the fellows who are in. The more they fight the cheaper he will buy the labor of the victors as well as the vanquished. The laborer must learn that every other laborer is his brother; that their lives are tied together by the universal law of brotherhood, which they can not violate without bringing vengeance down upon their heads; that an injury to one is an injury to all, and when they learn this they will quit throwing brickbats at each other and throw them at their real enemy.

September 19, 1896

intense that people can't even worship God under one roof, to say nothing about putting all their property in a common ownership? What a place for a banker or profit-monger a real Christian church would be! Where is the preacher that dares insist on the application of the REAL doctrine of Christ? Wouldn't he cause a sensation, though? When all property is held by the government for the equal use of all people, giving to each according to the time he or she has devoted to its production, it will be going a long way toward Christianity—and socialism.

February 6, 1897

Though not a Christian Socialist paper, the Appeal *nevertheless often reflected Christian and quasi-Christian ethics in its general outlook.*

J. A. Wayland's figurative prose still carries more power and clarity than many longer discussions of manufactured consent and false consciousness.

"Then they that gladly received his word were baptized: and the same day there were added unto them about three thousand souls. And they continued steadfastly in the apostles' doctrine and fellowship, and in breaking of bread and in prayers. And fear came upon every soul: and many wonders and signs were done by the apostles. AND ALL THAT BELIEVED WERE TOGETHER AND HAD ALL THINGS COMMON: AND SOLD THEIR POSSESSIONS AND GOODS AND PARTED THEM TO ALL MEN AS EVERY MAN HAD NEED."—Bible, Acts, chapter II.

This was Christianity in the time of the apostles. This was the doctrine as taught by the men whom Christ had selected to propagate his teachings. How many "steadfast in the apostles' doctrine" are in the churches today? How many make even the pretense of Annanias and Sapphira of following the doctrine? Christianity is all right, but where are its followers? Where is the "fellowship" in building many "kinds" of churches while people are freezing for houses? I wonder what Peter will say about the modern "fellowship" which is so

As I sit writing a canary bird is swinging in his cage, longing for the mate that never comes—a captive to give pleasure to the perverted taste of the feminine household. Born in the cage, its claws so long grown as to be useless in hopping when I force it out into the room, its wings so useless that a flight across the room almost exhausts its vitality, to free it would be to endanger its life. Freed, it tries to get back into its cage. But the cage is unnatural for it, nevertheless. The crime was in imprisoning its ancestors, but the crime could be righted by slowly according it freedom under favorable conditions and it would enjoy the rightful liberty it has never known. To me it is a symbol of the laboring people. So long denied their natural rights to the free use of the earth and the products of their labor, to give pleasure to the perverted taste of the robber class, they do not know what their right social condition is. Their stunted minds no more realize what liberty is than the canary knows of green fields and woods it has never seen. . . .

March 6, 1897

Some poor fellow who don't know any better writes to the San Francisco *Examiner,* protesting against the "invasion of foreigners," and takes the ground that the only way to get prosperity is to keep all foreigners out. I get out of patience trying to answer such tomfoolery. In the first place, such an argument is based on a selfishness so deep that ordinary Christian salvation will never save the soul of the man who makes it. In the next place, such an argument has no force unless it is assumed that a working man from abroad is not able, by his own labor, to supply his wants. Such an assumption is absolutely false. Every man capable of performing a fair day's labor can and does produce about three times the amount of wealth necessary to keep him and a family on the best of food, dressed in the best of clothes, and housed in the best of houses. That the foreign worker, or the American either, does not get it, is because he and every other worker is robbed, through the private ownership of the means of production, of four-fifths of what he does produce. The fault, my friend, is not with the foreigner, but with the cursed economic system that robs him after he gets here. Under our competitive system the American worker gets back as wages only 17 per cent of what he produces. Don't you honestly think it would be better to stop this robbery by the adoption of a better industrial system than to try to limit the number of the robbed? I believe in doing away with the robbers entirely.

October 16, 1897

Put two men in competition, let them set up in store, shop or factory and sell in the same territory, and see how they will grow to dislike each other and try to outdo and break each other up. That is the natural effect of such relations and can no more be avoided than the law of gravity. The success of each fully depends on the failure of the other. Now let these two men combine, form a partnership, and see how each will at once begin to work for the success of the firm which means the success of his partner. Neither can do anything for himself without at the same time helping his fellow. Mutual interest takes the place of self interest, love rules instead of hate. Can you give any valid reason why the same will not be true with three men instead of two? or of three hundred or three million instead of three? That is the principle of Socialism—that the industrial relations of men should be mutual instead of competitive, that all industries should be owned and operated by all the people collectively instead of individually. It would mean peace, plenty and pleasure for all.

May 7, 1898

You often see the white worker draw himself up in pride and say he does not care for the colored man and don't think the latter is entitled to as much wages for his time as the white. But that the whites must help to protect the blacks, that they are vitally interested in the condition of the blacks is plain enough if the workers were not so blind. Passing to the postoffice the other day I noticed that a colored barber had put the price of shaving down to 5 cents. There are four shops here run by white men. Do you think the white men are interested in what the colored man charges? If conditions are ever right it will be when every person is taught that their welfare is bound up with the welfare of every other worker, no matter what the color, creed, sex or vocation. The colored men are everywhere finding employment when white men are not wanted. They are more docile, willing to live on less, and thus are a factor in the reduction of wages. No change is worth the thought that does not include the entire race. It must be such that all can take advantage of it.

July 30, 1898

At the Mothers' Congress held in Washington last winter, Mrs. Helen Gardner, of Boston, the noted author of many works, said:

Self-abnegation, subserviency to man, whether he be father, lover or husband, is the most dangerous theory that can be taught to or forced upon a woman. She has no right to transmit a nature and a character that is subservient, inefficient, undeveloped—in short, a slavish character—which is either blandly obedient or blindly rebellious, and is therefore in either case set, as is a time-lock, to prey or to be preyed upon by society of the future.

If woman is not brave enough personally to demand and obtain absolute personal liberty of action, equality of status, entire control of her great and race-endowing function, maternity, she has no right to dare to stamp upon a child and to curse a race with the descendants of such a servile, dwarfed, time-and-master-serving character.

How many women have the faintest conception of what she means? Not many. As a whole women have no conception of the real character of their slavery—do not realize that they are slaves. So long have they been under the domination of men, the merest playthings of industrial slaves; themselves the victims of every social whim, that freedom is to them the most horrible of crimes.

History tells us not when women were not the chattels of man. Sometime, sometime, the words of Mrs. Gardner will have a meaning to women. Not now, not now.

August 13, 1898

Definitions of Socialism

A great many people believe that they know what socialism means, but they do not. They vainly imagine that it refers to bursting bombs, burning buildings, rapine and plunder. But these folks have never looked for the definition in *Webster's* dictionary which says that socialism is

A theory of society that advocates a more precise, orderly and harmonious arrangement of the social relations of mankind than that which has hitherto prevailed.

Of course that does not sound so very bad. Still for fear that Noah Webster may have been out of his head when defining socialism, let us go to some other authority and read carefully the definition in the *Standard* dictionary, which says that socialism is

A theory of policy that aims to secure the reconstruction of society, increase of wealth, and a more equal distribution of the products of labor through the public collective ownership of labor and capital (as distinguished from property) and the public collective management of all industries. Its motto is "Everyone according to his deeds."

Ha, Ha! "Everyone according to his deeds!" Are you in favor of a system which will give you all you earn? Do you want all the wealth you produce or do you prefer to give the Hannas and Rockefellers and Vanderbilts and Goulds a rakeoff on all the creations of your labor? But possibly you are not satisfied yet as to whether socialism has been properly defined or not. Let us get an up-to-date dictionary. Maybe things have changed since Noah Webster died. We have it here. The *Century* dictionary defines socialism as

> *Any theory or system of local organization which would abolish entirely, or in a great part, the individual effort and competition on which modern society rests, and substitute co-operation; would introduce a more perfect and equal distribution of the products of labor, and would make land and capital, as the instruments of production, the joint possession of the community.*

It is very sad, isn't it? You have been thinking all these years that you knew what socialism meant and it isn't what you thought it was at all, is it? But let us go the whole hog. Let us have *all* the authorities. Let us look into *Worcestor's* dictionary, which plainly states that socialism is

> *A science of reconstructing society on an entirely new basis, by substituting the principle of association for that of competition in every branch of human industry.*

But possibly some of you may not have one of the above named dictionaries and are suspicious— you may believe that we know your circumstances and are trying to trick you. Have you then an *Imperial* dictionary? It says that socialism means

> *The abolition of that individual action on which modern societies depend, and the substitution of a regulated system of co-operative action.*

Then, again, there are our religious friends who have vaguely, but wrongly, believed that socialism was the enemy of religion. What have you to say of this statement made by the *Encyclopedia Britannica*?

> *The ethics of socialism are identical with the ethics of christianity.*

November 18, 1899

"*The people of Buffalo are getting tired of paying two prices for inferior light, politely called gas, and they are not likely to tolerate needless delay on the part of members of the common council in affording them necessary relief. It has been practically decided that this relief can come only through a municipal plant. The board of public works is under instruction from the common council to procure a site and proceed with the construction of a plant as soon as funds are provided by a bond issue. There is no public business now pending before the common council of greater importance than the municipal lighting plant.*"—Buffalo, N. Y. Daily Courier.

Gentlemen, you forget yourselves. You should remember the poor capitalists who have been skinning you for many years are to be considered in this matter. Would you destroy the incentive of men to accumulate by taking the opportunity away from them? Would you tear down the fabric of society by such socialist innovations as permitting all the people to supply themselves with light? What if the people have been paying two prices for light—does that not make rich men and are not rich men indispensable to a high civilization? And inferior gas—why should not the people be satisfied with that? Is it not better and cheaper than candles? People do not have to use gas, they can live in the dark, you know, and better that than such slavery to the city as city ownership! Besides, where is this thing going to end? If the people find that public ownership of gas proves a benefit, they may want to own street cars and ride for one cent instead of five and that would reduce them to barbarism. Gentlemen, beware of such dangerous positions!

February 24, 1900

A nineteenth-century English writer and social activist who moved from a belief in romanticism to a commitment to socialism, William Morris remains best known for his utopian novel, News from Nowhere.

Revolution

WILLIAM MORRIS

The word Revolution which we Socialists are so often forced to use has a terrible sound in most people's ears, even when we have explained to them that it does not necessarily mean a change accompanied by riot and all kinds of violence, and cannot mean a change made mechanically and in the teeth of opinion by a group of men who have somehow managed to seize on the executive power for the moment. Even when we explain that we use the word revolution in its etymological sense, and mean by it a change in the basis of society, people are scared at the idea of such a vast change, and beg that you will speak of reform and not revolution. As, however, we Socialists do not at all mean by our word revolution what these worthy people mean by their word reform, I can't help thinking that it would be a mistake to use it, whatever projects we might conceal beneath its harmless envelope. So we will stick to our word, which means a change of the basis of society; it may frighten people, but it will at least warn them that there is something to be frightened about, which will be no less dangerous for being ignored; and also it may encourage some people, and will mean to them at least not fear, but a hope.

Fear and Hope. Those are the names of the two great passions which rule the race of man, and with which revolutionists have to deal; to give hope to the many oppressed and fear to the few oppressors, that is our business; if we do the first and give hope to the many, the few must be frightened by their hope. It is not revenge we want for poor people, but happiness; indeed, what revenge can be taken for all the thousands of years of the sufferings of the poor?

July 21, 1900

The U. S. Supreme Court's "separate but equal" doctrine was considered politically progressive in 1900. The Appeal's attempt to fuse socialist analysis with that doctrine yielded a mass of contradictions. White-administered literacy tests, such as that required in North Carolina in 1900, were commonly used to disfranchise black voters in the South and border states.

Two Wrongs Will Not Produce Right

The Democrats of North Carolina have passed a constitutional amendment that disfranchises nearly every colored voter in the state. The Republicans entered into the fight and assisted. They threatened personal violence to all citizens who opposed them. These are the Democrats who will be behind Bryan. They will do much for the laboring people! They kept the negro ignorant and now disfranchise him because he can not read! They love justice and socialists should help elect them! Socialism will solve the race problem in the only way it can be solved. That is not by disfranchising them, but by educating them, putting them under the best environments of employment and giving them the full results of their labor, but at the same time having them all located in sections of the country to themselves. Under socialism the workers in every department will have a voice in admitting all except their own class in the shop, factory or mine. This would make a condition in which the other races—Negroes, Chinese and others who are citizens—would have to segregate themselves in employment. They would get as much as others, according to their deeds, but would not be citizens of the same localities as the whites unless the whites should vote to admit them. A majority would rule. Nothing can ever be done by trying to do it the wrong way. The world is full of woe and injustice because of wrongly directed efforts to secure harmony.

August 25, 1900

Written in the language Eugene V. Debs used in his speeches, "The Co-operative Commonwealth" is a representative summary of his own and the Appeal's vision of the socialist commonwealth in 1900.

The Co-operative Commonwealth

Eugene V. Debs

There is an economic revolution in this and other countries in which modern industry has been developed in the past century. We have been so completely engaged in competitive labor that we are utterly oblivious of the fact. A century ago work was done by hand very largely, or with simple primitive tools. How to make a living was an easy question. The boy learned a trade, served his apprenticeship, and the skill inherent in the trade secured steady employment for him at fair wages, by virtue of which he could provide for his family, educate his children and discharge the duties of good citizenship. In that day the working man owned and controlled the tools with which he worked, and was virtually his own employer. Not only this, he was the master of what his labor produced. It was a very slow age, meagre of results; it required ten to sixteen hours daily labor to enable the working man to supply his material wants. It was then the machine emanated from the brain of labor; it was designed to aid the laboring man, so that he could provide for his social, moral and intellectual improvement.

At this point an industrial revolution began. The machine, the new tool of production, passed from the control of workingmen who used it, into that of the newly developed class. The small employer became a capitalist, and the employe be-

came a wage-worker, and they began to grow apart. The machine was crude and imperfect at first; it increased production, it began to displace the workingman, it pushed him out of the shop into the street. The workingman, forced into idleness, became a tramp. I have said again and again that I am with the tramp, and against the system of society that made him a tramp.

The machine became more perfect day by day; it lowered the wage of the worker, and in due course of time it became so perfect that it could be operated by unskilled labor of the woman, and she became a factor in industry. The owners of these machines were in competition with each other for trade in the market; it was war; cheaper and cheaper production was demanded, and cheaper labor was demanded. In the march of time it became necessary to withdraw the children from school, and these machines came to be operated by the deft touch of the fingers of the child. In the first stage, machine was in competition with man; in the next, man in competition with both, and in the next, the child in competition with the whole combination.

Today there are more than three millions of women engaged in industrial pursuits in the United States, and more than two millions of children. It is not a question of white labor or black labor, or male labor or female or child labor, in this system; it is solely a question of cheap labor, without reference to the effect upon mankind.

The simple tool of production became an excellent machine, it necessitated the co-operation and concentration of capital. The tool of production was no longer owned and controlled by the workingman who used it. It was owned by the class who didn't use it, and was used by a class who didn't own it. The owners of the machine want profit and the users of the machine want wages. Their economic interests are absolutely in conflict, diametrically opposite. What is good for one is not good for the other.

It is this conflict of interest that has given rise to the modern class struggle which finds expression in strikes, lock-outs, boycotts and deep-seated discontent. But I am not looking on the dark side of things. I am in no sense a pessimist. I am observing the trend of economic development. I realize it is only a question of time until this concentration of industry will be completed. One department after another is being monopolized in this march of concentration; the interests of these trusts are so completely interwoven that in the near future there will be a trust of trusts. In this trust the middle class, representing the small capitalists, is being crushed and ground beneath the upper millstone of concentration of capital and the nether millstone of vanishing patronage.

The workingman has been impoverished. Examining the reports I find that during the past fifty years of the age of the machine, his producing capacity had steadily increased; but upon the other hand, in the competitive pressure, his wage has steadily diminished. The more he produces the worse he is off. He cannot consume what he produces. The more he produces the more there is an over-production based upon under-consumption. The factories close down and he finds himself out of employment and the reason suggests itself; he no longer works for himself, he works for another, for a wage that represents but a small share of what his labor produces. This accounts for the fact that periodically the country is afflicted with over-production; this accounts for the fact that the large capitalists are struggling to open new markets for the sale of surplus goods, the very goods our own people here at home are suffering for the want of. In this great competitive system the mammoth department store is sapping the life currents of the small shopkeeper; the great bonanza farm is driving the small farmer to bankruptcy and ruin.

No power on earth can arrest this concentration. It is paving the way for a new economic system, a new social order. Socialists understand its trend; they are beginning to organize in every village and every hamlet, every town and every city, of every state and territory in the country. They are organizing their forces beneath the conquering banner of economic equality.

A century and a quarter ago this country witnessed a mighty struggle for political equality, the right of man to govern this country—and the formation of this republic was the crowning glory of the century. Today there is another struggle going forward for economic equality. If men are fit to be political equals, they are also fit to be economic equals. If they are economic equals, they will be social equals, class distinctions will disappear from human society forever.

Look over in the direction of Europe; we observe that the Socialists there are organizing day by day; that before their conquering march the thrones are beginning to tremble, and will, within the next few years, totter to their fall. The same movement is spreading over the United States. Its progress has not been so rapid here, for the reason that we have had a new country, and until recently there had been some opportunity for initiative. But no country on the face of the globe has been so completely exploited within so short a space of time as the United States of America.

Socialists are organizing for the purpose of securing control of this government. Having conquered the political power upon the platform that declares in favor of collective ownership in the name of the people, they will take possession of industry. It will already have been organized to meet co-operation, that is to say, self-operation, in the development of the capitalist system. Industry will be rescued from cupidity; it will be co-operative in every department of human industry. The badge of labor will no longer be the badge of servitude. Every man will gladly do his share of the world's useful work, every man can then honestly enjoy his share of the world's blessings. Every machine will be a blessing to mankind, because it will serve to reduce the number of hours constituting a day's work, and the work day will be shortened in exact proportion to the progress of invention. Labor will no longer be bought and sold in the markets of the world. We will not make things for sale, but will make things to use. We will fill the world with wealth and every man can have all that he can rationally use. Rent, interest and profit, three forms of exploitation, will disappear forever.

Every man will have the same inherent right to work that he has to live; he will receive the full produce of his labor. The soul will no longer be dominated by the stomach. Men and women will be economically free; life will no longer be a struggle for bread; then the children of men can begin the march to the highest type of civilization that this world has ever known.

The abolishing of the capitalist system does not merely mean the emancipation of the working class, but of all society. It will level up to higher and nobler elevation. This earth for the first time since it was flung into space will be an habitable globe; it will be fit for good men and good women to live in.

The existing system is unspeakably cruel; the life currents of old age and childhood are the tributaries of the bottomless reservoir of private profit. The face of capitalist society is blotched with the effects of a diseased organism. What is the estate of Christendom today? We boast of our civilization, and yet every Christian nation on the face of the globe is armed to the teeth. Against whom? Against heathens, barbarians, savages? No, against other Christian nations! And the world pays its highest tribute to that form of ingenuity that enables us to destroy the most human lives in the shortest space of time. Go to the city of Washington today with a device that will enable you to destroy one hundred thousand lives in a second, and your fame and your fortune are made. Is that civilization in the proper sense of the term? We must bear in mind, my friends, that competition is war; that war is the normal state of capitalism. With the end of capitalism comes the end of war, and the inauguration of peace.

In the march of invention space has almost been annihilated; the nations of the earth are being drawn into closer relation with each other. In the new social order each nation will have its place in the sisterhood of nations, just as every man wil. have his place in the brotherhood of men.

I will do what little I can to hasten the coming of the day when war shall curse this earth no more. I am not a patriot in the sense in which that term is defined in the lexicon of capitalism. I have no ambition to kill my fellowman, and I am quite certain that I have no ambition to be killed. When I think of a cold, glittering, steel bayonet being pushed into the soft, white, quivering flesh of a human body I recoil with horror.

Is it not possible to improve upon such a condition as this? Yes, by the intelligent application of Socialism. We live in the most favored land beneath the bending sky. We have all the raw materials and the most marvelous machinery; millions of eager inhabitants seeking employment. Nothing is so easily produced as wealth, and no man should suffer for the need of it; and in a rational, economic system poverty will be a horror of the past; the penitentiaries will be depopulated, and the shadow of the gallows will no longer fall upon the land. Co-operative industry carried forward in the interest of all the people, that is the foundation of the new social order; economic freedom for every human being on earth; no man compelled to depend upon the arbitrary will of another for the right or opportunity to create enough to supply his material wants. There will still be competition among men, but it will not be for bread, it will be to excel in good works. Every man will work for the society in which he lives, and society will work in the interests of those who compose it.

I look into the future with absolute confidence. When I strain my vision the slightest I can see the first rising rays of the sun of the co-operative commonwealth; it will look down upon a nation in which men and women—I say men and women, because in the new social order women will stand side by side with men, the badge of inferiority will be taken from her brow, and we will enjoy the enraptured vision of a land without a master, a land without a slave.

December 29, 1900

Appeal to Reason, January 9, 1904.

Say, Mr. Worker, haven't you been in the grip of this monster about long enough? Why not try the knife on him?

The early Appeal *advocated equal compensation for all, regardless of skill. That position softened considerably after J. A. Wayland died and Fred Warren left the paper.*

Superior Skill

Please explain if under Socialism superior skill would be entitled to greater returns. Mrs. Louise Lacey

No; unless one family can live and develop on less than another. But can it? What sense would there be in giving one more than it could consume and another less than it needed? This objection is raised on the hypothesis that there cannot be enough for all, and that some must do with less than is good for them. But this is not true. Enough for all who will perform the average number of hours of labor can be created and equitably distributed. If the architect, working four hours a day, receives enough to satisfy all his mental and physical wants, why should he have more? Should not the man who goes down into the deep foundation excavation and works four hours a day receive as much as will supply all his mental and physical wants, too? Especially so, when both can be supplied. And let us look at it in another light. Suppose the man cannot be found to go into the ditch—would not the architect have to go there himself, if there is to be any building? Surely. Now if the common laborer can and will go into the ditch, he takes the place of the architect—doing as much or far more than the office man could, and if he does the work and saves the architect, is he not then as valuable to society as the architect? And at the same pay, which job do you think the architect would take? Not hard to guess, eh? And from whom did the architect get his knowledge? From society that has slowly developed and preserved all the arts and sciences, and then took him from hard labor and gave him a schooling. Do you think society, that did all this for him, should have no consideration? His life has been more pleasantly surrounded than the one of the common laborer—and you still think that he should be paid greatly more because he has been so considerately treated all his life! That one of two men, each doing his best, should receive more than the other for the same time, is merely a matter of custom, without any reason in justice. And more than that, you do not believe it or practice it, except in some places. When you hire men to make laws for you in the state you pay them all the same wages, regardless of their ability or their industry; you do the same in congress; you do the same in judges; you do the same employing doctors, sheriffs, clerks, recorders. You do not pretend that the men who succeed each other are equally able or honest, but you do not differentiate the pay of the men for the same place. You know there is no rule by which you could arrive at such real worth. Any rule that differentiates compensation in co-operative results has no basis in reason. You pay the same fee to the capable and the incapable doctor, and do not know which one has the real ability, for the quack often has the greater practice. Further, what you term "superior skill," may not be skill, but cunning; may be bad instead of good; may be false teaching instead of true. Neither custom nor law can make right that which is wrong. When a machine will not run it is either built upon a wrong theory or else wrongly put together. The industrial system we have don't work—unless the turn-

ing out of murder, suicide, wretchedness and woe is right. Crime sits in high places and feasts on the fat of the land, while stupid, yet honest labor fasts and lives in wretchedness. Crime draws its greater income for its "superior skill." Justice will give each all they can consume. What more?

February 16, 1901

Activist, teacher, author of The Struggle for Existence, *and popular Socialist speaker, Walter Thomas Mills explains the major socialist implications of natural-rights theory in "A Defense of Private Property."*

A Defense of Private Property

WALTER THOMAS MILLS

That every man has a right to his life is no longer disputed. It would seem that such a proposition would be so simple that it never could have been disputed. But whatever power the master may have had over the life of his slave, whatever arbitrary authority aristocratic lords have exercised over their serfs, including the right to slay them at will, it is no longer disputed anywhere that each man has a right to his life.

Now, all property is the creation of labor, and labor involves an expenditure of life's energies. Inasmuch as every man has an inherent right to life, he also has, and by necessity, a right to the products of the expenditure of his life's energies. Thus the right to property becomes as sacred as is the right to life itself. The right to own carries with it the right to produce. Having produced, the right to own one's products must necessarily follow; but if the right to ownership is to be based upon the fact of production, then he who is able-bodied and produces nothing can be entitled to own nothing.

But production is no longer carried on by single handed enterprises. Production is carried on by great organizations with extensive equipments which no individual single handed could own or operate. Association in production is inevitable. The right to the opportunity to produce involves one's right to a place in associated production.

A child begins his life the owner of everything. He appropriates everything within his reach. So far as he is able to make use of all the earth, all the earth is his. He raises no question as to the propriety of his taking anything. He takes everything within his reach. He begins life's struggle with an effort to get possession of his hands and feet. His right to use these no one disputes. If he does not use them no one else can. His individual proprietorship in his own hands and feet no one questions; but when he undertakes to appropriate things beyond himself, others may use these as well as he, and the dispute for possession at once arises. If he does not use his own hands they go unused. If he does not use a biscuit for his dinner someone seated on the other side of the table may use the biscuit if he does not. It is the possibility of use by either which results in the struggle for possession. When the thing under consideration is the machinery, the organization, the process of production, there is not only the possibility that another may use, but there is the absolute necessity that the many must use these things together.

Who ought to own these great plants necessarily involved in associated production? Here it seems to me is the doctrine of collective and private property. The core of all ownership is in the right to use. That which one may use separately he may own separately; but that which men use together they ought to own together. Private ownership of that which absolutely pertains to myself, and to myself alone, can harm no other. There is no reason why my clothing should not be my own as absolutely as are my hands and feet. It is as necessary for my comfort, it is really a part of my personality. The old London sweat-shops, where the employer owned the clothing which his victims wore, while engaged at his tasks, involved a wrong against which Kingsley wrote, and about which Tom Hood sang with a matchless pathos. It in-

Publicity handbill for a speech by Walter Thomas Mills. Courtesy University of Colorado Historical Collections.

volved a wrong that the English speaking race rebelled against. All property which is for my individual, exclusive personal use . . . I ought to own alone. My right to it is as genuine and as sacred as is my right to my life—provided always that it is directly or indirectly the products of the expenditure of my life's energies, not the result of the exploitation of the toil of others. But the great plants involved in associated production I cannot use by myself. I cannot use their products by myself. I cannot operate them by myself. Association is necessary, is inevitable. Private ownership of these great industrial plants involves a great wrong. It places the tools necessary for one man's employment in the exclusive possession of another. It places the workman in a position where the only way by which he can produce his livelihood is to obtain the consent of some one else to use the tools of his own industry. It makes him absolutely dependent, not upon himself, but upon another. The toolless workman is helpless. The owner of the tools which I must use or starve is the master of my life.

. . . .

Here are the lines of economic and political warfare drawn squarely across the field. Capitalism contends for the right to privately own the things of common use even though the individual shall be deprived thereby of the ability to own the things of private necessity. Socialism contends for the opportunity for the individual to own the things of private use, even though it shall thereby deprive the individual of the power to own the things of common use. And this is no child's play. It means war to the finish. Capitalism must be dethroned in politics in order that it may be displaced in the market. Take sides. Get into line. Don't get between the lines. There is the place of greatest danger if not of certain disaster.

August 31, 1901

The Appeal *always enjoyed putting revealing government data to use. The comparative cost of city water in 1902 (nearly three times greater under private ownership than under municipal ownership) illustrates the profits "tax" charged by private capital.*

Municipal Ownership

The fourteenth annual labor report of the United States is devoted to an exhaustive investigation of the cost of production rates, wages paid, etc., of municipal and private owned water, light and gas plants. The figures are interesting and no doubt authentic. There are 1,787 municipal waterworks plants—more than half the total number in the United States; 460 municipal electric light plants and fourteen gas plants owned by cities.

[Below] the cost of producing water is given, showing the cost to be in private plants, $61.60 per one million gallons; while in municipal owned plants, the cost was $63.70. The wages paid for doing this work was in private plants $16.28; in municipal, $21.67.

	Private	Municipal	Page
Cost of production—			
one million gallons	61.60	$63.70	35
Wages—			
per one million gallons	16.28	21.67	31
Salaries—			
per one million gallons	14.33	10.60	31
Average price—			
per million gallons sold	160.00	59.00	42

The points in this official statement that should interest you as a citizen are these. That the cost to the users under city ownership is only $59, while under private ownership it is $160; that while the cost to produce is $2.10 more under public than private ownership, $5.39 more is paid out in wages, while the salaries of the kid-glove brigade is $3.73 less. But greater than even the getting of nearly three times the water for the same price is the taking away of the incentive of the private company to bribe your city officials. It is therefore plainly to the interest of every user of water and every wage-earner to have city ownership. As these are the great majority, why should they support the private ownership that overcharges and underpays them, and corrupts their officials and judges?

These are figures that are furnished by your government; by your Republican politicians. Now will you believe the hirelings of the corporations when they tell you that private ownership is the best?

February 8, 1902

Even during a period marked by much more public honesty than at the present, very few economic explanations were more illuminating than "A Plain Statement of the Capitalist Position" from the Bankers' Magazine. For a response to this "Plain Statement," the Appeal editors chose the work of Edward Bellamy, a socialist novelist who had been more influential in America than any other. Bellamy's own activism and his extraordinarily popular utopian novel, Looking Backward, had led to the founding of the widespread Nationalist move-

ment of the early 1890s. A lecturer and founder of the weekly New Nation, *Bellamy was also the author of* Equality, *a theoretical sequel to* Looking Backward.

A Plain Statement of the Capitalist Position

BY THE *BANKERS' MAGAZINE*

CONSOLIDATION and concentration of the forces of production and manufacture is the prominent feature of modern business operation. To accomplish great results, whether to conquer neighboring nations or to build pyramids, or to produce great quantities of iron and steel or oil, to build railroads or dig canals, it is necessary to organize humanity by the DIRECT or INDIRECT application of FORCE. The original and crude method of organization was by the application of force to the bodies of men. The MODERN and INGENIOUS method involves force applied to their MINDS. Under the rulers of Egypt and Assyria hordes of men were driven to work with sullen and unwilling minds. Nevertheless, the necessity of satisfying the mind while securing the service of the body was early recognized, and motives of CASTE and RELIGION, and so-called LOYALTY, helped to instill SATISFACTION with a man's lot in life, however hard and subservient it might be.

For centuries the mass of humanity has struggled to free itself from the visible chains of outward force and the more subtle influences which restrained and deadened their thoughts and feelings. Slavery, the admitted right of some men to dominate and control others, has been discredited and discarded by civilized nations. The equality of men in certain and radical rights is generally admitted. Nevertheless, the natural instinct of the race to conquer and bend to their uses the resources of the planet they dwell on grows stronger as the centuries pass. One achievement invites to greater and more ambitious efforts. The necessity of united effort grows more and more pressing.

Modern times, therefore, but lead the race in their efforts to secure their following by methods entirely different from those of the past. Patriotism in the old sense, loyalty to leaders because of supposed divine rights, have been so much weakened that they cannot be invoked to produce great results.

The welfare of the individual is the keynote of modern organization, whether for government or for business. In the United States the idea that the individual has the inalienable right to life, liberty and the pursuit of happiness is perhaps more fully acceded to in constitutions, laws and customs than among other nations. Nevertheless, in no country are men more fully organized and CONTROLLED for conducting industrial undertakings than in the United States. This result has been accomplished by INFLUENCES which CONTROL the MINDS of men, and in consequence their BODIES. The chief of these is the desire for property.

During the early part of the last century in the United States the democratic ideas of Jefferson dominated and flourished. Individual effort accomplished much, because there was room enough to give each individual a wide orbit; but the results of these ideas in business were not very conspicuous. The country grew because of immigration and the natural increase of population, but government was weak, business was conducted in a sporadic and disorganized fashion; there was no general system. Every man did what was GOOD in his OWN eyes; it was a formative period, chaotic, abounding in business explosions, crises, panics, and general tendencies to disintegration.

The Civil War was the epoch which opened the eyes of men to the possibilities of organization by means of capital. Never before had the possible resources of the country been realized even by the most advanced minds. The POWER of money was, by the great expenditures of the government, shown to MASSES of citizens. The construction of railroads necessary to overcome the expanse of territory gave a further impulse to the science of organizing human effort. Other enterprises requiring great organizing of men have followed. The problem, however, has been to effect this organization to secure the co-operation of the necessary human force without coming in conflict with the freedom of the individual as enunciated in the constitution.

The MODERN leaders of men CAN NOT ENSLAVE THE MASSES by DIRECT FORCE as the Pharoahs did. They cannot enslave them by false ideas of LOYALTY, of RELIGION, of CASTE, or of NATIONAL GLORY, as was done in later centuries. Their willing co-operation had to be secured, and this was done by what political economists characterized as CAPITAL. What capital consists of, it is not very easy to define. It includes money and all kinds of resources that can be directly turned into money, and many that cannot. Generally it is a power that enables SOME men to secure willing co-operation of OTHER men.

As the ideas of industrial development have expanded, the necessity of larger capital has been seen, and it has been secured by combination and consolidations, until the command of property and money, and through these of willing labor is practically unlimited.

How The People Were Harnessed

You have read in this issue of the *Appeal*, under the heading of "A Plain Statement of the Capitalists Position," from a sound-headed banker how the people are harnessed to do the will of the capitalist. The following chapter from *Equality*, written by Edward Bellamy, will give you a little clearer light on the subject. You remember that Mr. Bellamy's hero goes to sleep in the 19th century and awakens in the 21st. He undertakes to tell his new found friends, who are living under the Co-operative Commonwealth, how he and his compatriots fleeced the common people. Here is the story in the words of the young man

himself. Compare this bit of fiction with the truthful statement of the bankers of today:

Opening the inner door of the safe, I took out several drawers full of securities of all sorts, and emptied them on the table in the room.

"Are these stuffy-looking papers what you used to call wealth?" said Edith, with evident disappointment.

"Not the papers in themselves," I said, "but what they represented."

"And what was that?" she asked.

"The ownership of land, houses, mills, ships, railroads, and all manner of other things," I replied, and went on as best I could to explain to her mother and herself about rents, profits, interest, dividends, etc. But it was evident, from the blank expression of their countenances, that I was not making much headway.

Presently the doctor looked up from the papers which he was devouring with the zeal of an antiquarian, and chuckled:

"I am afraid, Julian, you are on the wrong tack. You see, economic science in your day was a science of things; in our day it is a science of human beings. We have nothing at all answering to your rent, interest, profits, or other financial devices, and the terms expressing them have no meaning now except to students. If you wish Edith and her mother to understand you, you must translate these money terms into terms of men and women and children, and the plain facts of their relations as affected by your system. Shall you consider it impertinent if I try to make the matter a little clearer to them?"

"I shall be much obliged to you," I said; "and perhaps you will at the same time make it clearer to me."

"I think," said the doctor, "that we shall all understand the nature and value of these documents much better if, instead of speaking of them as titles of ownership in farms, factories, mines, railroads, etc., we state plainly that they were evidences that their possessors were the masters of various groups of men, women and children in different parts of the country. Of course, as Julian says, the documents nominally state his title to things only, and say nothing about men and women. But it is the men and women who went with the lands, the machines, and various other things, and were bound to them by their bodily necessities, which gave all the value to the possession of the things.

"But for the implication that there were men who, because they must have the use of the land, would submit to labor for the owner of it in return for permission to occupy it, these deeds and mortgages would have been of no value. So of these factory shares. They speak only of water power and looms, but they would be valueless but for the thousands of human workers bound to the machines by bodily necessities as fixedly as if they were chained there. So of these coal-mine shares. But for the multitude of wretched beings condemned by want to labor in living graves, of what value would have been these shares which yet make no mention of them? And see again how significant is the fact that it was deemed needless to make mention of and to enumerate by name these serfs of the field, of the loom, of the mine! Under systems of chattel slavery, such as had formerly prevailed, it was necessary to name and identify each chattel, that he might be recovered in case of escape, and an account made of the loss in case of death. But there was no danger of loss by the escape or the death of the serfs transferred by these documents. They would not run away, for there was nothing better to run to or any escape from the world-wide economic system which enthralled them; and if they died, that involved no loss to their owners, for there were always plenty more to take their places. Decidedly, it would have been a waste of paper to enumerate them.

"Just now at the breakfast table," continued the doctor, "I was explaining the modern view of the economic system of private capitalism as one based on the compulsory servitude of the masses to the capitalists, a servitude which the latter enforced by monopolizing the bulk of the world's re-

sources and machinery, leaving the pressure of want to compel the masses to accept their yoke, the police and soldiers meanwhile defending them in their monopolies. These documents turn up in a timely way to illustrate the ingenious and effectual methods by which the different sorts of workers were organized for the service of the capitalists. To use a plain illustration these various sorts of so-called securities may be described as so many kinds of human harness by which the masses, broken and tamed by the pressure of want, were yoked and strapped to the chariots of the capitalists.

"For instance, here is a bundle of farm mortgages on Kansas farms. Very good; by virtue of the operation of this security certain Kansas farmers worked for the owner of it, and though they might never know who he was nor he who they were, yet they were as securely and certainly his thralls as if he had stood over them with a whip instead of sitting in his parlor at Boston, New York, or London. This mortgage harness was generally used to hitch in the agricultural class of the population. Most of the farmers of the west were pulling in it toward the end of the nineteenth century—. Was it not so, Julian? Correct me if I am wrong."

"You are stating the facts very accurately," I answered. "I am beginning to understand more clearly the nature of my former property."

"Now let us see what this bundle is," pursued the doctor. "Oh! yes; these are shares in New England cotton factories. This sort of harness was chiefly used for women and children, the sizes ranging away down so as to fit girls and boys of eleven and twelve. It used to be said that it was only the margin of profit furnished by the almost costless labor of the little children that made these factories paying properties. The population of New England was largely broken in at a very tender age to work in this style of harness.

. . . .

"As a representative of the nineteenth century," I said, "I can not deny the substantial correctness of your rather startling way of describing our system of investments. Still, you will admit that, bad as the system was and bitter as was the condition of the masses under it, the function performed by the capitalists in organizing and directing such industry as we had was a service to the world of some value."

"Certainly, certainly," replied the doctor. "The same plea might be urged, and has been, in defense of every system by which men have ever made other men their servants from the beginning. There was always some service, generally valuable and indispensable, which the oppressors could urge and did urge as the ground and excuse of the servitude they enforced. As men grew wiser they observed that they were paying a ruinous price for the service thus rendered, so at first they said to the king: 'To be sure, you help defend the state from foreigners and hang thieves, but it is too much to ask us to be your serfs in exchange; we can do better.' And so they established republics. So also, presently, the people said to the priests: 'You have done something for us, but you have charged too much for your services in asking us to submit our minds to you; we can do better.' And so they established religious liberty.

"And likewise, in this last matter we are speaking of, the people finally said to the capitalists: 'Yes, you have organized our industry, but at the price of enslaving us. We can do better.' And substituting national co-operation for capitalism, they established the industrial republic based on economic democracy. If it were true, Julian, that any consideration of service rendered to others, however valuable, could excuse the benefactors for making bondmen of the benefitted, then there never was a despotism or slave system which could not excuse itself."

February 15, 1902

───────────────

Many socialists were able to understand the conditions of life under capitalism, but very few were able to describe them as

effectively as J. A. Wayland. The following article begins to suggest why the federal government repeatedly sought to ban the Appeal.

THINK! It is beyond my understanding what interest in the present system you can have. If it gives you Peace, Plenty and Pleasure; if it affords you absolute security against want; if it makes you self-reliant citizens; if it gives you a voice in your employment—it would be something worth defending. But does it? Are you not under the authority of others? Are you not dictated to as to your wages, your hours and the price of what you spend your wages for? What system could be worse for you? Why, in many employments you have your dress prescribed and whom you shall buy it of and what you shall pay for it. Is this your idea of freedom? If so, what is your idea of slavery? No master could dictate more than that to his chattle slaves. Why should you be proud of great buildings or machinery in which you have no ownership, no voice? In olden times men strove to run away from their masters, but in these times you fight each other for the privilege of working for some master. Again, what interest have you in voting for and otherwise supporting the present industrial system? You are the underdogs in the fight, when you have the power to be on top if you will quit supporting the rules that place you underneath. You have little or no hope of ever being more than wage slaves. You have no hope that your children will be better off than you are under this system. You have no security against sickness or old age. You are bossed about by every employer and are employed only to make profit for him, and if you can find no man who thinks he can make something out of you, you have no employment. Do you never tire of such a condition? Is it the only system of employment you can think of? Do you never aspire to higher conditions? Do you never wish for a voice in the condition and pay of your employment? Does the system give you what you want, what you feel you are entitled to? Do you feel that you were born to serve others? Do you feel that your highest abilities can be developed under such conditions as you live? Do you never long for a good home, good clothing and time for pleasure and self-improvement of mind? Do you get it? What argument, what voice will instill into you action for realizing something out of life? Do you think the men who would give opportunity for a better life your enemies? Do your employers want you to have more than they give you? Is it to their interest to give you more and take less? You must be your own employers. To do this you must have the public own all the places of employment, and then you as a part of the public will have an equal voice in the management of the same. Would that help or hinder you? Would you be more or less a slave when given a voice with your fellows in directing the industry in which you worked? Wake up to the promise of the Twentieth century for the laboring people of the world. You alone can bring a change. You are in the majority. So long as you hold your slavish ideas, so long as you vote to uphold the present system of private capitalism you must remain as you are and your children must remain even lower, for day by day the trusts are tightening the bonds and making their power greater, which means that your power is lessening. Are you going to sit idly down in hopeless submission and say nothing can be done? Are you willing to surrender your manhood, surrender the future of your children to the tender mercies of the trusts that will own all the wealth of the nation? Are patriots made of such stuff? Are men who love their country and their fellows made of such stuff? Are MEN made of such stuff? Wake up to what the future portends. Get a move on your sluggish brains, that they may help you to better conditions. Capitalists use their brains to control you through your brains; they employ slick politicians; they employ what of the clergy they can; they employ all the wiles of kings to keep you doing the things and thinking the things that make you their slaves—human machines for their pleasure and profit. WAKE UP!

April 19, 1902

Socialist activist and writer Isador Ladoff's political beliefs remain best represented by American Pauperism and the Abolition of Poverty, *a book-length study of the maldistribution of American wealth based on 1900 census data, and by* The Passing of Capitalism and the Mission of Socialism.

Economics in Politics

Isador Ladoff

There is a constant war going on between labor and capital. The cause of this perpetual struggle between the producers of all material wealth on one side and the owners of all the means of production on the other side is generally known. The economic interests of these two classes of contemporary society are directly opposed to each other. The toiler strives to retain as much of the products of his labor as it is possible under the prevailing social economic conditions. The owner of the means of production, in his turn, endeavors to appropriate as much of the product of the toil of his wage slave as he may succeed in doing under the given conditions. The relations between the modern producer and his exploiting economic master are regulated chiefly by the prevailing social economic conditions, expressed and embodied in the ruling social economic institutions. The social economic institutions of a country make up in their entirety what we call briefly its STATE. The class that succeeds to control the state of a nation must of necessity be in power to modify the social economic conditions to suit best its interests. That class gains the power to dictate terms to all other classes of the nation. That class may enforce submission to its will in the name and by the authority of the state. Political power and economic power were, are and will always be concentrated in the hands of the ruling classes as long as class rule will exist. The ruling classes always used their economic power as a means to acquire political power and then used the last as a means to increase the first. All the his-

Justice:— "Say, Mr. Working Class, just swipe that parasite off the bag of Wealth—it is yours because you produced it. Refuse longer to be hypnotized into the belief that you and the capitalist are brothers. It is a lie so long so this system prevails."

Appeal to Reason, December 2, 1905.

tory of human kind is an illustration of this fact. On the other hand political dependence leads inevitably to economic dependence and vice versa. THERE CAN BE NO ACTUAL POLITICAL EQUALITY WITHOUT ECONOMIC DEMOCRACY.

The conclusions suggested by these general considerations may be applied profitably to the relations between capital and labor in the United States. Who actually controls our national, state and municipal administrations? Who spends millions of dollars on political campaigns? Who are the actual masters of our legislative and executive

institutions? Who are the real commanders of our army and fleet? Who owns the entire press, the pulpit, the institutions of learning? To put these questions means to answer them. The capitalists captured the state for all there is in it, and mainly for the SOCIAL ECONOMIC POWER it gives them "over the voting cattle." The laborer and small farmer are only NOMINALLY free citizens of the United States. Both capitalistic parties grossly flatter these nominal citizens before election and neglect, bulldoze and maltreat them all the rest of the time. The misfortune of the average laboring man consists in his failure to see the connection between his "job" and "ballot," between economics and politics. Trade unionism is obviously growing and developing in this country. Every clear sighted Socialist must rejoice in it as a healthy, normal development of the proletariat. But TRADE UNIONISM alone, trade unionism WITHOUT INDEPENDENT POLITICAL ACTION CANNOT SOLVE THE LABOR PROBLEM, as the history of trade unionism in England proved. Indeed only the better situated strata of skilled workingmen are comparatively easily crystallizing into unions. The great bulk of unskilled laborers remain stubbornly in the amorphous, unorganized state. The back bone of trade unionism is skilled or qualified labor. The marked tendency of modern machine production is however unmistakably in the direction of the elimination of skilled labor by the means of an ever increasing perfection of the tools of production. Another outspoken tendency of modern machine production militating against the institution of trade unionism is the ever increasing limitation of the number of laborers necessary for production. These two tendencies lead to the progressive increase of the industrial reserve army of unemployed, the army that is always ready to serve as a tool against organized labor. It has very little sense to vote the capitalists into power and then expect to win out against them in industrial battles by the means of strikes. Strikes may improve directly the condition of organized and indirectly of unorganized labor, but by the price of starvation, wrecked homes and ruined families.

As long as the capitalists control our national, state and municipal administration it will be managed in direct violation of the rights of labor. As long as the capitalists will spend millions in order to influence the voting cattle in political campaigns the political spoil will belong to them.

As long as the capitalists will make and execute laws, the laboring class will be compelled to break laws and be punished for it.

As long as the capitalists will remain the actual commanders of our army and navy, the tremendous physical forces will be used for the extermination of riotous strikers and for the conquest of new markets for capitalists.

As long as the capitalists will own the press, the pulpit, the educational institution, generations after generations will be trained in a spirit directly inimical to the interests of labor.

As long as the capitalists are allowed to monopolize the power and authority of the state, the laborer and small farmer will remain actually a slave of the social economic institutions of the country.

In order to have at least the ghost of a show of success in their struggle against capitalism laboring men must fight with weapons just as efficient as those of their adversaries, must meet their enemy on its own ground if independent political action. The laboring class must strike at the BALLOT BOX. . . .

September 6, 1902

Regardless of the Socialist party's policy of gender equality, Socialist men and party institutions often discriminated against women. The Appeal *sought to support women's (and feminist men's) efforts to achieve egalitarian gender relations, rights, and opportunities in practice as well as in theory.*

A Letter from an Enthusiastic Woman

Naomi McDonald Phelps

I would like to answer Comrade Wells' suggestion in regard to women, where he says he thinks women ought to be coaxed into the Socialist clubs, as they would talk the old parties to death in no time. He says he knows, because he has lived with one for thirty-five years. The very idea that HE had lived with one thirty-five years, and she was still alive, ought to have prevented him from slurring his wife in such a silly manner. The fact is, men have that principle so engrafted in their natures, i.e., speaking of women in regard to public affairs much as they would of imbeciles and children—"ha! ha! Johnny's got on his firstest pair of pants; thinks he will soon be old enough to vote"—that their invitations to women to join their clubs are couched in such a manner, and their treatment of "the talking sex" is so contemptuous that the self-respecting women resent it. We're not babies; we're not fools. If you had been our servants as long as we have been yours; if you had been obliged to minister to carnal appetites, with your limits subscribed by the four walls of the kitchen and nursery in one, with no time to read, the doors of schools closed in your faces, starved in soul and body, cook, cook, from morning to night, and a new baby every eighteen months or so, a half dozen trotting at your heels, whose wants were all laid upon your heart and tired hands—I believe with all my heart that you would have been a sex of blubbering idiots. By what twist of fortune's wheel men became so wise in their own conceits, fell so completely in love with their own preponderance of brains, is past the finding out of the wisest women.

· ·

But I want to give the male members of all political clubs a recipe for the tolling in of women. In the first place, do as churches, national, conventional and municipal assemblages, old party clubs, etc., do. Always get the first grip, while you urge her to take hold: see to it that you do the talking, while urging her to talk. Have Jones, Brown and Brewster all ready for the floor, and see that they keep it from the time your club meeting opens until the motion is made to adjourn. Prove your appreciation for her assistance as lecturer in the field by running all the consecrated, bifurcated gentry to the front, and filling all the places with the sex that God ordered to till the earth. Finish up by telling her that she's a daisy—when it comes to scrubbing—but it takes you with your wonderful preponderance of brains, to represent her interests. Give her to understand from start to finish that you represent the brain: deny her the right to

suffrage until—oh, until the millenium—and then, well, she won't want it. Thus, by your own egotism rob yourselves of the right wing of your army, and cripple your cause in the house of its friends. Do all this: nay, follow your Joans to battle, and after the victory, burn them for witches. That's the proper caper, if you profess to believe in our right to the ballot, our brain power, our adaptability to the lecture field, our power to win over men to the right, just keep on along the line I have marked out, and the way the women will flock to your standard will inspire you.

Well, I hope this will go in the *Appeal*, as men's attitude toward women in regard to the great issues of the day, destroys her usefulness, dwarfs her capabilities, kills her confidence, enlarges her disgust with self-conceit, and turns the volume of her patriotism back upon herself, and though her soul rebel, yet there is no way out of these annoyances, that hamper and annoy, until men shall LIVE the gospel they PREACH.

April 18, 1903

Born in Centralia, Missouri, converted to socialism at Missouri's socialist Ruskin College, Josephine Conger (later Conger-Kaneko) conducted the Appeal's *Woman's Department before moving on to edit and publish the* Progressive Woman. *Her works include* Woman's Slavery—Her Road to Freedom *and* Little Sister of the Poor.

The Prayer of the Modern Woman

JOSEPHINE CONGER

Unbind our hands. We do not ask for favor in this
    fight
Of human souls for human needs. We ask for
    naught but right,
That we may throw the burdens from backs and
    from our brains
The thrall of servitude. We are so weary of the
    pains

That crush our hearts, and cramp our wills reduc-
ing all desires
To childish whims, while great hopes lie like
smouldering fires
Within our brains, or burst distorted from some
weak, unguarded point,
Leaving ruin and sorrow in their track.
Since women are not free, the whole world's out
of joint—
For women are the mothers of the race. We cannot
boast
Of equal rights and liberty, while mothers of the
host
Must know they're classed in common law with
idiots and slaves,
Must stand aside with foreigners, with imbeciles
and knaves.
The sturdy sons nursed at their breasts cannot be
wholly free,
Since what the mother is, the child will in a mea-
sure be.
You are not granting favor when you give us equal
power
The shame is, you've withheld so long from us our
dower
Of earth's inheritance. We do not beg for alms or
charity.
We do not want our rights doled out; we want full
liberty,
To grow, and be, and do our part, as Nature meant
we should;
We want a perfect sister- as well as brotherhood.

May 16, 1903

Socialists were called upon to distinguish their principles
from those of the powerful populist movement of the 1880s
and 1890s. Ernest Untermann's responsibility in "Populism
and Socialism"—delineating the political differences while
also emphasizing the shared goals of the People's party and
the new Socialist party—was made the more difficult because ex–People's party leaders and Socialists were often

engaged in polemical debate and mutual attacks. Editor and
columnist for the Appeal in 1903, Untermann was well-known
in the socialist movement for his Marxian Economics: A Popular Introduction to the Three Volumes of Marx's Capital.

Populism *and* Socialism

ERNEST UNTERMANN

What is the difference between Populism and Socialism? That question is easily answered by a comparison of the platform of the People's party and the Socialist party.

The fundamental demands in the various People's party platforms may be summed up in these
words: Abolition of national banks; issue of legal
tender treasury notes in place of national bank
notes; free and unlimited coinage of silver; prohibition of alien ownership of land; a graduated income tax; public ownership of railroads, tele-
graphs and telephones; election of the president
and vice president and United States senators by
direct vote of the people; universal suffrage; endorsement of the eight hour law and of the minimum wage scale; declaration that "Wealth belongs
to him who creates it. Every dollar taken from industry without an equivalent is robbery. If anyone
will not work, neither shall he eat. The interests of
rural and urban labor are identical."

The fundamental demands of the Socialist
party are: Conquest of the political power by the
working class; collective ownership fo the essential means of production and distribution, under
the control and democratic management of the
working class, with equality of both sexes in all relations; production for use, not for profit, the producer to receive the product of his labor, un-
diminished by rent, profit and interest.

From the standpoint of the Socialist, the People's
party platform aims at symptoms without removing
the cause. Changes in the money system will not
bring the money into the pockets of the worker, as

long as production is for profit under the control of the capitalist class. Prohibition of alien ownership of land will not lessen the exploitation of the farmers by the trusts; a graduated income tax, if it could be enacted and enforced, would not help any working man, because the capitalists can shift the burden of taxation to the shoulders of the working class by increasing the prices of all the products. The universal eight hour day and a minimum wage can be met by the capitalists in the same way. Universal suffrage and the election of the president, vice president and United States senators, by the direct vote of the people, will be useless, as long as the working men elect capitalist politicians and leave the political and economic power in the control of the capitalist class. Government ownership of the railroads, telegraphs and telephones, under the control of capitalist parties, is an increase of power for the capitalists. The only really revolutionary statement in the People's party platform is that wealth shall belong to him who produces it; but the framers of that platform forgot to explain how the producer could obtain this wealth and be secured in its possession.

Now, the only way to accomplish this is to dethrone the capitalist class and change the system of production. Because the People's party did not recognize this, and because in spite of its appeal to the working class it sought to gain the political power through a fusion with a capitalist party, the Democratic party, therefore the People's party failed to accomplish its object.

But the Populists correctly stated that the interests of the rural and urban workers are identical. If they had added that these interests are also distinct from, and opposed to, the interests of all rural and urban capitalists, they would not have consented to a fusion with the very class which they are organized to defeat. But even then they would still have neglected the fact that capitalism is international, and that, therefore, the interests of the workers of the world are opposed to those of the capitalists of the world. Only an international party of the working class can meet international capitalism successfully, and the only party

that has boldly said so, and acted accordingly, is the International Socialist Party.

The Socialists recognize that the international wage system is the cause of all social evils; that this system is based on the exploitation of all working classes by all capitalist classes; that this results in economic and political class struggles between these two classes in all parts of the world where this system is in existence; and that in the United States this struggle can only be ended by a defeat of the capitalist class at the ballot box.

There is not the least doubt that the capitalist class will be easily defeated when the class lines are being clearly drawn. If all the wage workers and small farmers will vote for the Socialist party, and all the capitalists, great and small, for the capitalist parties, there will be no other class in control of this country but the working class.

And that is the reason why a Populist should become a Socialist.

June 27, 1903

Readers regularly asked how socialism would work in practice. These questions and the Appeal's responses made the paper a "school" for economic and political education.

As I understand it, under Socialism a worker has the full product of his labor, that a day's labor on one thing will exchange even for a day's work on another. If that is so, the workers have it all, and where do the sick people, the old people and the children get their share? The workers will certainly have to produce enough for all the people, and if they do, how will each worker get the full product of his labor?

C. A. ROSE

Socialism will give each worker the EQUIVALENT of what each produces. No worker wants all of WHAT he produces. For instance, if a farmer produces wheat he would not want wheat only, but a little of all things. Thus it will have to be arranged to give each the equivalent of what his labor produces. To do this the TIME cost of articles will be the only possible way of ascertaining the relative value of things. What cost an hour of this workman or group of workmen will equal the articles produced by another workman or group of workmen. This rule can be worked out ABSOLUTELY and no other can, for if there is to be a different wage, who is to decide it? If the persons doing the work, then can it be claimed that the present system of giving Rockefeller millions a year is right, for he decides the matter, and evidently considers himself entitled to it.

As you say, if the full average product were given direct, or the price of articles written in just the average time of actual production, there would be nothing to provide for accumulated capital, such as railroads, houses, factories, machines, schools, sickness, etc. Such being the case, it will be the duty of the statistical department to find out what percentage of the national labor it will require to provide the schools, the teachers, the appliances for school, clothing for the children and food and entertainment for them. If it should be found that such would equal 2% of the national labor, then 2% would be added to the price of articles for that: say 10% for the income to be paid to the old and sick and so on through the whole list of such national expenditures. While it may appear that each worker will not be getting the full results of these deductions, he actually does, for what is taken from him to care for the children is simply a repayment of the expenses on him when he was a child, and what is taken for the old or sick, will be his insurance in sickness and old age. Thus it will be that the interest of each will be the concern of all, for all will want protection in their incapacity, and as in insurance all will cheerfully pay the premium that will guarantee to him or her peace, plenty and pleasure in their old age or sickness.

September 12, 1903

Brief though it is, Andrew Carnegie's "greatest discovery" reveals more about the nature of capitalism than many longer explanations.

Mr. Carnegie says: "The greatest discovery of my life is that the men who do the work never get rich." Oh, that the men who do the work could wake to this discovery! Perhaps they might then ask the question, WHY?

October 17, 1903

The Marxist meaning of economic determinism—which included an understanding of men and women interacting with their social reality and actively making their own history—was explained often in the Appeal.

Question Box

Kindly give through the Appeal *the definition of Economic Determinism.*

E. W. C., *Bellingham, Wash.*

The idea expressed in the theory of Economic Determinism is that the economic conditions, or the methods by which the people gain a livelihood, in any given epoch, are the fundamental element in determining the nature of all social institutions. It is not asserted that this is the only determining element, but that it is the most important factor in shaping the social, legal and political institutions of the time.

The theory is stated by Frederick Engels in the introduction to the *Communist Manifesto* in the following language: "In every historical epoch the prevailing mode of economic production and exchange, and the social organization necessarily following from it, form the basis upon which is built up, and from which alone can be explained, the political and intellectual history of that epoch."

This proposition has now been demonstrated both practically and theoretically in a thousand different ways. The religious worker, the temperance reformer, the labor unionist, the charity worker, and the criminologist act more wisely and well because they see the correctness of this proposition—that down underneath every situation and every problem of the personal as well as the social life of man is the economic cause and condition. In the realm of social movements the discovery is of immense importance. It reveals the determining element in social motion, and turns the stream of energy which would make for human betterment upon the real issue and directs it at the strategic point.

It should be remembered that the theory of Economic Determinism, while it applies fundamentally to society in general, is not to be construed as the only motive influencing individuals. While the individual is largely influenced by economic environment, he also possesses the faculty of reacting upon environment and, to at least some extent, determines his own course of action. Many zealous converts to the theory have, in their enthusiasm, applied the theory where it doesn't apply; and thereby invoked justifiable criticism.

January 12, 1907

Comparisons between chattel slavery and more profitable wage slavery appeared in many forms in the Appeal. *This brief parable also reveals the unconscious racism prevalent in early-twentieth-century America and as well as something of the experience of Irish immigrants in the 1840s and 1850s.*

"Massah" Saw It; Do You?

"Massah!" a negro slave is said one day to have answered his master, who ordered him to climb on a steep roof and plug a leak, "Massah! If I go up that steep roof, and I rolls off, and I falls down, and I breaks my neck, Massah will lose $500. Now, if massah send up that Irishman whom massah is hiring for $1.50 a day, and he rolls off, and he falls down, and he breaks his neck, massah will lose nuffin."

The Irishman repaired the leak.

October 26, 1907

Understanding capital and capitalism as an historically specific set of social relations, at times the Appeal *had little patience with the confusion and mystification created by the capitalist press. Ferdinand Lassalle, socialist theorist and founder of the Social Democratic party of Germany in 1869, was influential in America primarily because of his emphasis on electoral activity as opposed to union organizing; John Mitchell was president of the United Mine Workers from 1898 to 1908.*

Question Box

"Do Socialists wish to abolish capital? Do you consider capital to be that portion of wealth which is used as a means of producing more wealth, as is taught by political economists? If not, please give your definition of capital, and state in what manner Socialism proposes to abolish it."

TRUTHSEEKER.

Socialists wish to abolish capital, but they do not regard capital as merely that portion of wealth which is used as a means of producing more wealth. They do not accept any of the definitions offered by alleged economists who have variously defined capital as "the saved portion of a man's income," as "the instruments of labor," as "hoarded labor" or as "products which are continually applied to further production."

Lassalle showed the absurdity of such definitions when he pointed out that according to all or either of them the bow and arrow of a wild Indian would be capital and their savage owner a capitalist. The intellectual apologists for the capitalist system of production have never given a definition of the term that would stand the test.

The word has been used so loosely by bourgeois writers that it has for the popular mind next to no meaning whatever. John Mitchell stated in a recent magazine article that the workingman's labor power is his capital, which, if true, makes capitalists of everybody and dissolved the conception of capital into nothing. Not infrequently some moralizer tells young men from the lecture platform that "character is capital," to impress the idea that the young man possessed of a noble purpose, though penniless, is a capitalist, and fit to meet the man of money in the economic struggle.

It is possible to make the definition of a specific thing so broad and so inclusive that it includes everything and consequently, means nothing. This is what the capitalistic writers have done with the term capital. They have made their definitions so broad that they have lost their depth, width and length; and in so stretching the meaning of a word to suit their immediate purpose they have virtually pulled it to pieces, and lost the pieces in confusion.

Briefly stated, capital is wealth used to exploit labor. Capital is wealth so manipulated that its owner derives a revenue from the labor of others. Capital is really more than the wealth used in such a process—it is both the wealth and the process. For capital to be capital it must be in motion functioning as an instrument in the process of exchange. It is peculiar to an industrial system in which wealth presents itself as a collection of commodities—that is, things made to sell.

Capital and capitalists had their beginnings when the old feudal institutions broke up and the serfs, transformed into free laborers, left the household or castle, where practically everything that was consumed was made. Theretofore things were made for the immediate use of the maker or his feudal master; thereafter things were made not for the use of either the worker or of his employer, but for sale on the market. Capital and capitalists

have developed as products have become commodities, and have been more and more produced for purposes of sale or exchange.

Capital enormously increased the productivity of the laborer, but the benefits of the increase are mostly for the owner of capital. In the days of serfdom the worker got enough of what he made to keep him in working condition and produce another generation to take his place. The wage laborer, though his standard of living has necessarily been raised as a necessary condition of the increased intelligence demanded by modern industry, gets practically the same reward for his efforts that the serf got, while the owners of capital have become more powerful than kings. The capitalists of today, because of what they have absorbed of the products of labor, are the power behind every throne and are the real government of all nations.

To abolish capital, therefore, is not to abolish wealth, but is to abolish that use of wealth by which the comparatively few owners of the earth and its contents are enabled to take the property which others have created and use it to the increase of their own wealth and power. The capitalists have by the operation of the capitalistic process become kings of industry. Like the kings of old, they hold the lives of the subject working class in their hands because they can give or withhold the employment which the worker must have to live. There is, therefore, the same reason for the abolition of capital that there was for abolishing the autocratic rule of kings. To abolish a kingdom is not to lay waste the lands of the king or raze his castles or disorganize society; it is simply to transfer the power of the king to some other form of government.

To abolish capital is to transfer the power of ownership now held by the owners of capital to a democratic government of industry under which each worker would receive the full value of what his labor would produce. The effect would be to divert all the wealth which heretofore has gone to the capitalists back to the producers thereof. And this would stop the process without which capital can have no existence.

November 2, 1907

Letters came to the Appeal from all quarters. Class consciousness and an understanding of political economy were not exclusive to radicals.

As a Capitalist Sees It

Bakersfield, Calif., Oct. 20, 1908.—Editor *Appeal*:—I frequently see copies of your paper, also *Wilshire*'s and a *Chicago Daily Socialist* paper. I have also read some leading books on Socialism, such as Chas. Vail's, Benson's, Engel's, etc., so that I think I am not so ignorant of your beliefs as some who write to you. I have also read many arguments against your theories but it doesn't appear to me that the arguments against tell the truth, not at least as I see it. They appear to me to be attempting to conceal the real arguments in their minds.

From my point of view I am better off now than I would be under Socialism. I do not want to do compulsory work for even four hours a day. The five or eight thousand a year income would not buy the things I have learned to enjoy. Our domestic force numbers six persons. Now if my chauffeur's or my wife's attendant's time was pitted against my own at equal value per hour, and I wanted their service for twelve or sixteen hours a day, where would I get off? I can't claim that I have given society an equivalent for every dollar I possess, but I have it and I want to keep it; and I want it to remain powerful, to exploit labor as you would say. I am now a personage looked up to in my home town.

I have been successful in accumulating dollars and I want to retain that prestige. I see smarter men every day and in every branch of human endeavor than I am and if I was debarred from excelling in my one specialty I would sink below the common level and be lost sight of. That to me

would be intolerable. Of course you can understand why I use my influence and money to head off your propaganda, and why I would favor resort to arms to defend the old standards of property rights.—Yours truly. W. D. Balfor

November 14, 1908

Support of equal rights and opportunities for women brought many accusations that socialists were in favor of breaking up the home and family. The findings of Theodore Roosevelt's Homes Commission gave the Appeal an effective basis to combat those attacks in the arena of public consciousness. Dr. William W. Sanger was the author of The History of Prostitution. *The national campaign against prostitution, alternately called white slavery and the Social Evil, dominated social reform activity during the first decade of the twentieth century.*

The Suppressed Report

The *Appeal* risks its mailing privilege by reprinting the following extracts from the report of the Homes commission appointed by Roosevelt to investigate conditions in Washington and New York. The report discloses such a vile condition existing in the homes of Republicans and Democrats that the senate declared the report unmailable and called on the department of justice to prosecute any one daring to circulate it. The *Appeal* dares this risk.

Investigation of prostitution was made in the city of New York. Here is what the Homes commission has to say relative to this substitute for the home that capitalism fosters so extensively:

"Of the 2,000 persons investigated 490 were married, 71 of whom still lived with their husbands; 103 left their husbands on account of ill usage, 60 were deserted by their husbands, 43 were deserted by husbands to live with other women; others left their homes on account of non-support, drunkenness, infidelity and in

75 cases no specific cause was assigned. There were also 294 widows in the general list. The author believes the principal conclusion to be drawn from the table which he presents is that the majority of this class of widows are DRIVEN TO A COURSE OF VICE FROM THE DESTITUTION ENSUING ON THEIR HUSBAND'S DEATH. It has been shown that a large number of them are very young and it can be scarcely necessary to repeat that any young woman in a state of poverty will be surrounded with temptations she can with difficulty resist. Much as this state of society may be deplored, its existence can not be denied.

The section dealing with hidden springs of the evil is of extreme interest. The causes assigned by the women themselves are as follows:

"Inclination, 513; destitution, 525; seduced and abandoned, 258; drink and a desire to drink, 181; ill treatment of parents, relations or husbands, 164; as an easy life, 124; bad company, 84; persuaded by prostitutes, 71; too idle to work, 29; violated, 27; seduced on board of emigrant ships or in emigrant boarding houses, 24.

"Doctor Sanger, in discussing the subject of inclination, adduces considerable evidence to show that if a positive inclination to vice was the proximate cause of the fall, it was but the result of other and controlling influences.

"Of the 2,000 cases examined with reference to previous occupation, 933 BELONGED TO THE SERVANT CLASS, 499 lived with parents or friends, 285 were dressmakers, tailoresses and seamstresses, and the remaining were engaged in miscellaneous occupations; 523 CLAIM TO HAVE EARNED ONLY $1 PER WEEK; 336, $2 a

Appeal to Reason, March 14, 1914.

Appeal to Reason, May 30, 1914.

week; 230, $3; 127, $4; 68, $5; 27, $6; 8, $7; 5, $8; two had earned over $20 a week and in 663 the question of earnings was not ascertained."—Page 223, Roosevelt's Homes Commission Report.

This is the situation under capitalism in Mr. Roosevelt's home city, New York. It is not Socialist talk, but is from the report of his own Homes commission, so carries with it capitalist authority. No wonder Roosevelt wanted to suppress it.

May 1, 1909

To the Appeal, freedom was the unconditional basis for human life to truly begin for both sexes. The setback for socialism that J. A. Wayland refers to in "Bully for the Women" is Job Harriman's defeat in the 1912 Los Angeles mayoralty election. Women had gained suffrage in California just months before.

Bully for the Women

Do Socialists condemn suffrage because women helped to defeat Socialism at Los Angeles? Bless you, no. There is not a true Socialist in America who is not just as ardently in favor of woman suffrage today as he was before that election. If men have been going through election after election without turning to Socialism, what right have we to be angry at the women because they did not stampede to Socialism the first time they got to vote? The women will get their eyes open yet and shame many of the men by their understanding of public good. Yet even if they did not, even if they always voted against Socialism, Socialists would favor woman suffrage. They couldn't help it, from the fact that woman suffrage is on the line of further democracy and hence an essential feature of Socialist agitation. Get this idea: Socialists seek only to give both men and women the power over their own lives, the power over their own jobs. We know that when they get this power they may

make mistakes; but that makes no difference. They should have the power anyhow.

December 23, 1911

The political parable of a postage stamp is classic J. A. Wayland; it was reprinted several times in the Appeal.

It Is Not Advertised

J. A. WAYLAND

There is a little article that everybody uses, and yet I never see it advertised. I look over the daily and weekly press in vain to find where it can be purchased. On this they are as silent at the tomb. In vain I look at the signs on the street, or in the shop windows for it. It is sold in every village and hamlet in the land, and yet no drummer ever carries samples of it and never takes an order for it. Its price never raises, and yet it pays handsomely all who deal in it. And strange to say there is usually but one place in a town that keeps it. There is always a supply of it—never too much nor too little. It is never taxed, no matter how many thousands dollars' worth are in stock. There has never been any corner or speculation in it and its price at wholesale or retail is always just the same. It has never made a millionaire or a pauper. That little thing is a postage stamp, and if all articles were produced and handled in the same way, there would be neither poverty, crime nor insanity in the United States. Try it.

April 6, 1912

"The Socialist and the Suffragist" sought to heal schisms between socialists and feminists. A leading socialist who never joined the party, Charlotte Perkins Gilman's posthumously published account of her life is The Living of Charlotte Perkins Gilman.

The Socialist and the Suffragist

CHARLOTTE PERKINS GILMAN

Said the Socialist to the suffragist:
  "My cause is greater than yours!
  You only work for a special class,
  We for the gain of the general mass,
  Which every good ensures!"

Said the suffragist to the Socialist:
  "You underrate my cause!
  While women remain a subject class,
  You never can move the general mass,
  With your economic laws!"

Said the Socialist to the suffragist:
  "You misinterpret facts!
  There is no room for doubt or schism
  In economic determinism—
  It governs all our acts!"

Said the suffragist to the Socialist:
  "You men will always find
  That this old world will never move
  More swiftly in its ancient groove
  While women stay behind."

"A lifted world lifts women up,"
  The Socialist explained.
  "You cannot lift the world at all
  While half of it is kept so small,"
  The suffragist maintained.

The world awoke, and tartly spoke:
  "Your work is all the same:
  Work together or work apart,
  Work, each of you, with all your heart—
  Just get into the game!"

September 28, 1912

Lack of formal education did not prevent Martha Baker, or many other Americans who wrote to the Appeal, *from under-standing what socialism would mean for both men and women.*

A Woman's Chance

MARTHA BAKER

I am a poor, uneducated girl, not a subscriber to the *Appeal* because I am not worth the subscription price. My health is too poor to do the work I can get to do. Therefore, I am dependent. I am uneducated. The greatest desire of my life is denied because poor working people have no chance for education and enlightenment. I am not a member of the Socialist party. I was born and raised in a state where few rights are granted to women, and to talk politics or to have a political opinion is considered unwomanly. But I have been reading the *Appeal* and trying to find out what Socialism is. Though it is too deep and broad and grand for my shallow brain and untrained mind to comprehend, I can see in it a great hope for the millions of working people who are struggling for existence. In the future, under Socialism, I can see equal privileges of life granted to all, the chance to grow and develop physically, mentally and intellectually. The people will be free from poverty, because they will not be robbed of what they produce. I can see the same right to live granted to woman as well as to man and she will not be kept down simply because she is a woman.

I can see real marriages—a union of heart and soul and not a ceremony performed just to give to one party the right to use the property of the other. I can see girls go where their hearts lead them and not have to sell themselves for food and raiment. I can see for everyone alike life and real life and the privilege of enjoying the earth and its resources. I can see less crime, fewer murders, fewer suicides, because I believe almost every crime can be traced to poverty as a direct or indirect cause.

When I think of the few who are enjoying the wealth that belongs to the millions who are living in poverty and want, who are starving both men-

Many of This Kind
He preaches that the rewards of labor shall be reaped in heaven.

Only a Few of This Kind
He preaches that labor should get a few rewards here on earth.

Appeal to Reason, September 9, 1922.

tally and physically, whose lives are one unbroken struggle for existence, I wonder that the poor people don't come together at once and demand their rights and show their masters that they will no longer be trodden upon.

Had I the money and education I would spend the rest of my life in trying to teach the working people sense enough to keep what belongs to them. But it is poverty that keeps us ignorant and ignorance that keeps us poor.

Perhaps I have not found the language that an educated person would have to express my sentiments. But I want to add my testimony to that of thousands of others—that wherever it finds them the *Appeal to Reason* and Socialism will bring new hope to the working people.

Suffolk, Va.
June 14, 1913

"What I Believe" summarizes Fred Warren's socialist belief in electoral activity rather than direct action at the point of production.

What I Believe

FRED D. WARREN

I believe in the confiscation of the productive property of this nation by the working class. I do not believe in confiscating it by piecemeal. That would be foolish and illegal. The plan I favor is that the working class shall first capture the political powers of the state and nation and then the job can be done without the danger of getting cracked skulls and prison sentences. This is the plan followed by the master class. It has been proved a success by the master. It will prove a workable plan for the slave.

The mission of the *Appeal to Reason* is to persuade the men who work to use their political power that it may be possible easily, quickly and without opposition to exert their industrial strength.

I believe the working class should capture the political powers of the cities as rapidly as possible. The capture of a municipality will not do the working class a great deal of good. What we want is ALL the wealth we create. The capture of a municipality will not give us all—not even a bit more. A Socialist administration of a city may succeed in raising wages and reducing hours and providing somewhat better conditions for a part of the working class. But this gain is quickly wiped out be increased prices of those things the working class as a whole must buy. Therefore we merely transfer from the pockets of a part of the working class what the more fortunate ones get in increased wages and shorter hours.

The capture of a municipality merely gives the working class a chance to "practice" administering public affairs. This experience will prove of great value later on.

I do not believe in sabotage. If a man steals my horse and I find it in his possession, it would be very foolish for me to hamstring the horse. It would merely be destroying my property and would not injure the thief. I should immediately take steps to recover my property. This is what the working class must do in its dealings with the capitalist class. The wealth of the world, having been created by the working class, rightfully belongs to the workers. It has been stolen by processes legal and otherwise, and if the workers are ever to recover possession they must take it. It will not be returned to them by their capitalist masters.

The working class cannot get possession of the industries until they have first taken over the police power, the courts and the law-making functions of state and nation.

A working man makes a rapid-fire gatling gun. He loads the gun with the latest improved ammunition—smokeless powder and deadly projectiles. He turns the gun over to his master. He then proposes a fight for possession of that weapon. I admire the dare-devil courage of the working man, but I would certainly condemn him as a foolish and unwise creature. The reward for his industry in making the gun and his courage in trying to take it, unarmed, from the man he had given it to, would be a mutilated body and an unmarked grave.

The gatling gun is the productive machinery of state and nation. Its political expression is the policeman's club and the soldier's gun.

The working man today possesses the ballot. It is not yet too late for him to use it for his own good and for the protection of future society. Tomorrow his ballot will be taken from him by the master class which is in undisputed possession, not only of the industries, but of the political powers of the state.

I have no conscientious scruples against the use of any method, direct or indirect, that will secure to the working class possession of the machinery of production. But I think entirely too much of my head to risk butting it against a stone wall in the shape of a policeman's club wielded by a man who takes his orders from capitalist politicians.

Be wise, Mr. Workingman, and exercise your right at the ballot box. When this plan has failed, it will then be time to discuss other methods.

November 8, 1913

"Who Does Your Thinking For You?" June 24, 1922.

"Socialism and the Negro" reflects the later Appeal's position on race. John Gunn, a young socialist journalist from the East, began writing for the Appeal in 1915 and remained a staff writer until the paper ceased publication.

Socialism and the Negro

JOHN WALKER GUNN

A reader asks if the negro would have equal rights with the white man under Socialism. You just bet your life a negro would have the same rights of freedom and opportunity that the white man would have under Socialism, and if I didn't believe so I wouldn't be a Socialist. A man once told me that he was opposed to Socialism because it meant equal rights for everybody, regardless of race. That is the only time I ever heard Socialism objected to on the frankly prejudiced ground tnat it stands for justice.

A Socialist doesn't necessarily believe in intimate social equality with the negro, in intermarriage between the whites and the blacks or any such thing. What every good Socialist must and does believe is that the negro has the same right to make a living and get it that the white man has, that the negro has the same right to political freedom, education and full opportunity to enjoy life and develop the talents that nature has given him. Any other view is viciously and brutally wrong and unfair, and springs either from blind prejudice or from the savage desire of one class or race to dominate another. Progress is merely a process of advancing away from this blind prejudice and this savage desire.

If every accusation against the negro were true—that he is ignorant, that he is without ability, that he is without moral restraint—this would be no reason for denying him the rights that Socialism offers. If the negro is ignorant, it is no reason why he should not be allowed to become intelligent; if he is without ability, it is no reason why he should not be allowed to develop ability or to use whatever ability he may possess; if he is without moral restraint, it is no reason why he should not be allowed to learn moral restraint. As a matter of fact, it is necessary to social progress that the negro be allowed to do these things. The negro is with us, we can't kill or deport him even if such a barbarous measure were desirable, and it is to our best interests and his to see that he is intelligent instead of ignorant, prosperous instead of poor, a good citizen instead of a bad citizen.

The negroes are an ignorant race, because until recently they were an enslaved race—and even now they are not perfectly free; in some portions of the south the negro is just as completely and brutally enslaved as he was in the days of chattel bondage. There is no question that the colored race has developed greatly, even with the little freedom it has had, since the so-called emancipation and that it has produced many brilliant, capable and estimable men.

The prejudice against the negro is found chiefly among the people of the southern states, where the negro is treated with the superior and reckless contempt that the master always exhibits toward the slave. This prejudice is and always has been impudent and insincere, dirty and damnable, the foul and illegitimate offspring of brutality and ignorance. It is a candid wonder that the negro is not a thousand times more vicious and immoral than he is, when one considers the contemptuous ignominy and violent persecution this unfortunate creature whose sole sin is the helpless possession of a colored skin has suffered at the cruel hands of the "respectable" whites, the light-skinned and light-minded aristocracy of the south.

The arrogant argument of the south is that the negro must be kept in subjection by the white race, in order to prevent him from becoming overbearing, impudent and inflicting violent injury upon the white man. There could not be a more transparent fallacy.

It is not on record that the colored race ever persecuted, injured or abused the white race; yet

Appeal to Reason, June 29, 1912.

The Same Old Nominee—Chicago—Baltimore

the history of the colored race in America, and especially in the southland, is one long and shameful record of subjection and abuse at the hands of the white race.

The white race it was that held the negro in chattel slavery for more than a century, robbing him of the fruits of his hard toil beneath the burning southern sun; inflicting the merciless lash upon his naked back; keeping him in ignorance and flattening his forehead with the slant of superstition, in order that intelligence might not bring the desire for freedom; separating families, tearing the black child from its weeping mother's bosom and subjecting the female of the race to the fierce lust of her lecherous master.

And after the black man, in the course of history, was relieved of his chattel chains it was the white man who continued to persecute him and wrong his rising race; it was the white man who continued, and continues to this day in the southern states, to hound and harry the negro as if his color were a crime, to insult and intimidate him and deny him the right given him by the federal constitution to exercise the rights of political democracy; it is the white race which has covered itself with disgrace in the south by lynching negroes in the heat of prejudice upon the barest thread of suspicion or upon no suspicion at all; it is the belief of many white men of the south that it is a good thing to lynch an innocent negro merely on general principles, and I have personally heard this brazen and barbarous belief uttered.

The white race has not stopped at enslaving and maltreating the negro, but has even gone so far as to cruelly oppress the unfortunate poor among the white race; and today the horrible employment of little children in southern cotton mills, the criminal exploitation of convict labor in southern prisons, and the inexpressible poverty and misery that darkens the life of the tenant farmer of the south stand as bloody and accusing blots upon the vaunted civilization of the dominant white.

If any protection against abuse is needed, it is plainly needed by the negro against the white race that has kept him in historic subjection, and that has persecuted him at every turn of history's highway. The objection to justice for the negro comes with ironical grace from that portion of the white race that has ever been the active exponent of injustice.

I repeat that I believe in freedom and opportunity as the equal and inalienable heritage of every human being, regardless of race, sex, creed or previous condition of servitude. This is Socialism, and it is dictated both by common sense and common humanity.

September 18, 1915

THREE

The Class War

Seek for food and clothing first, then the Kingdom of God shall be added unto you.—Hegel, 1807

The class struggle, which is always present to a historian influenced by Marx, is a fight for the crude and material things without which no refined and spiritual things could exist. Nevertheless, it is not in the form of the spoils which fall to the victor that the latter make their presence felt in the class struggle. They manifest themselves in this struggle as courage, humor, cunning, and fortitude. They have retroactive force and will constantly call in question every victory, past and present, of the rulers. As flowers turn toward the sun, by dint of a secret heliotropism the past strives to turn toward that sun which is rising in the sky of history.—Walter Benjamin, *Theses on the Philosophy of History*

America was dramatically transformed during the period between the Civil War and World War I. A predominantly rural, preindustrial nation in 1850, the United States was industrialized with unprecedented speed and thoroughness by the turn of the century. By the end of the first decade of the twentieth century, major industries such as mining, oil, steel, communications, transportation, and banking were consolidated in trust and monopoly ownership. Upon their control, American capital's growing influence ex-

tended across the continent and left few communities or lives untouched. The pace of urbanization increased with extraordinary swiftness as well; only one-third of the population remained on the farm in 1900. Chicago, a small city of 20,000 during the 1850s, grew to over 2,000,000 by 1910; in New York City, the population swelled from 500,000 to more than 3,500,000 during the same period as new immigrants arrived and Americans departed rural areas in search of work. By 1920 one-half of the country's population lived in fewer than fifteen cities. There and elsewhere they worked for corporations, the dominant new form of business organization. Fully 100 percent of transportation employees, 90 percent of those engaged in mining, and 75 percent of all manufacturing wage earners were employed by corporations. In a young country without a feudal background, one whose special destiny was to prevent a repetition of the social and economic inequalities of Europe, the appropriation of the bulk of the nation's new wealth by a small capitalist class created the conditions for a class war whose outcome was not decided until the aftermath of World War I.

The explosive growth of industrial and finance capitalism during the post-Civil War period created a world few had anticipated, a world radically different than anyone remembered. During the period between 1890 and 1912, national wealth increased from 65 to 187 billion dollars, a rise of 188 percent. The benefits of that increase, however, were not proportionately shared across the new class structure. Over virtually the same period of time, 1889 to 1909, the aggregate income of wage earners in manufacturing, mining, and transportation rose only half as much.[1] Sprung up to appropriate the wealth was a new class, small in number but great and at times unchallengeable in power, that did little or nothing more than own the tools which the great mass of working people used. Atop the hierarchy were seven "Greater Industrial Trusts," so called by John Moody in 1904 to distinguish them from smaller, if still powerful, combinations. The Money Trust, an interlocked group of some ten financial institutions, controlled American credit and capital. Dominating that small group were the House of Morgan, the First National City Bank of New York, and Rockefeller's National City Bank. Between them they controlled 112 corporations whose total resources in 1912 exceeded 22 billion dollars, an amount greater than the assessed value of all property in the twenty-two states and territories west of the Mississippi, an amount more than twice the assessed value of all property in the thirteen southern states.[2] Just how successful the new, owning class was in amassing the nation's growing wealth is revealed by conservative distribution-of-wealth figures used by the U.S. Congress's Industrial Relations Commission in 1915. Two percent of the population owned 60 percent of the nation's wealth, 33 percent owned 35 percent of the wealth, and the great majority of the population, 65 percent, was left to divide the small remainder, 5 percent. Put another way, two million Americans owned 20 percent more of the nation's wealth than the other 95 million Americans combined.[3]

Capitalist ideology was reproduced not only in American culture but, it is amply documented, in national and state legislatures as well. When necessary, both were bought and paid for by corporate bidders. Standard Oil, observed Henry Demarest Lloyd, "has done everything with the Pennsylvania legislature except to refine it." "A few individuals are becoming rich enough to control almost all the great markets, includ-

ing the legislatures." On the national level, U.S. senate seats were openly for sale to the highest bidders, in virtually every case the powerful new corporations. United States senators, observed William Allen White, a man hardly sympathetic with radical views, "represented principalities and powers in business. One senator, for instance, represented the Union Pacific Railway System, another the New York Central, still another the insurance interests of New York and New Jersey. . . . Coal and iron owned a coterie from the Middle and Eastern seaport states. Cotton had half a dozen senators. And so it went."[4] Capitalist assumptions came to permeate both dominant political parties so much that there was little practical difference, in either platform or administration, between Republicans and Democrats.

American capital assumed general control over the judicial system as well. As property ownership by corporations became dramatically concentrated, American courts moved broadly—almost automatically—to legitimize the new arrangement. "Unlawful assembly" and "disorderly conduct" were invoked throughout the United States to halt political demonstrations and strike-related activities such as picketing. State courts regularly issued injunctions upon employer demand. Governors, with very few exceptions, as easily declared martial law and used state militias to break strikes. At the workplace, courts cumulatively institutionalized capital's control over the conditions of employment. Laws beneficial to working people, which often had passed through legislatures or had been approved by voters after long decades of struggle, were repeatedly nullified by judicial decision. A host of labor-supported laws seeking, for example, to prohibit blacklisting, to protect workmen as members of labor unions, to limit the hours of employment, and to regulate the conditions of child labor were all overturned as unconstitutional interference with either the rights of private ownership of property or the rights of private contract. The Industrial Relations Commission, moved by investigation and testimony to describe American capital's manipulation of the courts as "another aspect of the control of the machinery of government by one class for the oppression of another," concluded in its *Final Report* that "legislatures, courts, and administrative officers under the domination of corporations have grievously wronged the workers."[5]

Domination of the economy and the political structures supporting it changed the very meaning of working for a living. The new industrial and financial barons, the men who made the decisions which affected not only millions of lives but entire regions of the United States, made their functional disconnection from the corporations they controlled unashamedly explicit. Other than in their rate of profit, the owning class divested itself of interest and responsibility. "We cannot pretend to follow the business itself," John D. Rockefeller, Jr., said of Colorado Fuel and Iron, one of the Rockefellers' numerous multimillion-dollar holdings. Asked if corporate directors were to any extent responsible for the working conditions at the companies they owned or controlled, J. Pierpont Morgan responded, "Not at all I should say."[6] The owning class had learned with Andrew Carnegie that, in a capitalist economy, it was impossible to amass a significant amount of money by working. After all, a John D. Rockefeller or a J. P. Morgan received more income every minute or two than an average agricultural worker or factory employee was paid in a year, more in an hour, awake or asleep, than a typical American worker could realistically hope to earn in a lifetime. Corporate and finance capitalists, socialists explained, reaped but ultimately did not sow. With their profits, appropriated from the unpaid wages of the men and women who did the work and created the value, they bought additional interests in yet more industries and hired managerial staffs to supervise and extend their small or larger empires.

Changes in technology, together with a new corporate structure that separated production plants from company headquarters in New York, Chicago, or elsewhere, changed the nature, conditions, and social relations of work for employees. Not only was significant policy control removed from the point of production, but the face-to-face relations between employer and employee of years past disappeared as well. During the 1850s, for example, the McCormick plant, America's largest manufacturer of agri-

cultural implements, employed less than three hundred men and was managed by Leander McCormick and four foremen. By World War I that modest form of production was rapidly becoming obsolete. The Ford plant employed over fifteen thousand men, factories employing six thousand to eight thousand men were common, and many plant managers did not know the names of even their oldest employees.[7] Replacing small-scale production was assembly-line work. Employees lost control over their time, saw their tasks become simplified and routinized, and felt their skills and status erode as they increasingly became anonymous cogs in huge, mechanized factories.

As new efficiency engineers devised speed-up and stretch-out procedures to increase productivity, work in the new factories became extraordinarily dangerous—more dangerous during the first few years of the twentieth century, John R. Commons found, than at any other place or time in recorded history.[8] Ten years later in 1914, in addition to 700,000 injuries forcing disability for four weeks or more, the U.S. Bureau of Labor Statistics found that approximately 35,000 persons were killed in American industry.[9] At least half of those deaths were judged preventable, but the courts had repeatedly absolved corporate officials from responsibility for accidents and there was little motivation under capitalism for human life to be balanced against increased profits.

Unemployment was common even for those who found work. A study of 105 plants during the period between 1912 and 1915 revealed that their "labor turnover" averaged almost 100 percent. Disregarding industries with significant fluctuation, such as harvesting and canning, the average American worker was unemployed between one-fifth and one-fourth of each year. Employers preferred to blame unemployment on strikes, but federal investigation determined that lack of work was responsible for two-thirds of unemployment and ill health responsible for a further one-fourth of lost time on the job. Strikes were responsible for less than 2 percent of the total. At the same time, a variety of elaborate investigations, encompassing all parts of the United States, found that a family of five needed a yearly income of seven hundred dollars to live at a level approaching decency. The Industrial Relations Commission was unable to determine precisely what proportion of wage-earning families engaged in manufacturing and mining the necessary seven hundred dollars put in literal poverty, but the figure was indisputably between one-third and one-half. In agriculture, although precise statistics were again unavailable, the proportion of impoverished families was "very much like that of the industrial workers."[10]

Between 1910 and 1920, approximately 25 million Americans yearly worked for wages. In 1915 the Industrial Relations Commission asked, and after investigation answered a question that was typical of economic discussion in America at the beginning of the twentieth century: "Have the workers received a fair share of the enormous increase in wealth which has taken place in this country . . . as a result largely of their labors? The answer is emphatically, No!"[11] Unable to buy the goods and services they produced, trapped in or on the edge of poverty, the majority of Americans faced hard realities of economic and human survival on a daily basis.

Challenges to capitalism's new order, consequently, were common. A rebellious element of the population took seriously American promises that opportunity and equality were essential to a just society, that a class of people should not be structurally subordinated to another class. It made little difference that, rather than by birth, membership in the new aristocracy was determined by ownership of the means of production: an economic system that physically and spiritually impoverished the bulk of the population had to be resisted and changed. The fact that the new economic and political order had come into being in little more than a generation intensified opposition. Hardly inured to economic inequality, adult Americans could remember and identify past and passing social relations. Nor was political economy significantly mystified: clarity was manifest in the very language of political and economic discourse. As letters to the *Appeal* and the explicit class analysis of the Industrial Relations Commission exemplify (and much other evidence confirms), workers perceived

themselves as workers and capitalists understood themselves as capitalists. Euphemistic disguises such as "free enterprise" did not yet exist. For turn-of-the-century American capital, putting a new industrial and financial structure in place, consolidating political power, and defeating a work force that wanted higher wages or a different economic arrangement altogether were more important priorities than controlling the consciousness of working people. As a result, many capitalists and radicals alike shared Jack London's belief in 1908 that contending forces in America would soon lead to open class warfare: "It is no longer a question of dialectics, theories, and dreams. There is no question about it. The revolution is a fact. It is here now. . . . Stop it who can."[12]

Class analysis was fundamental to the *Appeal* and to the socialist movement. While writers for the *Appeal* often defined class in stratified, quantifiable terms (the number of American wage workers, for example), the *Appeal* also understood class as social process—as the dynamic activity of men and women living their own history. In much the same way that class consciousness arises from the need for one class to combat the interests of another, a class dynamically comes into existence in the struggle itself.[13] Class conflict explained both the historical past and the many forms of antagonism between labor and capital in the present. "The history of all hitherto society," the *Appeal* quoted Marx and Engels, "is the history of class struggles."

Freeman and slave, patrician and plebeian, lord and serf, guild-master and journeyman—in a word, oppressor and oppressed—stood in constant opposition to one another, carried on an uninterrupted, now hidden, now open, fight—a fight that each time ended either in the revolutionary reconstruction of society at large or in the common ruin of the contending classes. In the earliest epochs of history we find almost everywhere a complicated arrangement of society into various orders, a manifold gradation of social rank. In ancient Rome we have patricians, knights, plebeians, slaves; in the middle ages, feudal lords, vassals, guild-masters, journeymen, apprentices, serfs; *in almost all of these classes again, subordinate gradations. The modern bourgeois society that has sprouted from the ruins of feudal society has not done away with class antagonism. It has but established new classes, new conditions of oppression, new forms of struggle in place of the old ones.*[14]

Class struggle, the manifestation of the ongoing human search for freedom, constituted nothing less than a philosophy of history for socialists. In turn-of-the-century America, as everywhere in the past, the human responsibility was to diminish the realms of necessity and limitation and expand the realms of freedom. In the conflict over the control of the means of life, the *Appeal* signed on with the working class as the agent of revolutionary change. In no other way could the classless society of the future be brought into being.

As a newspaper, the *Appeal* primarily sought to combat capitalist consciousness and to create socialist class consciousness in its place. Class struggle was ubiquitous in political and social life. Violent labor strife, the class war in its most overt, readily understood form, received detailed coverage in the *Appeal* because of its intrinsic importance and because it paradigmatically expressed the conflict between the working and owning classes. Class consciousness was often discussed in the paper's columns, but J. A. Wayland's explanation, based on an understanding of human slavery, was as definitive for the *Appeal* as any that appeared. It made no difference what wages one received, Wayland explained, or that some received ten times as much as others: in name or in fact, any economic system based on profit and human exploitation necessarily produced slavery. "Slavery was once thought to be right by the slaves. They became more intelligent and now refute slavery—such as existed ages ago. The masters, no longer able to control in the old ways, revise their methods and get the service of the working class just the same, while preaching the freedom of the race. The modern kind of slavery is called capitalism. It is the most profitable kind. Spurred by the hope of becoming masters themselves, the workers create more

wealth than in other forms, and the whole of this goes, sooner or later, into the hands of the most cunning. Being conscious of this state of things is what makes class-conscious Socialists, and not one who ever realized this condition ever got away from it."[15] For the *Appeal to Reason* and the insurgent movement it represented, only in a socialist society could men and women end slavery and begin to discover all that it meant to be fully human.

A Cleveland lawyer, William Babcock wrote on social and economic questions for both radical and reform papers.

Dives and Lazarus

WILLIAM AUGUSTUS BABCOCK

But whoso hath this world's goods and seeth his brother have need and shutteth up his bowels of compassion from him, how dwelleth the love of God in him?—1st Epistle of John, 3:17.

When the social fabric is on fire with pauperism, of all governments, republics are most endangered. Founded on the consent of the governed, there is danger of the securities or order burning away unnoticed before the flames appear in the superstructure.

The names of millionaires and the size of their fortunes, which have risen in a generation from the common level, are matters of common knowledge, while few have looked into the abyss which these fortunes have made in the misfortunes of others. Charles Spahr in *Distribution of Wealth in the United States* thus summarizes the [1890] federal census, classifying the people in families of five persons with their aggregate wealth:

Fortunes	Families	Total wealth	Average
Over $50,000	125,000	33,000,000,000	$264,000
From $5,000 to $50,000	1,375,000	23,000,000,000	16,000
From $500 to $5,000	5,500,000	8,200,000,000	1,500
Under $500	5,500,000	800,000,000	150
Total	12,500,000	65,000,000,000	$ 5,200

Appeal to Reason, October 19, 1912.

"Speak softly and carry a Big Stick"—T. R.

Classifying the people in hundreds, with the poorest at the bottom of the list, you must climb to the 45th man before you rise out of the class whose average wealth is $30 a head, or the price of a suit of clothes. From the 44th to the 89th man in the middle class, worth eight billions two hundred millions, or $300 a head on an average to the individual. From the 88th to the 99th inclusive are found 11% of the population owning nearly three-eighths of the wealth; and, finally, the hundredth man owns more than the 99. To speak accurately, 1% of the people owned 51% of the wealth of the United States in 1890.

The bottom 44%, who are steeped in poverty to the very lips, are two million tramps, flotsam and jetsam on the sea of life, the "hewers of wood and drawers of water," the exploited classes; the unemployed and the disemployed, who now sit with starving families by floorless cabins in the coal regions of five states; the hundreds of thousands from the silver mines of the Rockies in whose deserted villages the thistle nods over the wall and the wild fox looks out of the window; the vast army locked out of employment by trusts which close factories to limit productions; the larger army which the trusts and syndicates have squeezed into poverty; and finally those from the middle class, who, overtaken in debt, have been ruined by an appreciating standard of money, which has caused values in gold standard countries to fall to 60 cents on the dollar, or in other words, has appreciated 66% to the ruin of all debtors. It is hard to account for Mr. Rockefeller's income of 55 millions last year, when 27 million five hundred thousand of our people have been unable in their whole lives to save enough to pay the expenses of Christian burial. It is of interest here to note that one-tenth of all who have died in New York city during the last six years have been buried in the Potter's field. Where one falls into a nameless grave, it is a moderate estimate that two tremble on the verge even though they escape the fall. Dives and Lazarus live not alone in Bible story. They are here, and in these closing days of the nineteenth century their tribes have so increased as to mark them the conspicuous characters of the times. Lazarus stands idle, barefoot and hungry, at the closed gates of opportunity. Dives sits feasting in the halls of possession.

Daniel Webster once said: "Liberty cannot long endure in any country where the tendency is to concentrate wealth into the hands of a few." Either he was an alarmist, or the danger mark in this republic is reached.

October 2, 1897

Like "A Modern Pharisee's Prayer," a significant number of contributions to the Appeal *were written by authors who chose anonymity.*

A Modern Pharisee's Prayer

ANON

The drudgery I would not do,
O Lord, assign to others:
There's much to do of dirty work.
It will not hurt my brothers,
For they have not such souls refined

Nor slender milk-white hands;
I'd use my brilliant brain not brawn,
And thus possess the land.

A railroad king or merchant prince,
I'm fitted for I trow.
Then let my brothers serve me well,
With sweat upon their brow.
'Tis healthful for them, Lord to dig,
And delve in grimy soil—
The sweetest rest they sure will win
With unremitting toil.

And when at last Thy Kingdom comes,
For which devout we've prayed,
Appoint me to some upper place
In royal robes arrayed.
For my hard-working brain, dear Lord,
Will earn sweet promised rest,
Above my brothers (whom I love)
In mansions of the blest.

February 5, 1898

The correlation between technological advance and working-class poverty, now associated principally with Henry George's Progress and Poverty, *was a pressing, commonly addressed social question in turn-of-the-century America. George Allen White was a socialist and activist from Massachusetts.*

Lines of Human Progress

GEORGE ALLEN WHITE

With the aid of a three-horse sulky plow, a farmer in the United States is able to plow 150 acres in fifty days. With a harrow, a header and a thresher, he can perform in sixty-three days the labor necessary to grow and harvest three thousand bushels of wheat. Taking 113 days in all, in that space of time a man can procure wheat which, turned into bread, will supply one family with bread for two lifetimes, or two families for one lifetime. And yet the farmer on the western prairie is sometimes almost as destitute as the ignorant Israelite wandering through the wilderness with nothing but manna and a brass snake to comfort him. The Goodyear machine displaces eight men. With a McKay machine an operator can run through three hundred pairs of shoes a day, as against five pairs without the machine. A machine in the carpet industry does the work formerly done by one hundred men. One man, with the aid of a machine, can cut out as many hats and caps as once required six men. In textiles, where a spinner used to produce five banks of No. 32 twist a week, he can produce 55,000 banks a week now with the aid of a machine. Machinery has halved the time requisite for making a carriage. Go into a great metropolitan newspaper office, and they will tell you that the same force which turns out 48,000 papers an hour to-day, would have needed one hundred days instead of one hour, one hundred years ago. And so it runs throughout all industry. In his address at Buffalo, Dec. 15, 1892, [U.S. Labor Commissioner] Carroll D. Wright stated that he computed that under the old system of a few years back it would have required from fifty to one hundred million men to do the work now done by a few million. One man with the machine at his side has the potentialities of one hundred men of one thousand years ago. Man has reversed nature, harnessed the elements. His brain has teemed with wealth-making inventions. Appliance has succeeded appliance. Ever more brilliant has become the work of the human mind. If men could live in the days of Jesus Christ, every man not only ought to live, but ought to be a Crœsus and a king today. Yet, in chapter V of his autobiography, John S. Mill declares: "Suffice it [to] say that the condition of numbers in civilized Europe, and even in civilized England and France, is more wretched than that of most tribes of savages who are known to us." Invention astounds the nineteenth century student, and renders speechless the tongue; but when poor, unlettered man shot over the horizon

of history, he was a happier creature than are hundreds of millions of our fellow-men. Give us less rags and more reason; less twaddle and more justice. The wrong people own the machines. The man that owns the spindle is the man that owns the world.

August 27, 1898

Excerpts from W. G. Robbins's diary appeared not only in the Appeal *but in other radical publications at the turn of the century.*

Robbins Withdraws

W. G. Robbins handed in his resignation and quit the game in San Francisco a few days ago. He left a diary which may or may not prove of interest. To competition may be charged up this failure of society to properly perform its functions. Thousands of similar cases may be so charged and thousands of others will be. Did it ever occur to you that possibly some of you or yours might meet a similar fate? But read from Robbins' diary:

March 3.—No chance of getting anything here. What will I do? No money, no friends, no work—sick with heart trouble and asthma. God help me.

March 7.—Cannot find anything yet.

March 8.—I am living on doughnuts at 5 cents a day. Don't know where to go or what to do.

March 9.—My last quarter gone for room rent.

March 10.—God help me. Have only 5 cents left. Can get nothing to do. What next? Starvation or ——?

March 10, '99.—No work, no friends, no money; sick, alone and friendless. I have tried to get something to do—same answer everywhere—no help wanted. I have spent my last nickel tonight and am desolate and despondent without a friend to help or assist me. What shall I do or where shall I look for aid? Shall it be steal, beg or die? I have never stolen, begged or starved in all my fifty years of life, but now I am on the brink—death seems the only refuge. God forgive me for all.

March 11.—Went to see about two places the first thing this morning but had a chill at the time, so I could not get either. Sick all day—burning fever this afternoon. Had nothing to eat today or since yesterday noon. I'll have to starve or die now. No letter from Fred yet.

Saturday, 11.—No chance of anything today again. Nothing to eat since yesterday noon. My head, my head. Good-bye all.

April 8, 1899

Descriptions of the social customs of America's ruling elite appeared with some frequency in the Appeal. They made effective propaganda then and they remain instructive now.

Wonders of the Whitney Ball

New York Journal, DECEMBER 1900

Ninety-five debutantes danced in the cotillion, the greatest number ever assembled at a social function in New York.

Their aggregate fortunes amounted to $200,000,000.

With the dots which they may reasonably expect from their multi-millionaire parents, they will bring to their future husbands, $300,000,000.

Such a beauty show has never before been seen as that which graced the cotillion in the Louis XIV ballroom.

All New York's Four Hundred was there.

The jewels worn by the women were worth $1,000,000.

The Whitney mansion rivaled the palaces of the old world in its regal splendor.

The magnificence of the decorations excelled those of any similar function ever given in New York.

The palaces of the old world had been ransacked for the rare paintings, tapestries, rugs and house.

The sumptuous furnishings and decorations cost many millions.

For the floral decorations, every clime had been searched. Flowers from tropic Mexico were mingled with those from the frozen Alps.

The favors cost $50,000.

The floral decorations cost $10,000.

The supper cost $10,000.

The music cost $3,000.

The cotillion figures were the most novel ever arranged.

The ballroom itself was a wonderland of beauty.

One painting, exhibited for the first time, was the Rafael, valued at $150,000.

March 9, 1901

Grounded in an understanding of slavery, surplus value, and class conflict, J. A. Wayland explained class consciousness with his usual concision.

Consciousness of Being Slaves

J. A. WAYLAND

What do we mean by class consciousness? We mean the realization of being slaves—that the world is a slave pen in which the capitalists are the masters and all the rest menials. It matters not what wages one receives, the condition of slavery remains. Some slaves received enough to cover their necessities, but whenever men work for the profit of another there is slavery. It does not alter the condition because a slave may become master, or that some may be given ten times what others receive any more than it altered slavery because some were well groomed and attended their masters in their travels. The working people exist solely for making wealth for others to possess. When they realize this truth they will strive by every means in their power to abolish the system, just as they would if a law were made by which they were legally classed as slaves and their conditions prescribed as was the case in serfdom or chattel servitude. There are many forms of slavery, but one principle runs through ALL of them—that they are PROFIT-MAKERS for those who direct their labor. And that principle is the most prominent in the lives of the working class in modern life—no matter how many declarations or laws that slavery has ceased to exist. Slavery was once thought to be right by the slaves. They became more intelligent and now refute slavery—such as existed ages ago. The masters, no longer able to control in the old ways, revise their methods and get the service of the working class just the same, while preaching the freedom of the race. The modern kind of slavery is called capitalism. It is the most profitable kind. Spurred by the hope of becoming masters themselves, the workers create more wealth than in other forms, and the whole of this goes, sooner or later, into the hands of the most cunning. Being conscious of this state of things is what makes class-conscious Socialists, and not one who ever realized this condition ever got away from it.

It is the sphere of the modern state and church to prevent this view being realized by the working class.

July 18, 1903

The fear of "race suicide" was a turn-of-the-century fusion of xenophobia, racism, eugenics, and governing-class consciousness. In its best-known form, "race suicide" was President Theodore Roosevelt's response to the large numbers (and large families) of eastern and southern European immigrants, to their increasing presence and influence in the United States, and to their potential threat to continued domestic control by Anglo-Saxon and Nordic stock. Roosevelt's

anxiety-ridden belief in inherent racial ability meets a reply here from Mrs. Cy J. Cremler that had not entered his calculations.

Race Suicide

A LETTER TO THE PRESIDENT

Mr. President—

A month or two ago you wrote a letter to Mrs. Van Vorst in which you deplored the tendency to "race suicide." I did not see it for some time, as we do not take any newspapers or magazines, for reasons that will appear hereafter. But I have a sister who is a teacher in one of our city schools, who is not married, as it is the understanding that a married woman is very likely to lose her place as a teacher; and aside from that the position of teacher appears to be naturally incompatible with that of prolific motherhood. That is one thing that tends toward "race suicide."

My sister takes a monthly magazine, which she lets me read; and that is the way I happened to see your letter to Mrs. Van Vorst.

Permit me to suggest that you appear to have overlooked one matter of great importance. I will try to explain what I mean by reference to my own household.

Our family consists of my husband, myself, three children (between six and twelve years of age), and my mother, 65 years of age. My mother is useful about the house, but she is too old and feeble to work out for pay, so her support comes out of my husband's wages.

I read in that magazine of my sister's that the average earnings of the laborers in all the manufacturing establishments of the United States, according to the last census, were less than $450 per year. My husband earned a little more than that. His wages were $1.50 a day. He fortunately was in excellent health, and worked every day except Sundays and holidays—306 days—and his income was $459.

I had our eldest daughter, as practice in arithmetic, as a matter of business training, and to see to it that we did not run in debt, keep an exact account of our expenditures. They were as follows:

The sum total paid out for food materials was $328. That was a fraction less than 90 cents per day—15 cents for each of six persons, or not quite 5 cents a meal. I economized in every way to reduce the expense below that figure, but could not. A pint cup of bread and milk for one of the children costs more than that.

Our family occupies a three room house in the outskirts of the city. Of course we are badly cramped for space. There must be a bed in each room. Fortunately we have not much other furniture. We are always in a cluttered up condition, from the fact that we have no cellar. I do not see how we could get along with any smaller house. For this we pay $7 a month—$84 per year.

Our clothing, including hats, shoes, everything for summer and winter, cost a total of $30, an average of not quite $1.50 each. I cannot see how we could have got along for less.

We have but one stove in the house—an old broken concern that was second hand when we bought it. In the winter my mother lies abed considerable of the time to keep warm and give the rest of us a chance at the fire. I do not see how we could have been more economical than we were in the use of fuel, but it cost us $16 during the year.

Light costs us comparatively little. Sometimes—in summer—we used none whatever, for several evenings in succession. Probably we felt the deprivation less than we would if we had anything about the house to read. But in the winter, when darkness came early, I was sorry that the children had to go to school with lessons unlearned, which they might have learned if there had been lamplight by which to study them. Light cost us on an average of three-quarters of a cent a day—$2.75 for the year.

Last winter, because of getting my feet wet while wearing unmended shoes and sitting in a cold room, I was taken down with pneumonia, and was sick for a fortnight. As our house sits down flat on the damp ground my mother has become afflicted with rheumatism. However, we both get along without a doctor, or we would have had to add his bill to our other outlay.

To sum up, the year's expenses were as follows:

Food	$328.00
Rent	84.00
Clothing	30.00
Fuel	16.00
Light	2.75
Total	$460.75

You see, the very best we could do we expended a little more than my husband's earnings. And his work was not interrupted by sickness. There was no doctor bill to be paid for any of us. The furniture we bought the first year after our marriage before we had any children, is wearing out, but we have bought none to replace it; my husband spent not a cent for tobacco nor intoxicating drinks; he walked to his work every morning, even through the rain, without spending a cent for street car tickets; we have not been to church this year, for we will not occupy anybody else's pew, nor the pauper pew, and sit like a bump on a log when the contribution plate is pushed under our noses; we have not gone out on picnics, nor excursions, nor attended any entertainment of any kind. How could we? Few slaves on a southern plantation ever worked harder, or had less in the way of amusement or recreation in the course of the year, than we.

Dividing $459 by 6 gives $76.50 as the average annual expense for each member of our family—less than 21 cents a day. Our county board of supervisors allows our sheriff 25 cents a day for feeding prisoners in the county jail, and the same allowance is made for the paupers in the county alms house. It seems to me it is as much as I ought to be required to do to support our family—food, rent, clothing, fuel, everything on less than is paid out for food alone for paupers and criminals.

Our house rent can not be crowded down a cent, the landlord must have his pay, and that in advance, no matter what else may happen. Most of the other items of expense, as you see, are already at their lowest limit. If we expend anything for furniture, books, newspapers, entertainments, preachers, doctors, funerals, or other incidentals, it must come out of our food bill. For instance, by eating only 3 cents worth of victuals at breakfast this morning, instead of five, I saved 2 cents with which to buy the paper on which I am writing this letter. By eating a 3-cent dinner I save 2 cents with which to buy a postage stamp to mail it. The pen and ink I have borrowed from a neighbor.

I find in that magazine of my sister's the statement, deduced from the census reports and the bulletins of the Labor Bureau, that more than twelve million of the citizens of the United States—men, women, and children, the families of laborers—are living on even a less amount per day than we.

But to come back to my own family. You will observe that $76.50 is the average annual expense for each of us now, when there is no extra medical attendance on account of the advent of another child into the household. That would certainly mean more than $25 additional.

Now, Mr. President, I submit to your candid judgment whether it would not be the height of folly—worse than that, criminal recklessness—for us to make family arrangements that would necessarily involve us in an expense next year, and for indefinite years to come, of from $75 to $100 a year more than we have any reason to expect my husband's income will be, even in case he keeps his health, and work remains plentiful, and prosperity continues to reign?

(Mrs.) Cy J. Cremler, *Washington, D.C.*
August 15, 1903

The 1903–04 strike in the Cripple Creek district of Colorado pitted hard-rock miners and their radical Western Federation of Miners Union against the organized force of Colorado capital—the Mine Owners' Association, the state militia, martial law, Citizens' Alliances, and a militantly anti-labor governor,

James H. Peabody. The strike was smashed and the Western Federation was left in shambles. Nowhere in the United States was the class war more overt and violent than in Colorado: over 50 men died in the 1903–04 conflict, some 1500 were imprisoned in military bullpens, and at least 773 were forcibly deported from the state. Henry Morris's account from the scene of the strike is not exaggerated.

Miners' Property Destroyed

Henry O. Morris
Special dispatch to *Appeal to Reason*

Pueblo, Colo., June 7   Peabody's thugs and tin-horns are, at this hour, engaged in driving all the union men and their wives and children out of Teller county. The miners' supply store has been sacked by the leading bankers and millionaire mine owners. Over three hundred union men and their families are now herded in box cars on a siding. Every epithet and insult the blackguards can think of are hurled at the defenseless prisoners. The excitement is intense. Every police officer, deputy sheriff, constable, the sheriff himself, and court officers have been disarmed and run out by the "law and order" people. Who says the state of Colorado is in the United States?

Union Sympathizers Must Go
The Cripple Creek Citizens' Alliance Pushing Its Advantage
Associated Press Dispatch

Cripple Creek, Colo., June 10   Joseph Hamilton, chairman of the Democratic county central committee, was called before the Citizens' deportation committee today and asked concerning his sympathy with unionism. Mr. Hamilton acknowledged that he believed in unions, and he was told that he must leave the camp within the next four days. He was allowed this reprieve because of his standing in the community and because he is a member of the Masonic fraternity.

FARCE CORONER'S VERDICT

Pueblo, Colo., June 11   At Cripple Creek, yesterday, a so-called coroner's jury was empanelled to sit on the bodies of the men killed in the dynamite explosion which blew up the Independence depot. The jury was composed solely of members of the Citizens' Alliance mob, the Mine Owners' Association mob and strike breakers. The jury knew what it was organized for and so did the coroner who was not the duly elected coroner, but a paid usurper, placed in that position by the mob. In exactly forty-five minutes, this jury returned a verdict declaring the Western Federation of Miners guilty of the crime.

"Think of it, citizens of America, and render your verdict at the polls next November."

No more damnable outrage has been perpetrated than this last crime of the bogus coroner's jury.

Thousands of refugees are being run through Pueblo, in stock cars and passenger coaches, guarded by soldiers and members of the Citizens' Alliance mob.

The Western Federation has offered five thousand dollars reward for the arrest and conviction of the men guilty of the Independence explosion. Great excitement in Colorado. Citizens openly advocating murder of all union men; insolent khaki uniformed soldiers strutting about with brag and bluster.

[Adjutant General of the Colorado National Guard] Sherman Bell says from now on bullets will be the rule in Colorado. Before placing the refugees on the cars they are robbed of every dollar they may possess, even their watches and pocket trinkets stolen by the soldiers who are recruited from the lowest slums of Colorado, Wyoming and New Mexico.

A RECORD OF CRIME

Pueblo, Colo., June 10, 1904

Appeal to Reason, Girard, Kansas

The Portland mine of Victor, Colorado, the greatest mine in Colorado, and owned by the James Burns syndicate, employs 800 union miners. During all the trouble raised by the Citizens' Alliance mobs and scab herder soldiers "Jimmy" Burns has been loyal to his union men and the union men have been loyal to him. This made the Portland mine a source of trouble to the organization of law breakers known as the Colorado Mine Owners' Association.

Last night the militia and deputies armed with Krag-Jorgensen rifles, and a mob of Citizens' Alliance thugs, also armed with state arms, invaded the mine and closed it. The mob was in command of the swashbuckler hero suspect, Sherman Bell.

The miners were ordered to leave the county or be shot, and Jimmy Burns, who is now in Denver, was wired to stay in Denver to escape hanging.

The crime for which he is to be executed is employing union miners.

Yesterday afternoon the officers of ALL the unions, cooks, waiters, carpenters, blacksmiths, masons, clerks, electricians, drivers, hod carriers, railroad employes, engineers, firemen, barbers, etc., numbering in all something over seven thousand men, were told to take their choice of swearing allegiance to the Citizens' Alliance, leave the county or be hung or shot.

The employers were visited by an armed mob of Citizens' Alliance members and compelled to sign a declaration to employ no more union help, or hang.

I have not the least doubt many of the readers of this will question the truth of this statement, but I solemnly assert before the ever-living God what I have here written is the truth. But it is not the whole truth, because, should I write all I know it would be too horrible for any decent citizen to believe.

The Victor *Record* plant, which was destroyed by the Citizens' Alliance mob, was valued at eight thousand dollars.

Many murders have been committed by the soldiers and the Citizens' Alliance that have not been published to the world. Homes have been invaded, women ravished, children kicked and beaten and every species of deviltry known to the Citizens' Alliance indulged in without let or hindrance. No law save the law of brutes and cowards now governs the beautiful state of Colorado, and the chief thug and author of all is James H. Peabody, the accident governor.

Publish his deviltry that the workers of the world may read of the infamy of decaying capitalism.

Yesterday a prominent attorney of this city and a brother of a United States Senator told me that the evidence pointed almost conclusively to the detectives employed by the Mine Owners' Association as the authors of the dynamite explosion at the Independence depot. It was certainly not committed by miners. Considering the assassinations and mobbings perpetrated in the name of law and order, I feel sure that the attorney is correct.

June 18, 1904

Kate Richards O'Hare wrote periodically for the Appeal *for nearly two decades. An editor of the* National Rip-Saw, *a member of the Socialist Party's National Executive Committee, and an extraordinarily effective public speaker, she was imprisoned during World War I under antiwar legislation. "He Counteth the Sparrow's Fall" carries Kate Richards's power and feeling even now.*

He Counteth the Sparrow's Fall

Kate Richards O'Hare

"Yes, it is perfectly exquisite, Madame! Your deft fingers have made a reality of my hazy idea, and I am sure this will convince the girls that one can be modish and humane at the same time, and that it is not necessary to wear the bodies of dead birds to have a beautiful and becoming hat."

It was a sweet-faced girl whose elegant dress proclaimed her the daughter of wealth whom I overheard speaking to the smiling, deft little French milliner, who stood beside her holding a beautiful specimen of her art.

"I am so pleased that you like it," madame answered. "I remembered that your tender heart rebelled against the sacrifice of life for your adornment so I took particular pains with this that you might have something for your new ox-blood broadcloth. and here it is; ivory, velvet and ruby roses and no songster's life sacrificed."

"Thank you, you are very kind and I appreciate your thoughtfulness. My friends laugh at me, and I am glad you understand that I could not enjoy even the most beautiful of your handiwork if I knew that a bird's life had been needlessly taken, for you know He said: 'I count the sparrow's fall.' " And the tender eyes glowed with such sincerity and truth that it made my heart ache and I thought, "Poor girl! If she only knew! No life sacrificed, no songster missing from his woodland bower, and it is the essence of sacrificed life she looks at so complacently. Not bird life, but the lives of girls like herself and of little children."

Then my thoughts went back to on the brilliant, cold January morning when I took my place in the columns of the toilers' army that marched away to the great artificial flower factory in lower Broadway, New York. The cold and snap in the air made my blood flow briskly and as I hurried along in the rosy dawn I thought even the life of a working girl in New York was not all bad. Reluctantly I fell in behind the crowd of girls who rushed pellmell up the stairs to the factory. Most of them looked thin and blue and the cold air that made my blood bound seemed to chill their ill-nourished bodies to the very marrow and make even the horrible, odor-laden air of the workroom welcome to them, for it was warm.

Toiling slowly up the steps I came upon Roselie, the little Italian girl who sat next to me at the long work table. Roselie, whose fingers were the most deft in the shop and whose blue-black curls and velvety eyes I had almost envied as I often wondered why nature should have bestowed so much more than an equal share of beauty on the

Appeal to Reason, April 15, 1905.

Masthead, *Appeal to Reason*, March 31, 1906.

little Italian. Overtaking her I noticed she clung to the banister with one hand and held a crumpled mitten to the lips with the other. As we entered the cloak room she noticed my look of sympathy and weakly smiling said in broken English: "Oh, so cold! It hurta, it hurta me here," and she laid her hand on her throat.

Seated at the long table the forelady brought a great box of the most exquisite red satin roses, and glancing sharply at Roselie said: "I hope you're not sick this morning; we must have these roses and you are the only one who can do them; have them ready by noon sure."

Soon a busy hum filled the room and in the hurry and excitement of my work I forgot Rosalie until a shrill scream from the little Jewess across the table reached me and I turned in time to see Roselie fall forward among the flowers. As I lifted her up the hot blood spurted from her lips, staining my hands and spattering the flowers as it fell. There was a stir of excitement for a few moments and then the police ambulance clanged up to the door, and the surgeon raised Roselie from my arms and carried her away.

The blood-soaked roses were gathered up, the

forelady grumbling because many were ruined, and soon the hum of industry went on as before. But I noticed that one of the great red roses had a splotch of red in its golden heart, a tiny drop of Roselie's heart's blood and the picture of the rose was burned in my brain, and as I looked at the beautiful hat I could have sworn I saw a little brown spot in the heart of the largest rose.

The next morning I entered the grim, gray portals of Bellevue Hospital and asked for Roselie. "Roselie Randazzo," the clerk read from the great register. "Roselie Randazzo, seventeen; lives East Fourth street; taken from Marks' Artificial Flower Factory; hemorrhage; died 12:30 p.m." When I said that it was hard that she should die, so young and so beautiful, the clerk answered: "Yes, that's true, but this climate is hard on the Italians; and if the climate don't finish them the sweat shops or flower factories do," and then he turned to answer the questions of the woman who stood beside me and the life story of the little flower maker was finished. The woman who said no life had been sacrificed for her adorning never heard it, and the little brown spot in the heart of her rose could not whisper it to her even though it nestled among the golden tresses just above the tiny pink ear.

No life sacrificed! No life sacrificed! Again my thoughts went back to the morning when I stood in the office of a huge silk mill and asked for work, but was denied. Jobs are few and far between in a silk mill for women; little girls have nimbler fingers, and besides they are cheaper.

Philanthropists tell us patience and persistence will win, and it did. One day there was an opening in the factory where are made the silks to clothe the women who never toil and where the women who toil to make them are clad in rags.

There I saw women with stooped shoulders and dead faces, women whose lives seemed concentrated in their fingers. As little children they had gone into the factory and all the long, dreary years only their fingers had been trained or developed, until at twenty they were poor, mis-shapen, distorted creatures, with hands whose swiftness and accuracy were beyond comprehension and whose every other faculty was dead, starved by lack of use.

As I looked at the gleaming folds of velvet with the ivory whiteness of a woman's shoulder, and the downy softness of a baby's cheek, I saw not alone the long weaving room where life threads are woven into fabric but a picture of the cutting room rose before. A long room whose every beam, as well as walls and ceiling, is coated with pure white. I remembered that when first I saw it was in the early morning before the little ones had come to work, and as I looked at the soft white walls tinted with the pink glow of the rising sun I thought it looked like a fairy palace, but at night, as I looked again in the dull gray gloaming, it seemed only a horrible whitened sepulcher.

All day long I had checked the lengths of uncut velvet as it came from the sizing room where the nap had been stiffened with a thin solution of lime.

These lengths were placed on long tables and little girls scarcely out of the cradle, and who had never known a schoolroom, took tiny knives and slipping them into the first row or pile of nap ran down the long table cutting just one row as they went then back again, up and down, all day long and when the whistle blew in the evening they had traveled from fourteen to twenty miles.

The lime dust freed by the cutting floated out and settled alike on the walls and workers until both were covered by it—burning, corroding dust. All day long the children ran up and down breathing the death dealing dust, heeding not that it burned and scarred their tender skin or that their little feet and legs were swollen and distorted with continual running. Ceaselessly, noiselessly, uncomplainingly they trod the treadmill, making no murmur, voiceless martyrs to the god of Greed. Snatched from the cradle, helpless victims of the treadmill, they knew nothing of life but the ceaseless round of deadening toil. Beneficent nature seemed to have taken from them the capacity to suffer and they lived out their few short years of life unknowing, uncomprehending, not even capable of feeling grateful that outraged nature would claim her own and send the messenger of Death to close the door of the velvet mill for them.

Then the picture faded and I saw again the gentle, womanly face of the girl who would not wear the body of a dead bird and yet all unknowingly was wearing fabric woven from children's lives, dyed with the heart's blood of women, formed with the heart strings of the human race. But she does not know! She does not know! Deep down in my heart is that faith in God's creatures that makes me believe that they do not know. The work of every woman who does know is to tell the story of lives sacrificed until none can say, "I did not know." If you cannot speak the words that will reach the heart, help the woman who can. If you cannot write the words that burn, you can carry the printed page. If your hands are full and your heart is heavy with your own woes, you can still give your heart and soul, and that unvoiced prayer from a million women's hearts will reach even the uttermost ends of the earth.

November 19, 1904

*U.S. Labor Commissioner Carroll D. Wright's unemployment
figures, revealing American capitalism's inability to provide
regular employment for its working citizenry, were surprising
even to the Appeal.*

A Nation of Unemployed

	No. of unemployed part of time	Per cent of total number
1899 (census of 1890)	3,523,730	15.1
1899 (census of 1900)	6,468,964	22.3
1903 (18th Annual Labor Report)	14,500,000	49.81

Is the United States becoming a nation of unemployed workers? The 18th Annual Labor Report of the Commissioner of the bureau of labor statistics purports to make a detailed investigation into the state of unemployment, and finds that 49.81 per cent (not quite one-half) of the American workingmen are idle at some time of the year. This per cent varies according to occupation. Commissioner Wright's figures cover 25,000 working families in thirty-three states, and he thinks "are fairly representative of the conditions existing among the wage-workers in the whole country."

If this is true it would mean that practically one-half of the 29,000,000 workers in the United States are idle at some time during the year. The average length of idleness is placed at nine and one-half weeks. Multiply nine and one-half weeks by one-half of 29,000,000 and you get a total of 1,653,000,000 days. Assuming a working year of 300 days to the average man, it means that 5,510,000 are idle every day in the year in the United States during a period of time when General Prosperity is in the saddle. . . .

May 13, 1905

On February 17, 1906, Bill Haywood, Charles Moyer, and George Pettibone, the purported "inner circle" of the Western Federation of Miners, were secretly arrested in Denver by Idaho officials and as secretly (to avoid Colorado extradition procedures) abducted to Idaho on a special train on which they were the only passengers. There they were imprisoned and charged with the murder of ex-Idaho governor, Frank Steunenberg. After two trials, the union men were found not guilty and freed. "Arouse, Ye Slaves!" was the most militant position ever taken by Eugene Debs and the most notorious call to action ever to appear in the Appeal.

Arouse, Ye Slaves!

Eugene V. Debs

The latest and boldest stroke of the plutocracy, but for the blindness of the people, would have startled the nation.

Murder has been plotted and is about to be executed in the name and under the forms of law.

Men who will not yield to corruption and browbeating must be ambushed, spirited away and murdered.

That is the edict of the Mine Owners' association of the western states and their Standard Oil backers and pals in Wall Street, New York.

These gory-beaked vultures are to pluck out the heart of resistance to their tyranny and robbery, that labor may be stark naked at their mercy.

Charles Moyer and Wm. D. Haywood, of the Western Federation of Miners, and their official colleagues—men, all of them, and every inch of them—are charged with the assassination of ex-Governor Frank Steunenberg, of Idaho, who simply reaped what he had sown, as a mere subterfuge to pounce upon them in secret, rush them out of the state by special train, under heavy guard, clap them into the penitentiary, convict them upon the purchased, perjured testimony of villains, and then strangle them to death with the hangman's noose.

It is a foul plot; a damnable conspiracy; a hellish outrage.

The governors of Idaho and Colorado say they have the proof to convict. They are brazen falsifiers and venal villains, the miserable tools of the mine owners who, themselves, if anybody does, deserve the gibbet.

Moyer, Haywood and their comrades had no more to do with the assassination of Steunenberg than I had: the charge is a ghastly lie, a criminal calumny and is only an excuse to murder men who are too rigidly honest to betray their trust and too courageous to succumb to threat and intimidation.

Labor leaders that cringe before the plutocracy and do its bidding are apotheosized; those that refuse must be foully murdered.

Personally and intimately do I know Moyer, Haywood, Pettibone, St. John and their official co-workers, and I will stake my life on their honor and integrity; and that is precisely the crime for which, according to the words of the slimy "sleuth" who "worked up the case" against them, "they shall never leave Idaho alive."

Well, by the gods, if they don't the governors of Idaho and Colorado and their masters from Wall Street, New York, to the Rocky Mountains had better prepare to follow them.

Nearly twenty years ago the capitalist tyrants put some innocent men to death for standing up for labor.

They are now going to try it again. Let them dare!

There have been twenty years of revolutionary education, agitation and organization since the Haymarket tragedy, and if an attempt is made to repeat it, there will be a revolution and I will do all in my power to precipitate it.

The crisis has come and we have got to meet it. Upon the issue involved the whole body of organized labor can unite and every enemy of plutocracy will join us. From the farms, the factories and stores will pour the workers to meet the red-handed destroyers of freedom, the murderers of innocent men and the arch-enemies of the people.

Moyer and Haywood are our comrades, staunch and true, and if we do not stand by them to the shedding of the last drop of blood in our veins we are disgraced forever and deserve the fate of cringing cowards.

We are not responsible for the issue. It is not of our seeking. It has been forced upon us; and for the very reason that we deprecate violence and abhor blood-shed we cannot desert our comrades and allow them to be put to death. If they can be murdered without cause so can we, and so will we be dealt with at the pleasure of these tyrants.

They have driven us to the wall and now let us rally our forces and face them and fight.

If they attempt to murder Moyer, Haywood and their brothers, a million revolutionists, at least, will meet them with guns.

They have done their best and their worst to crush and enslave us. Their politicians have betrayed us, their courts have thrown us into jail without trial and their soldiers have shot our comrades dead in their tracks.

The worm turns at last, and so does the worker.

Let them dare to execute their devilish plot and every state in this union will resound with the tramp of revolution.

Get ready, comrades, for action! No other course is left to the working class. Their courts are closed to us except to pronounce our doom. To enter their courts is simply to be mulcted of our meagre means and bound hand and foot; to have our eyes plucked out by the vultures that fatten upon our misery.

Capitalist courts never have done, and never will do, anything for the working class.

Whatever is done we must do ourselves, and if we stand up like men from the Atlantic to the Pacific and from Canada to the Gulf, we will strike terror to their cowardly hearts and they will be but too eager to relax their grip upon our throats and beat a swift retreat.

We will watch every move they make and in the meantime prepare for action.

A special revolutionary convention of the proletariat at Chicago, or some other central point would be in order, and, if extreme measures are required, a general strike could be ordered and industry paralyzed as a preliminary to a general uprising.

If the plutocrats begin the program, we will end it.

March 10, 1906

Like the Appeal, *American newspapers and magazines at the turn of the century were much more overt in expressing their politics and social values than the media are at present.*

What Americans Should Do

The New York *Times* said: "The American laborer must make up his mind henceforth not to be so much better off than the European laborer. Men must be content to work for less wages. In this way workingmen will be nearer the station in life to which it has pleased God to call them."

The Chicago *Times* said: "Hand grenades should be thrown among those who are clamoring for higher wages. By this means they would be taught a valuable lesson, and other strikers would take warning from their fate."

A capitalist writer in *Scribner's Magazine* said: "The man who is compelled to travel in search of food has no rights except those which society bestows upon him. He has no more rights than the sow that wallows in the gutter, or the lost dog that hovers around the city square."

The Philadelphia *Times* said: "It would be a great relief if a few calamity howlers were quietly but firmly shot."

The Chicago *Tribune* said: "The simplest plan, probably, when one is not a member of a humane society, is to put a little strychnine, or arsenic in the meat or other supplies furnished tramps to eat."

Appeal to Reason, June 27, 1908.

"God Knows" Buttons.

Thomas Scott, millionaire and railroad president, said: "Give them [strikers] a rifle diet for a few days, and see how they like that kind of bread."

August 17, 1907

On occasion, the Appeal *enjoyed parodying class-based society columns.*

Society Among the Workers

Lemuel Simpkins is spending his vacation in the hospital. He finds recreation in fanning himself and fighting the flies.

John Jacob Gould is touring the southwest in a twenty-ton car. He reports that work is plentiful down there. He could be kept busy all the time paying for his meals.

William Thompson, the remarkable financier who supports a family of six on a dollar a day, has very simple tastes. He arises at four o'clock every morning and spends an hour digging in the garden before sunup, coming to breakfast with a splendid appetite. He eats heartily of cornbread and sowbelly, then rides in his handcar to his pick and looks over the ties till noon. He partakes of a simple lunch of cold hash, and then digs till six o'clock, when he wheels to his two-room mansion with a splendid appetite. He eats a light supper, whips his children all around and retires early to sleep soundly in spite of the heat and the flies.

Mrs. J. K. Almostkilt is a reigning belle at a famous watering resort. She makes as high as fifty

The Salvation Army's anti-suicide bureau has been gathering information showing the causes of suicide. Of 1,125 men who contemplated death as a relief from their ills, fifty-four per cent attributed their desperate state of mind to hopeless poverty or financial embarrassment from which they saw no escape; eleven per cent to drink or drugs or disease; nine per cent to melancholia, caused by illness in most cases; five per cent to crimes, such as forgery and embezzlement, which they had committed, and twenty-one per cent to general causes like accidents, sickness and unexpected misfortunes. It will be seen that the economic pressure is bringing about that mental condition which forces men to destroy themselves rather than face the uncertain future.

February 8, 1908

Preamble of the Industrial Workers of the World

The working class and the employing class have nothing in common. There can be no peace so long as hunger and want are found among millions of working people and the few, who make up the employing class, have all the good things of life.

Between these two classes a struggle must go on until the workers of the world organize as a class, take possession of the earth and the machinery of production, and abolish the wage system.

We find that the centering of the management of industries into fewer and fewer hands makes the trade unions unable to cope with the ever growing power of the employing class. The trade unions foster a state of affairs which allows one set of workers to be pitted against another set of workers in the same industry, thereby helping defeat one another in wage wars. Moreover, the trade unions aid the employing class to mislead the workers into the belief that the working class have interests in common with their employers.

These conditions can be changed and the interest of the working class upheld only by an organization formed in such a way that all its members in any one industry, or in all industries if necessary, cease work whenever a strike or lockout is on in any department thereof, thus making an injury to one an injury to all.

Instead of the conservative motto, "A fair day's wage for a fair day's work," we must inscribe on our banner the revolutionary watchword, "Abolition of the wage system."

It is the historic mission of the working class to do away with capitalism. The army of production must be organized, not only for the every-day struggle with capitalists, but also to carry on production when capitalism shall have been overthrown. By organizing industrially we are forming the structure of the new society within the shell of the old.

IWW Preamble, which continues to be available as a handbill.

Standard Oil's profits were difficult if not impossible to comprehend, but the Appeal sought to illuminate their dizzying magnitude by an explanation readers could grasp.

"All Hail the King!"

It may be a surprise to some of you simple minded folk when I tell you that one corporation in the United States has taken more dollars in net profits in the 25 years and six months just ended than was paid to all the kings of Europe and all the presidents of North and South American nations!

Just let that statement sink into your consciousness. Roll it around in your mind until it makes a sufficient impression to stick.

The Wall Street Journal places the net profits of the Standard Oil company for the past 25 years and six months at $929,000,000.00. This sum is so stupendous that it is impossible for the average mind to comprehend just what it represents. In order that you may make a comparison I publish below a list of the rulers of Europe and the presidents of North and South America with the

cents a day with her washing, and appears at her social functions with bare arms. She handles a larger wardrobe than any society bud in town.

Miss Mehytable Mayn is attending academy in the city. She reports that she sees much of society, as the department store where she is learning the business is a great resort for the rich and the fashionable. She loiters behind the ribbon counter all day, and is advancing rapidly as she almost pays her way now.

August 17, 1907

The Salvation Army's investigation of the causes of suicide substantiated the socialist belief in the primary role of economic determinism.

amounts paid them for their "service" and multiply the total by 25-½, the number of years covered in the report of the net earnings of the Standard Oil company:

British Royal Family	$2,910,000
Emperor of Austro-Hungary	3,875,000
King of Bavaria	1,412,000
King of Belgium	660,000
King of Denmark	227,775
King of Greece	280,000
King of Netherlands	250,000
King of Italy	2,858,000
King of Norway and Sweden	575,525
King of Portugal	634,440
King of Prussia	3,852,770
King of Roumania	237,000
Czar of Russia	12,000,000
King of Saxony	735,000
King of Servia	240,000
King of Spain	2,000,000
King of Wurtemberg	449,050
President of France	250,000
President of United States	50,000
President of Mexico	50,000
Governor General Canada	50,000
South American Republics	200,000
Total per year	$33,796,560
Total for 25 ½ years	$861,812,280
Rockefeller's income for 25 ½ years	$929,000,000

August 1, 1908

"Mother" Mary Jones was the most charismatic, nationally-famous woman labor organizer in the United States from the 1880s to the 1920s. She began agitational work with the Knights of Labor in the 1870s, became a socialist in the 1890s, organized textile workers, street carmen, metal miners, was the sole woman participant in the founding of the IWW, and was a paid organizer for the United Mine Workers for the better part of two decades. Very few written pieces by Mother Jones capture the power of her speeches as much as this account of her organizing experiences in Alabama.

Mother Jones in Alabama

When Mother Jones returned from her recent trip to Alabama she stopped in Girard long enough to write the following story of her experience for the *Appeal* and its readers, and then hurried on to other fields to continue her work of agitating and organizing workers to battle for their emancipation.

* * *

It had been thirteen years since I bid farewell to the workers in Alabama, and went forth to other fields to fight their battles. I returned in 1908 to see what they were doing for the welfare of their children. Governor Comer, being the chief star of the state, I went out to Abdale, on the outskirts of Birmingham, to take a glance at his slave pen. I found there somewhere between five and six hundred slaves. The governor, who in his generous nature could provide money for Jesus, reduced the wages of his slaves first 10 per cent and then 16.

As the wretches were already up against starvation, a few of them struck, and I went with an organizer and the editor of the *Labor Advocate* to help organize the slaves into a union of their craft. I addressed the body, and after I got through quite a large number became members of the Textile Workers union. I returned again inside of another week, held another meeting with them and another large number joined. I was also going to complete my work on Monday, the 12th, but I had to leave for southern Illinois. He has not yet discharged any of them nor has he threatened to call an extra session of the legislature to pass the vagrancy bill in case they struck against the last reduction. Of all the God-cursed conditions that surround any gathering of slaves, or slave pen, Comer's mill district beats them all. As you look at them you immediately conclude that they have been lashed into fear, but they still have some spirit of revolt in them. They work all of thirteen hours a day. They are supposed to go in at 6 in the morning, but the machinery starts up soon after five, and they have to be there. They are supposed to get forty-five minutes for dinner, but the machinery starts up again after they are out for twenty minutes and they have to be at their posts.

When I was in Alabama thirteen years ago, they had no child labor law. Since then they passed a very lame one, so-called. They evade the law in this way: a child who has passed his or her twelfth year can take in his younger brothers or sisters from six years on, and get them to work with him. They are not on the pay roll, but the pay for these little ones goes into the elder one's pay. So that when you look at the pay roll you think this one child makes quite a good bit when perhaps there are two or three younger than he under the lash. Then the governor runs a pill peddler, who is his nephew. There is two cents of every dollar knocked off of the 600 slaves to pay this doctor. You see it's all in the family. Then they have a Sunday school, and the chief guy of the Sunday school has a gold tooth in the front of his mouth, and when he is talking about Jesus, you can see him open up the mouth to show the golden calf. So the little ones pay particular attention to what he says. I found them all suffering from chills and fever and malaria; and whatever change they have left goes to the patent medicine doctor.

One woman told me that her mother had gone into that mill and worked, and took her four children with her. She says, "I have been in the mill since I was four years old. I am now thirty-four." She looked to me as if she was sixty.

She had a kindly nature if treated right, but her whole life and spirit was crushed out beneath the iron wheels of Comer's greed. When you think of the little ones that this mother brings forth you can see how society is cursed with an abnormal human being. She knew nothing but the whiz of the machinery in the factory. As I talked to her with many others she said: "O can you do something for us?" The wives, mothers and the children all go in to produce dividends, profit, profit, profit. This brutal governor is a pillar of the First Methodist church in Birmingham. On Sunday he gets up and sings, "O Lord will you have another star for my crown when I get there?" What a job God must have hiring mechanics to make stars for that black-hearted villain's crown "when he gets there." I saw the little ones lying on the bed shaking with chills and I could hear them ask parent and masters, what they were here for; what crime they had committed that they were brought here and sold to the dividend auctioneer.

Men and women of America, when will you stop your hypocritical actions and rise up in your might to protest against these conditions? When in Alabama 13 years ago these women ran from four to five looms. Today I find them running some 24 looms, and when you think of the high tension, when you think of the cruelty to their nerves, you may know why the glory of their lives is gone. The days when their labor was not a burden are gone; now it is all a hot rush and worry and incessant sweat. They scratch their bits of corn out of these hard days. Think of these young girls and children on their feet guiding that machinery for twelve or thirteen hours a day; running that machinery hour by hour; and in their fever at night I hear them moaning, "O what shall I do, I can't make the machine go, it won't wind." It is hell, worse than hell. Think of these children standing in the midst of these spindles every thread of which must be incessantly watched so that it may be instantly pieced together in a hot room amid its roaring machinery, so loud that one can not hear himself no matter how close at hand.

Amid the whizzing wheels and bands and switch racks that would snatch off a limb for one second's carelessness, all this in hot air so that in summer a great thirst scorches their throat, the weavers are encircled by twenty four terrific looms in a steamed atmosphere which is worse than hell. A method of communication has to be used as if they were dumb animals. At any moment a rebellious shuttle may shoot forth and knock an eye out. A loose skirt may be seized by a wheel or a strap, and then the horrors of the accident can better be imagined than told.

Their mentality is dwarfed, and if they say a

word the cruel boss, who is a scab, goes after them. They tell me that when they get thirsty they cannot get water enough to drink. They are all victims of some ailment. They are never free from headache. Owing to the necessity of cleaning machinery they do not eat at noon. An unpleasant odor comes from the oil and grease, while the rumbling of shafts and drums with squeaking of wheels and spindles make them sick. They rise at 4 o'clock in the morning to prepare to enter that slave pen at half past five. They are all pale, dyspeptic, hollow-chested, and it seems as if life has no charms for them. They cannot go and seek other employment because the energy has been all used up from childhood in their particular line of industry. Mr. Roosevelt makes no allusion to these undesirable citizens who murder these children for gold. I believe that the god of justice will yet rise and take it into his own hands and punish the devourers of children's life for profit.

This is the Democratic south, my friends—this is a Democratic administration. This is what Mr. Bryan and Mr. Gompers want to uphold. I stand for the overthrow of the entire system that murders childhood. I stand for the overthrow of a system that can give $6,000 jobs to labor leaders who have betrayed these infants in their infancy. I stand for the teachings of Christ put into practice, not the teachings of capitalism, and graft and murder.

I stand for the day when this rotten structure will totter of its own vileness. I stand for the day when the baby will live in God's fair land, enjoy its air, its food, its pleasures, when every mother will caress it warmly, when there will be no parasites, no slaves, when $2,000 won't be paid for a hat to cover the skull of the desirable citizen's daughter, when the child shall not be taxed for such diabolical infamy, when poodle dogs will not be caressed on the life blood of innocent childhood, when these children of Comer's hell-hole will live under God's heaven without any master to rob them of their lives.

The high temperature of the mills combined with an abnormal humidity of the air produced by steaming as done by manufacturers makes bad material weave easier and tends to diminish the workers' power of resisting disease. The humid atmosphere promotes perspiration, but makes evaporation from the skin more difficult; and in this condition the operator, when he leaves the mill, has to face a much reduced temperature which produces serious chest affections. They are all narrow-chested, thin, disheartened looking.

I found very few of them who could read or write as I went to take their names to register it for their charter. I found they would come and ask me "you write his or her name," whoever they voted for. No wonder the governor could send his daughter to the sea shore, no wonder he could have the audacity to drive miners back at the point of the bayonet. No wonder men and women commit suicide. They are too tired out at the end of the day to engage in any mental pursuit. They want something or someone to cheer them up.

As Rudyard Kipling says:

Comer, go reckon our dead
By the forges red
And the factories where your slaves spin.
You've eaten their lives,
Their babes and wives,
For which Roosevelt says you're a desirable citizen.
It was your legal right, your legal share.
If blood be the price of your god-cursed gold,
God knows, these slaves have paid it dear.

October 24, 1908

The Class Struggle

The fundamental fact of the Socialist movement is
the class struggle. Without this such a movement
as international Socialism would not only be impossible but unthinkable.

The antagonisms of capitalist society increase
with its development and the more clear-cut and
acute these become the stronger the working class
movement and the earlier its triumph.

The present social system is called the capitalist
system for the simple reason that it is dominated
by the capitalist class. The capitalists own and control the sources of wealth, the machinery of production and the means of exchange; as a corollary
they also control politics, including the judiciary,
and as a result the entire machinery of government
is operated in their interest. On the other hand the
working class do not share in such ownership or
control. All they have is their power to labor, and
in the capitalist system they are compelled to dispose of this at the market price to the capitalist
class, thus being in antagonistic relation to that
class and having no interest in common with that
class.

It is from this fundamental antagonism, this in-
disputable historic fact, that the Socialist movement springs, and this antagonism and this fact
must be clearly kept in mind and never lost sight of
if the movement is to preserve its uncompromising character and be saved from the bogs of confusion and the rocks of destruction.

The capitalists and the workers represent two
separate classes and these two classes are at war,
the one beating down labor power and the other

seeking to raise it up, and this class-cleavage must
be recognized clearly as a fundamental principle of
both economic and political organization if the
aim is to abolish the wage-system and establish a
Socialist commonwealth.

The class struggle may grate offensively upon
the ears of some and if so it is because they are too
sensitive to face the fact and grapple with the situation as it is. . . .

July 3, 1909

Court Crookedness in Fresno

Some time ago the *Appeal* printed a story about
the fight on free speech at Fresno, signed by
Mrs. W. F. Little, a comrade of that city. The story
resulted in Mrs. H. H. Roberts, of Connecticut,
getting trace of a relative who had engaged in the
fight and who was in jail at Fresno. F. W. Boyle, of
Humboldt, Kan., and A. F. Boyle, of Dunneweg,
Mo., also discovered that their cousin, Frank Little, was one of the prisoners of the free speech
fight. The result has been a protest from various
sections of the United States. It would be well for
all acquainted with these parties and others to
write to the chief of police and the police judge
and the mayor of Fresno protesting against the
imprisonment of these people. Following are
some further facts furnished the *Appeal* relative to
the fight by Comrade Mrs. Little:

"Before the I.W.W. was organized at all the chief of police told my husband, 'You mustn't organize the common workers, for we have a raisin crop here that must be handled cheap.' A painter belonging to the painters' union here gets $4 a day and works eight hours. A man digging a ditch or picking raisins gets $1.50 to $2 a day and works ten hours. Both are out of work a good deal of the time.

"In spite of the chief of police and his cheap raisin crop, my husband did his best to organize the common workers in the I.W.W., and shortly after a small local was formed. For some reason the chief of police got the idea into his head that the workers wouldn't join the I.W.W. anyway, so he graciously allowed us to speak on the street. The chief was mistaken, and our local grew from fifteen to over a hundred in a couple of weeks. Then the chief took our permit to speak on the streets away from us. He informed my husband that he knew where his bread and butter came from.

"We called a meeting for the park Sunday afternoon to protest against our being denied the right to free speech. The supervisors refused to allow us the use of the park: but we get out our advertising just the same; and when hundreds of people gathered in the park that peaceful Sunday afternoon, they were met by the clubs of over a dozen policemen, some in uniform and some in plain clothes. Everyone asked why? For the park had, hitherto, been used freely by anyone who cared to address the public from its platform. From then on it was turned over to the ministerial union, for religious purposes only, and educational purposes were neglected. From that time we have not been permitted to speak on the streets of Fresno or in the park, with the exception of one or two addresses. The Salvation Army and other speakers have been allowed the use of the streets all that time.

"However, we went quietly about our business of organization and were building up our local. The police couldn't stand that. The raisin growers were after the police, also the packing house employers, and the railroad officials to get them to do something. So the police commenced arresting men on the charge of vagrancy and disturbing the peace. They would come up to a bunch of men talking industrial unionism on the street and order them to 'move on.' They would see a number of I.W.W. men on the street as early as nine o'clock and order them to go home.

"They arrested a number of men as vagrants, and the men proved that they were working at the time of their arrest. They arrested my husband, his brother, and two other I.W.W. men for disturbing the peace, and brought perjured testimony against them. My husband had such a clear alibi that they were forced to discharge him, but they convicted my brother-in-law and sentenced him to thirty days' imprisonment. After a great deal of trouble my husband secured a warrant for one of the men who committed perjury. He was tried, found guilty and bound over to the superior court. He is out on bond, and it is needless to say will never be punished.

"With the encouragement and help of other locals, our local decided that as long as they were to be harrassed by the police, they might just as well obtain the use of the streets while they were about it. But first they again asked the chief of police for a permit to speak on the streets. It was refused. Then they went to the mayor and the trustees of the city and presented them with a written request to be allowed to speak on the streets; this also was refused. Then one night eight boys, one after another, got on the soap box on the street. The first one got to talk a few minutes, after that all the men could say would be 'fellow worker' and the police would grab him and take him to jail.

"There was no street speaking ordinance, and so they charged the men with vagrancy or disturbing the peace. Later they made an ordinance against street speaking.

"There are about one hundred I.W.W. men in jail now with different charges, but all are arrested for the same offense. Only a few of the I.W.W.

men have been tried. Some of the best speakers were tried and convicted of vagrancy, by juries of business men. Four of them got six months apiece, although they proved that they were not vagrants. Many of the boys have been imprisoned fifty-one days today, without trial. For a long time they were not allowed to see anyone. Now they can see the people who call on them. Men accused of nothing worse than disturbing the peace or vagrancy held 51 days without a trial, part of the time not allowed to see their friends, and this happened not in Russia, but in sunny California, that you read so much about, where every prospect pleases and only man is vile.

"Frank Little was arrested on the charge of vagrancy. Frank is one of the 94 I.W.W. men confined in a bull pen, 47 x 28 feet. The officers of the state board of health say that there is air enough in the pen for 5 men. Most of the men confined in the bull pen have been out in the open air only once or twice since they were arrested. A good many of the men have been in there 53 days today. Only a few have been tried. Frank has not been tried as yet."

February 11, 1911

Scabs, persons hired to take the jobs of striking union members, were commonly imported from far away to break strikes. Scabbing was regarded as class betrayal and was often far more dangerous than its wage of two to three dollars a day justified.

The Battle of McComb

STRIKER

McComb City, Miss., Oct. 17 The men went out on the I. C. railroad September 30th, ten crafts. Tuesday evening, October 10th, the company brought in thirteen coaches of scabs from Philadelphia, Pa., and New York, the hardest looking gang of criminals a man ever looked at. As the train hit the state line the scabs began to do their dirty work, tearing up little towns along the road, and insulting women in every way.

They got in McComb City about 3:30 p.m. When within one mile of town they stopped the train and loaded up with cobble stones and bricks. As the train pulled by the depot they began to shoot and throw stones. They hit several women and children. One poor old man was struck in the head with a brick.

The I. C. company pulled the train down in the car sheds, where they slopped like a gang of pigs.

The people demanded the sheriff to deputize enough men to go down and put them all under arrest, but he would not interfere. Instead, he wired the grafting governor for the militia.

The citizens took the case in their own hands, so when the train left the shop yards 150 armed men opened fire and what they did to the train was a plenty. The company is trying to keep it quiet, how many were killed and wounded, but I learned from reliable sources that seventeen were killed and forty-five wounded. The dead were buried in the swamps near New Orleans. The company left two coaches of these scabs in McComb under heavy guard, but the next morning they refused to go to work and made the company take them out of town.

Now we are entirely surrounded by soldiers. Nearly every company in the state is here. They want to go home, most of them saying when their time is up they never want to belong to another company. I am proud to say 90 per cent are strike sympathizers. They all say that there is no need of them here. They want to go home. But our lovely governor, Noel, is the scoundrel who is getting the grapes out of this at present.

The company has about thirty men at work, about four mechanics in all. Some hired as machinists and boiler makers who never saw a railroad shop. Some are professional scabs.

October 21, 1911

Appeal to Reason, June 6, 1914.

SPIRIT OF CAPITALISTIC LAW

The Ruling Spirit When Labor Seeks Justice.

The consequences of capitalism's class division sometimes compelled the Appeal *to respond with sardonic humor.*

The Class Struggle

A man was arrested and fined in Chicago because he wore woman's clothes to get jobs as a washerwoman.

John Redpath, a civil war veteran, with his wife, was found starving in East Brooklyn in spite of a small pension he was drawing.

Exploited women workers in a macaroni factory in Fort Worth, Tex., get $4 a week. Enough for them to buy the holes in the macaroni they make.

A concrete building rising in Indianapolis fell during the noon hour and killed four workmen, eating their lunch. Fortunate is the laboring man who can hope to die on a full stomach.

An Akron, Ohio, man, thirty-five years old, has just been sent to the penitentiary for fifteen years because he stole $10 from a candy store. The way society stole the rest of his life span was like taking candy from a baby.

Table butter went to forty-five and fifty cents a pound retail in Chicago last week, the highest mark for this season of the year since 1888. High butter helps grease the way for the social method of food distribution.

Fred Whiteside, a state senator from Montana, told the late irrigation congress that thousands were actually starving in his state because of the government's red tape delay in working out irrigation projects for which the money is raised.

An Indian witness in a case at Fergus Falls, Minn., who sold his testimony, declared in court that he "would do anything for $7,000." The Indian is a crude and costly device compared with the ordinary plute banker who will turn any trick known for $10.

Hundreds of men are applying to the police to be arrested, reports the Cleveland *Press*. They are those who cannot find work and have no friends, yet they are still so in love with life that they do not want to starve, or freeze to death in the wintry streets. Absurd fellows!

A Wisconsin paper manufacturer overworked his girl employes, thirteen hours at a shift, all night, in spite of the law which limits night work to eight hours. But last week he was made to pay dearly for his cruelty in pursuit of profits. He was arrested and fined every cent of $10!

The National Founders' association recently met and resolved that it was time for confidence to return and business to boom through the suppression of the agitator and co-operation "more friendly" between capital and labor. Doubtless the "peace of Los Angeles" will bring about these divine conditions the founders speak of so lovingly.

Laura Stallo, beneficiary of one of the late Standard Oil millionaires, got into court as a spendthrift when her guardian explained that while the girl's income is a mere $18,000 a year, she spends an average of $21,000 annually. Poor dear! She's like the average working man who with an income of $450 a year finds himself continually living beyond his means.

A form of peonage on the Colorado sugar beet farms where city derelicts recruited from the slums are held in a veritable state of bondage was described by James Bodkin, of Colorado, before the "Sugar Trust", investigating committee. By a labor contract system, the sugar company tied up

Russians, Hindus and other poor, miserable devils, and worked man, wife and children sixteen hours daily at back-breaking toil an American would scorn to do.

December 23, 1911

The Lawrence strike, begun on January 12, 1912, when 25,000 textile workers walked out of the mills in Lawrence, Massachusetts, concluded two months later with the mill workers and their IWW union victorious. A spontaneous revolt by predominantly immigrant workers, more than half of whom were women and children, the conflict became famous as the "Bread and Roses" strike when a woman striker was photographed carrying a banner which read, "We want bread and roses too." The strike succeeded despite the arrest of union leaders, beatings by local police and the state militia, and the planting of dynamite by agents of the mill owners.

Dynamite Witness Suicides

By Telegraph to Appeal to Reason

Boston, August 27 Rather than testify before the grand jury now investigating the responsibility for the planting of dynamite during the Lawrence strike, Ernest W. Pittman, a Lawrence mill owner, committed suicide today. John J. Breen, Lawrence school commissioner, prominent politician and extremely active in the leading Catholic circles, was convicted some time ago of having planted this dynamite last January in an effort to discredit the strikers. Every effort has been make to hush up the matter and shield the mill owners who are believed to have been behind Breen. The suicide of Pittman is now accepted as a confession of guilt and also of fear of the vengeance of the other members of the woolen manufacturing and dynamiting trust. Other mill owners are being examined by the grand jury and sensational developments are almost certain.

September 7, 1912

John Kenneth Turner's account of the Akron rubber strike and employers' strike-breaking tactics illustrates why he was one of the finest investigative reporters at work in America during the 1910s.

Labor Union and Socialist Local Infested With Corporation Spies

BY JOHN KENNETH TURNER
STAFF CORRESPONDENT *Appeal to Reason*

Akron is a typical American trust city. It is the home of the manufacturing end of the Rubber trust—of which, by the bye, the Rockefellers and the Aldriches are controlling figures.

As a manufacturer of rubber goods Akron has no rival. The value of the annual product runs to about $100,000,000, nearly all of it rubber. The three largest companies are the Goodrich-Diamond, the Goodyear and the Firestone. The capitalization of the Goodyear climbed from $100,000 in 1903 to $10,000,000 in 1913, the Firestone from $500,000 in 1910 to $4,000,000 in 1912, and on this four million it made a 30 per cent profit. The largest concern is the Goodrich-Diamond, with a capitalization of $90,000,000, of which $60,000,000 is muddy water.

The retail prices for the same class of goods, respectively, turned out by the various Akron factories, are identical.

Mountains of gold have been piled up from rubber in the past decade. But neither the farmhands in rubber, nor the artisans in rubber, have come into possession of any gold mountains—nor even of gold mole-hills.

A good deal has been written of the rubber slaves of Putamayo, of the Congo and of Mexico. Little is known of the rubber slaves of Akron. There are 22,000 of them   22,000 in a population of 70,000. They are driven under the Taylor speeding system, some as long as from 11 to 13 hours a day. Piece-work is the rule. One per cent of the workers are fairly well paid. An investigation

by a committee of the state senate, ordered because of the strike, proved that the vast majority are unable to live decently on their wages.

Twenty-two thousand slaves cannot associate together without drawing comparisons between their lot and the lot of their masters, and plotting to get more of the stuff of happiness for themselves. The first step toward getting that stuff of happiness is to organize, and ever since rubber became king in Akron the slaves of rubber have been reaching out toward organization.

The masters, for their part—fully appreciating human nature—have taken every precaution to keep their employes divided.

Every applicant for a job was investigated and catechised in order to make sure that he came clean of any taint of unionism. Every worker was kept under close surveillance and discharged the moment he developed evidences of rebellion. In order to make sure of a body of unemployed to fill the places of these incipient rebels, standing advertisements of "Men Wanted" at Akron were kept in the newspapers of neighboring cities.

The Goodyear company launched a feudalistic scheme of home-building for its employes. The scheme offered a home to be paid for in twelve years by installments, and was so cunningly contrived that the employe who went on strike would lose everything.

The chief work of preventing organization, however, was let by contract to one of the fifty defensive concerns that are specialists in anti-union—anti-Socialist warfare—namely, the Corporations Auxiliary company, with headquarters at Cleveland, Ohio.

The Corporations Auxiliary company, as an instrument for the repression of labor, is a special protege of the National Association of Manufacturers, which has officially assisted in the formation of several agencies for "industrial defense," as these silk-hatted bandits politely term their war upon wage-earners.

Unlike Bergoff Brothers, Waddell & Mahon, Baldwin & Felts, and others, the Corporations

Auxiliary company does not furnish gunmen armies. Instead, it specializes in "Industrial Inspection." As will be observed by an extract from its confidential advertising printed in another column, in place of destroying labor unions with machine guns, its policy is to lead and officer them, and so bring about gradual disintegration. By "calm argument" of representatives specially educated for that purpose, it lays bare "the fallacies of Socialism" and points out the joys of meekness and humility.

Ever since the smoke began to rise from the tall chimneys at Akron the Corporations Auxiliary company has had scores of "operatives" (pretended workingmen) in the factories "inspecting," reporting upon and discharging the rubber workers. In spite of all this surveillance the latter actually succeeded in making a number of starts in the formation of a union.

On the first occasion the "industrial experts" committed burglary to get the names of the members in order to discharge them. On the second the custodian of the books was bribed to give up the names. Still another time one of the companies actually signed an agreement with 350 of its union employes, simply to find out WHO were union members in order to get rid of them.

During this period the Corporations Auxiliary company carried out its policy of officering and leading the unions. Among the spies exposed were John Washer, now a United States secret service man; John E. Sebree, who had become president of the Molders' union and secretary of the Central Labor Council and organizer of the Carpenters' union.

At the time of the strike last year all the local officers of the I.W.W., except one, were "operatives" of the Corporations Auxiliary company. The recording secretary of the Socialist party local was a Corporations Auxiliary "operative," while other "operatives" were members of the I.W.W., the Socialist party and the A.F. of L. unions of the city.

The great rubber strike came February 11, 1913. It originated in the Firestone factory and was the re-

sult of a dispute with a comparatively small number of men. Once the ice was broken, between 15,000 and 16,000 of the employes quit work.

The season was specially favorable for a successful strike and the permanent organization of the workers in the rubber industry. The factories were overwhelmed with contracts and stood to lose immense sums by a shut-down.

But the strike was put in the hands of the I.W.W., and the I.W.W. was in the hands (locally) of Corporations Auxiliary company spies.

Before proceeding to show precisely how the Corporations Auxiliary company broke the strike, it may be worth while to devote a few paragraphs to the deportment of the pillars of Akron society in the premises.

Said the Akron *Times*:

Not since the civil war has local citizenship and patriotism been in such thorough accord. Set on a hill, where its light cannot be hid, what a glorious flame of patriotism shines across the city! How its radiance spreads the glory in the heavens! Old men, young men, learned men, ignorant men, rich men, poor men, professional men, laboring men, ministers, lawyers, doctors, teachers—stand together on the broad base of a common patriotism! What a glorious sight! What manly forms, what open faces! And that little yellow badge, shining in the spring sunshine over hearts of gold!

This is only a sample. There was poetry, too. For example:

> *After all—*
> *'Tis freedom wears the loveliest coronal;*
> *Her brow is to the morning; in the sod*
> *She breathes the breath of patriots;*
>   *every clod*
>   *Answers her call*
>   *And rises like a wall*
> *Against the foes of liberty and God!*
> *Just one more:*
> *God gives us peace!*
> *Not such as lulls to sleep,*
> *But sword on thigh,*
> *And brow with purpose knit—*

And, let our ship of state to harbor
  sweep,
Her ports all up, her battle lanterns lit,
And her leashed thunders gathering for
  their leap!

Sounds like "Remember the Maine"; or "On to Mexico"; doesn't it? What can it all mean?

Simply this, that the pillars of Akron society had been gambling in rubber stock. Old men, young men, learned men, ignorant men, ministers, lawyers (and editors!) were caught with rubber stock on their hands! The strike "beared" the market and a "glorious flame of patriotism shone across the city!"

Whether or not the Corporations Auxiliary company was prepared to call mercenary gunmen to its aid will never be known, for, as it turned out, no mercenaries were needed.

A thousand patriots, yearning to bleed for their country, volunteered to club the stuffing out of the rubber workers. Led by two ministers of the gospel, wearing little yellow badges over their hearts of gold, armed with maces and guns, the rubber stock gamblers assembled their manly forms at 5:15 every morning, their battle lanterns lit for the foes of liberty and God, ready to do or die for freedom. What a glorious sight!

The gambler-patriots were formed into a semi-military organization known as the "Citizens' Welfare league." Sheriff Ferguson duly deputized them in the name of law and order. The Rev. George P. Atwater, after leading in prayer, was named commander-in-chief and selected a good, strong mace for himself.

(Rev. Atwater, by the bye—he was pastor of the Episcopal church—was rewarded with a fine automobile, the gift of the Goodrich Tire company.)

The rubber-stock defenders of liberty were not maneuvered on foot, like common infantrymen; they rode in automobiles—125 automobiles of the most expensive makes. Their purpose was, first, to prevent picketing, which they did; second, to intimidate the strikers into returning to work; third,

to fight the strike by any other means that might occur to their devoted consciences.

When the local Scripps paper, the Akron *Press*, persisted in telling the truth about the strike, the patriots made an assault upon its advertising, and with such success—it is claimed—that the *Press* finally surrendered.

Some manly fellows broke into the strike headquarters at night, stopped up the water-pipes and flooded the hall, with the result that the strikers were forced to vacate.

The Mayor, Frank W. Rockwell, helped, by sending out a circular letter to every other mayor in the United States, urging that the public be warned against forwarding funds to aid the strikers, as the "agitators" were stealing it all.

The regular police helped, and was afterwards rewarded by the Goodrich Co. with $2,000 for its pension fund "for patriotic services rendered during the strike."

Police Judge Vaughn, member of the firm of Vaughn, Voorhies & Vaughn, rubber company attorneys, helped by refusing jury trials to men arrested for picketing and parading and giving them the limit in the work-house.

The City council helped, by rushing through an ordinance multiplying by ten the penalty for parading; and the mayor showed his heart of gold by declaring that he wished the paraders could be given six years in the work-house, instead of two!

Meanwhile an investigation by the state senate—which was not so patriotic—revealed the fact that the patriotic Goodrich Company had criminally swindled the U.S. government on certain hose contracts.

The Goodrich company, however, was never prosecuted for the theft—probably because the U.S. government was more patriotic than the Ohio senate!

It was not the thuggery of the Akron gambler-patriots, however, that broke the strike, but the Corporations Auxiliary company and its wonderful "system" of Industrial Inspection.

Rockefeller's Gunmen Murder Women and Children in Colorado

Blood of Slaughtered Babes Calls for Immediate Action

"MY COUNTRY, 'TIS OF THEE"

Gunmen Army Riddles Tent Colony With Bullets, then Burn Bodies in Coal Oil

Scores of Miners, Their Wives and Babies Slain in Cold Blood by Mine Magnates Private Army of Gunmen —Truce Bearer Receives 51 Bullets.

EXPLOSIVE BULLETS USED ON HELPLESS BABES

Bloody Incidents of French Revolution Outdone by Greedy Exploiters Headed by Rockefeller—While Wilson Sends Military Forces to "Civilize" Mexico, Colorado is Soaked With Blood of Disinherited. Militia Company Mutinies When Called Out.

By Telegraph to APPEAL TO REASON.

Denver, Colo., April 23.—*Twenty-eight bodies of striking coal miners have been recovered from the ruins of the Ludlow tent colony, and at least thirty more are believed to have been burned by the gunmen militia in a huge funeral pyre of bullet ridden and suffocated bodies.*

Masthead, *Appeal to Reason*, May 2, 1914.

For the inside story of how the trick was done I am indebted to John W. Reid, an old-time labor spy who began under Farley and who for over five years was in the pay of the Corporations Auxiliary company at Akron. Last January, having been discharged by the Corporations Auxiliary company, Reid made affidavit to his connection with the strike. In February I had a long talk with him, and he confessed freely, furnishing me with many details that had not been given in his affidavit.

The Akron Rubber Workers' union (I.W.W.) was organized August 14, 1912, at a neighboring town, Barberton.

Why not at Akron? For fear of spies. But the latter did not mind the trip to Barberton. According to Reid, half of the charter members were Corporations Auxiliary company spies.

Not only that, but the spies got possession of the offices. From the day of organization until after the strike, Corporations Auxiliary company men held all but one of the offices.

At the start the spy officers were: V. G. Williams, president; Ed Dickerson, vice-president; J. G. Glendenen, cor. sec'y; John W. Reid, conductor. At the beginning of 1913 Williams and Dickerson were re-elected. Reid was made secretary-treasurer; A. G. Shepley, another spy, recording secretary. C. A. Miller and Charles Gross, also spies, were elected trustees.

This was the I.W.W. line-up when the strike came.

"The rubber workers were determined to have an organization of some kind," Reid explained to me. "We (the spies) had orders to keep the local alive, but to hold it in our hands."

Reid went on to say that D. G. Ross, vice-president and general manager of the Corporations Auxiliary company, had told him at one time: "We're spending thousands of dollars a year to down the I.W.W. We have a man in the national headquarters at Chicago—right on the inside."

This corresponded with the statement previously made to me by W. A. Mundell, Pacific Coast manager for William J. Burns, that: "The Burns agency has many men in the I.W.W. In fact, I brought one of them, an organizer, all the way from New York, to make street speeches while we were working up the case against the hoppickers."

So thoroughly did Williams, Dickerson, Reid and Miller have the affairs of the Akron local, I.W.W., in their hands at the time of the strike, that they were known to their fellow-workers as

"The Big Four." All four had for years been working for wages in the various rubber factories, and the utmost confidence was placed in them. Reid declares that Miller, who had been in Akron for more than 10 years, had previously been a labor spy in the great teamsters' strike in Chicago, where he had been exposed and had made a quick get-away.

Williams, president of the I.W.W., was also recording secretary of the Akron Socialist local, and at the time of Reid's confession was a delegate to the Socialist state convention and candidate for state secretary. Miller was a member of the Socialist press committee and very active in the party. Reid was an active member of the Socialist local, as were many other of the Corporations Auxiliary men.

Spies Williams, Dickerson, Miller, Reid et al were under orders to prevent a strike. They failed to prevent the strike, but they succeeded in making a fiasco of it, and by the following methods:

1. By quietly advising the unorganized strikers against joining the I.W.W., the argument being that there would be plenty of time to join when the strike was won.

2. By "making monkeys of" (Reid's words) the I.W.W. organizers who came to Akron from the outside. Corporations Auxiliary money was spent freely for drinks, with the result that several well-known I.W.W. organizers were kept drunk most of the time, and when they attempted to do their work they usually made fools of themselves.

Reid said laughingly to me: "It was easy to keep ⸺⸺⸺⸺⸺⸺ and ⸺⸺⸺ drunk all the time, but ⸺⸺⸺ was a tank."

3. By quietly stirring up race hatreds and circulating tales calculated to split the strikers up into factions.

4. By wasting the funds of the organization. The spies placed two of their number, Miller and Dickerson, on salary at $12 a week each. Thousands of dollars were spent in futile ways. Reid claims that soon after the strike started, Ross, general manager of the Corporations Auxiliary company, tried to get him to abscond with all the funds of the organization—at that time $3,000—but that he refused to do it.

5. By delaying the presentation of the demands. Fifteen thousand poverty-stricken rubber workers, living from hand to mouth, were on the streets. Their only chance lay in a quick fight. The spies, in control of the wage-scale committee, took three weeks to frame the demands. And when the demands were finally framed they were so exorbitant and unwieldly as to be worthless.

6. Another maneuver of the Corporations Auxiliary company was to cause the organization of an A.F. of L. Rubber Workers' Local, in opposition to the one already in existence. A man by the name of Neal—who it is claimed was afterwards proved to be a spy—was chosen for this work and became president of the opposition union. The usual A.F. of L. vs. I.W.W. controversy followed.

As fast as the rubber workers joined the union their names were turned over to the C.A.C., and by the C.A.C. to the rubber companies. The Big Four "led" the strike in the day-time, and met nightly at the home of one or another of the quartette to chuckle over their villainy and to write their reports to their bosses.

In three weeks the strike was practically broken and in six it was officially called off. The strikers, properly disciplined, went back to work under the old conditions. The I.W.W. local dwindled to a membership of fifteen.

So were blasted the hopes of 22,000 slaves of rubber. Had the strike been a success a great union would have been organized, and there is little doubt that the Socialist party would today have a voting majority in Akron.

But that was not to be. Government by Gunmen had scored another victory.

SPIES TO FIGHT SOCIALISM
The following paragraphs are from a confidential letter sent out to large employers of labor by the

Appeal to Reason, March 7, 1914.

President Wilson says that when warm weather comes everything will be all right for the unemployed.—News Item.

Corporations Auxiliary Company, Chamber of Commerce building, Cleveland, Ohio:

"In view of the present labor conditions we believe you will be interested in the enclosed pamphlet, entitled Industrial Inspection which describes in a very general way the inspection system operated by this company.

"Wherever our system has been in operation for a reasonable length of time, considering the purpose to be accomplished, the result has been that union membership has not increased if our clients wished otherwise. In many cases local union charters have been returned without publicity and a number of local unions have been disbanded.

"Our experience has convinced us that the best way to control labor organizations is to lead and not to force them. We are also convinced that the conservative ele-

ment in all unions will control when properly led and officered, which we are prepared to do.

"We help eliminate the agitator and organizer quietly and with little or no friction, and further, through the employment of our system, you will know at all times who among your employes are loyal and to be depended upon.

"You will also be advised of any loss of time and material, and will be furnished such information as will assist you to increase the efficiency of your working force and promote economy of operation.

"In view of the rapid increase of Socialism, which is the real mischief-making influence in the industrial world today, we would particularly call your attention to the educational feature of our work. Our representatives are educated along industrial lines for the express purpose of combatting by calm argument the fallacies of Socialism. In a number of instances our men ARE EMPLOYED FOR NO OTHER PURPOSE THAN TO RESIST THE SPREAD OF SOCIALISTIC THEORIES."

July 25, 1914

Joe Hill, Swedish immigrant, IWW organizer, poet, and song writer, was shot by a Utah firing squad on November 19, 1915, for the murder of a Salt Lake grocer and his son. Neither objections to the trial's many irregularities, massive protest, nor an official request for a thorough reconsideration of Hill's sentence from President Woodrow Wilson to Utah's governor prevented Joe Hill's execution. The IWW has had many martyrs, more lying in unmarked than in marked graves, but none has lived on as much as Joe Hill, the man who "never died." Of the dozens of songs Joe Hill wrote, "The Preacher and the Slave," "Casey Jones—the Union Scab," and "There's Power in the Union" are still sung in the United States. "Don't waste any time in mourning," Joe Hill wrote to Bill Haywood, general secretary of the IWW, before he was shot. "Organize."

"I Am Innocent!" Swears Joe Hill, at Death's Door

The following letter by Joseph Hillstrom, known among labor agitators as Joe Hill, was sent from prison by the condemned man to the *Salt Lake Telegram*. The letter is a convincing protest against unjust punishment, and rings with Joe Hill's dauntless defiance of the rotten rulers who would put a bullet in his heart as the penalty for being a class-conscious rebel against present conditions. Joe Hill is ready to die like a man, but the workers for whose cause he lived and is about to die are guilty of great ingratitude if they permit him to be murdered without making a mighty protest. The same anarchy of the law that permits

the murder of innocent Joe Hill because he is an "undesirable" agitator will permit, if allowed to go unchallenged, the persecution and murder of any workingman who is big enough to stand for justice and bold enough to speak against anarchy and the legalized murder of innocent workingmen. Strike now for Joe Hill, for yourself and for the whole working class. Write NOW to the governor of Utah, Salt Lake City, and DEMAND that Joe Hill be given another trial.

State Prison, August 15, 1915.

Editor, *Telegram*, Salt Lake City, Utah:

Sir—I have noticed that there have been some articles in your paper wherein the reason why I discharged my attorneys, F. B. Scott and E. D. McDougall, was discussed pro and con. If you will kindly allow me a little space, I think I might be able to throw a little light on the question.

There were several reasons why I discharged, or tried to discharge, these attorneys. The main reason, however, was because they never attempted to cross-examine the witnesses for the state, and failed utterly to deliver the points of the defense.

When I asked them why they did not use the records of the preliminary hearing and pin the witnesses down to their former statements, they blandly informed me that the preliminary hearing had nothing to do with the district court hearing and that under the law they had no right to use said records.

I picked up a record myself and tried to look at it, but Mr. Scott took it away from me, stating that "it would have a bad effect on the jury." I then came to the conclusion that Scott and McDougall were not there for the purpose of defending me, and I did just what any other man would have done—I stood up and showed them the door. But, to my great surprise, I discovered that the presiding judge had the power to compel me to have these attorneys, in spite of all my protests.

The main and only fact worth considering, however, is this: I never killed Morrison and do not know a thing about it.

THE TRAP

Appeal to Reason, July 22, 1922.

He was, as the records plainly show, killed by some enemy for the sake of revenge, and I have not been in this city long enough to make an enemy. Shortly before my arrest I came down from Park City, where I was working in the mines. Owing to the prominence of Mr. Morrison, there had to be a "goat," and the undersigned being, as they thought, a friendless tramp, a Swede, and, worst of all, an I.W.W., had no right to live anyway, and was therefore duly selected to be "the goat."

There were men sitting on my jury, the foreman being one of them, who were never subpoenaed for the case. There are errors and perjury that are screaming to high heaven for mercy, and I know that I, according to the laws of the land, am entitled to a new trial, and the fact that the supreme court does not grant it to me only proves that the beautiful term, "equality before the law," is merely an empty phrase in Salt Lake City.

Here is what Judge Hilton of Denver, one of the greatest authorities on law, has to say about it:

"The decision of the Supreme Court surprised me greatly, but the reason why the verdict was affirmed is, I think, on account of the rotten records made by the lower court."

This statement shows plainly why the motion for a new trial was denied and there is no explanation necessary. In conclusion I wish to state that my records are not quite as black as they have been painted.

In spite of all the hideous pictures and all the bad things said and printed about me, I had only been arrested once before in my life, and that was in San Pedro, Cal. At the time of the stevedores' and dock workers' strike I was secretary of the strike committee, and I suppose I was a little too active to suit the chief of that burg, so he arrested me and gave me thirty days in the city jail for "vagrancy"—and there you have the full extent of my "criminal record."

I have always worked hard for a living and paid for everything I got, and my spare time I spend by painting pictures, writing songs and composing music.

Now, if the people of the state of Utah want to shoot me without giving me half a chance to state my side of the case, bring on your firing squads—I am ready for you.

I have lived like an artist and I shall die like an artist.

Respectfully yours,

JOSEPH HILLSTROM

A staff writer for Life, *Ellis O. Jones wrote occasionally for the* Appeal *during its later years. For all its tone of good humor,* "Police Club Capitalists" *is a revelatory description of police strike-breaking tactics.*

Police Club Capitalists

ELLIS O. JONES

Nowhere, U.S.A.   Upon the advice of detectives the police yesterday broke into the stockholders' meeting of the American Dividends company, known as the Dividends' Trust, which has a monopoly of many of the necessaries of life. It has been suspected for some time that the stockholders expected to strike for higher prices. Anticipating this, a squad of police were secreted in an anteroom, and when the meeting was at its height, they broke in, scattered the assembly and confiscated their records. Those who resisted were clubbed. Mr. Portly Goldgrabber, president of the company and well known philanthropist was placed under arrest.

At the same hour, the police in other parts of the city were also busy. Some of the capitalists having received a tip that trouble was coming had arranged to send their children abroad on the Gigantic. These children were seized and will be held as witnesses.

At three-o'clock, the Chief of Police issued an order to the effect that all halls and public streets should be closed to the meetings of those who are trying to increase dividends. All capitalists found riding in the park or other public places will be looked upon as conspirators and summarily dealt with. This gang must be broken up, the police declare. Human life is not safe as long as they are allowed to run at large or conspire behind closed doors. We are interested in law and order and the welfare of the people.

At three-thirty, Chief of Detectives Popully, who has worked up the case, gave an interview to the press. He said: "I have gone into this case very thoroughly. That they are a very lawless crowd doesn't admit of the slightest doubt. They are a serious menace to the public for they will go to any lengths to increase dividends. I have traced scores and scores of crimes and outrages to their machinations. Among the most important of these, I may mention mine explosions, railroad wrecks, wholesale poisonings from adulterants, deaths from fire owing to insufficient safeguards, hundreds of deaths due to diseases caused by overwork and undernourishment. Every one of these crimes is due to the fact that these men consider dividends more important than humanity."

When one of the lawyers for the defense asked the Chief of Police if he wasn't exceeding his authority and violating constitutional rights, he admitted that he probably was. "But," he explained, "it has been the practice for the police to invade constitutional rights in dealing with the poor. Why should we make an exception of the rich?"

August 12, 1916

Scott Nearing was a teacher, a prolific writer, a socialist, an anti-World War I activist, a communist, and an ecologist during his eventful life. Fired from the University of Pennsylvania's Wharton School in 1915 for his political beliefs, in 1916 he briefly taught at the University of Toledo. His autobiographical The Making of a Radical *is a convenient starting point for understanding Nearing and the America he lived in.*

What Chance Has Worker to Become a Capitalist?

PROF. SCOTT NEARING

The maximum amount of income which the workingman may earn is limited. To be sure, there is always a possibility of the workingman rising out of the ranks of the workers and becoming a manager or a capitalist. The existence of the chance to rise has never been questioned though its mathematical boundaries are not always under-

stood. Consider, for example, one of the greatest single industries in the United States, the Railroad Industry, employing nearly a million and three-quarters of men. What are the possibilities for advancement in this industry as shown by the statistics of the Interstate Commerce Commission?

There were, in 1910, 5,476 general officers directing the activities of a million and three-quarters employes. Therefore, in the business life of the general officer and the business life of the employe, each employe should have one chance in three hundred of becoming a general officer at some time during his life, provided that the employes live as long as the general officers, and provided further that all the general officers are drawn from the ranks of the employes. Neither of these assumptions, however, is correct, because, in the first place, insurance tables indicate that the life of the general officer is somewhat longer than the life of the average workingmen. In the second place, the general officers are not always drawn from the ranks. Leaving these two considerations out of account, however, it is apparent that the mathematical probability that the average railroad employe will become a general officer is about one-third of one percent.

Consider another phase of the situation. Suppose that you are a railroad trainman. Mathematically you have one chance in three hundred of becoming a general officer at some time during your life. On the other hand, you have one chance in twenty of being injured, and one chance in one hundred of being killed during each year that you are at work.

Suppose that your total term of service is twenty years, the chances are one to one that during that time you will be injured and one to six that during that time you will be killed; so that the chance of your being injured is three hundred times as great, and of your being killed is fifty times as great, as your chance of becoming a general officer in the company which is employing you.

A similar condition exists in the manufacturing industries.

IN SHORT, THE TENDENCY OF
MODERN INDUSTRY IS TOWARD A
FORM OF ORGANIZATION WHICH
WILL REQUIRE THE WAGE WORKER
TO REMAIN A WAGE WORKER. The rail-
road does not expect a brakeman to become president or general manager, but instead to become a
conductor. In the same way, section hands make
section foreman, and locomotive firemen make locomotive engineers. The railroad manager is not
looking for an engineer who will make a general
superintendent, but for an engineer who will be
and will remain a good engineer.

August 12, 1916

FOUR

The Land Question

The outstanding feature of the Homestead Act was that until the settler proved his use and occupancy, his presence constituted his only claim to the land. Or, in other words, the title remained with the government while the settler enjoyed the usufruct thereof. Relinquishment of claims could be sold, but only to purchasers who agreed to live on and work the claim. Thus, only farmers who farmed the land could possess the gift of Uncle Sam. Under this form of land tenure, which, so far as I know, was a purely American invention, absentee ownership was excluded. The tragedy of American farm life is that the Homestead Act was not made perpetual.[1]

Socialists agreed with the logic and assumptions of the American land reformers of the 1840s and 1850s. If a portion of the public domain was to be made available to settlers, no criteria for title to that land could be more just or democratic than use and occupancy. Implicit in the Homestead Act of 1862 was a set of endemically American assumptions so powerful that they had held constant, regardless of changing economic and social realities, for more than a century. Jefferson had apotheosized the yeoman farmer as the ideal man and ideal citizen: "The small land holders are the most precious part of a state." The cultivation of land and their close relation to nature made smallholders a chosen people and made agriculture, for Benjamin Franklin, "the only *honest*

way" for a nation to acquire wealth.[2] The farmer lived by the sweat of his own brow, not another's.

The settlement experience itself led to a natural justification of land tenure: "God made this earth to be free to all; and whoever takes wild land, and clears it, and cultivates it, makes it his own—he's a right to it."[3] The philosophical underpinning was provided by a broadly shared doctrine of natural rights. Since men and women had a free, inalienable right to existence, they had necessarily the corollary right to the means of that existence. The earth was an inherent part of the collective human inheritance. If its ownership—determined naturally, by use and occupancy, not by artificial title—were denied, the right of many to exist except as instruments of another's profit disappeared with it. The *Appeal* approached the land question—the presence of vast land monopolies, the crop lien system, increasingly high rates of mortgages and foreclosures—as it approached impoverishment elsewhere: common ownership of the means necessary for life had to be restored in order for human life, in its full dimensions, to flourish.

The transformation of the American political economy during post–Civil War America left no significant area of life unaltered; only escapist nostalgia permits us to cling to the myth of the happy yeoman independently cultivating and harvesting his fields. Social and economic realities were dramatically different. Only one settling family in eight to ten obtained "free" homestead land. Of those, two-thirds failed by 1890. For every industrial worker who amassed the money necessary for transportation, stock, and equipment, and then succeeded on the land, twenty farmers' sons were dispossessed and driven into the cities to survive. Historically, the Homestead Acts came too late to break, much less prevent, the developing pattern of land monopoly and speculation. By 1886, for example, twenty-nine foreign land syndicates and individuals had amassed 20,747,000 acres.[4] Although substantial in its way, that total is modest when compared to the railroads' appropriation of public land. In addition to hundreds of millions of dollars extracted from federal and state legislatures, as well as from towns and cities, the railroads obtained some 200,000,000 acres, a private domain roughly one-tenth of the continental United States or, as the *Appeal* usually put it, an area the size of France and Germany combined.

The dimensions of the railroads' landgrab made effective propaganda, but the place of the railroads in the new capitalist order was even more significant. Although an ideological legacy remained, the day of the comparatively independent farmer was gone from many areas of the United States and was quickly disappearing from yet others. By the beginning of the twentieth century, the American farmer and his family rarely produced for local needs, but for distant markets in Chicago, New York, and Europe instead. Post–Civil War farmers were systematically trapped by railroads demanding and receiving all the traffic would bear, by a deliberately contracted money supply, and by a powerful new class (primarily composed of grain elevator owners, eastern and local bankers, railroad owners, and manipulators of commodity markets) that arose to appropriate much of the value of the crops produced in the plains and prairie states. As Fred Shannon writes in his fine study of nineteenth-century American agriculture, "When the farmers of Iowa, Nebraska, or Kansas complained that it took the value of one bushel of corn to pay the freight on another bushel, or when the Minnesota or Dakota

farmers said the same of wheat, often this was no exaggeration and sometimes it was an understatement." In 1869, when the Erie Railroad Ring pocketed twelve million from the Minnesota wheat crop, the farmers received eight million; in 1896, when the price of corn stood at $1 per bushel in New York, farmers in Iowa burned corn rather than coal. The price offered them per bushel was 15¢. By 1900, nearly one-third of American farms were mortgaged and the percentage of sharecroppers and tenants had risen in every area of the country. In the northcentral tier of states, stretching from Kansas through the Dakotas to Minnesota, stood gaping areas of abandoned farm land. Mortgages and foreclosures outnumbered the families that remained.[5]

In the South, although ownership of large estates shifted northward, the brief period of reconstruction did not fundamentally alter the ante-bellum landholding pattern of large plantations, yeoman smallholders, and tenant farmers. Onto this structure, in many areas dramatically changing it, was imposed control and demand for tribute by victorious Northern capital. The South was treated as a conquered territory; credit was granted to landlords and furnishing merchants who would profitably supply the cotton or sugar needed in the North. The result was a new form of bondage, a crop lien system that led to degradation and, in response, to a succession of reform and radical protest movements.

General Sheridan had boasted, after his mission of devastation, that a crow could not fly over the Shenandoah Valley without carrying its own provisions. Sheridan's crow would have had to carry its own money as well. There were neither banks nor virtually any money in broad areas of the South after the Civil War. Confederate currency was worthless, many Southern banks had failed, and the contraction of the money supply—the national circulating supply of $31.18 per capita in 1865 shrank to $20.10 by 1870—had sent shocks through the economy. The nationwide per capita figure, moreover, is misleading unless distribution by area is considered: Massachusetts had five times the national bank circulation of the entire South. The per capita figure for Rhode Island was $77.16; for Arkansas it was thirteen cents.[6] For farmers struggling to survive between crops, or farmers who had mortgaged shortly before the war, the reduced purchasing power, coupled with falling crop prices, made both their debt and payments significantly more than they had bargained for. These economic realities, particularly as they reflected the growing control over the political economy by northeastern capital, begin to reveal why the money question was so crucial during the latter part of the nineteenth century and why the crop lien became so dominant in Southern agrarian life.

The crop lien, aided by the political and legal superstructure erected to enforce it, bound sharecropping farmers to the furnishing merchant differently, but almost as securely, as slaves were bound to the plantation owner before the Civil War. Only infrequently did either slaves or farmers escape. The merchant, typically operating on money borrowed at eighteen to twenty percent interest from northeastern lenders, furnished whatever seed, implements, fertilizer, and food were absolutely necessary for the sharecropping family. As collateral, the merchant held title to the crop. He had as well legal guarantee that the cropper could not buy supplies or sell his crop elsewhere. Either could bring a sheriff's attachment and sale of the crop, the costs of the procedure borne by the sharecropper. Only rarely did money change hands between the merchant and the cropper. The prices of supplies were not marked, nor were they sold. Instead they were "furnished," commonly at credit rates of 50 to 200 percent.

Cotton was king before the Civil War, and after the conflict its production intensified. A dependable cash market for it existed; unlike corn, for example, it was not perishable and the farming family could not eat it. Unless the furnishing merchant was dissatisfied with the sharecropper and his "force"—not merely the mule power, but the age, number, and health of the farmer's wife and children—inevitably, at final settling time, the "value" of the cotton amounted to less than the "indebtedness." If the merchant was dissatisfied with the rate of profit on his investment, the family was simply "turned out" to fare for itself somehow, and an-

other indigent family installed. This cycle of bondage, enmeshing millions of black and white farming families, was replicated throughout the South for decades. By the 1890s the crop lien governed three-quarters of all Southern cotton field workers. By 1900 white sharecroppers outnumbered blacks, and the crop lien system swept into the Southwest, into eastern Texas, Oklahoma, and southeastern Missouri. The accompanying rise of tenancy in the South and Southwest—20 to 30 percent during 1870–1880, 50 percent by 1920, testifies clearly, if unemotionally, to the loss of smallholder land. The rising tenancy figures do not, however, include the millions of indebted farmers who somehow managed to hold onto their land titles, but whose material existence barely differed from the day-to-day realities of landless renters. The crop lien system, more than any other factor, created a two-class structure in much of the rural South and Southwest. Desperately impoverished, the bulk of Jefferson's indebted yeomen were part of an underclass that included tenants, sharecroppers, and migrant farm workers. On the edge of tenant farming themselves, Southern and southwestern smallholders composed the most radical element of populist and socialist insurgent movements.

Unlike the People's party, whose very beginnings were forged from agrarian conditions, the Socialist party at the national level initially gave little attention to farmers' concerns. Instead of recognizing the radicalizing effects of populism on hundreds of thousands of farmers and renters, mechanically doctrinaire notions on the part of largely eastern Socialist leaders about "the idiocy of rural life" led to a provincial misunderstanding of agrarian radicalism and the politicized awareness that so commonly arose from it. The land question was additionally entangled for Socialists by a factional demand from the inner-party left for collectivized farming. During national conventions in 1901 and 1904 the party was unable to do more than debate and recognize the need for an agricultural program. In 1908 the party passed a left-sponsored resolution demanding the immediate nationalization of all land. Not until 1912, in response to farmers' programs developed by socialists in Oklahoma, Texas, and the Dakotas, was the party able to agree on an agrarian policy. Faced with a chain of inequities—exploitation of farmers and renters, widespread impoverishment and debasement, children working in the fields rather than in school or at play, severe shortages of food in the cities and "overproduction" on the farms—the *Appeal to Reason* understood the land question earlier and better than the Socialist party.

The debate surrounding the land question was crucially important for Socialists. Looming behind the discussion was the practical issue of how to recruit the mass of rural Americans. Prior to 1912, party organizers principally sought to recruit farmers and tenants around the Socialist position that use and occupancy, with ultimate title residing in the commonwealth, would prove a far stronger entitlement to land than private ownership in a capitalist economy. The spreading recognition that renting was a broken rung on the agricultural ladder proved fertile ground for the Socialist argument; even more effective as evidence were the rising mortgage, foreclosure, and tenancy rates in the United States. Ultimately, however, the Socialist organizing enterprise ran aground on the here and now. As successful as Socialist campaigns were in certain rural areas of the United States, a party exclusively proposing collective ownership and collective farming of land could not realistically hope to win a majority of the agrarian population to its side. Desire for land and distrust toward any state, cooperative or not, was too strong.

The *Appeal to Reason*'s position on the land question anticipated the Socialist party's gradual recognition that its inherited assumptions needed to be modified for American conditions. Wayland and Warren believed unswervingly in the natural, inalienable right to existence as well as the right to the means of that existence without being subject to exploitation and another's profit. The *Appeal* agreed with Marx that the "foundation of the capitalist method of production is to be found in that theft that deprived the masses of their rights to the soil, in the earth, the common heritage of all."[7] Like private ownership in the industrial sphere, private ownership of land led to concentrated holdings of the agricultural means of production and

inequitable use of common resources. Private ownership of land introduced profit and compelled the agricultural laborer to accept less than the value of his production. "As soon as land becomes private property, the landlord demands a share of almost all the produce which the laborer can either raise or collect from it."[8] To the *Appeal*, this dependent, hierarchical relationship between landlord and tenant was a form of slavery. The *Appeal* also used Herbert Spencer's writings to show that private title to land originally arose from violence, fraud, and cunning—the prerogatives of force. There could be no just individual possession of the soil, Spencer argued: the right of all humankind took precedence.

Influenced by its Kansas location and knowledge of rural conditions, the *Appeal* gradually set itself against exclusive demands from the Socialist party left for collective farming and immediate nationalization of all land. Those demands rested on the uninformed assumption that all small farmers were labor-hiring petty capitalists, an assumption the *Appeal* knew to have too little basis in fact to form the basis for party land policy. The *Appeal* supported the concepts of socially-owned farms and a public agricultural service, but not to the exclusion of privately operated farms. The contradiction that some found in this position was a false one: socialist theory required social ownership of socially-operated means of production, not of every enterprise; nor did it deny choice in non-exploitative matters. The *Appeal* argued for the right of individuals and families to operate small farms if they wished. However, the paper's socialist writers doubted that many families would ultimately prefer to farm privately in a cooperative commonwealth. Although access to land in a socialist state would be free, the necessity to buy expensive farm machinery, remain healthy, and work uneconomically long hours on the land would too much replicate old farming conditions under capitalism. To do so, the *Appeal* believed, would make no more sense than for a doctor to buy a hospital to practice in it or for a teacher to buy a school to teach in it. The advantages of cooperation would prove practical and unavoidable. The *Appeal* did not diverge from its socialist use and occupancy principles, wherein ultimate land title resided in the commonwealth. No other position promised the mass of farmers access to the land.

The development of a farm program in Oklahoma and its acceptance in 1912 by the Socialist party provide illuminating measures of the *Appeal*'s influence. During the early years of the socialist movement, before local and regional papers sprang up, the *Appeal* was not only the largest but in many areas the only socialist newspaper. The *Appeal*, consequently, brought the first awareness of socialism and a means of understanding the land question to many thousands of farmers and tenants. That pattern held true in Oklahoma where, for years, the *Appeal* was the voice of the socialist movement. In no other state were socialists better organized than in Oklahoma; into no other state did the *Appeal* put more ongoing commitment. In 1912 Socialists polled 17 per cent of the vote in Oklahoma (42,000 votes, virtually the same number as *Appeal* subscribers in the state); in 1914 the percentage increased to 21 per cent. The paper was an integral organizing tool. The *Appeal* publicized issues and state news, announced and reported socialist encampments, provided socialist speakers' dates, and unified people in their political struggles.

In 1907 Oklahoma led the United States in subscribers to the *Appeal* with 22,000. A year later Oklahoma was also first to have its own state edition of the *Appeal*. Moreover, as James R. Green writes, Oklahoma's grass-roots radicals were commonly members of the *Appeal*'s subscription army. They "organized locals, spoke at schoolhouse meetings, conducted evening educationals, circulated radical literature, and campaigned for Socialist candidates."[9] Socialist organizers in Oklahoma were almost everywhere confronted with poverty and debasement among tenants and smallholders. With the help of analysis and publicity from the *Appeal*, they constructed an agrarian program that emerged organically from actual conditions, a program that remained consistent with use and occupancy principles but called additionally for tax exemptions for small farms, state farm insurance, the expansion of the public domain for tenant use, graduated land taxes to prevent speculative landholding, and state-

sponsored cooperatives.[10] The principles of the Oklahoma Renters' and Farmers' Program were accepted by the Socialist party on the national level and, with variation for regional conditions, they became the model for other states as well. The *Appeal*'s role in the process was crucial. The organizing success and political influence of Socialists in Oklahoma and Texas, aided and then nationally reported in the paper's columns, provided the authority southwestern Socialists needed to resolve inner-party debate in their favor, an essential factor in the Socialist party's development and adoption of agrarian policy. As an agitational paper, the *Appeal* could not have been more influential. Agrarian socialism, like the larger socialist movement itself, would be fractured by federal and local repression during World War I and its Red Scare aftermath. However, before the jailing of Socialist leaders, the widespread destruction of party locals, and the delegitimization of domestic radicalism, the *Appeal* community and agrarian Socialists created an insurgent movement, a party, and a culture that gave hope and practical meaning to their lives.

The *Appeal*'s pages provide not only discussion of the land question but a richly textured picture of life on the land, a picture drawn by staff writers, Socialist organizers, and by farmers themselves. The accounts of their conditions, their anger, sometimes their despair, and their political beliefs reflect the unity between writer and audience that the *Appeal* captured so successfully. The *Appeal* was the voice of the disinherited because in their letters, complaints, hopes, and work together they spoke directly through it.

J. A. Wayland wrote for many audiences during his years at the Appeal, *but his explanations of capitalist dynamics were never more clear than when addressed to tenant farmers and small freeholders.*

See here, my tenant brother, you would quite probably be offended if I should compare you with cattle, but let us logically consider your relationship with the man who owns you and the cattle—the landlord—the lord of the land. He has a piece of land, and from that land he desires to draw a living without work. He begins to make calculations. Fine cattle would be profitable, but cost too much; he figures on a commoner, scrubbier, cheaper kind and find they too will cost more than he has. He must get something still cheaper, cattle that will produce a profit and cost no further investment—and he looks about for tenants. They are not hard to find—and cost nothing. He begins to draw his profit. The tenant stands in the same relation to the lord of the land that cattle do—mere objects of profit. If the landlord ever has means, he figures, according to the soil, which kind of cattle will bring him the greatest net profit—two-legged or four-legged cattle—man or beast. Say, my brother, are you not tired of being, living and working on the same level as a beast for the profit of a useless, idle monster? There can be no profit out of land, except by your consent. Only by law is the right to hold land and force you to rent it given. Why not rise above the cattle level, use your mind some instead of your muscle all, and abolish landlordism by establishing socialism, under which there is no holding land to get rent or profit out of it? Can you rise? Will you read?

July 10, 1897

Marxist theory was usually recast in accessible, American terms by Appeal writers, but Marx was quoted on more than an occasional basis in the paper.

The Planet On Which We Live

"The foundation of the capitalistic method of production is to be found in that theft that deprived the masses of their rights in the soil, in the earth, the common heritage of all."—Karl Marx

"We have seen that the expropriation of the mass of the people from the soil forms the basis of the capitalistic mode of production. That is, private property in land results in an inequitable dis-

tribution of wealth, deprives laborers of access to natural resources and concentrates wealth in the hands of the few."—Karl Marx

January 28, 1899

Many Populist supporters joined the Socialist party after the People's party was defeated by compromise, fusion, and by the Republican party in the 1896 national election. The work of onetime Populist organizers was particularly important to Socialist party growth in areas of the South and Southwest. One of the most experienced figures in the early Alliance movement, from which the People's party developed, was J. F. Willits.

They Will All Be Socialists

In the old days of the Farmers' Alliance movement its best known worker in all the nation was J. F. Willits of this state. On an old letter head of the executive department of the Alliance, and which calls to memory days that were pregnant with possibilities, and on fire with the zeal of a mighty revolution that had come up from the western prairies and the sunny land of Dixie, but now only records broken promises and wrecked hopes, he writes us the following letter:

McLouth, Kansas, Aug. 22, 1903
Dear Comrades:—Inclosed find one dollar. Don't muzzle the press. Every pulsation of its mighty machinery breathes hope and proclaims liberty to the plundered victims of chartered crimes in every capitalist cursed country round the grey old world.

In 1890 I was elected governor of Kansas, but counted out by the ruling party. I lacked but one vote of getting the seat of John J. Ingalls in the United States senate. I was elected lecturer of the National Alliance in '91, and preached the gospel according to the Alliance dispensation, equal rights to all and special privileges to none, in every

Appeal to Reason, October 26, 1895.

state and territory in the Union; met our people in great picnics by the acre; organized state Alliances in Iowa, Washington, Ohio, New York, and New Jersey. I was afterwards elected president of the National Alliance. Designing unprincipled leaders sold the People's party to the Democrats, in the hope of getting a place at the pie counter. The PARTY IS DEAD BEYOND THE POWER OF RESURRECTION, and now to the thousands of brethren I have looked in the face in the past, I want to say, VOTE THE SOCIALIST TICKET AND GET ALL WE HAVE EVER ASKED FOR AND MORE, by the success of the Socialist party.

I have spent my life of 70 years on the farm. It is as good a farm as there is in the land. I do not owe a dollar on it, or a cent to any one, and yet I am one of the fool farmers who believes that Socialism is the only salvation of both the farmers and the wage workers, and that in the class struggle the farmer must perform his full share in the overthrow of capitalism.

J. F. WILLITS
September 12, 1903

Private title to land was challenged by various methods in the Appeal. The paper's readers were instructed and entertained by the following tale.

Ready to Fight for it Again

Snob—"Hello, here, man, what are you doing on my property?"

Tramp—"Jes takin' a rest, boss."

"Well, sir, who gave you permission to come in here?"

"No one, cap'n, what ov it?"

"Why, fellow, I want you to git off of my land immediately."

"How did dis yere land come to be yourn, Colonel?"

"Why, you impudent puppy, my father gave me this piece of property."

"Well, General, where did yer dad get it?"

"My father, sir, got this piece of land from his father."

"And where did yer granddad git it, governor?"

"Sir, my grandfather got this piece of land by fighting for it."

"And did dat make it hisn?"

"Why, certainly it did."

"Well, den, peel yer coat. It's bout time dis piece ov land was bein fit fer agin."

May 7, 1904

Natural rights, human freedom, and non-exploitative social relations were at the foundation of the Appeal's approach to the land question.

Serfs, Wake Up!

J. A. WAYLAND

Every human being has the NATURAL RIGHT to work, to use as much of the earth, air and water as necessary to produce, and to pay no man for the use of them. No being has any right to profit off any other human being. Such profit is slavery. Slavery consists solely in one being used for the pleasure or profit of another. Chattel slavery was one set of beings working for the pleasure and profit of the master, receiving only their necessary food and shelter out of their toil. Wage slavery does the same thing. The wage-workers are employed for the pleasure or profit of the master class, receiving in wages only enough to feed and shelter them, the surplus above this going to the masters. Serfdom was a condition in which the serfs worked for the feudal lord two or three days in each week, and the balance of the time they had all the land they could use, and paid no other kind of profit or taxes. Land tenantry today takes from

SENATOR TILLMAN'S ALLEGORICAL COW.

This cartoon, designed by Senator Tillman, shows his idea of the present American situation. The cow, symbolical of natural resources, is feeding on the farmers out west, while her golden milk is all drawn by the gentlemen of ability in Wall street.

Appeal to Reason, March 14, 1896.

HIS GUARDIAN ANGELS.

Under our present social condition the farmer is stricken down, and he is food for carrion birds. Brother are you doing your duty to save your neighbor?

Appeal to Reason, January 18, 1896.

the workers one-third or one-half the crop—just the same as serfdom, but puts an additional burden on them of taxes, and a profit is taken out of what remains on everything they buy. The present land system in this country today is worse to that extent than was the serfdom of the Middle Ages. As the serfs then raised up under that system were unable to see the robbery they suffered, and were mostly satisfied, so you, tenants of today, raised up under the private ownership of the soil, pay your rent, or serfage, and do not see the wrong under which you live. Because you have always seen land bought and sold, and rent paid for it, you have never thought that there was anything wrong with such a system that takes from you half of your products, and gives it over to those who have cunningly got hold of the land. Private ownership of land is a crime, and the landless, who are in a majority, should use their ballots to elect men to office who will change it, that every child, when it grows up, will have the use of land, without paying other human beings for what God made a free gift to man. If each has all the land he or she can use, what would they want with more, except to deny others the right to use the earth, that they may levy tribute on them? Wake up.

March 21, 1903

Quoting capitalism's best-known political philosophers, Adam Smith and Herbert Spencer, for socialist purposes was a subversive twist of readers' expectations. This strategy was not uncommon in the Appeal.

Labor's Just Reward and Why He Does Not Get It

Fred D. Warren

"The produce of labor constitutes the natural recompense or wages of labor. In that original state of things which preceded both the appropriation

of land and the accumulation of stock, the whole produce of labor belonged to the laborer. He had neither landlord nor master to share with him. Had this state continued, the wages of labor would have augmented with all those improvements in its productive powers to which division of labor gives occasion. All things would have become gradually cheaper. They would have been produced by a smaller quantity of labor; and as the commodities produced by equal quantities of labor would naturally in this state of things be exchanged for one another, they would have been purchased likewise with the produce of a smaller quantity. . . . But this original state of things, in which the laborer enjoyed the whole produce of his own labor, could not last beyond the first introduction of the appropriation of land and the accumulation of stock (capital). . . . As soon as land becomes private property, the landlord demands a share of almost all the produce which the laborer can either raise or collect from it. His rent makes the first deduction from the produce of the labor employed upon lands. . . . It seldom happens that the person who tills the ground has wherewithal to maintain himself till he reaps the harvest. His maintenance is generally advanced to him from the stock of a master, the farmer who employs him, and who would have no interest to employ him unless he was to share in the produce of his labor, or unless his stock was to be replaced to him with a profit. This profit makes a second deduction from the produce of the labor employed upon the land. The produce of almost all other kinds of labor is liable to the like deduction of profit. In all arts and manufactures the greater part of the workmen stand in need of a master to advance them the materials of their work, and their wages and maintenance till it be completed. He shares the produce of their labor, or in the value which it adds to the materials upon which it is bestowed, and in this consists his profit."

These are the words of Adam Smith, a political economist who wrote one hundred and twenty-five years ago. Now, note: "In the original state of things, the laborer enjoyed the full produce of his own hands." He had not yet arrived at that stage of civilization where he would meekly give up to a landlord or master a portion of what he garnered from the earth. I can imagine my paternal ancestor some thousands of years ago taking a swat at the man who would have the nerve to demand a portion of the crop which he, with his own hands, aided by the resources of nature had laid by to supply himself and family until next harvest. Had the other fellow insisted on taking a portion no doubt there would have been some tall scrapping. But in the original state of things, there was probably little of this sort of thing done, because it was easier to gather directly from nature's resources. Men lived in groups in those olden days and the collective product was more than sufficient to supply the simple needs of all the members of that group.

But there came a time when all this was changed. With the introduction of private ownership in land came that period in the history of the human race when some man by reason of his superior strength or cunning, or some group of men, by reason of greater numbers, took possession of the land being used by another group and made slaves of the latter. Discussing this question of when and how titles to land passed to the individual, Herbert Spencer, the English political economist made the following observations on the origin of title deeds, which so aroused the English aristocracy that it was suppressed, and the ruling class refused permission to circulate it among the outraged subjects of the British Isles:

"Passing from the consideration of the possible to that of the actual, we find yet further reason to deny the rectitude of property in land. It can never be pretended that the existing titles to such property are legitimate. Should any one think so, let him look in the chronicles. Violence, fraud, the prerogative of force, the claims of superior cunning—these are the sources to which those titles may be traced. The original deeds were written with the sword, rather than with the pen; not law-

yers, but soldiers, were the conveyancers; blows were the current coin given in payment; and for seals blood was used in preference to wax. Could valid claims be thus constituted? Hardly. And if not, what becomes of the pretensions of all subsequent holders of estates so obtained? Does sale or bequest generate a right where it did not previously exist? Would the original claimants be nonsuited at the bar of reason because the thing stolen from them changed hands? Certainly not. And if one act of transfer can give no title, can many? No; though nothing be multiplied forever, it will not produce ONE. Even the law recognizes this principle. An existing holder must, if called upon, substantiate the claims of those from whom he purchased or inherited his property, and any flaw in the original parchment, even though the property should have had a force of intermediate owners, quashes his rights.

" 'But time,' say some, 'is a great legalizer. Immemorial possession must be taken to constitute a legitimate claim. That which has been held from age to age as private property, and has been bought and sold as such, must now be considered as irrevocably belonging to individuals.' To which proposition a willing assent shall be given when its propounders can assign it a definite meaning. To do this, however, they must find satisfactory answers to such questions as, How long does it take for what was originally a WRONG to grow into a RIGHT? At what rate per annum do invalid claims become valid? If a title gets perfect in a thousand years how much more perfect will it be in two thousand years? And so forth. For the solution of which they will require a new calculus.

"Whether it may be expected to admit claims of a certain standing, is not the point. We have here nothing to do with considerations of conventional privilege or legislative convenience. We have simply to inquire what is the verdict given by pure equity in the matter. As this verdict enjoins a protest against every existing pretension to the individual possession of the soil; and dictates the assertion that the right of mankind at large to the

Appeal to Reason, September 5, 1903.

earth's surface is still valid, all deeds, customs and laws notwithstanding.

"Not only have present land tenures an indefensible origin, but it is impossible to discover any mode in which land CAN become private property."

It should be borne in mind, that while both Smith and Spencer wrote as quoted they believed in the prevailing social order which we today know as the capitalist system. These writers were simply telling the story of progress of the race from primitive man to the present. Little heed was given to their words by their contemporaries. A hundred years ago when Smith wrote and fifty years ago when Spencer wrote, there were still continents where land was plenty and it only required the transfer of one's person to America, Australia or Africa to at once become a landlord in your own right.

Today the available land for farming purposes is so meagre that we witness the spectacle of 100,000 persons in a frantic scramble for 2,500 small plots of ground, as occurred at the opening of the Rosebud Indian reservation in South Dakota last month.

If men understood that the land is one of the great natural resources on which life depends, that it is the natural heritage of all men, and not a few, and it was so recognized through the long ages of savagery and barbarism, and that no title deed was recognized until civilization, so-called, made its appearance, I believe few would be willing to submit longer to the tyranny of the landlord and the master.

But the landlord, once the dominant factor in the work of exploitation, has been in a very large measure superseded by the captain of industry. Not only is the land controlled and owned, but, also the machinery of production   the tools by means of which men transfer the simple products of nature into articles of use—is privately owned and used as means of exploitation.

But, back of it, we see that the modern system

of forcing the greater part of the result of human labor into the coffers of the idle rich, had its origin and beginning with the writing of the first title deed to land in the blood of the captive. . . .

August 13, 1904

The Socialist party's most respected authority on the land question was Algie Simons, author of The American Farmer *and* Social Forces in American History. *Simons's conceptually powered economic history is well represented in the following article.*

The Children of the Farm and the Farmer

A. M. SIMONS

When Uncle Sam first counted up his children in 1790, he found that about ninety-seven per cent of them lived in the country. By 1900 more than half of them had moved to town, and more were going every day.

Did you ever see a magnet thrust into a plate of iron filings? All the tiny particles leap up into piles around the magnet. Each one attracts the one next to it. Even those too distant to touch the magnet directly turn toward it, ready to leap in its direction at the first jar.

Our society is today like that plate of iron filings, with the city playing the part of the magnet. The faces of all are turned toward it. The millions that have gone on before draw their friends after them. Great heaps of human atoms are piled up here and there.

Why does this great migration go on? What is the magnetic force that is drawing these multitudes from the farm to the city?

It is not because the city offers a pleasanter place in which to live. Smoke is not so refreshing to the lungs as pure air. The crowded tenement and the narrow alley, or the paved street are a poor exchange for the old farm house and the broad, shady highway. To be sure, there are museums, libraries, theaters, lectures, grand balls and beautiful palaces for those who have wealth and leisure. But such things are not yet for those who do the work of the world, either on the farm or in the city.

Nevertheless, these great, congested spots on the social body continue to fester and spread, and to carry the infection to ever greater multitudes of the healthy country corpuscles.

What is the motive power, then, that sets this great army in motion and causes it to grow larger each year?

THESE PEOPLE GO TO THE CITY BECAUSE THEIR WORK WENT ON BEFORE THEM.

When ninety-seven per cent of the population lived in the country it was because nearly all the work of the world was done upon the farm. They lived there to do that work. Most of the city industries of today then lived on the farm.

Carding, spinning and weaving were as much a part of agriculture as raising sheep or planting cotton. Meat was prepared for the kitchen by the same hands that cared for the animal. The report of the first census tells us that certain "doubtful articles" were excluded from the statistics of manufacture, which "from their very nature were nearly allied to agriculture, including cotton pressing, flour and meal, grain and saw-mills, barrels for packing, malt, pot and pearl ashes, maple and cane sugar, molasses, rosin, pitch, slates, bricks, tiles, saltpetre, indigo, red and yellow ochre, hemp and hemp mills, fisheries, wine, ground plaster, etc." How many farmers of today recognize even the names of all these early children of agriculture, so long has it been since they left the old homestead? Some, about whose inclusion with agriculture there was not even a question at that time, have since left the farm. Cheese-making was first classified as a manufacturing industry by the census of 1870, while butter did not follow its elder brother until ten years later, and cotton-ginning was only classified apart from agriculture in 1900.

Agriculture is the great ancestral trunk from which all other industries are descended. It is the parent of all our modern industries, although many of its children have wandered far away. While young and small these children stayed close to their parent. As they grew older and stronger they left the farm and wended their way to the city. The spindle and the loom, the flour mill and cheese press, the dye vat, soap kettle, slaughter-house, and even the churn, have gone to the city, or are on their way there. But however far they have gone, or however great the changes through which they have passed, they are none the less the children of agriculture.

When agriculture itself was thus going piecemeal to town the farmer was compelled to follow.

THE CHILDREN OF THE FARMER WERE FORCED TO FOLLOW THE CHILDREN OF THE FARM.

They could do nothing else. Their work had gone on before them. Since the world began man has ever been forced to follow whithersoever his work might call him.

Like many a man and woman, these industrial children of agriculture changed greatly in appearance and habits when they took up city life. The plain, simple tools of the farm became strange, complex machines, glittering with paint and polish. Their slow pace was quickened. They were herded together in great prison-like buildings called factories. They turned night into day and whirled on with feverish speed for a few years. Then they were worn out and thrown upon the scrap-pile to rust away.

Following the tools came the workers. After these industrial children of agriculture came the farmers' boys and girls. They, too, underwent a great transformation in changing their residence. They, like the machines, are herded in prison-like barracks. They wear shoddy, eat poisonous adulterations, and work day and night until worn out and flung aside to die. Worse still, the machines produce so much and men receive so little for tending them that there are more workers than work. A great host of the children and grand-

If having to work 3 days a week for the **Feudal Lord** was **Serfdom**, what is **giving half your crop for land rent ?**

OVER A
Quarter Million Circulation
WEEKLY.

No. 376 ...

This is Number 375.   *25 Cents a Year.*

Appeal to Reason.

Published Every Saturday.

OWNERSHIP of the EARTH
By ALL the People, and Not by Part of the People.

J. A. Wayland.

Girard, Kansas, U. S. A., February 7, 1903.

IT WAS JUST A PIECE OF PAPER CUT FROM THE APPEAL, WHICH BORE A NAME. IT WAS not unlike hundreds of others which I have handled in the past two months, and yet there was something about it that called into action that subtle power of instinct which warned me that I was confronting something unusual. And I was. The name was not uncommon, but the state was Georgia, where the Appeal is just beginning to grow, and the person is the sole subscriber in the town of Trenton. Not a word of comment accompanied the pledge. It was eloquent in its silent expression. Something had stirred this comrade's mind and aroused his nature to action, and he has pledged himself to send 260 subscribers to this paper during the next twelve months. I turned from the paper before me and went through our subscription books, and found over FIFTEEN THOUSAND NAMES OF PERSONS WHO ARE THE SOLE SUBSCRIBERS AT THEIR RESPECTIVE POSTOFFICES. I stopped and pondered long, and this is what I thought: HOW CAN I AROUSE THIS HOST OF MEN AND WOMEN TO ACTION? Comrades, we are living in a time of distress as dire as a Famine in India. Men, women and innocent children are freezing at our very door; thousands of poor humanity are enduring a living hell in every city. Distress and suffering are beyond all human description, and this while granaries are bursting with plenty, and the earth is rich with fuel. The barons of capitalism eat of the fat of the land, banquet their dogs, cats and monkeys and protect them from the cold, while humanity shivers and starves. We give our law makers $5,000 per year to make laws for capitalists, and we shiver over an empty grate. We give Rockefellar $50,000,000 a year, while the light in our humble cottage goes out. We even pay one of our labor leaders a luxurious salary, while we accept a pittance. And yet we are the cause of it all. We are paying the price of our ignorance, and ignorant slaves we will ever be until we LEARN HOW TO BE FREE. The working-class will be slaves until they arise in their power as a united class and by the power of the might of ballots overthrow the capitalist system, and take control of the capital their united labor has created. IGNORANCE has no CONQUEROR but TRUTH. Truth will never come to the masses until it is uttered in words that shock and startle by their intensity and boldness. In my mind's eye I can see you when you scan these pages---in my subtler senses I can feel the intensity with which you read these lines. I know that I address a MULTITUDE, but ever is there an unsatisfied feeling in my mind. I think of the millions of men and women crushed by this accursed system who do not read these pages and who are ignorant of the means of their salvation. I AM GRASPING FOR THE UNCONVERTED. This is why I am driving YOU out for subscribers. THIS IS WHY I CANNOT LET YOU REST. Beset with enemies on all sides, defamed by the same kind of high priests who cried to the multitude to crucify Jesus, and labor betrayed by many false leaders, who are seduced by the hellish dollar of the capitalist, the Socialist party stands as the sole defender of the suffering people. We boldly come not to mend, but to END this strife in order to end strife. We in order to destroy all class destinc-hood forever. The working class is declare our intention. We have system. We must ENGENDER must array CLASS against CLASS tions, and make humanity a brother-under the hypnotic spell of capitalist

Volunteer No.
(Do not use above space.)
J. A. Wayland, Editor Appeal to Reason, Girard, Kansas:
Comrade:—You may enter my name on the roll of Five Thousand for the
"Twelve Months' Campaign" for a Million Circulation.

Masthead, *Appeal to Reason*, February 7, 1903.

children of the farmers are drafted into that most desperate of all armies, the army of the unemployed, whose death rate is far higher than that of any body that ever followed the flag of militarism.

While tool and worker were both changing, the relation between these two became transformed. On the farm the connection between the tool and the man was simple and direct. The tools belonged to the worker and he kept what he made. The producer owned the means of production and the product. But when the farmer's child reached the city he found that the tool which he had followed now belonged to someone else, and could be used only after the user had agreed to give up to this new owner all the product save a bare living.

Nor is the relation between the farmer and these city-dwelling descendants of the farm less significant. When these industries left for the city they did not lose connection with the farm or the farmer.

Weaving, spinning, grinding, slaughtering, transporting, storing, once but mere babes at the knee of agriculture, now have grown to such giant proportions that they threaten the existence of their parent. Large as they are, and loudly as they swagger, they still consider that they have a "vested right" to "live on the old man."

Perhaps we can understand this if we take as an illustration the industry of transportation. When the Declaration of Independence had just been written (and while it was still supposed to mean what it says) the farmers' crops were carried to market in the old lumber wagon, drawn by oxen, mules or horses.

When the farmer of today wishes to send his wheat to the far-off market he finds that the old farm wagon has changed into a long line of fifty-ton pressed steel freight cars, hitched to a great Mogul locomotive, which will move more grain in a minute than the old methods could transport in a year. The farmer's son may still drive the new steed, but, nevertheless, there has been a great change in the social relations of the farmer to his means of transportation.

While the farmer or his son owned the old farm wagon and the team, NEITHER father nor son own the railroads. Yet the farmer still supplies the load, and the son drives the rig as they always have done. The OWNERSHIP of the tools have somehow got out of the family, while the WORK still remains.

A new social class has entered upon the scene, which seems to have nothing to do but own something that all the rest of the world must use. It looks very much as if some confidence men must have met the team and wagon, loom and spindle, cheesepress, soap-kettle, blacksmith shop and slaughter-house on their way to town, and, while they were still somewhat green as to city tricks, become possessed of these tools of society. By the time the farmers' sons and daughters came along in pursuit of the tools these confidence men had changed the names and altered the appearance of them so that the original owners, being also somewhat new to city ways, were unable to prove their property. These new owners pointed out that the old simple tools of the farm had now become an aristocratic something called "CAPITAL," and that all "Capital" belonged to a new social class, whose members had been named after the thing they owned, and were called "CAPITALISTS."

These new machines made it possible for the workers to produce from five to a thousand times as much as they could have produced with the old simple tools. The workers cannot live unless they can get a chance to use these new tools called "Capital." But the capitalists will not let the workers use these tools unless they agree to give up to the owners, the capitalists, all above the living wage that was produced with the old crude implements back on the farm. Consequently, it was not long until the capitalists began to get possession of everything the rest of the family produced. "They toiled not, neither did they spin," but just held fast to their title to the machines while the farmer and his sons did the work.

Steadily more and more of the wealth of the world came into the hands of the capitalists. During the last few years, there being almost nothing that this class did not already own, its members have turned upon each other in a cannibal-like fight, until at the present time less than ten per cent of the population, and this the most idle, useless portion, owns more than half of all the wealth in the country.

We can get some idea of how much the very biggest of the capitalists have got when we remember that the total wealth of the United States in 1860 was valued at only a little over $16,000,000,000, and that the trusts now own over twenty-five billion dollars' worth of wealth, and that less than twenty men are able to control this whole vast sum. In other words, if a few of our trust magnates (less than could crowd into even an ordinary workingman's home) had been alive at the beginning of the Civil war, with the same amount of money that they now possess, they could have bought all that lay between the Atlantic and the Pacific, between the Canadian border and the Gulf of Mexico—all the cities, with all the stores and factories, mills, mines and railroads, all the chattel slaves of the South, and the cotton fields in which they toiled; all the farms, and horses, cattle, sheep and hogs of the North; paid all the expenses of the four years of fighting, and still had enough small change left to purchase a half dozen European nations to take home to their children.

The command of these vast sums of money enabled the capitalists to secure control of the government in all its branches. Then their legislatures made laws, their courts interpreted them, and their mayors, governers and presidents enforced them, saying that all things done by the capitalists were right. Then the newspapers were bought, colleges endowed, churches, libraries and missionary societies given large donations, until "public opinion" gave its approval to this whole state of affairs.

When the farmer wishes to use the railroad to ship his products to market he is charged "what the traffic will bear," until the fruit for which his children and grandchildren in the city are dying rots in the old home orchard. When he wishes to convert his live-stock into meat, he finds that the Meat Trust, that owns the machines for transporting, slaughtering and preparing the meat, will only pay him enough to barely keep body and soul together, while the price of meat to the children in the city climbs ever higher and higher.

At different times in the past the farmer has grown indignant, and organized Alliances, Wheels, Granges, etc., with the purpose of doing terrible things to this class of idle owners. Sometimes the farmers have even captured the offices of a few states, and made laws fixing the amounts to be charged for the use of some of the new tools—particularly the railroads and elevators. Again they have enacted legislation designed to "bust the trusts." But the capitalists simply had their supreme court declare the laws illegal, or else ignored them altogether, and the farmers became discouraged.

At any rate it is now too late for the farmers alone to do anything politically. They are in such a hopeless minority that they can never carry an election. At the present time they make up less than forty per cent of the population, and are so scattered, geographically, that they cannot effectively use what political strength they have. It should begin to dawn upon that portion of the family that has remained at home that alone they are helpless to overthrow their exploiters.

The children, who are tending the machines in the factories, are also having battle after battle with the idle owning class. At first they fought only for a little larger share of the tremendous product they were creating. Whenever they refused to work, and sought to better conditions,

soldiers and police shot and clubbed them back into submission. Then they went to the political parties owned by their masters and asked them for better legislation. Sometimes they were laughed at; sometimes the laws were given to them, and then, before their shouts of rejoicing had died away, the supreme court declared the laws unconstitutional. Finally, some of the brightest of the workers began to ask why they should not own the tools with which they worked. They did not see any reason why the great machine that was made and cared for by workers should not be owned by those who made and used it, just as the plain, simple tool from which the machine came had been owned before either tools or men came to town.

They are reaching their hands across the seas to all the sons of all the farmers, all round the world, to organize a political party, whose object is to change the laws so as to return the ownership of the machines and their products to the makers and the users of those machines. But the wage-workers of the city are also too few to accomplish this task unaided. The capitalists recognize this fact and seek to keep the farmer and his wage-working children fighting among themselves. They tell the wage-worker that the farmer is a member of the capitalist class, and wishes to exploit the workers. They tell the farmer that the laborers want to get his farm away from him. All this unmindful of the fact that the farmer could not exploit the laborer, or the laborer run the farm, if he had a chance.

Don't you think it is about time the family got together politically to fight the capitalist who is robbing both? The farmer, fighting the capitalist owner of the instruments by which his crop is transported to market and prepared for use, should join hands with his children, who are fighting with that same capitalist for a chance to use those same tools and get what they produce.

Just because the different processes of industry are scattered all over the country; and just because simple tools have given place to great, complex machines, are no reasons why a class of idle owners should be permitted to live upon the labor of those who made and use the things with which wealth is produced and consumed.

All the processes of production were once a part of agriculture. All the work has always been done by the farmer and his descendants.

The family is now so scattered, and the processes of production so divided, and the machinery so complicated, that it is no longer possible to restore all the old conditions of ownership, and let each member of the family own some one individual link in the chain of production.

THE WHOLE PROCESS, WITH ALL THE TOOLS AND RAW MATERIAL, MUST BELONG TO THE WHOLE RE-UNITED CO-OPERATIVE FAMILY.

This family, as a whole, must own the farm and the factory, the mill and the mine, the railroad, store, slaughter-house and elevator. All will co-operate in doing the work, all will unite in the ownership, all will share in the product.

Whenever the family gets together politically they can accomplish this. The overwhelming majority which their combined numbers will give them assures victory. Victory at the polls will enable them to restore the tools and the product to the farmer and his children. It will unite the industrial and social family.

THAT WOULD BE SOCIALISM.

September 30, 1905

Many personal accounts of conditions on the farm appeared in the Appeal. *For many renting families, the cycle of poverty produced apathy and defeated despair. In other families, however, privation created political awareness and barely controlled rage.*

The Independent Farmer

H. D. CALWALER, ADAIR, ILL.

Editor *Appeal*: A sample copy of your paper fell into my hands recently. I would like to subscribe,

but haven't the 50 cents. I am a renter with a family of six. The small renter is worse off than the factory hand. Here is my last year's statement:

Rent of 40 acres at $6.25	$250.00
Seed oats for 38 acres at 30¢	.34.20
Binder to cut oats at 60¢ per acre	.22.80
114 lbs. twine to tie same at 12 1/2¢	.14.25
Threshing 1,463 bu. oats at 2¢	.29.26
Boarding 20 men two meals at 10¢	.4.00
Clothing for six one year	.60.00
Six pair of shoes at $1.50	.9.00
15 sacks of flour at $1.25	.18.75
10 pounds of coffee at 15¢	.1.50
1 pound of tea	.30
50 pounds of sugar	.2.50
2 brooms	.50
Fuel	.12.18
Doctor for setting boy's arm	.12.00
Total	.$471.24
Credit 1,463 bushel oats at 25¢	−365.75
Deficit	$105.49

Thus you will see that after giving the landlord all the crop my wife must sell chickens, eggs, butter and I must go out and work by the day to make up the difference.

How much longer is this condition to exist? Do the parasites expect us to bear this forever? Do they never feel the rumbling that must come up in our hearts at the injustice, the slavery, the despotism of it? Do they think they can always live on the best while we perish miserably in poverty and hopelessness? I often feel that it would be better to die as are the Russians in an effort to better conditions than to die miserably piecemeal, year in and year out.

January 27, 1906

In 1908 the Appeal *asked farm readers why they voted the Socialist ticket. These replies, written by farmers who distributed extra copies of the paper, typify the responses.*

The Farmer Division of the Appeal Army

"My reason for voting the Socialist ticket is because I want my wife and daughters to be free from bondage so they can have a vote in making the laws under which they have to live. It is the best policy I have ever read or heard of." Luke Fugate, Madisonville, Ky.

"You ask me, as a farmer, why I voted the Socialist ticket. I voted the Socialist ticket because I am a laboring man, and it seems to me that every intelligent thinking laboring man could very plainly see that the Democratic or Republican parties never have or will do anything in favor of the farmer or laboring man only to screw them down a little tighter in favor of the money sharks." R. Loomis, Anna, Mo.

"At your request, I will give my reasons for voting the Socialist ticket this fall. I am a farmer. Two years ago I was a Republican. I learned by reading the government's reports fifty years prior to 1904 that the working people of the United States owned 67 per cent of the wealth of the United States, and that in 1904 they owned only 10 per cent. I figured from this that in less than 50 years from 1904, under the present form of government unmolested, the working man would not own anything. A reform of government being our only hope from capitalistic slavery, I joined the Socialist party heart and soul." W. H. Nichols, Boswell, Okla.

"In answer to your ad to farmers asking them to write and give their reasons for voting the Socialist ticket this fall, I voted for Grover Cleveland when he was elected the first time and I have not voted in the presidential election since till this fall. I quit voting because I could get no good of my vote. I may be a slave all my life, but I will not cast my vote to keep on being one. I voted for Debs because I have read and thought and find that Socialism under your platform is all the way for poor people to break their bondage. I think if every workingman will stop and think he will see like I do." John Tyler, Weleetka, Okla.

"I was reared a Democrat, voted twice for Bryan and once for Parker and at the last election I voted for Eugene V. Debs. I am 34 years old, and up to a year and a half ago, I had never read a Socialist paper of any kind. I have been reading the *Appeal* that long, and will give the paper credit for my conversion. It is the only party for the working class, guarantees equal opportunity for all men, women as well." Harry Stephens, Montague, Mo.

"Of all the slaves with their different trades and occupations, we farmers feel and know that we are the worst oppressed; that we are compelled by sheer want to labor longer hours each day and receive less in return for the same than our other brothers who have a trade and are working for wages. Our wives, our sweethearts and our mothers and little daughters are forced to work in the fields day after day, year in and year out, in order that we may find a landlord who will rent us land to tend the coming year. We have organized and have stored and held our cotton for a minimum price, only to see the price go steadily down until we were forced to sell. Brother farmer and comrade, the foregoing are facts and you know it. By and through Socialism and the ballot box we will appropriate all our labor creates enabling us to own and beautify our home as well as our lives and that is why I have voted the Socialist ticket in the recent election." Clarence E. Broom, Manitou, Okla.

"Although my post office is in Randolph county, I live in Webster, and I have to travel eight miles through the rocky fastnesses of the Allegheny mountains to get to my voting place. Being quite a distance from home, teaching school, in 1904, I had to travel, mostly on foot, a distance of twenty-six, and this year sixteen miles, in order to get to vote for Debs and Hanford; but each time when 'The official vote of Webster county' was published in our county paper it appeared that no one had been voted for for president except the two old party candidates. Several of my immediate neighbors, in whom I repose the utmost confidence, informed me that they voted the prohibition ticket; but their votes, like my own, were 'not accounted worthy' to appear in 'The Official Vote!' While this is certainly discouraging, I shall, if I live that long, vote the national Socialist ticket again in four years from now! In the meantime I certainly shall try to ascertain 'the reason why' my vote was not counted, or rather not recorded, this time!" W. E. Ashburn, Pickens, W. Va.

"Complying with your request in the issue of December 5th, will state why I became a Socialist. I was born a Republican and accepted the dope until three years ago, when a friend persuaded me to investigate the Socialist philosophy. I began by subscribing for the *Appeal to Reason*. That the farmer and his city cousin were both getting it in the neck was much in evidence, and not consistent with a square deal, considering the number of multi-millionaires we were turning out. This we know—that labor creates all wealth. But what we did not know was the process by which those who did not labor managed to get control of the wealth the laborer had created but did not get. Well in my case it was this way. After reading the *Appeal to Reason* for about a year in connection with other Socialist literature it oozed into my know that the solution of the economic problem was based on the class struggle, whereupon, I capitulated to that evil thing so undesirable to the welfare of knaves and became a class-conscious Socialist." Earl A. Parrett, North Manchester, Ind.

December 26, 1908

The Appeal *was repeatedly asked if farmers were capitalists. The paper's position in 1909 follows.*

Are Land Owners Capitalists?

Please tell me whether a land owner is a capitalist. I maintain that land is a means of production and that the owner thereof is a capitalist. My friend is of the opinion that the man who owns land is a farmer who works hard and gets little for the products of his labor, and is therefore not a capitalist.

R. J. B. S., *Omaha, Neb.*

A land owner may or may not be a capitalist. Whether he is or is not a capitalist depends not on his ownership of land or other forms of property, but on the use he makes of such things.

Mere ownership of the means of production does not make the owner a capitalist. If that were true the carpenter who owns the hammer with which he labors and the Indian who owns his bow and arrow would be capitalists. It is equally untrue that the man who owns land is a farmer. There are many land owners who are not farmers in any sense of the term, and there are others who are farmers by proxy—who do not farm the soil but rather farm the real farmer.

A capitalist need not necessarily own any land or any property. He may rent the one or borrow the other. The essential act which makes the capitalist is his activity in the use of land, or wealth of any description as a means of exploiting labor.

The man who engages in commerce, industry, speculation or any other of the common means by which he acquires values produced by others without rendering an equivalent is a capitalist. The wealth he uses in the process of such accumulation is capital whether it consists of land, money, pig-iron or saw-dust.

The man who owns only so much land as he can till by means of his own labor and who actually cultivates that land without hired help is essentially a non-capitalist. He may at some time participate in an advanced value given to his land by society, and that interest identifies him slightly with the capitalist element; but that is of comparatively too little consequence to consider when it is remembered that practically all his income is the product of his own labor.

But were a farmer to own land which he would not farm but would rent it or hold it purely for speculative purposes he would become because of the use made of his land a capitalist in the full sense of the term. Such a man is an exploiter the same in principle, though possibly not to the same degree as the owner of a factory or railroad.

There was a time when many farmers hired help and operated their farms on a wage basis, but in recent years conditions have so changed that many can no longer afford to hire help. The effect of this is significant in the fact that it has transformed them from capitalists into exploited laborers without even taking their farms away from them.

January 16, 1909

"Independent" farmers were often lectured by Appeal writers about the benefits of publicly owned and controlled institutions of exchange.

That Old Coffee Pot

You sell your wheat at $1 per bushel and go to the store and get four pounds of coffee for the dollar. The four pounds of coffee costs the importer, jobber and retailer only about 30 to 40 cents. So you see how much you *really* get for your wheat—about forty cents a bushel. When the wheat is sold to the slaves in South America they give twenty pounds of coffee for it. Now if the public owned the business of exchange you would get as much coffee for a bushel of wheat as the coffee workers pay for it, less the necessary cost of delivering it to you. In that way you would get the present equivalent of $2.50 a bushel for your wheat when exchanging it for coffee. And this would be true on

an average with all other things. The farmers are the most skinned class on earth—and they think they are prosperous! It is out of the difference between the amount of coffee the farmer gets for a bushel of wheat and the amount of wheat the coffee workers get for a hundred-weight of coffee, that the palaces of the rich are built. This is true of *all* commodities. Can you not see why the men who skin you do not want the public to own and operate the industries? Isn't it plain why they warn you against the paternalism of government? Why are you so stupid? Socialism will give you the *full* products of your labor—that is, it will give you as much sugar, coffee or other products for your products as others pay for your products. Get that through your skull bones.

April 23, 1910

The Appeal's answer to what would happen to large land owners and their acreage in a socialist America was part of an ongoing debate in the Socialist party.

Landlords Under Socialism

What will become, under Socialism, of the men who own thousands of acres of land, which is more than they can use themselves?—Georgia.

They will be unable to get hired help to farm this land, for the reason that those who have hitherto hired out can then work for the public and get their full product. They will not be able to rent the land, for the reason that there will be public land which can be had under more favorable terms. They will not be able to sell the land at an advance over what they paid, for the reason that men will then be able to use land without buying it. As they can make nothing out of any except what they can use, it will be worse than a bad investment, it will be an expense, and they will let the land go back to the public as being preferable. At the same time, the removal of the speculative title to their land, which will be voluntarily surrendered when the possibility of speculation is at an end, will not in the least invalidate the use title, but rather make it stronger than it is now. What they can use themselves will be secure to them.

January 21, 1911

For J. E. Nash, who often sent poetry to the Appeal, *explaining capitalism and capitalist consciousness to farm readers was easy work.*

The Farmer and Financier

J. E. Nash

A financier drove out to see
A farmer, who professed that he,
   (Although his farm was rented),
Had found the surest means to take,
And own the wealth which others make,
   Yet keep his dupes contented.

The farmer proudly led him out,
To see his oxen strong and stout,
   His pride and greatest treasure;
They came, almost before he spoke,
And placed their necks beneath the yoke,
   Apparently with pleasure.

"What makes them come?" the other said,
"With nothing but a nubbin fed;
   Indeed, I don't see through it."
The farmer smiled, and said, said he,
"I broke them in as calves; you see;
   They're educated to it."

"They do my will, my word obey,
Without reward, not even hay,
   Although I let them pass
An hour at noon and all the night

Down in the pasture, out of sight,
   A hunting 'round for grass."

Thus spake the financier then.
"You deal with cattle, I with men,
   Whose toil has greater worth,
Financially, I reign a king,
Invest in nearly everything,
   Some day I'll own the earth."

"Men come to me in sorest need:
They beg for work; implore and plead;
   If I a job assign,
The highest wage I ever give,
Is fixed by what it costs to live,
   The product, sir, is mine."

"Your nubbin represents the wage
For which the working class engage,
   To live so mean and humble;
And grind out profits, don't you see,
That comes to me, yes, comes to me,
   What cause have I to grumble?"

"I serve the farmer much the same,
Ha! Ha! But they are easy game,
   And think they're independent,
I set the price and profit well
On all they buy; on all they sell
   And roll in wealth resplendent."

"And price or wage, which e'er it be,
The system soon returns to me
   In interest, profit, rent.
Yet, all the same my victims cheer
And shout with joy when I appear,
   So well are they content."

The farmer asks: "What makes them toil,
For you to plunder, rob and spoil?
   Gee whiz! It beats the nation."
"Ah, well! they are taught as babes, you know,

Appeal to Reason, July 6, 1912.

That God Almighty wills it so;
   'Tis all in education."

"I pension men to teach our youth
As I direct; to hide the truth,
   And regulate instruction.
For, if the truth were known, you see,
My dupes no more would give to me
   The fruit of their production."

March 4, 1911

The Socialist party's farm program was the culmination of lengthy and sometimes acrimonious debate within the party.

The Farm Program

ARTICLE 1.

The retention and constant enlargement of the public domain:

By retaining school and other public lands.

By purchase of arid and overflow lands and the state reclamation of such lands now held by the state or that may be acquired by the state.

By the purchase of all lands sold for the non-payment of taxes.

By the purchase of segregated and unallotted Indian lands.

By the retention of leased lands after the expi-ration of leases and the payment of the improvements thereon at an appraised valuation.

ARTICLE 2.

Separation of the department of agriculture from the political government by means of—

Election of all members and officers of the board of agriculture by the direct vote of the actual farmers.

Introduction of the merit system among the employees.

ARTICLE 3.

Erection by the state of grain elevators and warehouses for the storage of farm products; these elevators and warehouses to be managed by the board of agriculture.

ARTICLE 4.

Organization by the board of agriculture of free agricultural education and the establishment of model farms.

ARTICLE 5.

Encouragement by the board of agriculture of co-operative societies of farmers—

For the buying of seed fertilizer.

For the purchase and common use of implements and machinery.

For the preparing and sale of produce.

For the working of land by groups.

ARTICLE 6.

Organization by the state for loans on mortgages and warehouse certificates, the interest charges to cover cost only.

ARTICLE 7.

State insurance against disease of animals, diseases of plants, insect pests, hail, flood, storm and fire.

ARTICLE 8.

Aid and encouragement to be given the actual workers of the farms in the formation of district co-operative associations which shall be given the power to issue bonds for the purchase of suitable farming lands—bonds to be redeemable in forty years. Individuals purchasing such lands shall pay the purchase price of land in share or cash annual or semi-annual rentals extending over a period of forty years, or may at their option pay in full in any given number of years.

ARTICLE 9.

Exemption from taxation and execution of dwellings, tools, farm animals, implements and improvements to the amount of one thousand dollars.

ARTICLE 10.

A graduated tax on the value of rented land and land held for speculation.

ARTICLE 11.

Absentee landlords to assess their own lands, the state reserving the right to purchase such lands at their assessed value plus 10 per cent.

ARTICLE 12.

Land now in the possession of the state or hereafter acquired through purchase, reclamation or tax sales to be rented to landless farmers under the supervision of the board of agriculture at the prevailing rate of share rent or its equivalent. The payment of such rent to cease as soon as the total

amount of rent paid is equal to the value of the land and tenant thereby acquires for himself and his children the right of occupancy. The title to all such lands remaining with the commonwealth.

June 8, 1912

Born in a rented shack on a Texas cotton plantation, Nat L. Hardy wrote often for the radical press on tenant farming and the land question. In 1912 he was editor of the Dallas Laborer.

Tenantry in the South

APPALLING FIGURES SHOWING GROWTH OF LANDLORDISM
NAT L. HARDY

William Hunter owns thirty sections of land in the south part of Dunklin county, Mo., which is cultivated by over one hundred tenants. This is a typical farm and cultivated under typical conditions. The land is so badly drained that it can hardly be said to be drained at all. It is low flat country between the St. Francis and the Mississippi rivers. This year being a wet year the land has been under water much of the time and crops have been almost ruined in many instances. Hunter's fields resemble a forest almost as much as they do cultivated fields. The stumps and standing trees are very thick. It is impossible to use any up-to-date implements in cultivating the land. Weeds grow prolifically in the rich wet soil and it takes heart-breaking work with plow and hoe to cultivate a very few acres. Hunter steadily raises the rent on this land. Last year the men paid $5 per acre and this year they are to pay $6. The tenants must sign a contract that requires them to pay their rent by the 15th of October or sooner if any of their crop is sold. It requires them to keep all fences repaired and to keep fences and ditches cleared of weeds and rubbish. This requires an immense amount of very hard work and is plainly the duty of the landlord. The renter must bear all loss of crops from invading stock and of improvements by fire or storm. And after the men have bound themselves up in this slave contract to him he will not help them secure the necessaries of life. Nor will he provide accommodations worthy to house swine for them to live in.

What is said of Hunter's farm is what can be said of all Dunklin and adjoining counties. The same is practically true of every rented cotton farm in the United States. The houses that these people live in are a shame and a disgrace to even capitalist civilization. They would be a disgrace to the lowest savages of Africa. No words of mine can give you an idea of what they really are. Mere ragged little coops made from logs or the scraps from the lumber mills. Not a foot of real lumber in them. Scarcely ever a shingle used and in a country where shingle mills are located at every village. Little two and three room shacks! Low, ragged, filthy dens, places that intensify the heat in summer and offer no substantial protection from cold in the winter and little shelter from the frequent rains. Little places where whole families are forced to sleep in the same room; where there is no room for furniture, and no room for any, except their dirty beds and a few chairs and boxes. Not a picture, not a book, not one bright thing to make the place a home. Never has the writer seen worse habitations except the temporary brush huts of Mexican laborers in the dry warm southwest. The worst mining camp I ever saw, which consisted mostly of Mexicans and was altogether unorganized, did not present as bad a spectacle as the places the nineteen hundred tenant farmers of Dunklin county, Mo., are forced to exist in. The slaves that dig in Hunter's swamp fields are in scarcely any worse condition than the rest of the three and one-half million tenant farmers of America.

If Dunklin county was the only accursed spot it would be an easy matter to buy the people out of their slavery but this is a great social question; an evil that is sapping and ruining agricultural life in the United States. It is a growing evil. There is scarcely a state in which tenantry has not made a great advance during the past ten years. The following table for the four greatest cotton producing states shows something of its growth:

PER CENT OF FARMS OPERATED BY TENANTS

	1910	1900	1890	1880
Georgia	65.6	59.9	53.6	44.9
South Carolina	63.0	61.1	55.3	50.3
Texas	52.6	49.7	41.9	37.6
Mississippi	66.1	62.4	52.8	43.8

Every other southern state would show the same record. Ask your congressman to send you the Agricultural Bulletin: Farms and Farm Property, Live Stock, Principal Crops and Farm Expenses for 1910 for your state and see what per cent of your neighbors are living on rented farms.

In every county that the production of cotton is unusually high the percentage of tenantry is unusually high. The higher valuation that is put on the land the less of it is worked by its owners. In Mississippi the five greatest cotton producing counties have percentages of tenants ranging from 90 to 95 per cent. Texas shows about the same rates, with her ten greatest cotton producing counties ranging from 60 per cent up occupied by tenants, Collins and Ellis counties being the highest with 69 per cent each.

Burke County, Ga., shows 85.4 per cent tenants with Merriwether county second with 77.4 per cent. South Carolina's ten leading cotton counties have from 60 to 80 per cent of their farms occupied by tenants. In Oklahoma 55 per cent of the farmers were renters in 1910 where only 44 per cent were in 1900, while many Oklahoma counties show a percentage of renters above 80 per cent.

Some may think tenant farming is confined to the south but look at this table of the ten greatest cereal producing states:

PER CENT OF FARMS
OPERATED BY TENANTS

	1910	1900	1890	1880
Illinois............	41.4	39.3	34.0	31.4
Indiana	30.0	28.6	25.4	23.7
Missouri	29.9	30.5	26.8	27.3
Iowa	37.8	34.9	28.1	19.3
Nebraska..........	38.1	36.9	24.7	18.0
Ohio	28.4	27.4	22.9	19.6
North Dakota.......	14.3	8.5	6.9	—
South Dakota.......	24.8	21.8	13.2	—
Kansas............	36.8	35.2	28.2	16.3
Minnesota.........	21.0	17.3	12.9	9.1

The cereals haven't quite as bad a record yet as cotton but then they are coming along very well. The same rule applies in the cereal states as in the cotton states as to the higher the yield and the higher valuation the land is held at the greater the percentage of tenants. This rule works in every state given here except Missouri. In that state we find the same high tenant percentages as in the cotton producing states.

In North Dakota, a frontier state, where one would scarcely think of finding tenant farming at all and where the average for the state is very low, 14 per cent, the heavy wheat producing counties range from 19 to 30 per cent. Indiana, where the percentage for the state is lower than any of the older settled farming states, the ten counties with the largest corn yield show percentages of from 5 to 24 per cent higher than the average for the state. Benton county has the highest percentage of tenants, 53.7 per cent. In Illinois the ten richest counties run from 47 to 64 per cent tenants. Iowa's ten best producing counties have from 37 to 53 per cent of their farms cultivated by others than their owners. And in every other state, the same story is told by the census figures of which enough has been given here to convince any intelligent man.

To those who would like to blame these conditions on the negroes and foreigners we would say that in Dunklin county, Mo., where conditions are worse among the tenants than were conditions in the negro quarters in Georgia before the war, so we were assured by many old timers, that of the 1,936 farm renters in the county only two were colored and two foreign born while there were eleven foreign born and four negro farmers in the county that owned their farms.

There is one bright spot in the darkness revealed by the growth of tenant farming and that is the rapid growth of Socialism among the farmers. When I stood on Hunter's farm near Hunter's school house and looked at the scenes of suffering and desolation, the knowledge that nearly all of Hunter's tenants were readers of the *Appeal to Reason* and that at Hunter's school house a Socialist local met every week with nearly seventy-five members was very encouraging. Also the man that was teaching the school was a class-conscious Socialist and was doing his duty in teaching the young people to think straight for themselves.

This is the situation most everywhere. In Texas alone, in great big old rackrented Texas, there are twenty-four regularly routed Socialist organizers besides a host of volunteers and over thirty big camp meetings are being held there this summer. The *Appeal* has a circulation of nearly 40,000 in that state and the Socialist party has a membership of over 6,000 and the movement is composed almost entirely of farmers, the majority of whom are tenants.

The farm renter is waking up to a knowledge of how he is being robbed, not alone by the landlords, but also by the railroads and the trusts that buy his products at their prices and sell back to him at their prices also. That is why he is in revolt against this robber system that is causing him to work twelve and fourteen hours a day the year around and keeping his children out of school to work them into ill-health and ignorance all for a dirty coop to live in, enough bread and bacon to keep alive on and enough calico and ducking overalls to hide their nakedness. It is high time that the people voted the Socialist ticket to put an end to this infernal tenant system that is sapping the fertility from our American fields and the vitality and intelligence from our American manhood and womanhood that must live by tilling the soil.

August 31, 1912

A socialist refugee from the establishment press, John Kenneth Turner came to the Appeal in 1910 after his series of articles on political conditions in Mexico, later published in book form as Barbarous Mexico, was suppressed by the American Magazine. Turner had an extraordinary ability to get inside events and reconstruct their human as well as political dimensions.

Bankers Squeeze Out Last Drop of Blood of Poor Tenant Farmers

JOHN KENNETH TURNER

Madill, Okla.—I have just finished a ten-day trip through five of the southernmost counties of Oklahoma, Love, Marshall, Bryan, Choctaw and Pushmataha.

I fully expected to find the conditions in these counties better than those in Carter county, which I have described at some length. I found them worse in almost every particular.

In general the system is the same. According to a report of the state board of agriculture, published in the fall of 1911, 76 per cent of the farms in the counties I have visited are operated by tenants. My observation leads me to believe that the figures are too conservative; 90 per cent would be nearer the truth.

These tenants surrender one-fourth of their cotton crop and one-third of all other crops for ground rent.

They pay from 20 to 50 per cent to the banks and farm loan companies in cash loans.

They pay from 15 to 40 per cent above cash prices to the credit merchants for food and clothing.

There is no market for anything they raise ex-

cept cotton, and there being no real competition in the buying of their cotton, they are invariably forced to sell below the market price.

The result is that not one in ten is able to make ends meet, year in and year out, and not one in one hundred has made ends meet this year.

With hardly an exception, they are in debt and are never able to get out of debt. In my trip through the five counties mentioned above I did not meet nor even hear of but ONE working farmer who was not in debt.

That the debt is not the result of extravagance, but of absolute necessity, is evidenced by the way in which the farmer and his family live.

The women and children work in the fields a great part of the year; cotton is always considered before school.

All are miserably clothed. Fifty-cent overalls are patched and patched until they are all patches. The cheapest calico is the best the women can afford. The snow finds many children without shoes.

A man of wealth would not stable his horse in such houses as these people live in; the food that they eat would be spurned by a well-fed dog.

Many of them at this moment are in the actual throes of acute starvation. Many have already been stripped of their poor possessions and turned out in the cold, with no shelter, nowhere to turn, and not a penny in their pockets. And many more will have met the same fate by the time this article reaches the reader.

So much for generalities.

My investigations on this ten-day trip were conducted precisely as in Carter county. I talked with farmers who had come to town to dispose of their cotton, and drove out in the country to visit them in their hovels as well. I also interviewed many persons of other occupations.

In Love county I found a wealthy merchant, S. Westheimer, brother of the Westheimer of the merchant firm, Westheimer & Daube, which takes rich tribute from Carter county farmers. This Westheimer is not only a merchant, but a director of the First National Bank of the county seat, Marietta, a large landlord and a cotton buyer, thus combining within one personality the functions of all the various Interlocked Parasites of the First Degree.

I found this prosperous gentleman very rapidly absorbing Love county's 1914 cotton crop. If he did not take it as landlord, he took it as usurer, if not as usurer then as merchant, if not as merchant then as cotton buyer; for I was informed that Mr. Westheimer monopolizes the buying of Love county very much as Love & Thurmond monopolize the buying of Carter county.

I was told of instances where Mr. Westheimer was put to the trouble of hiring men and paying real money to have the cotton picked, since certain farmers, being hopelessly in debt, and knowing that if they picked they would be picking only for Mr. Westheimer, left their cotton in the field, left their teams and tools, which were mortgaged also, and walked away with their families, carrying their poor possessions—ran away from their peonage like refugees from fire, flood or war.

This, from the point of view of Mr. Westheimer, was killing the goose that laid the golden egg. The Interlocked Parasites of the cotton sections want men to work for them, not to run away from them. And, during this trip, I found Mr. Westheimer and others doing their best to keep the tenant peons on their farms *at least until after the cotton was all picked.*

For this reason, in Love county, as elsewhere, the closing-out process had not been resorted to in a great many cases. Mr. Westheimer as merchant was still doling out a little corn meal. Mr. Westheimer as banker was still slipping a dollar here and a dollar there, as the farmer came in and turned over a bale of cotton, reporting progress in the picking.

But in general the farmers were not allowed to have more than one week's rations ahead, and all predicted a complete shutting down of credit about January 1. One voiced the prevailing sentiment when he said to me: "Our New Year's reso-

lution will have to be not to eat anything, wear anything, or HAVE anything until after the 1915 cotton crop is harvested next fall!"

In Marshall County, which I visited next, I was told by E. S. Hurt, a noted lawyer and a fighting Socialist who is feared and hated by the Interlocked Parasites of southeastern Oklahoma, that they were closing out an average of a dozen farmers a day.

The three banks of Madill, the county seat, absolutely dominate the situation in the county. The banks loan all the money and hold all the mortgages. They have a blacklist. They keep the merchants informed as to whom they may extend credit and to whom they may not. *The merchants file their credit accounts in duplicate in the bank and when the farmer pays his grocery bill he pays it at the bank.*

The banker does not permit the farmer to pay his mortgage first and let his grocery bill stand, but credits the payments to the merchant's account until the latter is settled. This is done in order that the surest lien on the farmer's property may be held over his head to the last.

"For miles around this town you won't find a horse that is not owned by the banks," Hurt told me. "The farmers are using them—and feeding them. When a banker wants a horse he goes and takes it, wherever he finds it. They're taking some now, and they're waiting until the cotton's all picked to take others. . . . The bankers are giving the farmers a little credit yet—just enough to get through picking their cotton. A banker told me yesterday: "I JUST GAVE A FELLOW $12.50 ON FOUR BALES OF COTTON THAT HE BROUGHT IN, SO THAT HE COULD FINISH THE PICKING. AFTER HE'S BROUGHT IN HIS LAST BALE THERE'LL BE NOTHING MORE DOING WITH HIM!"

While the Madill banks are in a position to close out a vast majority of the cotton peons, they will not close out so many as a majority, even after the cotton is all picked, ginned and delivered.

They want to collect on their usurious loans and they want to reduce the 1915 acreage. For these two reasons they will strip scores of families clean of their last belongings. But they will "carry over" a certain number. *The one and only reason is that they want somebody to raise cotton for them next year.*

The arrangement which the Madill banks have adopted to carry over a certain number of their rural "customers" is a sad commentary on "independent farming" as it is found in the sovereign state of Oklahoma. On the Saturday before my first visit to Madill the three bankers of that city held a conference and entered into an agreement conceived toward the end that the carrying over process might be accomplished with the least possible outlay to themselves. The essentials of the scheme are as follows:

First, a blacklist and a whitelist: the blacklist comprising the names of the farmers to be given no extension of credit, either by banker or merchant, but to be closed out and driven from the county; the whitelist comprising the names of farmers to whom the individual banker, at his option, may give an extension of credit, but only under the following conditions:

1. That the entire 1914 crop be turned over to the banker holding the mortgage.
2. That a new mortgage be made out at the usual usurious rates, and made to cover the entire possessions of the farmer, regardless of the value of those possessions or the amount of the loan.
3. That the farmer make affidavit to the effect that the property listed is all that he has and that there are no other liens upon it except the first mortgage that is now being written to cover it.
4. The bankers agree among themselves that there shall be no second mortgages, the farmers must likewise agree; every possible precaution is taken to prevent the farmer from getting any money except what the banker has decided to advance him.

These are the precautions taken to protect the banker for the outlay that he is about to make. Next, as to that outlay.

5. The bankers agree not to pay the loan in a lump sum, but to dole it out monthly, this in order that the farmer may never come and say: "I have spent it all. Let me have a little more before the harvest, or I starve."

And how much a month? That is not to be determined by the amount of the security, but purely by the absolute needs of the farmer and his family to save them from actual death by starvation during the year 1915. For example, if it is a family of four the banker will dole out $10 monthly, if a family of eight he will dole out $15 monthly.

This is the scheme. Read it over once more, carefully, and do your own commenting.

For seven years there have been no prosecutions in Marshall county for violations of the compulsory school attendance law. When the cotton peons are notified that they must comply with the law or show the reason why, they simply file an affidavit with the school board alleging that the labor of their children is needed at home to help support the family; *and they invariably have the evidence to back them up.*

One of the long rides that I took in this investigation was from Aylesworth, out through Cumberland, to Linn, and on beyond. Cumberland is a little town at which, in a speech just before election, Judge Hurt ventured the guess that 90 per cent of his audience had not had any meat of any kind in their houses in 30 days. A grizzled farmer rose from his seat and said: "*I want to make a correction. You should have said 99 per cent.*"

On this little journey I did not find anybody enjoying the benefits of modern civilization in any degree. The Aylesworth liveryman would not rent me a single rig because he declared no horse was equal to drawing a buggy alone over the rough roads.

The tumble-down log cabin was common, sharing honors for numbers with one and two-room shacks of thin walls, quite as ancient and rotten as its neighbor.

Of both I found more dilapidated examples than any I had seen in Carter county. The ridge-pole of one sagged like the outline of a swaybacked horse. In another the cracks between the logs are as wide as those between the boards of a cattle car. Many had no window-panes at all. Some had mere holes for windows. The windows of others consisted of swinging doors of rude boards, while still others presented absolutely nothing in the nature of windows; one home-made door afforded the only opening except for cracks and knot-holes.

One old log house that I saw near the road looked so far gone that it was hard to believe it harbored human beings. But, looking closely, I could make out thin smoke rising from the ruined and half-fallen chimney. As I turned in from the road I heard a shot, and from a clump of trees came an intelligent young man holding a dead rabbit by the hind legs.

"It's the only meat we're getting nowadays—and mighty scarce at that," he said.

We went into the house, invited by a young wife who had not yet worked years enough in the field to become lean and scrawny, like her neighbors. She had two small children. The house had one room, one door, one bed, one chair, and no stove. The family cooking was done over the fire-place.

"I made seven bales of cotton," the young farmer told me. "It's all delivered and I have $1.50. We are getting ready to move. I came here from Arkansas. In Arkansas we had more to eat, because we could grow it ourselves. But nobody ever has any money there. Still, I wish I were in Arkansas."

Out on the road it was cold—cold—cold. I saw unpicked cotton in the field, but saw few pickers. I asked a farmer why.

"Too cold," he said. "It numbs the fingers. We can't pick when it's so cold." He glanced at the spot in the sky where the sun was obscured by clouds. Less than half an hour later I came upon three little children, one boy and two girls, very near the road, dragging their long sacks, bending forward, putting out one little hand and then the other. All three were barefooted.

"Mamma's gone to get dinner," said the boy, in answer to my questions. "Once I picked a hundred pounds, but not on a day like this."

"Once I picked nearly a hundred pounds," said the larger of the little girls.

"O-e-o-oh! It's so-o co-o-ld!" murmured the smaller of the little girls.

I ate dinner with a farmer who considered himself prosperous—that is, comparatively prosperous. There were seven in the family, and as the house had but two rooms, they used the smoke-house for a kitchen and dining-room. Certainly the farm was unusually well equipped; for it had a smoke-house! . . . So we ate in this smoke-house. The floor was dirt. There were two holes for windows. In one corner was a pile of cotton seed.

"This has been our dining-room for nine years," remarked the farmer.

Our dinner consisted of dry salt pork, corn bread, coffee; no sugar or milk.

I came across a number of instances of foreclosure in this one-day trip.

To satisfy a note for $200 the Madill State Bank had just descended upon M. M. Whistman and taken three cows, four calves and two mules; value at least double. There are three Whistman children.

"*What are you going to do, Mr. Whistman?*"

"*I don't know.*"

Henry Stewart is an old man with a family of twelve. His banker took everything except his household furniture. He was unable to budge from his rented dung-hill. The dilemma was met by his son-in-law, a Texas renter, who drove to Linn in a wagon and moved the cotton refugees away.

The name of another of the early sufferers is Reed. Reed could not pay the note of the Madill State Bank. He had a span of mules and a wagon, a cow and calf and some "fattening hogs." The property is now for sale by the Madill State Bank.

"*What are you going to do, Mr. Reed?*"

"*I don't know.*"

At Aylesworth I was told of an old man whom the agents of the bank found sick in bed. Nevertheless, they took everything but his household goods to satisfy the note. The next day the old man died. His neighbors say it was from excitement and despair attending the foreclosure.

Those who were closed out were unlucky. For if they had possessed less—if they had had no cows or hogs, for example—they might have been carried over another year. For I was told, both in Marshall and other counties, that *where the banks are able fully to satisfy their notes they are most apt to foreclose; and, on the other hand, are most apt to carry over those farmers whom to foreclose would profit them little.*

The most vivid picture that I retain of this little drive is of a very old woman at a country store. I had stopped at the store to talk and warm by the stove. The old woman came with two chickens.

"Are you buying chickens today, Mrs. Blank?" asked the old woman of the store-lady.

The store-lady looked at the chickens, took them in and weighed them. "We're paying ten cents," she said.

The price came to $1.05. But nothing was said as to payment.

"Aren't you paying—cash?" asked the old woman.

"We can't pay cash when we're giving ten cents," was the reply.

The old woman tottered. Her voice changed, breaking with each word.

"Well—I—guess—I—can take it out. I need—some meal."

She steadied herself by grasping the counter.

"But—I—wish—I would much rather have the cash!"

The final words came out with a rush. The old woman leaned forward, her wasted body shaking with dry sobs.

January 2, 1915

The Nonpartisan League, a broadly socialist and insurgent farmers' organization, flourished in the Northwest until 1924. For a time the League included labor elements as well, and in 1919 its candidates and political programs swept to success in North Dakota. John Gunn's writing and reporting was one of the Appeal's strongest features as the paper neared dissolution.

Awakening of Farmers Is Shown in Growth of Nonpartisan League

John W. Gunn

The spectacle presented by the Nonpartisan League, aside from any wider radical significance it may have, is that of a large and tremendously, fundamentally, important class fully awakened to the fact that it is being robbed, clearly aware of the forces that are robbing it and firmly united to utterly undo this robbery. From the point of view of the class struggle in modern society, it represents a gratifying degree of class-conscious resistance to class rule; from the point of view of democracy, it represents a gratifying degree of alert and progressive citizenship.

The figures showing the League's growth give a forceful illustration of how substantial and widespread is this awakening of the farmers of the Northwest. Bear in mind, too, that the majority of the membership of the League has been secured through the personal solicitation of League organizers, of whom there are at present a few more than two hundred. The League largely represents the results of a farm-to-farm canvas, a man-to-man propaganda. Many members are of course gained through meetings.

At the end of its first year—in March, 1916—the League had, approximately, a membership of 25,000. This number does not include the friendly supporters of the League in the cities, those not occupationally eligible to membership in the organization. It means that in one year's time 25,000 earnest farmers were induced to join in a serious organized effort to free themselves from exploitation. This is a tribute to the amazing activity of the League organizers, and likewise is testimony to the profound importance and pressing reality of the economic forces that really produced the League.

The second year of the League was closed with a membership of 70,000—more than doubling its record. It closed its third year with 150,000 members. When I visited the national offices of the League early in June, I was informed that it then had a membership of about 210,000. As an indication of the rapid rate of its growth, I can state that in a single week, in the month of May, 3,500 members were enrolled. In North Dakota, in one week, 1,410 members were enrolled; 564, or 40 per cent of this number, were new members. These figures indicate that the League is not only constantly and substantially gaining ground but that it is holding the ground it has previously gained. When I was in St. Paul, I was told that the League expected soon to be able to make a regular monthly enrollment of 20,000 members, counting both those newly enrolled and those re-enrolled.

The League is more or less active in eight states: North Dakota, Minnesota, South Dakota, Montana, Idaho, Wisconsin, Nebraska and Colorado. In these states its active organization work is being conducted; but its influence spreads throughout the whole Northwest. In seven of these eight states it has made perceptible dents in the reactionary armor of "old gang" politics. In North Dakota, as the whole country knows, the League is politically supreme and its control, apparently, there is none to seriously dispute; in Minnesota it has 33 members in the state legislature—and it confidently plans to carry the state in the next election; in Montana it has 21 members in the state legislature; in Idaho it has 24 members in the state legislature; in South Dakota it has 18 members in the state legislature; in Nebraska it has eight members in the state legislature; and in Colorado it has four members in the state legislature.

Of course the reader will understand that in those states where the League has not yet attained to a formidable strength, it has not yet carried on the determined, vigorous and sweeping propaganda which characterizes it. The men who are managing the League believe greatly in concentrated and efficient effort; to use a coarse yet clear colloquialism they are not inclined to "bite off more than they can chew." They may long for the whole loaf, but they are content to take it gradually in the shape of slices.

Just now the League is intent upon separating the Minnesota slice from the Northwestern wheat loaf; it is no secret that the League expects to win in its next peaceful assault, via the ballot box, upon privilege in this state; the capture of Minnesota is especially important, as it is here, in the Twin Cities, that the grain grabbers of Big Business in the Northwest are strategically entrenched. In Minnesota the situation is not so simple as it was in North Dakota, as the united strength of the farming element alone is not sufficient to carry the state. The cooperation of organized labor is essential to victory here. Recent events point strongly to the fact that this cooperation will be forthcoming in a decisive manner.

At the annual convention of the Minnesota state federation of labor in July a program was adopted for the formation of a Working People's Nonpartisan Political League, and steps have already been introduced to bring forward a close working agreement and affiliation between this party of the organized city workers and the party of the organized farmers. Such a union spells certain disaster and oblivion for the political parties of privilege in Minnesota. It has sent sensational shivers down the spine of every grafter and gangster in the state. In this Minnesota labor convention the following significant statement was made by S. S. McDonald, president of the North Dakota Federation of Labor:

"I used to be against political action on the part of labor, but I have found I was badly mistaken in my views. In the last North Dakota legislature labor had

two members of the house and none in the senate. The legislature was controlled by the Nonpartisan League farmers.

"We asked them for nothing. They exacted no pledges or promises from us. All they did was to inquire what laws organized labor in North Dakota wanted passed. We submitted eight measures. Every one is now on the statute books of the state, and it cost organized labor just $10.

"Before that we had been dealing with old-line party politicians, spent thousands of dollars and got nothing. There is no state now in which the labor men wouldn't give $100,000 to get the laws labor got in North Dakota for $10."

. . . .

There is a state committee in each state, a national committee and a national executive committee, these committees being given wide and virtually unlimited powers of management, within the organization itself; this does not include political power as exercised in the selection of candidates, which is reserved to the membership. All officers and candidates of the League are chosen by conventions, with the exception of the national executive committee. The members of the League in each voting precinct elect a delegate to a legislative district convention; the delegates to this convention elect a delegate to a state convention and select a nominee for the state legislature. The state convention selects the nominees for state offices.

This procedure is also followed in selecting the various organization committees within the League—precinct, county, district and state. Each state has a committee of from three to five men: the national committee consists of the chairmen of the different state committees, and the national executive committee. The national executive committee of three men is selected at two, four and six year periods by the national committee.

Every member of the League is shown a complete draft of the League program when he is asked to join, so that he is fully informed as to the nature and purpose of the organization at the time he is asked to give it his approval and support; as

the membership is constantly being renewed every two years, when every member has the opportunity to rejoin the organization or depart from it, it will be seen that the principles and program of the League are thus regularly checked up to a virtual vote of the rank and file. The membership fee carries with it a two years' subscription to the *National Nonpartisan Leader*, now located in St. Paul, Minn., and to the state paper of the League, there being a paper in each state where the organization is sufficiently strong to warrant such an organ. Thus every member of the League is kept in touch with the progress of the organization through its own press.

The League's press is a powerful factor. It not only keeps League members informed of the practical organization work of the League and exposes the conspiracies of Big Business to undermine and wreck the League and counteracts the falsehoods that are circulated to mislead the farmers; but in addition to this necessary task it gives the farmers truthful accounts of events and movements and political issues of national and even international interest, and combines this with a decidedly progressive editorial policy which as a means of education among the farmers of the great Northwest is of far-reaching and enduring value.

In its press the League enters into discussions of a far wider scope than it does in its political state platforms. It favors industrial democracy, upholds the cause of labor, scores the profiteers and plutocratic traitors of the people of the nation, opposes all schemes for militarism, defends the right of self-determination for Russia and all other nations, denounces imperialism and secret diplomacy and favors real efforts toward bringing world peace. In short, it carries the message of truth and justice to thousands of farmers who are thus effectively removed from the pernicious propaganda of the plutocratic daily press. It is really preparing the farmers for the most intelligent participation in solving the problems that face modern democracy.

In addition to its national and state papers,

there are other League papers not directly owned by the League. There are two daily papers in North Dakota—the Fargo *Courier-News* and the Grand Forks *American*—that are owned and controlled by League members. These papers are excellent examples of what journalism can become when it is genuinely independent and emancipated from capitalistic influences; they are harbingers of progress and bearers of the truth, ably and honestly edited, and they make the art of lying as practiced, often with incredible clumsiness, by capitalist journalism, an exceedingly perilous and uncomfortable practice for the editors of other North Dakota dailies. Before very long the organized labor forces and the Nonpartisan League forces will cooperate in establishing a daily paper in Minneapolis, and then the Twin Cities *Daily* liars will do well to walk warily and "lie low."

More than a hundred small weekly newspapers in North Dakota, with a few in other states, possessing various degrees of minor and local influence, are champions of the League; and in Fargo there is an office maintained for the especial purpose of helping to promote the circulation of these papers, aiding them to introduce auditing and accounting systems, joining in promoting and selling stock for the enlargement of existing papers or the establishment of new papers; this office conducts an advertising agency and sends out weekly a very able and up-to-the-minute news and editorial service; it arranges for the purchase and sale of newspapers, and is preparing to extend its services so that it can provide printing material and machinery, print paper and supplies. Altogether, it is a venture in independent, popular, democratic journalism that promises manifold and magnificent results. A weekly state paper, printed in the Norwegian language, is just being started in North Dakota for the benefit of these foreign-speaking farmers.

Another feature of the League propaganda in North Dakota, which will doubtless be extended to other states as the women gain the right of suffrage, is the Women's Auxiliary League. Conducted by women for women, this branch of organization work—a comparatively recent one—is designed to arouse the same interest and maintain the same standard of solidarity and effort among the farmers' wives that exists among the farmers. To be sure, the farmers' wives have never been indifferent to the League, but from its very beginning have been greatly interested in the cause and have assisted it immensely. But the maintenance of this special and distinct bureau for propaganda among the women is not underestimated, and is gradually being widened in activity and importance. The Women's Auxiliary League rendered particular aid in the recent referendum fight to sustain the new educational program of the League in North Dakota, a feature of legislation in which women naturally display an intimate interest.

But the actual organization work of the League, and thus its primary and basic propaganda, is carried on by the organizers who go out into the rural highways and byways and who constitute the "far-flung battle line" of the League. These organizers go to the farmer's home and there, in the midst of the scenes of farm life and farm toil, they explain to the farmer how he can secure for that life and toil their true reward: as a line officer, in the thick of a critical engagement, rallies his men to save the day by pointing to the battleflag that is the visible symbol of their cause, so these line officers of the League, figuratively speaking at least, can rally the farmers individually to the fight against their exploiters by pointing to the waving wheatfields—the wheat that must be rescued from the grip of the forces of exploitation.

The organizer can lay his plan before the farmer without interruption, he has ample opportunity to fully outline the cause for which he is working, and he can reinforce his appeal by arguments and illustrations with which the farmer is familiar; it is seldom that the organizer leaves a farm without having enrolled the farmer in the League. This plan of propaganda, while slow, is sure and thorough and has abundantly proved its efficacy. Walter Thomas Mills, who is a speaker and organizer for the League, discussing this plan of organization, said:

"Heretofore public meetings, newspaper publicity and public gatherings on the street had been depended upon in every effort to promote progressive organizations. The men who created this organization realized that the only place to reach a man and always find him at his best was at his home and in the midst of the things which most vitally concern all capable and serious-minded citizens. In order to reach men in their homes, a group of organizers was made acquainted with the plans and then set to work in a house-to-house canvas of all the farmers of North Dakota.

"This was done without newspaper notoriety. It was done without any public gatherings. It was done by a campaign based entirely on the power to produce results by meeting face to face and man to man the persons most vitally concerned. Before the enemy was aware that the work was under way the day had already been lost by them and gained by the League."

The League still relies chiefly upon its organizers. Of course it now has its press which backs the original work done in the field, which gives this work permanence, which educates the membership in modern citizenship and affords it a wide, steady and intelligent view, not only of what the League is doing, but of what the nation and the world is doing. The League has its public meetings, its picnics and rallies, too. These picnics and rallies are wonderful and inspiring things. The farmers and their families, including Old Dobbin (or Tin Lizzie) and Old Dog Tray turn out in tremendous throngs and a pleasant and instructive and splendidly enthusiastic time is had by all. Parades miles in length, containing automobiles packed with farmers' families, have covered the countryside like a conquering army in the League campaigns. This human or holiday element exhibited in the League campaigns is one of the greatest demonstrations of the popularity and profound realism of the movement.

September 6, 1919

The wholesale shooting of blacks in Elaine, Arkansas, in 1919, followed by planter-controlled trials, brought a temporary halt to black tenant farmers' resistance and to their organization, the Farmers' and Householders' Progressive Union. Their struggle was an inspiration to members of the Southern Tenant Farmers' Union, an inter-racial mass movement formed fifteen years later on the Arkansas Delta.

White Landlords, Robbing Negro Tenants, Let Loose Arkansas Reign of Terror

Repeated and strenuous efforts have been made to extradite Robert L. Hill, a negro, from the state of Kansas to Arkansas, where he is indicted for murder. He has not been delivered up to the Arkansas authorities, and his extradition would be a deep and shameful stain upon the state of Kansas. For Hill's is no common murder case. The question of his fate is linked with the larger question of economic justice to an exploited race. It isn't for murder, really, that Hill would be tried if he were sent back to Arkansas; the real charge against him is that he was active in helping to organize the negro tenant farmers of southern Arkansas that they might remove some of the burdens of landlordism and virtual slavery from which they have cruelly suffered.

Hill is the president and organizer of the Farmers' and Householders' Progressive Union of America—a union of negro tenant farmers. The story of this union and of the present effort to extradite Hill into Arkansas cannot be understood without explaining the general situation existing in Arkansas.

First let us recall the lurid excitement that prevailed in Phillips county, Arkansas, of which Helena is the county seat, in October, 1919. It will be recollected that the Associated Press sent out to the rest of the country stories of a formidable negro plot to terrify and exterminate the white race in Arkansas, with the news that negroes in Phillips county had uprisen and wantonly killed 21 white men. For several days Arkansas was crimsonly featured in riot stories, and the patriotic fashion in which the white men of Phillips county suppressed the uprising and upheld law and order was dramatically chronicled. Federal troops were called to the scene, and the whole affair made the nation gasp in horror and fright for several days. For of course ninety-nine out of one hundred who read this highly colored, melodramatic news implicitly believed every word of it. They saw visions of an immediate race war.

The only truth in the Associated Press reports was that a number of men, both white and black, were killed. Aside from this fact, the whole impression of what happened in Arkansas was deliberately and utterly falsified. The true story of the massacre in Phillips county, and the highly important economic situation out of which it sprang, has never been told to the American people. The facts about this negro massacre in Phillips county, Arkansas, as gathered by an *Appeal* correspondent, are as follows:

Practically 90 percent of the farm labor of the rich delta country of Arkansas, in which Phillips county is located, is done by negro labor, and practically all of the land is owned in large plantations by white people, many of whom live in the northern cities and operate their plantations by superintendents and by what is known as "share-croppers." The owner of the plantation either employs the manager or superintendent on a salary or leases the farm to him for a net price per acre, including teams and implements necessary to work the land, and then, the manager or superintendent has the land worked in cotton by the negro farm laborers, on the shares, under an agreement that the manager furnishes the land and teams, implements and a house necessary for the cultivation of the land, and the negro farm laborer furnishes the labor necessary to work the land and makes and gathers the crop for one-half. Since the poor negro laborer has no money with which to purchase

his supplies until he makes and gathers his crop, the manager or superintendent operates a store on the plantation where the negro is forced to purchase the supplies necessary for him and his family to live while they are making their cotton crop. The laws of Arkansas give the landlord a prior lien upon the tenant's crop for all indebtedness that the tenant owes him, and make it a felony for the tenant to sell or dispose of his own crop before all his accounts to the landlord are paid. Therefore the poor unfortunate negro is not allowed to sell his cotton to anyone but his landlord, and is not permitted to buy supplies from anyone but the landlord, or whom the landlord dictates.

This system has been in operation for years, in fact since the Civil War, and as a result the negro has been kept in a perpetual state of degrading poverty and ignorance. Of late years, the younger generation of negroes have, in spite of poverty, learned a few things, and have become more or less unruly. For the past three years these negroes have made unusually good crops and cotton has sold for an unusually high price, and they know that they should receive something more for their share than the bare existence that they have been receiving.

In 1918 most all the negro tenants were advised to hold their cotton for better prices, the managers or superintendents shipped the cotton presumably to some warehouse, but they declined to render any accounting to the negro tenants for the sale of their cotton, nor would they give the negroes a statement of their indebtedness, but gave them such sums as they desired, and in many instances they whipped the negro who had the courage to demand a statement of either his cotton or his account. This condition grew intolerable even to the poor negroes.

Early in 1919, some of the young negroes who had returned from the army began an organization of the negro share croppers, under the name of "Farmers' and Householders' Progressive Union of America," for the purpose of getting relief from the abuses their people were made to suffer. The charter and constitution of the organization was drawn up by two prominent white lawyers at Winchester, Ark. The organization was looked upon with much disfavor from the start by the land owners. So the plans of the organization had to be carried on in secret, but it met with instantaneous approval of the negro laborers. The organization arranged that friendly and trustworthy counsel was furnished the negroes who would bring suit and force the land owners to make a settlement with the negroes and in many instances they were forced to pay back to them hundreds, and some instances, thousands of dollars that they were stealing from their tenants.

These negroes had grown a bumper crop this season, some families making as much as fifty bales of cotton, twenty-five of which was theirs. Cotton this season in this locality was selling at from fifty to seventy-five cents per pound, or $250 to $300 per five hundred pound bale, or over $5,000 for the tenant's share of the crop, while everything they purchased at the land owner's store was sold at 50 to 100 per cent higher than at cash stores in nearby towns. These negro tenants were due to have several thousand dollars as their share of the crop for their work. This the land owners could not allow for various reasons. If the negroes got out of debt, they might leave the farm, then they would not trade at their stores if they had the cash to buy from mail order houses or the cash stores in the towns.

The land owners began to make arrangements to again ship the negro's cotton without asking his consent, or rendering him a statement of his store account. The negroes went to their organization for aid and counsel. A representative of their organization went to a prominent white attorney for counsel, whom they knew was a friend to all labor organizations. This attorney was not in his office at the time the delegation called, but his son, who was in charge of the office in his father's absence, advised the delegation to get their members together and he would come out and meet them, and investigate their claims. The representatives of the negroes returned and called a meeting in one of their churches, to advise their members.

Evidently the land owners had spies in the negro organization, for soon after the negroes began to congregate at the church a car from Helena, the county seat of Phillips county, stopped near the church and a deputy sheriff and a special agent or railroad detective, ran up to the church and began to fire into the church and put out the lights. No violence had been contemplated or thought of by the negroes, but some of the younger men had revolvers on their persons from which they returned the fire, killing the detective and wounding the deputy sheriff.

The killing of a white man, a railroad detective, spread like wild fire. A slanderous report was put into circulation that the negroes had planned an insurrection, and had marked twenty-six prominent white men for assassination. White men began pouring into Elaine from all nearby towns, and began to hunt down the negroes, and question them. Any negro who did not answer as they desired was arrested or shot down in cold blood, in many instances. The negroes hurriedly armed themselves with such arms as they could secure and prepared to defend themselves from attack. As a result, five white men were killed and twenty negroes were officially acknowledged killed, but many of the prominent white citizens of Helena boast that over one hundred negroes were killed.

Several hundred soldiers were sent from Camp Pike to restore order, and hundreds of negroes were placed under arrest and huddled together in a stockade where they were denied the right of counsel, or the right to communicate with friends or relatives, where they were tortured and beat and threatened with death until they gave the evidence that the authorities in charge wanted, to convict the several union officials of murder.

The young white lawyer who at the negroes' request came to make an investigation was arrested, chained between two negroes and made to suffer every humiliation known to their fiendish minds, taken to Helena, and kept in jail for a

The Boss: Don't think; stay on the job.

Drawn by Art Young.

Appeal to Reason, August 26, 1922.

month, and finally released on his own recognizance on a charge of barratry (soliciting litigation).

Another young Socialist lawyer who had represented negro tenants in the courts was forced to flee for his life. An armed mob broke into his office and private room and seized all his private papers. After the excitement had somewhat died down, he returned and was also indicted on a charge of barratry and was released on a $200 bond.

Six of the negroes were jointly indicted for murder in the first degree and placed on trial. None of them was allowed to make any defense, as counsel was assigned to them by the court, then the negro defendants were brought into court and placed on trial. Their counsel did not consult with them, no witnesses were allowed to testify for their defense, the jury, composed of white land owners or agents, was not challenged, no defense

was made, the testimony forced from some of the negroes was introduced, the whole trial was over in fifteen minutes, and the court sentenced the defendants to death by electrocution. In all twelve negroes were sentenced to death and eighty were given prison terms varying from one year to life. The father and brother of the young attorney who was arrested were not allowed to come to Helena nor to assist him, under threat of assassination.

Certain public spirited and liberty-loving citizens of this state have taken up the matter of a defense fund. Competent legal counsel is now in charge of their defense and appeals of all the cases are being prosecuted. The attorneys feel sure of success if the proper publicity can be had. Every paper in the state is dominated by the same powers that are trying to railroad these poor negroes to death.

February 14, 1920

Editor of the IWW's Solidarity *during World War I, Ralph Chaplin was sentenced to prison in 1918 for antiwar activities. Poet and author of the autobiographical* Wobbly, *Chaplin was pardoned in 1923. He wrote the song known as American labor's hymn, "Solidarity Forever."*

The West Is Dead

RALPH CHAPLIN

What path is left for you to tread
    When hunger-wolves are slinking near—
Do you not know the West is dead?

The "blanket-stiff" now packs his bed
    Along the trails of yesteryear—
What path is left for you to tread?

Your fathers, golden sunsets led
    To virgin prairies wide and clear—
Do you not know the West is dead?

Now dismal cities rise instead
    And freedom is not there nor here—
What path is left for you to tread?

Your fathers' world, for which they bled,
    Is fenced and settled far and near—
Do you not know the West is dead?

Your fathers gained a crust of bread,
    Their bones bleach on the lost frontier;
What path is left for you to tread—
    Do you not know the West is dead?

June 10, 1922

FIVE

The Socialist Party and the *Appeal*'s Socialist Culture

Socialism is coming. It's coming like a prairie fire. . . .

The *Appeal to Reason*, May 3, 1902

Socialism established deep and diverse roots in the United States decades before the founding of the Socialist party in 1901. Immigrant and native-born Americans alike recognized during the early 1800s that basic economic and social inequalities could not be meaningfully corrected without changing the economic structure that created and institutionalized them. Initially, socialism found practical expression in many utopian communities (the Owenite, Fourierist, and Icarian settlements most influential among them) that arose in the East and Midwest during the early and middle years of the nineteenth century. However, as America industrialized and as capitalism's influence broadened, new forms of socialist opposition developed: the Farmers' and Mechanics' Protective Association in 1850, the General Working-Men's League and New York Communist Club of the same decade, the National Labor-Union of the 1860s and 1870s, and the Socialist Labor party founded in 1877. As the impact of the new industrial and financial order became more severe in the 1880s and 1890s, middle-class Americans were also propelled into widespread socialist reform movements such as Bellamyite Nationalism, Christian Socialism, and the

American Fabian Society. The Socialist party, both a culmination of past socialist activity and a response to changing economic and political realities, unified elements of radical labor, Milwaukee Social Democrats, Christian Socialists, a faction from the Socialist Labor party, and radical populists from the Southwest. A nonsectarian party with great regional and cultural diversity, composed of both native-born and immigrant citizens, the Socialist party was the political expression of what until 1919 was a powerful mass movement.[1]

From its very beginnings the Socialist party was conceived as a broad-based, democratically-administered organization, one with room for both gradualist and revolutionary politics. American political tradition demanded the presence of a Socialist party, one that would educate men and women to a socialist analysis and simultaneously be a factor in both national and local life. Conceived as a revolutionary party, Socialists meant by revolution a thorough, fundamental change of capitalism's structure and relations. Relatively few considered the revolutionary process as necessarily violent. Instead, since the governing class was few, the working class many, the avenue to state power was popular victory at the polls. Upon that victory, Socialists believed that incremental, structural transformation of capitalism and the state would gradually bring an egalitarian, social- ist society into being. Virtually all Socialists were agreed that though the process would be protracted, socialism would be achieved in their lifetimes. That optimism empowered Socialists at the turn of the cen- tury, and it was an integral part of the socialist move- ment.

Until World War I an electoral transition to power seemed more than mere possibility. In 1900 the Presi- dential ticket of Eugene V. Debs and Job Harriman re- ceived 97,000 votes; thereafter, until the mid-term elections of 1914, the Socialist party's support at the polls grew more quickly than any radical party in American history. More than any other Socialist, Debs symbolically united the diverse party. Born in Terre Haute, Indiana, in 1855, first a railroad fireman, then secretary-treasurer of the Brotherhood of Locomotive Firemen, Debs organized the American Railway Union in 1893. Jailed in the aftermath of the Pullman strike in 1894, Debs became a socialist shortly after his release from prison. Socialist candidate for Presi- dent five times, charismatic, intensely human and ac- cessible as a man, no figure personified American so- cialism as fully as Debs.

In 1904 Debs and Ben Hanford, a New York printer famous for creating the fictional Jimmie Hig- gins (a rank-and-file Socialist who performed the unrecognized tasks crucial to the success of the movement), polled 402,000 votes. Aided in the weeks prior to the election by the *Appeal*, which published a series of effective, widely distributed campaign issues, Socialist strength stretched out of eastern cities, the major source of popular sup- port in 1900, into the Midwest and West. Wayland and the *Appeal*'s editorial staff showed in article af- ter article that Socialist principles were consistent with the egalitarian American ideals that capitalism had sprung up to deny: social equality, economic as well as political freedom, a world in which men and women would no longer be degraded instruments of another's profit. The dramatic increase in elec- toral strength in 1904 gave Socialists confidence that they were on the correct side of history.

The results of the 1908 national election, 420,000

votes, represented more a consolidation of earlier gains than a setback. In 1908 Socialists were orga- nized in 39 states; their party numbered 41,000 mem- bers organized in more than 3000 locals. The mar- ginally larger vote for Debs belied socialism's increasingly influential presence in America, a pres- ence which compelled Theodore Roosevelt to de- clare it "far more ominous than any populist or similar movement in time past."[2] Republican party leader Mark Hanna predicted that by 1912 socialism would be the most significant issue in America, and as party membership tripled between 1908 and 1912, events proved him correct. Running for the fourth time, Debs received over 900,000 votes, 6 percent of the total cast.

The Socialist party was stronger in 1912 and 1913 than ever before, more vital in retrospect than it would be again. In 1912 the socialist press included eight foreign-language and five English dailies, 262 En- glish and 36 foreign-language weeklies, and nu- merous monthlies. Led by the *Appeal*'s 694,000 (761,000 in 1913) average weekly circulation, the *Na- tional Rip-Saw*'s 150,000 and the *Jewish Daily For- ward*'s 140,000, socialist circulation totaled some two million copies weekly. Over 1200 Socialists held elec- ted public office (the majority in towns of 10,000 or less) a total that included twenty state legislators and seventy-nine mayors in twenty-four states. Among AFL unions, socialists controlled the Machinists, the West- ern Federation of Miners, the Brewery Workers, exer- ted significant influence in others, and led state feder- ations of labor in Pennsylvania, Illinois, Wisconsin, and Missouri.[3] At the same time, however, the gains of 1912 masked a crucial division within the party itself, one that erupted when a conservative leadership fac- tion engineered the recall of Bill Haywood from the party's National Executive Committee. A leader of the IWW as well as the Socialist left, Haywood advocated militant, direct action and a general strike rather than compromised political work leading to victory at the ballot box. Unaware that the Socialist vote of 1912 would prove an electoral high point, unaware as well of the international and domestic effects of the com- ing world war, the majority of Socialists endorsed the more conservative electoral strategy of their national leadership and voted for Haywood's recall. Thousands of Socialists exited the party as a result.

The war years saw the party change in composition and in certain of its political positions. Party membership, socialist influence in unions, and the diverse socialist press all lost ground. In the off-year elections of 1914 the Socialist vote dipped significantly downward. When Debs refused to run in 1916, *Appeal* columnist Allan Benson mounted an antiwar but dispirited campaign against the popular Woodrow Wilson, "the man who kept us out of war." The disappointment of only 585,000 Socialist votes cast doubt on the Socialist party's electoral strategy and indicated that the party's membership was moving toward the left. The fundamental cause of that leftward turn was World War I.

The relative ease with which foreign Socialist parties capitulated to nationalist imperatives and supported their countries' war efforts destroyed the Second International (which, in part, had been formed to prevent Socialist participation in international capitalist conflict) and revealed to American socialists the compromised nature of their European counterparts. A critical examination of gradualist Socialist party policies, which focused less on class struggle than on reformist demands and popular American appeal, was not long in coming. Consequently, as the United States was pushed first into jingoism and finally into war, the majority of American Socialists responded by moving to a more overtly antiwar position. They were joined by a large proportion of foreign-language federations, semi-autonomous organizations that had affiliated with the Socialist party after 1910. From less than 15 percent in 1912, foreign-born party membership in 1916 had climbed to 35 percent. Apparent in the 1916 party platform, which for the first time urged a general strike to prevent America from entering World War I, the leftward impetus was so strong that in April, 1917, the Socialist party declared itself against the war by a resounding majority. The United States had entered the conflict less than a week earlier.

In the 1918 midterm elections, Socialist candidates attracted a large measure of popular support,

so much so, Paul H. Douglas estimated, that in a national election the Socialist party would have received some four million votes.[4] Part of the midterm vote, however, was deceptive. As the only political party opposed to the war, the Socialist party attracted a significant number of antiwar votes from nonsocialists. Also, strong popular support was concentrated in areas where the party temporarily remained well organized, such as Ohio, New York City, and Chicago; elsewhere, wartime repression destroyed party organizations and criminalized Socialists as a threat to the American war effort. More than 1500 Socialist locals were destroyed by federal and state authorities. An additional event, however, was to affect the socialist movement dramatically. On November 7, the day after the midterm elections, the Bolsheviks seized power in Russia.

The Russian Revolution could not have occurred at a more crucial time for American Socialists. Federal and state governments had responded to the Socialist party's antiwar politics by declaring a domestic war on radicals, one that was intensified by the electoral support given to Socialists for their opposition to the war. Domestic repression of radicalism and the Socialist party resulted in the arrest and imprisonment of party members and officials, attacks on locals and on antiwar meetings, and wholesale censorship and removal from the mails of socialist periodicals. For elements of the embattled Socialist left, increasingly defenseless before the criminalizing machinery and power of the state, the need to develop new strategy arose. The Bolshevik seizure of power seemed an obvious model.

As an insurrectionary, mass action analysis formed, it was met by the argument of party leaders that political conditions in the United States did not even remotely justify a strategy of open revolt. That response, however, only helped to crystallize division within the party. Additionally, Lenin's belief that socialism could not succeed in one country alone was underscored when the Soviet Union was invaded by American and Allied troops in support of the counterrevolutionary White Army. The political ground, then, was more than prepared for what occurred: polarized division within the Socialist party and a split late in 1919 into three major fragments, the Communist party, the Communist Labor party, and what remained of the Socialist party itself. After a repressive, Red-scared year had passed, the fissured radical parties were left without the strength to play a significant role in national life. From nearly 110,000 Socialist party members early in 1919, the total membership of the three fragments had dwindled to some 36,000 a year later.

For Socialists, the popular support given Debs in the 1920 presidential race, 919,000 votes, could not be interpreted optimistically. In only a handful of states had the party been able to maintain a viable organization. Elsewhere the party was weak or not even on the ballot. Debs's proportion of the popular vote, moreover, had dropped as a consequence of the Nineteenth amendment, which gave suffrage to women. In 1921 the Socialist party's national membership totaled a little over 11,000. In the 1924 presidential election the Socialist party lent its support to Wisconsin Senator Robert LaFollette's Progressive party candidacy. Broken apart by the consequences of World War I, political repression, the 1919 fissures, and unable to support a ticket of its own, the Socialist party acknowledged by supporting LaFollette that it was no longer the dominant political expression of the American left.

Only a part of the Socialist party's political history appears in the *Appeal to Reason*. The *Appeal* was designed to educate and convert readers to socialism, not to focus on the Socialist party or be an official party vehicle. Nevertheless, the paper's columns record 25 years of Socialist campaigns and elections, political conditions in towns and cities throughout America, as well as reports on Socialist administrations in cities and towns such as Milwaukee, Wisconsin, Schenectady, New York, Berkeley, California, and Butte, Montana. With accounts of national elections available elsewhere, the *Appeal*'s record of local organizing, of the day-to-day realities otherwise lost to history, become even more significant. The paper tells much about Debs's meetings and speeches, but it also discloses the conditions faced by John W. Bennett when he organized in rural North Dakota during the winter of 1903; why Martin Roskay of Detroit and J. T. White from Connorsville, Indiana, voted the Socialist ticket in 1908; why A. E. Farnham, from Russell, Minnesota, would have voted for socialism had she been permitted to; and what it was like when Caroline Lowe organized in LaBette County, Kansas, in 1913. Their accounts and hundreds similar to them reveal not only a great deal about the social texture of working-class life, but they also reveal that Socialists were not made passive victims of the wrenching social and economic changes in turn-of-the-century America. The *Appeal* shows clearly that Socialists created a rich and varied culture opposed to capitalism, one that merged indigenous American traditions with a vision of nonexploitative life that provided direction and richness to their lives.

A sometimes amorphous concept, culture here means "the special sets of behavior, norms, loyalties, beliefs, etc., manifested and internalized" by the community of people sharing them. Implicit in behavior, as Clifford Geertz suggests, "culture is not behavior but the complex of rules and values which generate and guide behavior."[5] Socialist culture was animated by two dominant forces, one general to the movement itself, the other more specific to locally determined conditions. In its general dimensions, shared belief in the principles of socialism informed behavior and created a shared identity that was intensified by the values of fraternity and community. Binding Socialists together as well was the understanding that, although their circumstances might differ, they were all engaged in a mutual struggle against capitalism. Resistance to capitalism and its manifestations created a new consciousness, one that did not so much reject received cultural values as it redefined and reshaped them. Nowhere was the culture, the politics, and the confidence so central to early twentieth-century socialism better expressed than in the closing words used by thousands of Socialists when they signed their letters: "Yours for the Revolution."

For the *Appeal*, the more specific dimension of socialist culture arose from the geographic region it inhabited and expressed. The *Appeal*'s Debsian socialism was conditioned by different material and cultural factors than the German- and Polish-influenced socialism of Milwaukee, the socialism found in Finnish halls in the Mesabi iron range, or the sophisticated, sometimes avant-garde socialism of the *Masses*. The *Appeal*'s primary territory, a vast expanse west of the Mississippi, stretching north and south as well, was marked by smallholder and tenant farming, mining and manufacturing, a limited number of significant urban centers, and by numerous small towns and cities. The ethos of the area was predominantly "American"; for the most part its population was composed of native-born Americans who had come to America from northern and western Europe prior to 1890. Traditional institutions such as the family, church, and home were powerful; various denominations of Protestantism held sway. The cultural values and moral codes were traditional as well: a belief in honesty, personal dignity, the value of hard work, and self-improvement. Not far beneath the surface was the legacy of populism, people's empowering belief in themselves and in the legitimacy of insurgent politics. A crucial reason for the *Appeal*'s success, therefore, was the extraordinary convergence it established between traditional culture and Debsian socialism. In Debs's speeches, and in virtually every issue of the *Appeal*, traditional values were invested with new, radical meaning. In the process, a people's resistance to the effects of capitalism was transformed into a people's active opposition.

No paper fused socialism with midwestern American values more effectively than the *Appeal*. J. A. Wayland, Fred Warren, Eugene Debs, and many of the *Appeal*'s other editorial writers during the paper's early years were born and culturally rooted in the Midwest. Their belief in quasi-Christian morality, home, family, and community were authentic, not rhetorical. The *Appeal*'s adherence to existing cultural values, however, was critically edged. Only in a socialist America could those traditional values be realized in new, humane form. Capitalism was everywhere subjecting the family to stress, forcing children into fields and factories, uprooting communities, and, far from reinforcing traditional morality, had elevated self-interest and profit above ethical behavior. Received

cultural values had to be given new shape and meaning if they were to attract Americans to a socialist analysis.

Socialist redefinition of traditional American culture took many forms. The meaning of family, for example, was enlarged from an independent unit, a refuge from the realities of work and survival, to mean the interdependent human family. Socialist Sunday schools, bands, and songs emerged from the process of cultural redefinition to enrich social dimensions of life. Meetings of Socialist locals, debating societies, and socialist women's groups reaffirmed community and redefined the purpose of education. Study and discussion of social questions redefined self-improvement: its meaning was broadened to include the responsibility for improving others' lives. As winning control over a profitable spoils system increasingly came to characterize capitalist politics on the local and national levels, Socialists mounted clean, fair campaigns. At a time when municipal corruption, what Lincoln Steffens called "the shame of the cities" was a widely recognized if deplored reality, Socialist administrations of towns and cities were free from graft and the abuse of power. Debs and other Socialist candidates everywhere propounded the value of serving rather than governing the people. Few institutions, however, reveal as much about socialist culture and its formation as the widespread Socialist encampments.

Modeled on religious camp meetings and Populist encampments of the 1890s, socialist encampments brought the secularized gospel of economic salvation to thousands of dirt-poor farmers and rural people. Extending from Oklahoma and Texas south to Florida, northward from Missouri and Kansas into the Dakotas, and commonly scheduled in late August and early fall—after crops had been harvested—the encampments were a renewal of community, an education, and a rich cultural celebration. The first socialist encampment occurred in Grant Saline, Texas, in 1904; in 1914, apart from the hundreds of one- and two-day socialist picnics, there were 125 encampments in Texas and more than 100 in Oklahoma alone. Towns competed for encampments and integrated them into local life. It was not unknown, as Oscar Ameringer recounts in *If You Don't Weaken*, for chamber of commerce members to decorate telephone poles leading to the campgrounds with socialist flags. Displayed in the shop windows of merchants were red flags of human brotherhood.

The encampments characteristically lasted three days to a week. At times they drew as many as 20,000 people. Seeing so many socialists for the first time, the more nervous citizens of the small towns must have thought the revolution was not merely inevitable but just weeks away. Music was always a staple at the encampments. While young children rode the ferris wheel and played at games, their parents sang socialist songs, many put to the melodies of religious hymns. If Ameringer and his three sons were present, they played not only traditional American music but arrangements of classical music. Socialist skits and theatrical performances drew large crowds. Part of the day was spent in educational classes and discussion. One of the most effective lecturers was Walter Thomas Mills, whose classes in social economy had been sponsored by the *Appeal*. A. M. Simons held classes on the land question. Books, pamphlets, and socialist newspapers were available on literature tables. Local and national speakers, such as Eugene Debs, Kate Richards O'Hare, Mother Jones, and Caroline Lowe spoke in the afternoon and evening. For members of the audience, in Ameringer's words, "radicalism was not an intellectual plaything. Pressure was upon them. Many of their homesteads were already under mortgage. Some had actually been lost by foreclosure. They were looking for delivery from the eastern monster whose lair they saw in Wall Street. They took their socialism like a new religion. And they fought and sacrificed for the spreading of the new faith like the martyrs of other faiths."[6]

Biblically-sanctioned morality and millenarianism were an unashamed part of Debsian socialism. In an ethos in which the social implications of Christian morality had significance in people's lives, the consequences of capitalism were not simply wrong but were evil. "Economic salvation" and "conversion to socialism" bespoke a wholeness and commitment

that extended far beyond cognitive agreement with abstract economic principles. Socialism fused with traditional culture at the encampments and elsewhere in a profound critique of capitalism. From that fusion emerged an authentic socialist culture.

The Socialist party was the dominant expression of insurgent politics as the twentieth century began. However, as socialism was more than political theory, the party was more than an institution. Neither the popular vote nor the many socialist demands accepted later as part of American life are adequate measures of its significance. The party was embedded in a larger socialist movement, one which gave purpose and hope to people's lives. Few dimensions of personal life were not enriched by movement culture and its varied oppositional forms. In creating those forms, Socialists were empowered by a purpose and vision far richer, and far more to be respected, than the competitive, lonely search for personal wealth that even then was an important part of capitalist culture. Recognizing the futility of individual solutions to collective problems, socialists thought of others as well as themselves. The new consciousness that socialism provided was briefly expressed by Debs as well as by anyone in the movement. "I could have been in Congress long ago," Debs told the court before he was sent to prison under the new Espionage Act in 1918.[7] Socialists chose their politics and, when their movement was turned back, relatively few took it as personal defeat. There are many signs of defeat, but an ongoing commitment to building a cooperative commonwealth for all to inhabit equally is not one of them.

The International School of Social Economy, which primarily attracted socialists from the Southwest and Midwest, was one of the earliest socialist counterinstitutions. Students Kate Richards and Frank O'Hare, married in 1902 in J. A. Wayland's home, would become significant figures in the socialist movement. The founder of the School of Social Economy, Walter Thomas Mills, moved on to other organizing activities,

Enrollment form, *Appeal to Reason*. Courtesy Special Collections, Pittsburgh State University Library.

and the School later merged with the socialist People's College in Fort Scott, Kansas.

International School of Social Economy

A CORRESPONDENCE AND TRAINING SCHOOL FOR SOCIALISTS

Walter Thomas Mills will remove his Correspondence School from Chicago to Girard, Kansas. He will establish here a training school for Socialist party workers.

The course of study will cover the present work of his correspondence school in social economy and will add short and practical courses in political and economic history, voice culture, practice in speaking, correction of common errors in speech, practice in the preparation of addresses and in methods of study, training in the work of a canvasser and organizer and parliamentary drill.

The school will open with a twelve-weeks course on Wednesday, October 9th.

All who take this course of study and desire to do so, will be given work in the field for Socialism and on proving their ability to do the work will be kept constantly at work as speakers and organizers, and their living will be provided for.

Mr. Wayland has put himself on a salary and will devote all the earnings of the *Appeal to Reason* and of his printing office in excess of expenses to this work. Mr. Mills also has a salary and all of the receipts of the school in excess of expenses will be used in the same way. This will provide at once a sufficient sum to keep a large number of workers constantly in the field. The paper is now earning several hundred dollars a week and the receipts from both sources will rapidly increase as the work goes forward.

The demand is for men who can and will do this work. The workers ought to be young men or women with no one but themselves to support and who are willing to give four or five years of their time to the cause of Socialism. . . .

August 17, 1901

Questions and Answers

The *Appeal* has been permitted to look over the examination papers of the students of the International School of Social Economy, which closed its first term in Girard, Kan., December 30. The following questions and answers have been selected as showing the scope of work embraced in the course of study. Prof. Mills has reason to feel gratified at the result of the first term of the training school.

To whom does the earth belong?

The earth, being necessary for man's existence and man being the highest development, it must belong to living mankind. As the right to life is admitted to be inalienable, the right to the means of life must be inalienable, and necessarily must belong to all the human race.—Mrs. R. C. Massey.

Why is Socialism the only platform upon which all workers, including farmers, can be united?

Because it is the only one ever devised broad enough to include all of the toilers of all of the earth, in the equal rights to all. The trade union provided for the wage workers, the grange and alliance for the farmer, but Socialism embraces them all.—Miss Kate Richards, Kansas City, Mo.

Trace the origin of the trusts. Why must it be a world trust? What of the strikes, tariffs and competing companies under a world trust?

The formation of the trust has been similar to the formation of both ancient and mediaeval world powers. They were military, it is commercial, but the principle is the same. Machinery and commerce outgrew the power of the individual manager and a corporation was formed, borrowing the power of the state to further its aims. The law of expansion is relentless; the corporation must fight forever wider markets, or be overwhelmed. The stronger absorbed the weaker, and the struggle waxing ever fiercer threatened ruin and bankruptcy to even the victorious—union was the only relief. This was primarily caused by the fact that machinery had been constructed of fully twice the capacity required by the market, the trust could dismantle the unproductive and unprofitable plants; and having the power to arbitrarily fix prices, continue to pay dividends to the owners of nonexistent factories. To prevent being fleeced in turn by other combinations, the trust must continue to extend its range to include all other branches of productive industry and transportation till it becomes universal. It must, to keep its factories running, contrive to reach out for ever wider markets to continue its surplus until it becomes world-wide. When it ceases to expand it must perish. It cannot in its very nature tolerate competition, and the strike cannot hope to affect it unless the labor organization is even more extensive than the trust. In the event of a strike in one country the factory is exported, or unorganized laborers imported and the strikers held down by the powers of the state, which are essential to the trust. The only vulnerable point for the people to attack is this same political power. That is the key to the entire situation.—E. Backus, Carthage, Mo.

Does rent, interest or profit rest in any necessary factor in production? State reasons.

Neither rent, interest or profit rests on any necessary aid to production. The land was here before the landlord came, and will remain after he is gone. Whether the landlord receives rent or not, does not in any way affect the productivity of the soil. Under any other system of allotment of products, the land would reward the toil of labor as well. The rewards of the soil are yielded to labor, not to ownership. Interest is said to be the reward

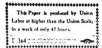

This Paper is produced by Union Labor at higher than the Union Scale, in a week of only 47 hours.

364

This is Number 363.

25 Cents a Year.

Appeal to Reason.

Girard, Kansas, U. S. A., November 15, 1902.

Published Every Saturday
— FOR THE —
OWNERSHIP of the EARTH
By ALL the People, and Not by Part of the People.

TREMENDOUS SOCIALIST GAINS EVERYWHERE!

Masthead, *Appeal to Reason,* November 15, 1902.

of abstinence; as such it is a negative virtue and contains no principle of productivity, whereas we know interest compounded today has power to deprive the laborer of his products in excess of all the powers of nature to respond to his labor. Interest is now called a guaranteed share in the profits; as such it must stand or fall with the question of profits.

Profit is said to be the reward of superior equipment increasing in ratio between the poorest and the best managed enterprises and is reaped by the sagacious manager. Today the greatest profits accrue to those who have no knowledge of the management of industry, and the trust has wiped out the poorly equipped factory, but profits in the thoroughly equipped concern which covers the whole field are greater than ever.—J. H. Backus, Houston, Texas.

January 11, 1902

The Appeal's national circulation made the paper a better source of information than the Socialist party's generally underfinanced National Committee, which in 1903 was headed by William Mailly of Massachusetts.

Organize a Local

How the Thing Is Done
You Should Read This Carefully

The *Appeal* is flooded with questions on how to organize a local and to whom to send for a charter. We have bombarded Comrade Mailly and all the state secretaries for weeks and still they come.

Now comrades I am going to tell you how the thing is done in this article and I want you to cut it out and paste it up in some convenient spot where you can see it every day. To begin with, it takes five to organize. We will suppose you live in a territory or state that has as yet no state or territorial organization. In that case you will get five or more together at some comrade's house or in a hall or under the trees, or any old place that is convenient. Then you will proceed to elect a chairman for the one session. Next elect a recording and financial secretary who will serve for six months or a year as you may elect. Then an organizer, and then a literature agent who will each serve for the same length of time as the secretary. But wait a minute. Before doing all this have each member sign the following pledge:

I, the undersigned, recognizing the class struggle between the capitalist class and the working class, and the necessity of the working class constituting themselves into a political party, distinct from and opposed to all parties formed by the propertied classes, hereby declare that I have severed my relations with all other parties; that I endorse the platform and constitution of the Socialist party, and hereby apply for admission to membership in said party.

Now you are ready for business as stated above. Next collect ten cents dues from each member. Your secretary will then draw up a paper like the following: we, the undersigned votes of _____ having complied with all the requirements for membership in the Socialist party hereby make application for charter as a local. Don't fail to enclose the dues for each member with the application. You will find Comrade Mailly's address given below, and he will be immensely tickled to receive your application, and will send you a charter of which you will be proud. If you live in any of the organized states given below you will send to your state secretary, acting precisely as outlined above. Your own state official will be just as much pleased as the national official. Now we fully believe that hundreds of locals can be formed in the next 30 days, and we are going to keep a record in the columns of the *Appeal* of the result, so just as soon as you have organized send us the particulars on a postal card. It won't take but a moment and we will smile all over the office every time a card comes in. Who will report first?

July 18, 1903

By reporting Socialist activities in the various states, the Appeal helped to bind Socialists into a national movement.

How We Move in Alabama

F. X. Waldhorst, State Sec'y

Socialism in the South—in Dixie! Well, who would have thought such a thing possible? Only two years ago we had two small locals in the state and no agitation. To-day there is a good state organization. In 1902 we had nominees for state office and polled 2,312 votes, with absolutely no campaign money, no organization worth mentioning. To-day we are claiming and getting the attention of the public to such an extent that the plutocratic dailies are giving us space every time we ask for it. There has been but little said against the cause, sometimes some ridicule, and such arguments as rain-bow chasers. The Socialist movement in the South has such peculiar conditions to contend with as probably are found in no other section of the country. The race question, for one, and the conservative, reactionary, dominant Democratic party, for the other. As the negro is practically disfranchised in this state, he cannot help us much, but there are signs that the negro is taking to Socialism when he gets the chance to study it;

as he is the most class-conscious "work mule" there is, he will soon become a factor. In this state the Democratic party has been on top since the war with but little interruption, not because it is the strongest party, but because the voters have mostly stayed at home for various reasons. The Populists, who were quite a factor in politics for a short time, were sold out, like in other places, and do not go to the polls at all. About 45% of all the registered voters stayed at home at the last election. At that time, on the adoption of the new constitution, which was framed almost exclusively by railroad attorneys, or their friends, it was openly admitted and gloried in, that the election in the past went Democratic under any circumstances in order, it was said, to keep the negro from dominating the state. Counting out is an open fact and from what can be learned, it is not a lost art to-day.

But conditions are changing fast, and the old Populist element is coming to the front again, and that old daring spirit of the men who stood for five years in defense of what they thought and believed was right, is asserting itself to such a degree that great strides will be made from now on. Apparently the people are accepting Socialism faster here than they are in the East. The farming element predominates so far, but the industries are growing fast, and are teaching the people what to expect from them, by taking the little white children and working them 12 to 13 hours a day, while the negro goes to school. Audiences accept our lectures in a very respectful manner, though much is an unknown quantity to them. In a very short time, when we have been before the people longer, the comrades in other parts of the country will be surprised at the result of a few dimes expended in organizing this state, and not enough praise can be given to the *Appeal to Reason* for its influence in this work.

We have 20 locals in the state now, and the number is constantly increasing. The Comrades are working hard and we expect to take our place in the front ranks at an early date.

September 5, 1903

Pennsylvania's Outlook

FRANKLIN H. SLICK, STATE SEC'Y

In no state in the union is there a more fertile field for Socialism than in the Keystone state. Here the trusts, corporations and corrupt capitalist politicians hold sway. The Socialist party is the only organized political force arrayed against these powers of greed, corruption and oppression. Previous to the anthracite coal strike it was almost impossible to convert the workers to join our party. The arrogance of the coal trust, Baer's declaration that he and his class were divinely appointed to take care of the working people, opened the eyes of the wealth producers and they showed their recognition of the class struggle by increasing our votes from 4,861 to 21,910 in the November election of 1902.

The trick of the last legislature in passing the miners' bills at the end of the session, thus allowing the governor to veto them, has confirmed the prediction of the Socialists that the tools of the corporations and business interests would not grant the mine workers any relief. The repudiation of the award of the coal strike commission by the coal trust has also convinced the mine workers that they will not be given justice by any representatives of the class whose god is profit. The indications are that our vote will be increased in the coal region if we can afford to keep our agitators in the field.

A strike of 100,000 textile workers is now on in Philadelphia. They asked for a reduction of the hours of work from sixty to fifty-five. The manufacturers have combined to starve them until they give up the strike. Our speakers are calling attention to what tariff laws have done to enrich the manufacturers and the prospects are good that thousands of workingmen who voted the old parties' tickets will vote for Socialism this fall.

All we need is money to carry on our propa-

ganda work to put Pennsylvania's vote at the head of all other states.

September 5, 1903

George Goebel's account of his organizing activity in the South captures part of the life of a national organizer for the Socialist party.

What the National Organizers Are Doing

Geo. H. Goebel reports his work in Virginia as follows: opened at Norfolk Aug. 21 with open air meeting and good audience. On Sunday went to Ocean View with thought of reaching the large crowd of people who visit there Sundays, but the trolley company, being thoroughly class conscious, declined to permit any meeting. Monday spoke to a good sized and much interested open air audience at Newport News, and on Tuesday at Portsmouth to a fair crowd and good attention shown. Next day at noon spoke to the employes at navy yard, getting fine reception for my message. At night spoke in Norfolk again and despite rain had a fair audience. After meeting, a well-educated man asked a question, which led to more questions, a new crowd gradually gathered until we had a larger number than before, which really meant two meetings for the night. Next two nights were at Newport News, one open air and one indoors, several new members being obtained.

From there went to Richmond, which I found to be ripe for Socialist agitation, because of the car strike which was just coming to a close with the men defeated. Spoke Saturday night in hall. Sunday afternoon went to a public park intending to speak. Was told by police that only religious speaking was permitted there, and the moment I attempted anything else I would be hauled down. I said, "All right, I guess I know how to make a

183   *The Appeal's Socialist Culture*

religious address." Had a fine audience and wonderful attention. One old lady remarked at close it was the finest religion she ever listened to, and I guess she was right, for it was as good Socialism as I had to offer. Spoke again at night in hall.

On Monday went to Petersburg and found the only active Socialist in the town packing his grip to go to New York, because of being black-listed for his trade unionism and all-round cussedness from the capitalist standpoint. This left me nothing to work on, but by calling on a number of union men I finally got hold of some that seemed interested and arranged for meeting on Wednesday night. In the meantime I returned to Richmond to speak there in the open air on Tuesday night. Had a permit but was given the information that it would be the last.

When I started I called attention to statement of chief of police and suggested that there could hardly be any law against talking on the street, for if there was he would not dare give permission for its violation, therefore it must be the chief was assuming to make law himself, and I served notice that we proposed to have not only this but future meetings. Presently a policeman appeared and said he was sent to tell me I must stop talking. I said, "I might obey that order in some towns but I certainly will not obey it in Richmond, Virginia, within 200 feet of the church in which Patrick Henry took his life in his hands by standing for the right of free speech," and then asked how many in the audience would go my bond, a half dozen responded, but the officer, seeing we were not to be bluffed, suggested I go with him and see the chief. I replied that I did not feel any anxiety to see him, that if the officer wanted me to see him all he had to do was to arrest me. Finally the policeman went off and returned with word we could go ahead. So we had the first test of the right of free speech in Richmond, with first blood in favor of the working class.

On Wednesday when I went to Petersburg, I found nothing had been done owing to diphtheria breaking out, so was disappointed in getting results hoped for. I have, however, some

union men circulating a charter application, and the Richmond comrades have promised to go over and finish the work. It is only a question of time when a local is gotten there.

Went next to Lynchburg and found old local was dead, but with information given me by Comrade Hek went to work. Was given opportunity to talk in Trades Union Hall, a union meeting adjourning so that I could proceed. Got ten signers to application and comrades are confident they will get many more. Went next to Roanoke, but it had rained for two nights and could not even hold outdoor meetings. Went next to Pulaski, where I organized a local with eight members.

Goebel began in Tennessee at Knoxville on September 4th, and afterwards visited Harriman, Nashville and Memphis, beginning in Arkansas Sept. 14th, under direction of State Secretary Perrin, for eleven dates. Comrades Hall, of Newport News, and Chapelle, of Richmond, wrote in high praise of Goebel's work. Goebel's financial report for July 20th to 31st inclusive, shows: Expenses: Salary $36; Hotel, $4.08; Railroad fare, $23.06; Miscellaneous, $5.61: Total, $68.72. Receipts, $34.05. Cost to National Office, $33.77. Addressed thirteen meetings, organized two locals. . . .

September 26, 1903

━━━━━━━━━━━━━━━━━━━

As John W. Gardner graphically explains, a brief notice hardly described the commitment of Socialist party organizers.

Propagating Socialism in the Dakotas

DISSMORE, N.D., DEC. 18, 1903

Dear Comrades: I wish to make a few comments on the following, copied from the *Coming Nation*, of December 12th:

"Comrade John W. Bennett is braving the cold blasts of North Dakota's winter winds to plant the seeds of Socialism."

It is said that no person can realize what pain is unless they have had actual experience.

For the same reason, very few who read the above extract will realize the volume of self-sacrifice, inconveniences, discomforts and actual SUFFERING experienced by the comrades in active service.

In view of the above a short account of Comrade Bennett's trip thru Nelson County, N.D. may be interesting.

Comrade Bennett entered this county on the 2nd day, inst., and spoke that evening at Petersburg to a crowded house. The next morning, December 3rd, was very stormy and he went by rail to Michigan City and addressed a fair sized audience there that evening. The next morning he joined Comrade Robt. Grant, of Lakota, who had met him at Petersburg, and together they drove in Comrade Grant's rig to Lakota, a distance of twelve miles. The day was cold and stormy and the drive was anything but a pleasant one. Bennett spoke that evening to a large and appreciative audience and tho he did not succeed in organizing a local, the prospects of one later are considered excellent. The next day he and Grant drove to Bartlette (in Ramsey county), a distance of four miles, and it being a pleasant evening a large audience greeted him and he organized a local of, I think, seven charter members and the same evening drove a distance of nine miles to the country home of Comrade Grant, where he remained over Sunday. The morning of the seventh was cold and blustery and it continued so during the day and evening.

Comrades Grant and Bennett arrived at my home, a distance of seven miles from Grant's, at five o'clock, and after supper we drove two miles to the school house where an intelligent audience of farmers greeted the speaker and where he succeeded in organizing a local with eleven charter members. I wish to add that this local admitted three new members at the first meeting and confidently expects to increase the membership to twenty, or more, before spring.

The afternoon of the 8th, Comrade Bennett and I started with a horse and buggy for McVille, where Bennett was billed to speak that night.

When we left my home, a storm, at times approaching a blizzard stage, was raging and grew in severity until, after we had traveled about twelve miles, it became so blinding we were compelled to seek shelter at a convenient farm house. After an interval of about forty minutes, the storm having abated somewhat, we thanked our involuntary host for the shelter and the offer of more so freely extended, and once more plunged forward, arriving at the home of Comrade R. H. Carr about one hour later where a hearty welcome awaited us. After supper, seated by a cheerful hard coal fire with the storm raging outside, what a temptation to say: "There will be no one at the meeting place tonight, let us remain at home." But the thought that a few might have braved the elements in order to hear the truth compelled us, Comrades Mr. and Mrs. Carr, Bennett and myself, to drive two and one-half miles to the place of meeting and we were amply rewarded by the close and even eager attention with which the fifteen persons there assembled listened to the speaker. While no local was organized that night, I confidently predict that one will be formed there in the near future.

On the morning of the 9th, a howling blizzard was holding high carnival on the cold, bleak, dismal prairie, and the prospects for filling the date at Aneta, "the Queen City of the Upper Cheyenne," that night were far from bright.

Fortunately, however, the storm became less severe after noon and Comrade Carr hitched his team to a sled and took us to Aneta, a distance of eighteen miles, where we arrived cold and hungry, but happy, at about six o'clock. We were met by Comrade John P. Sundquist, who, tho in poor health, had done all in his power to make the meeting a success, having individually paid for the advertising in the local paper besides paying ten dollars for the use of the opera house. We had a satisfactory meeting that night and the next morning bade Comrade Bennett a regretful farewell, as he was no longer to work under our direction. He is an earnest and fluent speaker and is doing a world of good which, tho perhaps not immediately apparent, will be shown in an increased Socialist vote next fall. During the time that he worked under the direction of the Nelson county comrades, he spoke at seven different places and cheerfully faced the cold and storms in buggy and sled for a total distance of more than seventy-five miles.

In closing this short detailed account of a very small portion of the work of our loyal and earnest Comrade Bennett, I desire to say: if the reading of the above inspires one comrade to renewed effort in behalf of the cause we all love, I will feel amply repaid for writing it. Yours faithfully,

JOHN W. GARDNER

January 9, 1904

G. H. Lockwood, a political cartoonist and illustrator for the early Appeal, *was persuaded in 1904 to write an account of his years traveling America in a Socialist propaganda van. At that time an Appeal van was operating locally out of Girard and another was the prize in an Appeal subscription contest.*

The Socialist Lecture Van in America

By G. H. Lockwood

Dr. C. W. Wooldridge, formerly of Cleveland, O., was the first Socialist in this country to conceive and put in operation the idea of the Socialist Lecture Van. In the winter of '96 he designed a wagon for this purpose and had it constructed by the Labor Exchange Branch at Ashtabula, O.

The van completed, he advertised in the old *Coming Nation* for a companion, and, after a preliminary correspondence, selected the writer of this article, who was at that time living the life of a recluse in the woods of California preparing for the Socialist platform.

Together we went to Ashtabula, outfitted the van, and started what I believe to be the most effective method of Socialist propaganda ever designed.

The first van was a very clumsy affair. The wheels were low, the reach was long, and it was decidedly top-heavy. Many is the time I have on a bike followed the trail of that old wagon for miles by the snake-like track that it made; for like the Socialist agitators who went with it, it was not built to run in the ruts of a capitalist road bed.

Over an eighteen inch deep wagon bed a 6 x 12 foot platform was constructed covered by a canvas top over six foot high, making the extreme top of the wagon 12 feet, eight inches from the ground. An ordinary load of hay could go places where we were sure to get stuck and many bridges and railroad culverts, especially in Tennessee and Kentucky, we could not go under without first "dismantling the riggings."

Unfortunately, Dr. Wooldridge's wife was stricken with nervous paralysis soon after our start and he was compelled to abandon the project, much to his sorrow, for if there ever lived a man whose soul was in the Socialist movement, and who was willing to sacrifice and who did sacrifice for the cause, that man is Dr. Wooldridge.

In the fall of '97, after working during the summer in Ohio, the van, manned by the writer and a young stenographer from Cleveland, O., named Joe Beardsley, a fine singer and pianist, made the trip from Cleveland to Ruskin Colony, Tenn.

Beardsley was not a Socialist at the start but got off on a month's vacation to make the trip for the sake of his health. In three weeks' time he was a thorough convert to the cause in general and the van propaganda in particular, and threw up a good job to cast his lot with, what we at that time called, "The Wagon Mission of the Co-operative Commonwealth."

After a very successful trip, everything considered, we eventually landed in Ruskin Colony, stored the outfit for the winter and spent our time working with the colonists, with the exception of

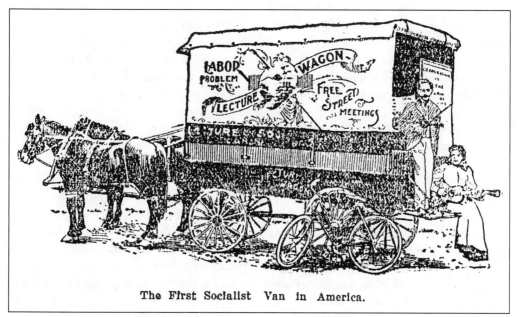

The First Socialist Van in America.

Appeal to Reason, February 13, 1904.

a two months' propaganda trip to Nashville, then the home of our National Secretary, Wm. Mailly, who was an active assistant in our work in that city.

Early in the spring of '98 the van left Ruskin Colony for Chicago. This trip we had a male quartet of singers on board, having added A. S. Edwards, former editor of the *Coming Nation*, and another singer named Garken, to the outfit.

The old comrades at Paducah, Evansville, Vincennes, Terre Haute, and other points along our trail will testify that we stirred up the animals wherever our four lusty voices broke loose.

About this time the Cuban war excitement was at its height and we found the propagation of Socialism "up hill business" until we hit on the plan of advertising to talk on "War from the Socialist Standpoint," thus attracting large crowds who would listen to any kind of talk if they thought it had anything to do with the war, and inasmuch as the Cuban war was a product of capitalism, the text was a good one for our purpose, in more ways than one.

At Chicago we attended the first convention of

the Social Democracy, or what has been called the Debs movement, which resulted in a split and the organization of the Social Democratic party by the minority faction, which stood for political action, while the majority faction soon went to pieces on a utopian colony scheme.

After the convention Edwards and Garken left the van, the former to take the editorial management of the *Social Democratic Herald*, Beardsley and myself again hit the trail, this time for Toledo, O. Starting out in the hole over five dollars we met all expenses, including repairs on our wagon from an accident, and landed in Toledo with about twelve dollars in our treasury, all of this money coming from the sale of Socialist literature.

At Toledo the best looking girl in old Tennessee came up and joined the mission, and after that the Lockwoods had complete charge of the destiny of the van.

We took our wedding trip in the van and were only prevented from being married in it by the collection of a crowd of curious people from whom we took refuge in the friendly home of Rev. Geo. Candee, who married us without money and without price—fact is that I was about as near broke at that time as—as a Socialist agitator generally is.

It would be useless, at this time, to try and follow the trail of this old Socialist Lecture Van to the time when the severe illness of Mrs. Lockwood forced us to abandon the ship. We spent four years of active service with it covering over five thousand long, weary miles of country, dispersing Socialist philosophy and recitations interspersed with music and supplemented with literature sales.

It would require a book to give an adequate account of the interesting and exciting experiences incident to the pioneer work we were doing.

During the four seasons we worked with the old van, we were, most of the time, in territory wholly unorganized and depended on voluntary contributions and the sale of literature for our support. I was prejudiced at that time against the idea of taking public collections, which undoubtedly would have yielded us a better living than our book sales and the few dollars that were given to us by our friends.

As it was, book sales were light, there being comparatively little interest or sympathy with the movement at that time, especially so, outside the cities. As the Irishman expressed himself: "The only way we kept up our expenses was by keeping them down."

Many is the meal we made on graham mush prepared on our little gasoline stove, for we always kept house, and the house was always the same, 'tho we frequently moved our back yard.

By the majority of the people we were considered as dangerous "anarchists," or at the best rattle-brained cranks.

We frequently worked for weeks without meeting a comrade and those who were friendly to us in our audiences were usually afraid, or ashamed, to manifest it by any act more than a kindly look, 'tho our book sales was evidence that we had created an interest. Practically we were outcasts in our own country.

We traveled during the day. Invading the towns at night, we rang our gong, advertised our meeting, lit our lights, played violin and organ duets, such as they were, to attract the crowd, then went after them with illustrated lectures and recitations and closed our meetings with book sales. And after it was all over we drove out of town in the darkness and camped like gypsies along the country highways, frequently taking the precaution to get several miles out of town before we pulled in for the night. At 4 o'clock the next morning we were again hitting the pike, 'tho we generally tried to have a good rest at noon, having usually reached a camping ground near to our night's stand. In the afternoon, while the horses were picking grass along the roadside, Mrs. Lockwood would do her house work and I would get on our bike and go down to reconnoiter the enemy's country and lay out the plan of attack.

It was a hard life, especially for a woman, but the Spirit of the great Social Revolution was on us; we had seen the vision of the "New Heaven and the New Earth," and the old one could no longer satisfy us. Day after day, week after week, month after month, we hit the trail, seeking new fields in which to plant the seeds of social discontent that might some day, we knew not when, blossom into our beloved Co-operative Commonwealth. That we did good work will be attested by thousands of comrades in Illinois, Indiana, Ohio, Kentucky and Tennessee, who first heard of Socialism through the medium of the old "White Elephant" as the boys nicknamed our van.

After abandoning the old van, that was much the worse for wear, we went to Minnesota and took an active part in the work in that state. As state secretary and organizer of local Minneapolis, I started the movement for the building of the Minnesota State Van, which has done such excellent service the past season under the management of State Secretary Holman, manned by Etherton and Martin. This van was planned and partly builded by myself and was run the first season by the Lockwoods. That the van was a success from

Appeal to Reason, May 7, 1904.

the start the Minnesota comrades will gladly testify.

Partly through our influence the *Coming Nation* boys started the van proposition that has resulted in the building of three excellent vans, which will be started out as soon as the weather is favorable in the spring.

After coming to Girard we started another van agitation that resulted in Comrade Wayland purchasing a complete outfit for local work.

With the exception of a van that was operated in California one season, '98, by Job Harriman, and the Lockwoods' new auto, these are the only Socialist Vans in the country of which I have any knowledge.

I have gone somewhat into the history of this matter to show that my enthusiasm for this method of propaganda is not altogether the result of theorizing. Basing my opinion on my past seven years of experience I am HEARTILY IN FAVOR of the Socialist Lecture Van.

There is room for 100 vans in this country. The van, aside, of course, from the weekly Socialist papers, is the cheapest and most effective method of propaganda yet devised. If, seven years ago, two people could invade the enemy's country and carry on an active and successful propaganda without the aid of organizations and at a time when the question of Socialism was not in the public mind, what a field the country now offers for this kind of work backed up by a powerful organization and a quickened public interest.

The strong points in favor of the van method are these: it saves car fare and puts the time of starting and stopping at the disposal of the operators. It saves hotel bills, or inconvenience to friends. It saves advertising expenses and work. It saves hall rent. But best of all and more important than anything else, it catches the crowds, furnishing a good light and fine rostrum from which the speaker can pour forth hot broadsides into the rotten old capitalist hull.

You can do more effective advertising with a good van in half an hour than with any other method in a week's time.

Everything put together, it is a sharp axe for cutting tall timbers compared with a dull jack knife or a stone implement.

A Socialist Van won't run itself; it must be operated, and it is certainly important that the right kind of people operate it. But we already have plenty of bright young Socialist agitators who are capable of doing good work with this kind of a tool and the *Appeal* is going to give them a chance to get an outfit that is complete in every particular.

Nothing that the *Appeal* has done, or can do, in my estimation, in the way of premiums can equal the one it is now offering. And the conditions of the contest are such that every one has an equal show to get out and hustle. . . .

February 13, 1904

Socialism was much more an accepted part of American life during the decade before World War I than at any other time, but state, local, and federal officials did not always respond to Socialist street meetings as though they were Salvation Army gatherings.

"Sweet Land of Liberty"

Where Policemen Club Women and Free Speech Is a Crime—The Police of St. Louis, Acting Under Orders from Mayor Wells, Break up Socialist Meeting and Destroy Banners Bearing the Pictures of Washington, Lincoln, Jefferson and Patrick Henry

Section 14, Constitution of Missouri.—"That no law shall be passed impairing the freedom of speech; that every person shall be free to say, write or publish whatever he will on any subject, being responsible for all abuse of that liberty."

From *St. Louis Globe Democrat*

The Socialist party was prevented from holding a meeting at Olive and Twelfth streets last night by the police, who, with their clubs, charged the dense crowd, striking right and left.

Promptly at 8 o'clock the Socialist party parade, with more than 100 men in line, marched west on Olive street and turned into Twelfth.

G. A. Hoehn, editor of *Labor*, bearing the banner of Thomas J. Morgan of Chicago, mounted the box. He was no sooner up than he was down.

He attempted to open the meeting with three cheers for Morgan, when a policeman's club came in contact with his head and the box was kicked from under his feet. Then the wild scramble began.

The policemen in hiding rushed from their covers, and, charging into the confused crowd, hammered men and boys right and left with their clubs. The badly frightened Socialists ran in all directions; hats were battered to pieces, women were knocked down, and their screams added to the general confusion. The police finally finished their job by attacking the surprised banner bearers. Banners bearing the pictures of Washington, Jefferson and Lincoln met the same fate as those bearing Morgan's.

From *St. Louis Post Dispatch*

"I wish the police would raid our meetings every night. It spreads the cause of Socialism and brings us recruits," said Mrs. W. F. Humstock, of 2823 South Eighteenth street, to a *Post Dispatch* reporter Tuesday. Her arm was slightly injured in the crush which followed the raid.

"Liberty cannot be crushed. I had been under a doctor's care for three months, but the brutal way in which the police acted, and the good that will come to our cause from their action, has been a tonic to me. I feel almost well."

From *St. Louis Star-Chronicle*

Disinterested spectators who witnessed the attack of the police upon the Socialists generally expressed the opinion that their action was arbitrary. The Socialists conducted themselves in an orderly manner, and the first outbreak was made by the police.

October 7, 1905

The inegalitarian effects of patriarchy in the socialist movement were often a subject of criticism by the Appeal. *Appeal editors were unable to conceptualize the socialist movement apart from the full and equal participation of women.*

Woman in the Movement

The influence of woman is not sufficiently evident in the Socialist movement. This is distinctively a weakness which should be remedied. It is true that we have a limited number of women who are active in our propaganda of speech and letters and who have done and are doing excellent service, but the number is far short of what it should be for the good of the movement. It is likewise true that in many of our branches women, more or less active, are enrolled, but here again the number is too small compared to the whole.

The Socialist movement, above every other, is woman's as well as man's on terms of exact equality. Above every other, its mission is to destroy oppression of man by man, sex by sex; to abolish self-assumed superiority and self-imposed inferiority and blot out the last vestige of the barbarous doctrine that woman is a secondary consideration. The Socialist movement is in fact the only great political and economic movement committed unreservedly by its philosophy and its platform to the proposition that woman shall be with man an equal citizen of the world.

This being true, woman should not be an incidental feature, but an equal factor with man in the movement.

Woman owes it to herself to take the initiative in socializing the Socialist movement. It is her movement as well as man's and it can not be wholly for either unless it is equally for both.

Woman has an influence and power peculiar to her sex and nature which the Socialist movement needs and must have and without which it must surely fail.

There is a certain spirit which only woman can impart to the movement and a certain work that woman is better fitted to perform than man. For these and many other reasons woman's presence should be more conspicuous, her counsel more frequent and her influence more pronounced in all our meetings.

To this end the women themselves should throw aside all ancient folly which masquerades as modesty and join the movement and take active part in all its affairs. There should be as many women as men in local branches, in office, on the platform and delegates to our conventions.

Prof. Otis Mason says: "All the social fabrics of the world are built around woman. It matters not whether we regard the history of the remotest past, or the diverse civilizations of the present, the emancipation and exaltation of women are the synonym of progress."

There is wisdom in these words; sense in this conclusion. We can never build a Socialist movement by leaving woman behind. She must be with us wholly and any policy that aims to keep her in the background or in a minor role, is vulgarly and fatally out of place in the Socialist movement.

When the crisis comes the need for woman's sustaining influence will be felt even more than now. The pains of travail are borne by her and her spirit is supreme in the crucial hour of revolution.

May 4, 1907

A query from the Appeal brought many reasons why its readers intended to vote for socialism in 1908. Like many columns, stories, and autobiographical accounts in the paper, these explanations indicate why millions of unknown and unrecorded Americans responded to the socialist cause.

Why I Shall Vote the Socialist Ticket

I shall vote the Socialist ticket because I am a working man, and the Socialist party is the only political party representing the interests of labor. Knowing the old parties to be capitalist parties, and knowing that they would perpetuate capitalism, with all its miserable results, and knowing the conflicting interests between labor and capital, I would be a fool to vote any other than a Socialist ticket. James O. Blythe, Cecil, Ark.

The Only Logical Remedy
1. Because Socialism proposes the only logical remedy for the many political, industrial and social evils so generally prevalent. 2. I prefer to vote for what I want and not get it than to vote for what I don't want and get it. 3. It is a duty which I owe to myself, my family, my friends and to our enemies as well. A. D. Marble, Oklahoma City, Okla.

The Earth For All
I am going to vote the Socialist ticket next fall because it is the only party which favors the ownership of the earth by the whole people, to be directly governed, politically and industrially, by the

"His only crime is loyalty to the Working Class"

WILLIAM D. HAYWOOD
Who will go from a prison cell in Idaho to the Governor's Chair in Colorado.

Bill Haywood, Socialist party candidate for Governor of Colorado, 1908. Courtesy University of Colorado Historical Collections.

people who do the world's work. This is a common cause, and I believe any man who will study Socialism, or even the platform, with any sense of justice to himself and all others, will do the same thing. Jas. B. Eltan, Marling, Mo.

It Demands What He Wants
I am going to vote the Socialist ticket because wage slavery is wrong, and because the Socialist party is the only party trying to abolish it. Because I will not support that class that is perpetuating wage slavery. Because I am not an anarchist, a supporter of individualism, as are the beef-witted capitalist candidates. I am a Socialist because I know that any system that robs a man of four-fifths of what he produces is unjust, and causes poverty and disgrace, ignorance and superstition; and this system is not worthy of a man's support. I have never voted any other ticket than the straight Socialist and never will. Martin Roskay, Detroit, Mich.

I shall vote the Socialist ticket because there are nearly 2,000,000 children forced to work in the mines and factories under the most degrading conditions of poverty, where body and mind are being so dwarfed as to render them unfit for the battle of life—thus forcing our sons to be criminals and our daughters to sell their bodies for bread; because if I refuse to vote to relieve these slaves I become accountable for all this crime and misery; because under capitalism we must pay usury, and interest is dishonest. W. C. Hood, Verona, Mo.

WILL VOTE FOR SUCCESS

I vote for Socialism because production of wealth by all for all will give plenty to all, while the present grab game gives too much to a few, a bare living to the workers and keeps an army of unemployed on the edge of starvation. I'd be a fool to vote myself two hours' pay for ten hours' work when I can vote myself a time check entitling me to my share of the nation's wealth. I want national scale production, not petty private production.

I vote for myself and brother workingmen; not for the leeches; for success, not continued failure. Frank Warren Cotton, Fulton, Kans.

A WOMAN WHO KNOWS WHY

I am a woman and cannot vote. I am compelled to pay taxes, which I have no voice in appropriating. I must obey laws that I do not help to make. I would vote the Socialist ticket if I could, because Socialism would give me the same privileges as all other citizens and because air, water, land and all other necessaries of life should be free—publicly owned. So long as someone else owns what I must have to live on, he can compel me to obey him or die. I am his slave. A. E. Farnham, Russell, Minn.

MORE NOT WANTED—LESS DOESN'T SATISFY

I can imagine nothing more absurd or unjust than that in a "free country" three-fourths of the people must forever remain the hirelings and servants of a few job-owners. The laboring people of today are practically slaves. They sell themselves to the highest bidder, and must accept such employment un-

der such conditions as their masters provide. Shall this condition exist forever? It is for us to answer. Socialism provides the only remedy. "To the producer should belong his full product." No honest man wants more. J. T. White, Connersville, Ind.

WOULD ABOLISH ALL SLAVERY

I was born in West Virginia. Am 68 years old. Know all about chattel slavery and the tactics of the government and the courts to foster and protect it. I saw its blossom and its withered leaf. I saw it evolve into wage slavery, a system more cursed and inhuman, with more arbitrary legislation and court decisions to crush the very life out of labor. I saw that there was something wrong in a government where those who do the most have the least, and where the loving and tender-hearted eat a crust. I saw that those great wrongs could be righted once and forever by the greatest of all labor laws, Socialism, which says every man and woman that labors shall have the full product of his or her labor. This is working class justice, and for this I shall vote. My hope is that I may see wage slavery perish off the earth as I saw chattel slavery. A. Pifer, Richmond, Fla.

TO OWN WHAT HE MUST USE

The day of industrial production, when the worker had a kit of tools or small machine and owned his product, is past. Production is now carried on in great plants which workers must use on the terms of capitalists who control both machine and product. The farmer is only apparently an exception. He may own land and tools, but he must use railways, stock yards, packing houses, elevators, etc., on their owners' terms, to market his product. Socialists demand collective ownership of natural resources and all machinery of production and exchange, that the laborer may reap the full benefit of his labor. James Beattie, Wise, Mo.

A SOLDIER GAVE HIM AN *Appeal*

Firstly: The Coeur d'Alene "bull-pens" of '99 started me to thinking. Secondly: The big street

Eugene V. Debs campaigned by train during the 1908 presidential race. The Red Special comprised an engine, a sleeper, a dining car, and a baggage car filled with socialist literature. Courtesy University of Colorado Historical Collections.

car strike of 1900 in St. Louis, where my union was broken and members maltreated by Democratic police and Republican deputy sheriffs stimulated my think-tank. Thirdly: I then heard Socialism expounded for the first time from the top of a soap box, thereby putting me on the right track, and then one night a SOLDIER handed me a copy of the *Appeal to Reason*, clinching my half-formed ideas, and later a dose of the blacklist got my fighting blood up and I joined the *Appeal* Army. Howard Lindsay, M.D., St. Louis, Mo.

HAS HAD A SUFFICIENCY

My reasons for voting the Socialist ticket, in less than a hundred words, are as follows: I already have had enough of the bronco buster's administration. Am no hog, and can tell when I have had enough. W. C. Daly, Huntington, Indiana.

IN JUSTICE TO WOMEN

I will vote the Socialist ticket because I believe in woman's suffrage. The population of any nation is composed of about equal parts, men and women. It is very unjust for half of the people to be governed without having a voice in the making of the laws that govern them, so if you have a wife, mother or daughter you should be interested. Charles E. Crosby, Indianapolis, Ind.

THE GOSPEL OF THE POOR

I intend to vote the Socialist ticket because Socialism is no pernicious doctrine preached by irresponsible fanatics, but is the natural outcome in the evolution of the human race. 'Tis the gospel of the poor. It stands for economic sanity and industrial equality; for the elimination of the pauper and the millionaire, the hovel and the palace, the curse of poverty and the evils of capitalism and its resultant wage slavery; to save my children from the curse of wage slavery and the deadly competition for jobs; to save the homes, the health, the peace and the wealth of the nation from the vultures of capitalism. O. M. Schroer, Terre Haute, Ind.

May 23, 1908

"From the Depths."

Appeal to Reason, December 29, 1906.

Stupendous Socialist Encampment

Our fifth annual Socialist encampment at Grand Saline, Texas, August 17th to 22nd, fulfilled the most optimistic predictions, and was easily the largest Socialist meeting ever held in the solid south. It was a phenomenal success in every respect, and the immense amount of splendidly effective propaganda work accomplished momentous and counting results for Socialism, and made telling inroads on the ranks of the Democratic party. On Thursday, preceding the opening of the encampment on Monday, people eager for the message of economic salvation began to arrive in crowded covered wagons and pitch their camps for the occasion. By Friday the train of covered wagons that continued coming in ahead of time resembled a pioneer immigration to the west fifty years ago in prairie schooners. Some of these first arrivals came for hundreds of miles over land, calculating to arrive early and in plenty of time, so as not to miss any of the good things in store. This irregular inflow soon changed to one ever increasing continuous stream that incessantly poured in all day Saturday and Sunday and never slackened for the night. When the rose tints of dawn illuminated the eastern horizon Monday morning, which was the opening day for the great historic meeting, fully ten thousand people were on the ground, busily bustling about, preparing their camps and getting ready to participate in the festive and instructive event. Several days before the encampment opened it was evident that the attendance would exceed the most sanguine expectations and that the twenty acre camp ground would not hold the people who had arrived and accommodate those en route. On every hand the greeting for a committeeman was, "where are you going to put this ocean of people?"

William D. Haywood was scheduled to make the opening speech Monday, and when the speaking hour arrived approximately 20,000 people were on the grounds. Some disappointment was manifested when Haywood failed to arrive on the morning train, as arranged, but a telegram advising he was unavoidably delayed and would arrive as soon as possible rapidly restored enthusiasm. Clinton Simonton, of Iowa, was introduced and made the opening speech. Haywood arrived in time to make the night speech, and spoke to a vast, attentive audience. Three speeches were made daily during the week, by different speakers, to large audiences eager to know "what's the matter in America?" Among the speakers on deck were William D. Haywood, Winfield R. Gaylord, Hon. Lee Rhodes, Clinton Simonton of Iowa, Hon. J. C. Rhodes, Socialist candidate for governor, Rev. M. A. Smith, state organizer, W. W. Buchanan, Richey Alexander, W. A. Shivers, J. L. Scoggin, Dr. B. F. Bell, W. A. Blackburn, and many others. For six days and nights the great concourse listened earnestly to the discussion of every phase of scientific Socialism, by as able speakers as are on the American platform. The people weighed, thought, and considered, and many political sinners repented, realizing Socialism was the only avenue of escape from economic damnation. Intensely serious and impressive attention, combined with frequent and vigorous applause for every speaker, evinced a superb spirit of revolt and presaged the demise of the decadent Democratic party. The attendance ranged from 5,000 to 20,000 daily. Over $70 worth of five and ten-cent pamphlets were sold. The revenue derived from the sale of privileges for attractions and amusements was sufficient to defray all expenses of the big six days' meeting. Over $100 was spent for advertising alone. Many people came by rail from a distance, taking advantage of reduced rates that were granted for the occasion. The Texas Short Line railway ran a special train Monday to accommodate people from northern points. Old party people everywhere are wondering how the Socialists managed to get up such a tremendously suc-cessful meeting. Richey Alexander, General Secretary-Treasurer for fifth annual Socialist encampment.

SOUTH TEXAS ENCAMPMENT

The South Texas encampment, to be held at Hallettsville, September 17 to 19 inclusive, will mark an epoch in the movement in that part of the state. With their characteristic determination the Meitzen boys are putting their whole energy in the work of preparation and every detail is being carefully looked after to make it a grand success. Special excursion rates have been secured from all points on the S.A. & A.P. There will be three speeches or more daily by different speakers, all lecturers of ability. Bohemian and German Socialist speakers will be present to address the people of these nationalities. Attractions of all kinds for pleasure seekers will be there. Camping tents on the grounds. Good water and shade. Wood, water and camp ground free. Turn the cows out; let the hogs go to the brush; hitch up the mules; tuck the wife and children in the old wagon; throw care to the winds; and go to the camp for a week's pleasure and recreation. If you "miss it" you will miss it.

September 5, 1908

The Socialist party Platform and Demands changed some-what in response to changing conditions in America, but the 1908 Platform, General Principles, and party Demands are representative of Socialist political philosophy during the century's first decade.

Socialist Party Platform

DECLARATION OF PRINCIPLES

Human life depends upon food, clothing and shelter. Only with these assured are freedom, culture and higher human development possible. To produce food, clothing or shelter, land and machinery are needed. Land alone does not satisfy human needs. Human labor creates machinery and applies it to the land for the production of raw materials and food. Whoever has control of land and machinery controls human labor, and with it human life and liberty.

Today the machinery and the land used for industrial purposes are owned by a rapidly decreasing minority. So long as machinery is simple and easily handled by one man, its owner cannot dominate the sources of life of others. But when machinery becomes more complex and expensive, and requires for its effective operation the organized effort of many workers, its influence reaches over wide circles of life. The owners of such machinery become the dominant class.

In proportion as the number of such machine owners compared to all other classes decreases, their power in the nation and in the world increases. They bring ever larger masses of working people under their control, reducing them to the point where muscle and brain are their only productive property. Millions of formerly self-employing workers thus become the helpless wage slaves of the industrial masters.

As the economic power of the ruling class grows it becomes less useful in the life of the nation. All the useful work of the nation falls upon the shoulders of the class whose only property is its manual and mental labor power—the wage worker—or of the class who have but little land and little effective machinery outside of their labor power—the small traders and small farmers. The ruling minority is steadily becoming useless and parasitic.

A bitter struggle over the division of the products of labor is waged between the exploiting propertied classes on the one hand and the exploited propertyless class on the other. In this struggle the wage-working class cannot expect adequate relief from any reform of the present order at the hands of the dominant class.

The wage workers are therefore the most determined and irreconcilable antagonists of the ruling class. They suffer most from the curse of class rule. The fact that a few capitalists are permitted to control all the country's industrial resources and social tools for their individual profit, and to make the production of the necessaries of life the object of competitive private enterprise and speculation is at the bottom of all the social evils of our time.

. In spite of the organization of trusts, pools and combinations, the capitalists are powerless to regulate production for social ends. Industries are largely conducted in a planless manner. Through periods of feverish activity the strength and health of the workers are mercilessly used up, and during periods of enforced idleness the workers are frequently reduced to starvation.

The climaxes of this system of production are the regularly recurring industrial depressions and crises which paralyze the nation every fifteen or twenty years.

The capitalist class, in its mad race for profits, is bound to exploit the workers to the very limit of their endurance and to sacrifice their physical, moral and mental welfare to its own insatiable greed. Capitalism keeps the masses of workingmen in poverty, destitution, physical exhaustion and ignorance. It drags their wives from their homes to the mill and factory. It snatches their children from the playgrounds and schools and grinds their slender bodies and unformed minds into cold dollars. It disfigures, maims and kills hundreds of thousands of workingmen annually in mines, on railroads and in factories. It drives millions of workers into the ranks of the unemployed and forces large numbers of them into beggary, vagrancy and all forms of crime and vice.

To maintain their rule over their fellow men, the capitalists must keep in their pay all organs of the public powers, public mind and public conscience. They control the dominant parties and, through them, the elected public officials. They select the executives, bribe the legislatures and corrupt the courts of justice. They own and censor the press. They dominate the educational institutions. They own the nation politically and intellectually just as they own it industrially.

The struggle between wage workers and capitalists grows ever fiercer, and has now become the only vital issue before the American people. The wage-working class, therefore, has the most direct interest in abolishing the capitalist system. But in abolishing the present system the working men will free not only their own class, but also all other classes of modern society: the small farmer, who is today exploited by large capital more indirectly, but not less effectively than is the wage laborer; the small manufacturer and trader, who is engaged in a desperate and losing struggle for economic independence in the face of the all-conquering power of concentrated capital; and even the capitalist himself, who is the slave of his wealth rather than its master. The struggle of the working class against the capitalist class, while it is a class struggle, is thus at the same time a struggle for the abolition of all classes and class privileges.

The private ownership of the land and means of production used for exploitation is the rock upon which class rule is built; political government is its indispensable instrument. The wage workers cannot be freed from exploitation without conquering the political power and substituting collective for private ownership of the land and means of production used for exploitation.

The basis for such transformation is rapidly developing within present capitalist society. The factory system, with its complex machinery and minute division of labor, is rapidly destroying all vestiges of individual production in manufacture. Modern production is already very largely a collective and social process. The great trusts and monopolies which have sprung up in recent years have organized the work and management of the principal industries on a national scale, and have fitted them for collective use and operation.

The Socialist party is primarily an economic and political movement. It is not concerned with matters of religious belief.

In the struggle for freedom the interests of all modern workers are identical. The struggle is not only national, but international. It embraces the world and will be carried to ultimate victory by the united workers of the world.

To unite the workers of the nation and their allies and sympathizers of all other classes to this end is the mission of the Socialist party. In this battle for freedom the Socialist party does not strive to substitute working-class rule for capitalist class rule, but by working-class victory to free all humanity from class rule and to realize the international brotherhood of man.

PLATFORM FOR 1908

The Socialist party, in national convention assembled, again declares itself as the party of the working class, and appeals for the support of all workers of the United States and of all citizens who sympathize with the great and just cause of labor.

We are at this moment in the midst of one of those industrial breakdowns that periodically paralyze the life of the nation. The much-boasted era of our national prosperity has been followed by one of general misery. Factories, mills and mines are closed. Millions of men, ready, willing and able to provide the nation with all the necessaries and comforts of life, are forced into idleness and starvation.

Within recent times the trusts and monopolies have attained an enormous and menacing development. They have acquired the power to dictate the terms upon which we shall be allowed to live. The trusts fix the prices of our bread, meat and sugar, of our coal, oil and clothing, of our raw material and machinery, of all the necessities of life.

The present desperate condition of the workers has been made the opportunity for a renewed onslaught on organized labor. The highest courts of the country have within the last year rendered decision after decision depriving the workers of rights which they had won by generations of struggle.

The attempt to destroy the Western Federation of Miners, although defeated by the solidarity of organized labor and the Socialist movement, revealed the existence of a far-reaching and unscrupulous conspiracy by the ruling class against the organizations of labor.

In their efforts to take the lives of the leaders of the miners the conspirators violated state laws and the federal constitution in a manner seldom equaled even in a country so completely dominated by the profit-seeking class as is the United States.

The congress of the United States has shown its contempt for the interests of labor as plainly and unmistakably as have the other branches of government. The laws for which the labor organizations have continually petitioned have failed to pass. Laws ostensibly enacted for the benefit of labor have been distorted against labor.

The working class of the United States cannot expect any remedy for its wrongs from the present ruling class or from the dominant parties. So long as a small number of individuals are permitted to control the sources of the nation's wealth for their private profit in competition with each other and for the exploitation of their fellow men, industrial depressions are bound to occur at certain intervals. No currency reforms or other legislative measures proposed by capitalist reformers can avail against these fatal results of utter anarchy in production.

Individual competition leads inevitably to combinations and trusts. No amount of government regulation, or of publicity or of restrictive legislation will arrest the natural course of modern industrial development.

While our courts, legislatures and executive offices remain in the hands of the ruling classes and their agents, the government will be used in the interests of these classes as against the toilers.

Political parties are but the expression of economic class interests. The Republican, the Democratic and the so-called "Independence" parties, and all parties other than the Socialist party, are financed, directed and controlled by the representatives of different groups of the ruling class.

In the maintenance of class government both

the Democratic and Republican parties have been equally guilty. The Republican party has had control of the national government and has been directly and actively responsible for these wrongs. The Democratic party, while saved from direct responsibility by its political impotence, has shown itself equally subservient to the aims of the capitalist class whenever and wherever it has been in power. The old chattel slave-owning aristocracy of the south, which was the backbone of the Democratic party, has been supplanted by a child slave plutocracy. In the great cities of our country the Democratic party is allied with the criminal element of the slums as the Republican party is allied with the predatory criminals of the palace in maintaining the interest of the possessing class.

The various "reform" movements and parties which have sprung up within recent years are but the clumsy expression of widespread popular discontent. They are not based on an intelligent understanding of the historical development of civilization and of the economic and political needs of our time. They are bound to perish as the numerous middle class reform movements of the past have perished.

GENERAL DEMANDS

1. The immediate government relief of the unemployed workers by building schools, by reforesting of cut-over waste lands, by reclamation of arid tracts, and the building of canals, and by extending all other useful public works. All persons employed on such work shall be employed directly by the government under an eight-hour work-day and at the prevailing union wages. The government shall also loan money to states and municipalities without interest for the purpose of carrying on public works. It shall contribute to the funds of labor organizations for the purpose of assisting their unemployed members, and shall take such other measures within its power as will lessen the widespread misery of the workers caused by the misrule of the capitalist class.

2. The collective ownership of railroads, telegraphs, telephones, steamship lines and all other means of social transportation and communication and all land.

3. The collective ownership of all industries which are organized on a national scale and in which competition has virtually ceased to exist.

4. The extension of the public domain to include mines, quarries, oil wells, forests and water power.

5. The occupancy and use of land to be the sole title to possession. The scientific reforestation of timber lands and the reclamation of swamp lands. The land so reforested or reclaimed to be permanently retained as a part of the public domain.

6. The absolute freedom of press, speech and assemblage.

INDUSTRIAL DEMANDS

7—The improvement of the industrial condition of the workers.

(a) By shortening the workday in keeping with the increased productiveness of machinery.

(b) By securing to every worker a rest period of not less than a day and a half in each week.

(c) By securing a more effective inspection of workshops and factories.

(d) By forbidding the employment of children under sixteen years of age.

(e) By forbidding the inter-state transportation of the products of child labor, of convict labor and of all uninspected factories.

(f) By abolishing official charity and substituting in its place compulsory insurance against unemployment, illness, accidents, invalidism, old age and death.

POLITICAL DEMANDS

8. The extension of inheritance taxes, graduated in proportion to the amount of the bequests and to the nearness of kin.

9. A graduated income tax.

10. Unrestricted and equal suffrage for men and women, and we pledge ourselves to engage in an active campaign in that direction.

11. The initiative and referendum, proportional representation and the right of recall.

12. The abolition of the senate.

13. The abolition of the power usurped by the supreme court of the United States to pass upon the constitutionality of legislation enacted by congress. National laws to be repealed or abrogated only by act of congress or by a referendum of the whole people.

14. That the constitution be made amendable by majority vote.

15. The enactment of further measures for general education and for the consecration of health. The bureau of education to be made a department. The creation of a department of public health.

16. The separation of the present bureau of labor from the department of commerce and labor, and the establishment of a department of labor.

17. That all judges be elected by the people for short terms, and that the power to issue injunctions shall be curbed by immediate legislation.

18. The free administration of justice.

Such measures of relief as we may be able to force from capitalism are but a preparation of the workers to seize the whole powers of government, in order that they may thereby lay hold of the whole system of industry and thus come to their rightful inheritance.

October 10, 1908

Numerous American towns and cities voted Socialist, Milwaukee, Wisconsin; Berkeley, California; Schenectady, New York; and Butte, Montana, most notable among them. Although specific to Butte, the programs instituted by Montana Socialists are illustrative of those put into effect by Socialists elected elsewhere in the United States.

The Work in Butte

A. G. EDMUNDS

The Socialist victory here last spring was not the result of a sudden rising of public indignation, as capitalist newspapers would like to have it appear. It was the legitimate outcome of a long, hard, forceful, never-ceasing campaign to bring the working class of Butte to a class-consciousness that would make them see that their interests are the interests and purpose of the Socialist party.

After the fall election, which showed a surprising increase in the Socialist vote, the time seemed ripe for the launching of a Socialist paper, and so, in December, the *Butte Socialist* was brought forth under the auspices of the city central committee. Following the plan adopted in Milwaukee, the pa-

per was distributed free to every house in Butte. The first edition contained 8,000 copies, the second, 10,000, the third, 11,000, and now we are distributing 12,000 copies. At first the paper appeared monthly, but prior to the election in the spring it was changed to a semi-monthly and has so continued.

It was evident at once that the paper had appeared at the psychological moment. The people received it gladly and watched for the succeeding copies eagerly. As the election drew near extras were printed every other day and faithfully distributed to the people. It was purely a literature campaign, there being only three meetings held during the entire time. We launched our platform two weeks ahead of the other parties and it was of such a character that it left the old line politicians not a plank to stand on.

In the meantime we had secured the services of the state organizer, and altogether, we made the campaign what it was afterward pronounced to be by the old party war horses, "the most perfectly managed campaign ever seen in the city of Butte."

It accomplished its purpose, for the working class vote was practically unanimous for the

Appeal to Reason, March 4, 1911.

How Miss Socialism Will Work.

Socialist party, and we elected the mayor, city treasurer, police judge, and five aldermen. This leaves us still in the minority in the city council, but we are bending every effort to make it a Socialist city council in the next election.

Meanwhile, these are some of the things the Socialists have done in the two months of their tenure of office:

Established economies of from $5,000 to $7,000 per month.

Established a clean city for the first time in ten years.

Recommended and accomplished a plan for the purchase of city horses for street work.

Purchased materials and instituted a policy for doing public improvements by city whenever and wherever state laws favoring a contract system could be evaded.

Proposed a new license bill designed to secure additional revenue from corporations and large business institutions heretofore exempt.

Discontinued the old practice of blackmail on women of the red light district.

Submitted to the city council an ordinance providing for the funding of the warrant indebtedness of the city, which if adopted will mean an immense saving in interest to the city.

August 19, 1911

Masthead, *Appeal to Reason*, April 6, 1912.

"Why You Should Vote for Socialism" provides both the Socialist political (or electoral) analysis and a sense of Eugene Debs's oratorical passion and effect.

Why You Should Vote for Socialism

Eugene V. Debs

There are ninety million reasons why you should vote for Socialism in America this year and every one of them is a pulsing, breathing, human reason!

You must either vote for or against your own material interests as a wealth producer; there is no political purgatory in this nation of ours, despite the desperate efforts of so-called Progressive capitalist politicians to establish one. Socialism alone represents the material heaven of plenty for those who toil and the Socialist party alone offers the political means for attaining that heaven of economic plenty which the toil of the workers of the world provides in unceasing and measureless flow.

Capitalism represents the material hell of want and pinching poverty of degradation and prostitution for those who toil and in which you now exist, and each and every political party, other than the Socialist party, stands for the perpetuation of this economic hell of capitalism.

For the first time in all history you who toil possess the power to peacefully better your own condition. The little slip of paper which you hold in your hand on election day is more potent than all the armies of all the kings of earth. To that ballot the will of despots must bow; before its alchemy the mythical power of money melts away and is as the fleeting mists before the morning sun.

Upon the political battlefield the worker meets the millionaire upon terms of absolute equality.

On any chosen day, you who toil may vote out of existence the system which robs and plunders you, for you are many and your oppressors are few.

You who toil are the arbiters of your own destiny in a sense never before realized by the workers of the earth.

In a single bloodless battle you can put an end to poverty; you alone possess the key which will unlock the fetters that bind you to a life of unrequited toil.

At your command, the millions of child slaves now toiling in the factories and mines of capitalism will troop forth to joyous freedom.

Either you must vote for capitalism, with its ever increasing poverty and prostitution for the workers—with its army, its militia, its police and its courts, with which it enforces its bestial conditions upon you—or else you must vote for Socialism which proclaims industrial peace in place of war—plenty in place of poverty—love and chastity in place of vice and prostitution.

I care not by what name the political parties of capitalism are called, Republican, Democrat, Progressive, they are all one and stand irretrievably committed to the preservation and perpetuation of capitalism with all its horrors of vice and corruption, in city, state and nation.

For you, the workers of this nation, there is but one issue in this campaign and that issue is Socialism vs. Capitalism. Beside this issue all other questions pale into insignificance. In the name of civilization, Socialism challenges capitalism to justify its right to exist.

Appeal to Reason,
September 21, 1912.

Can the Leopard Change His Spots?

Here we have a primal political issue as incapable of misconception or misunderstanding as was the issue between the advocates of human slavery and the abolitionists of half a century ago.

Today capitalism stands stripped in all its hideous nakedness. Its political spokesmen of whatever name or brand must justify the almost universal poverty which it visits upon the useful workers of this nation. They must justify the multi-millionaire and the pauper. They must justify the slaughter of the workers in the mines and mills, the factories and upon the railways of capitalism.

They must justify the ever present army of the millions of unemployed. They must justify the employment of millions of wives and mothers, daughters and sisters, at a wage which drives six hundred thousand of them into the brothels of capitalism.

They must justify a child slavery which chains more than two million helpless little ones to the chariot wheels of modern capitalism.

They must justify the civic and political rottenness which permeates the institutions of capitalism like a living leprosy, debauching alike the policeman on his beat and the judge upon his bench.

They must justify the prostitution of the press and pulpit, of schools and colleges, which serve the interests of capitalism and thereby poison the very fountainhead of the nation's source of information and intelligence.

Beside these terrible facts of capitalism how puerile, how utterly imbecile is the chatter about the "tariff," "the control of corporations," "the dignity of the courts," "the theft of delegates to national conventions of capitalist parties" and half a hundred other so-called "issues" with which capitalism seeks to cozen the worker out of his vote!

Can you, my fellow-worker, justify a vote of confidence in capitalism in the face of this terrible indictment? Surely the daily experience of your own life and the experience of those who are dear to you is a more terrific indictment of capitalism than mortal man can pen.

In the name of peace and plenty; in the name of honor and virtue; in the name of manhood, in the name of the womanhood and in the name of the childhood of this nation, you should cast your ballot for Socialism.

In the name of human liberty Socialism invites you to rally to its standard. Behind the ramparts of capitalism, buttressed by soldiers and costs, cower the latest beneficiaries of human slavery. They are the modern captains of industry—the owners of this and every nation of earth.

As long as *you* must *use* the things *they own*, the modern machinery of production and distribution, just so long will you be slaves. Just so long will your wives and daughters fill the brothels of the rich. Just so long will your children be sacrificed upon the altars of human greed. Just so long will the vast army of the unemployed, our brothers, tramp the highways and byways of this nation denied even the poor privilege of earning a mere existence.

Just so long will you and your brother workers fill the jails and the asylums—the penitentiaries and the poor houses—oblations to the greed and avarice of a plutocracy, compared with which the greed of the chattel slave master was respectable.

In the name of that democracy which, in its final interpretation, spells universal brotherhood, you should vote for Socialism. It is the universal bond that binds the workers of all tongues and of every nation and its password is "Love and Liberty."

August 31, 1912

The socialist vote in 1912 was something of a disappointment for optimistic socialists, but the following table is a revealing record of socialist influence in America.

Official Socialist Vote Over 900,000

At last the Socialist vote is complete. A study of the table printed herewith will show there has been a steady advance in Socialism from its inception in America. The one thing most clearly shown by the last election is that Socialism has ceased to be confined to the cities or to one section of the country. It is now a national party as absolutely no other party in America is. It has a vote, sometimes small but nevertheless a start, in practically every county in every state of the union.

A most remarkable showing is that of the south. Following is the vote of the southern states. The increase is great in all except three. Adverse election laws, and, in Florida, the dismissal of thousands of cigar makers since the 1908 election, account for the decrease. The increases have been helped by a southeastern secretary appointed by the national committee and a southeastern edition issued weekly by the *Appeal*. The vote in the southern states is as follows:

States	1908	1912
Georgia	224	1,014
Kentucky	5,239	11,647
Louisiana	1,641	2,675

Mississippi	23	2,061
North Carolina	437	3,100
Oklahoma	24,707	41,678
South Carolina	70	164

In some states as in Alabama and Texas, Debs ran second. It shows that the south will admit Socialism in preference to Republican policies.

The west also showed a remarkable gain. Sometimes this gain was more than 100 per cent. This is worthy of consideration from the fact that in many of the states farming is the leading industry and there are no big cities. Wisconsin lost, perhaps because of the agitation of the Progressives and the personal popularity of some who opposed Socialism. Following is the vote in this group of states:

States	1908	1912
Colorado	9,608	16,418
Iowa	9,685	16,487
Missouri	19,957	28,148
Kansas	16,994	26,907
Minnesota	14,527	27,505
Nebraska	6,721	10,214
Nevada	3,637	4,500
New Mexico	1,056	2,859
Idaho	6,400	11,960
Utah	4,889	9,889
Washington	15,994	39,994
Wyoming	2,155	2,715
Montana	5,412	10,828

The middle states also made remarkable gains. These are for the most part states where big cities are located. They indicate that the wage earner is not losing interest in Socialism. Four years ago these states polled more than one-half the votes in America. This year they polled about one-third of them. This is not because of lack of increase in these states, for they kept up their percentage of increase well, but because of the growing diffusion of the Socialist movement. In Pennsylvania, Indiana and Michigan, *Appeal* specials helped. The vote:

States	1908	1912
Illinois	49,896	81,278
Indiana	19,632	36,951
Michigan	18,363	27,363
Ohio	62,356	88,022
Pennsylvania	59,690	81,837

The northeast, while gaining in some states, lost in others. The loss may be accounted for in Connecticut by the personal popularity of Robert Hunter, who two years ago polled a phenomenal vote. In Massachusetts the strikes conducted by the I.W.W. worked against Socialism, although Socialists did all in their power to bring about justice. So many of the I.W.W. people, while appealing to Socialists for aid, refused to participate in political action that the vote decreased.

The General result is very encouraging to Socialists. We have reached the farmers. Socialism has become an American movement. These things were decided by the last election.

December 21, 1912

Effie D. Lallement's romance illustrates how deeply the Appeal *penetrated the life and culture of many of its readers. Lallement was the* Appeal *Army editor in 1913, having replaced Grace Brewer.*

Appeal Army

Effie D. Lallement

Here is a charming little romance in which the *Appeal* played the part of Cupid. The first act opens in Buffalo, Mo., a small country town nestling among the Ozark hills.

Frank Robinson, though that is not his real name, was 22 years old. His father was a bitter partisan Republican. He had served under General Grant in the Union army. Shortly after the war he moved to this Missouri community. Most of the

Votes by States

States	1900	1904	1908	1910	1912
Alabama..............	928	853	1,399	1,633	3,019
Arkansas.............	27	1,816	5,842	9,196	8,153
Arizona	—	1,304	1,912	—	2,934
California............	7,572	29,533	28,659	47,819	*77,000
Colorado	684	4,304	7,974	9,003	16,418
Connecticut..........	1,029	4,543	5,113	12,179	10,038
Delaware	57	146	240	556	356
Florida	603	2,337	3,747	10,204	4,826
Georgia	—	197	584	224	1,014
Idaho	—	4,954	6,400	5,791	11,960
Illinois	9,687	69,225	34,711	49,896	81,278
Indiana.............	2,374	12,013	13,479	19,632	86,931
Iowa................	2,742	14,847	8,287	9,685	16,487
Kansas	1,605	15,494	12,420	16,994	20,807
Kentucky	770	3,602	4,185	5,239	11,647
Louisiana............	—	995	2,538	706	5,055
Maine...............	878	2,103	1,758	1,641	2,675
Maryland	908	2,247	2,323	3,924	3,996
Massachusetts	9,716	13,604	10,781	14,444	12,650
Michigan	2,826	8,941	11,596	10,608	*26,000
Minnesota	3,065	11,692	14,527	18,363	27,505
Mississippi...........	—	393	978	23	2,001
Missouri.............	6,128	13,009	15,431	19,957	28,148
Montana	708	5,676	5,855	5,412	10,828
Nebraska	823	7,412	3,524	6,721	10,219
Nevada..............	—	925	2,103	3,637	4,500
New Hampshire	790	1,090	1,299	1,072	1,980
New Jersey...........	4,609	9,587	16,253	10,134	15,901
New Mexico	—	162	1,056	—	2,859
New York............	12,869	36,883	38,451	48,982	*60,000
North Carolina	—	124	345	437	3,100
North Dakota	518	1,017	2,421	5,114	6,740
Ohio................	4,847	36,260	83,795	62,356	89,930
Oklahoma	815	4,448	21,779	24,707	41,674
Oregon..............	1,495	7,651	7,889	19,475	14,856
Pennsylvania	4,831	21,863	33,913	59,090	81,337
Rhode Island.........	—	956	1,365	529	1,950
South Carolina	—	22	101	70	164
South Dakota	169	3,138	2,846	1,675	4,192
Tennessee............	410	1,354	1,870	4,571	3,397
Texas...............	1,846	2,791	7,870	11,538	25,742
Utah................	717	3,767	4,895	4,889	9,023
Vermont.............	371	844	547	1,067	928
Virginia	145	218	255	987	728
Washington	2,006	10,023	14,177	15,994	40,445
West Virginia.........	268	1,572	3,679	8,152	15,248
Wisconsin	7,095	28,220	28,164	40,053	34,120
Wyoming.............	—	1,077	1,715	2,155	2,715
Total................	96,981	408,230	424,488	607,674	909,142

*Estimated

settlers were Democrats who had fought for the "lost cause."

Across the street lived Noah Bigler—an "unreconstructed" Democrat. He had a daughter, age 18, a slip of a girl with dark brown hair, who responded to the name of Margaret. The two young people were often together. It was the same old story. They plighted their troth and promised lifelong devotion to each other. Then came on the political campaign of 1904. Politics waxed warm. During a heated argument between father Bigler and his neighbor Robinson, blows were narrowly averted by interested friends. Both men retired to their respective homes, breathing dire threats against each other.

At the gate Bigler met his daughter and her sweetheart, Frank Robinson.

Without much ceremony Frank was ordered from the place by the irate and highly incensed father.

"Don't you ever dare come on this place again," shouted Bigler, shaking his fist in the face of the young lover. Turning to the daughter, who by this time was in tears, he ordered her to the house, forbidding her to see young Robinson in the future.

Frank, much surprised at this rather unexpected outburst on the part of Margaret's father, turned and went to his house across the street. Here he found his father in a towering rage.

"Where have you been?" shouted the elder Robinson. Frank informed him that he had just returned from Margaret's home. At the mention of the name of a member of the Bigler family, the father's wrath against his neighbor blazed forth anew.

"As your father, I forbid you to see that girl again, and if you disobey me I shall disown you and drive you from my house."

If Frank and Margaret had been story-book young folks, they would have defied their parents, run away to the village parson and got married and then returned to the parental roof for the regular story-book blessing. But they were just ordinary country boy and girl. They had a great deal of respect for their parents.

There was nothing for Frank to do in the little town of Buffalo and they were both too sensible to do the foolish, though romantic, act of facing the world empty-handed.

That night Frank packed his belongings and boarded the train for St. Louis. For eight years he wandered from city to city and from country to country. As this is a true story, we will let him tell what happened.

"I arrived home last night," he said to a traveling man who had met him on the train eight years before, as he was leaving home. "I have come back to marry the sweetheart of my boyhood. It happened this way: after several years of wandering, I landed in Rock Island, Ill. I obtained employment in the machine shops at that place. Next to me worked an old man who talked little. One day he handed me a paper with an article marked with a blue pencil. He asked me if I would read it. I nodded my head, took the paper and read the marked article. It did not make much of an impression on my mind. The next week he marked another paragraph. I read that. It interested me. I read more of the paper. The next week I asked him for another copy. I shall not soon forget the knowing smile that lit up his face. Afterward he told me that he saw from my interest that I would soon become an enthusiast. The paper was the *Appeal to Reason*. I became an ardent admirer of it, then a supporter; finally I joined the Socialist party. Naturally I looked about for converts. I thought of father at home. I wouldn't have dared hand him a copy of the *Appeal*, but I was willing to risk sending it through the mail to him. I heard from mother regularly. Once she mentioned what father said about the paper. It wasn't very flattering. Several months passed. One day I received a letter from mother which contained the startling, but none the less pleasing, news to me, that father had embraced the Socialist principles. Then it occurred to me that what was good for my father would likewise be good for my sweetheart's father, so I sent the

Appeal to Noah Bigler, and that's how I happen to be here today. Mr. Bigler, so I learned afterward, greedily devoured every word in the little old *Appeal*. He sings its praises from every street corner and on every occasion. One night he handed in his application for a membership in the Socialist local. There he met father. The two old neighbors had not spoken since that eventful day eight years previous. The reconciliation was complete, save my absence. I was sent for. The marriage will take place tomorrow night. Yes, I love my sweetheart, but I guess there is just about as warm a spot in my heart for the little old *Appeal*, but Margaret isn't a bit jealous."

May 3, 1913

Born in Ontario, later a school teacher in Kansas, Caroline Lowe became a Socialist in 1903, a party organizer in 1908, and then General Correspondent of the Socialist party's Woman's National Committee. Lowe remained a Socialist, became a lawyer, and practiced in Girard until her death in 1933.

Work in Labette County

Caroline A. Lowe

The work in the county is beginning splendidly. The first meeting was at Montana, with a crowded house both nights. We reorganized the local with 11 members, five of whom were women. Comrade Z. L. Cook was elected secretary. Each member paid one month's dues and the secretary was instructed to report the organization to E. G. Fisher of Parsons, county secretary.

At Liberty school house the meeting was almost the first Socialist lecture ever given, and the time is hardly ripe for organization.

At Oak Grove, despite the dark, stormy night, the house was well filled, and the enthusiasm was great. A local should be organized here at once.

A good crowd came out at Labette and the women, especially, seemed interested. The comrades here have done good work in bringing in speakers and much of the old prejudice has been removed.

At Stover revival services were in progress, but the church members decided to dismiss their services at eight o'clock and unite with us to hold our meeting in the church. We gladly accepted the invitation and a large crowd was present. About half the audience consisted of women and I managed to speak personally to nearly every one of them. With two exceptions, they were all in sympathy with our cause, and several declared themselves Socialists and requested application cards to join the party. It was decided not to push the organization at this meeting.

At Campbell school house the meeting was small, consisting almost entirely of Socialists. I made a special effort to induce the women to join the local. A meeting was arranged for November 29th, at which they all promised to be present. An amusing incident occurred at this place. The secretary, not satisfied with the collection of sixty cents, asked me what my terms were. I told him I was working upon the same terms as all state speakers in Kansas received, collections and book sales. But that it was customary in most states to pay the speaker $3 and expenses. To my astonishment, he returned in a few moments with the three dollars. This is the first time in my nearly three months' work in the state that this has happened and my collection has gone below a dollar many times, one night consisting of one lone dime. My receipts for October averaged almost $1.50 per day.

During the past week have visited seven school rooms and talked to about 175 pupils.

The four meetings at Chetopa were successful from every standpoint. A vacant store building had been secured and made ready for the meetings by active comrades. The well-directed work of these comrades made the meetings a success. Before the second night the whole town was talking Socialism, and by the third lecture, the hall was packed and many standing. At the close of the fourth meeting we organized a local with 21 members, ten of whom are women. Walter White was elected secretary; the women were elected into a woman's committee, with Mrs. White as local correspondent; Comrade Bannon, one of our enthusiastic comrades, young at three score years and ten, was elected literary agent. They are already planning an entertainment and another series of meetings. I visited the schools and the older pupils and the teachers all came out to the lectures.

At Bartlett the meeting was well attended, every seat being taken. The local here consists of 20 members. I hope our meeting shall result in bringing some women in. Their help is all that is needed to make a great force of our movement in Bartlett.

December 6, 1913

In the 1916 national election, the Socialist party sought to use electoral strategies proven successful in Milwaukee and Oklahoma. The dispiriting vote for Allan Benson, running in place of the well-known Eugene Debs, signaled a falling off of popular support for socialism. J. Louis Engdahl, editor of the American Socialist, was soon to be sentenced to 20 years for interfering with military recruitment. He was freed on a legal technicality.

Organization—The Road to Power

J. L. ENGDAHL

Editor's Note—By a special arrangement made between Walter Lanfersick, national executive secretary of the Socialist party, and the *Appeal to Reason* this paper will conduct a special campaign to get new members of the party. Below is an article especially written for the *Appeal* and is of a series which will convince any Socialist sympathizer that his place is in the organization. The *Appeal* urges every reader of this paper to join the ranks and help "Organize for 1916." The dues generally are 25 cents a month, of which 15 cents is retained by the local organization, 5 cents by the state organization and 5 cents by the national organization. Drop a postal card to Desk B, *Appeal to Reason*, Girard, Kan., and we will gladly give you the necessary information to get you in touch with the nearest local secretary. Do this today as the party needs you.

"Organization for 1916" is the slogan that is now cheering the forces of Socialism wherever they gather anywhere in the land. One year of active preparation and intensive organization is needed to make the Socialist party the challenging force it ought to be in the 1916 campaign.

Before it is possible to build an organization it is absolutely necessary to have numbers. The great armies massed for slaughter on the frontiers of Europe number millions of men, each with his appointed task, all a part of the big murder machine. The world has never before beheld such an example of organized effort among men as is now being displayed on the European battle fronts.

The organized Socialist party is the army of peace. It is the only worth-while organization opposed to war. It must have many soldiers, millions of them, and its forces must be well organized and educated.

As the numbers of new recruits to the Socialist movement increased, and as its organization was more and more perfected, it was able to achieve greater and greater victories. Villages, towns, cities, counties, state legislative and congressional districts were captured. Some of these strongholds have been temporarily lost because the party organization was not strong enough to hold them. In other places we just missed victory because of some slight weakness.

FAILED FOR LACK OF ORGANIZATION
We carried Milwaukee, Wis., Schenectady, N.Y., Butte, Mont., Berkeley, Cal., and smaller cities,

and then lost them. We put our mayors into the city halls and were then compelled to withdraw them. The big fault was with our organization. We did not have a worker in every precinct, in every city block, agitating for Socialism, so that the lies of the capitalist press would have no effect, so that the falsehoods of our enemies would find a answer before they were uttered. There were too many vacancies in our ranks and so we were compelled to retire temporarily for re-enforcements.

We started with the soap-boxer—the lone agitator. He did heroic and very necessary work. The nation first heard the message of Socialism from the soapbox. Yet it is impossible to build an organization around a soap-boxer who may be agitating in some other city or hamlet tomorrow. But he usually left behind him the nucleus of an organization. Those who had come to show their interest by pelting the soapboxer with rotten eggs usually finished by joining the party and becoming active members. And today the agitators for Socialism are not rotten egged. They are elected to all the seats of government—to Congress, state legislatures, city councils, county and school boards. We won because of or in spite of the fact that we were organized. If we did not continue to develop our organization we ceased growing.

There were no soap-boxers in the 1910 campaign that swept Socialism into power in Milwaukee. They had evolved into "speakers," who addressed monster gatherings in big halls that overflowed with eager humanity. Milwaukee was developing an organization. Instead of a soap-boxer trying to win the workers of the city from a street corner, there were precinct workers, Socialists who canvassed the homes and in the shops, putting Socialist literature into their hands and by word of mouth delivering to them the message of Socialism. Milwaukee was the first city to be so organized for Socialism. Because of that organization Socialism is electing more and more representatives to the places of power in Milwaukee. And it is the building up and strengthening of that organization that will again win Milwaukee for Social-

ism next April. What the Milwaukee Socialists are doing for their city the Socialists of Oklahoma are doing for their entire state. "A committeeman in every precinct in the state" is the aim of the Oklahoma Socialists, and an enthusiastic committeeman in every precinct will easily carry that state for Socialism in 1916.

One diligent worker ought to be able to carry a precinct. Yet the Socialists in Washington are going even further. They have issued a call for "a captain for every precinct—a leaflet for every house every month!" So the precinct captain will enlist in his support a company of workers.

Many other states will soon join these two in a similar effort to place a worker in every precinct. What Oklahoma has done, and what Washington is striving to do, every other state organization can also do, during the year of preparation for the 1916 campaign that now confronts the Socialist party.

Few men make good soap-boxers. It takes considerable courage to face a prejudiced if not hostile audience. But the prejudice against Socialism is rapidly waning. It is difficult to find hostile audiences. That is why Socialism has passed the agitation stage. It has now entered upon a period of organization and education. And this work is easier and more agreeable because the Socialist message is welcome and there are more minds and more hands to plan and do the work.

And it all seems so easy that the wonder is that every city is not a Milwaukee and every state is not an Oklahoma. Let every Socialist official, local, county, state and national, in the land, memorize a sentence just taken from the *Party Builder* of the Washington Socialists, which reads as follows:

"WORK UNTIL YOU GET A GOOD CAPTAIN FOR EVERY ONE OF YOUR PRECINCTS!"

The secret of success in commanding an army of workers is to keep it continually busy. There should not be an idle moment for a soldier in the Socialist army. The is why the plute parties of Oklahoma are in a continuous tremble—the

Oklahoma Socialist army of precinct workers is always doing something. Right now they are working to secure the passage of an election law that will make it possible for every voter in the state to cast his ballot with the knowledge that it will also be counted. At the last election the Oklahoma Socialists learned that the ballot is a poor weapon if it doesn't hit its mark.

The greatest task for the precinct workers is the periodical distribution of literature. The *Appeal to Reason* did much to help build a strong, militant Socialist party in the United States when it provided for a monthly distribution of leaflets.

The literature distributor is the new agitator for Socialism. He has taken the place of the soapboxer. In the cities and along the highways of the rural districts, the industrial and farm worker anxiously await his coming. Socialism is today being welcomed to the homes of the nation where labor dwells. All that is needed is a vast army of messengers to carry the message to those awaiting it.

There is one year to enlist and train this army in its task. Now is the time to prepare. The 1916 campaign must not find us unprepared. The first thing to ask yourself is this, "What am I doing to carry my own precinct for Socialism?" Then, "What am I doing to help my local, county, state and national officials put a worker for Socialism in every other precinct?" When you have answered these questions satisfactorily to yourself then you can be assured that the problem of Socialist agitation, organization and education has been settled for the neighborhood in which you live. And while you are doing this for your little community be assured that thousands and tens of thousands of other workers will be doing the same thing in their communities. After we win the precincts we will get the cities and counties, then the states, and then the nation.

A few thousand more precincts organized during the coming year of preparation, a few thousand more precinct workers on the job, means that the 1916 presidential campaign will mark an historical epoch in the rapid progress toward the Co-op-

erative Commonwealth and the emancipation of all labor from the profit system.

August 21, 1915

The diminished vote for socialism in the 1916 general election was the subject of considerable disappointment and reflection among socialists. Rather than mistaken electoral strategies, however, the reasons for the decline in popular support are to be found in the domestic repression and delegitimization of American radicalism during World War I.

A Criticism
and
a Confession

THE NATIONAL SOCIALIST VOTE

1900	96,116
1904	402,321
1908	420,973
1912	901,062
1916 (Estimated by National Secretary, Socialist Party)	597,000

For the first time in the history of the Socialist movement in this country our national vote has shown a loss. To be frank, the loss is even greater than it appears in the above table, for there were about 3,000,000 more votes cast in 1916 than in 1912. Moreover, it is not only the loss in the national vote that we have to sorrowfully record. Our party organization has about half as many dues-paying members at this time as we had a few years ago. And our party press has suffered a severe slump in circulation and effectiveness.

We believe it our duty to make these facts known to our thousands of loyal supporters and hundreds of thousands of faithful readers. Nothing is gained by hiding the truth. If we are to grow in the future we must honestly examine the facts as they are and act accordingly.

For twenty-two years the *Appeal to Reason* has been the champion of the rights of the disinherited, fighting their battles as best it could under capitalism and ever educating them to the necessity of inaugurating a social system more just and efficient than the present one. To find that after twenty-two years of untiring efforts on the part of the *Appeal* and seventeen years of organized activity on the part of the Socialist party that our numbers have diminished and our common influence has lessened is to find SOMETHING RADICALLY WRONG. . . .

February 3, 1917

SIX

Poetry and Fiction

Our lives shall not be sweated from birth until life closes;
Hearts starve as well as bodies; give us bread, but give us
roses!—James Oppenheim, "Bread and Roses"

"I want some more." —Oliver Twist

Like the vast majority of American newspapers at the
conclusion of the nineteenth century, the *Appeal* integrated poetry and, to a lesser extent, fiction into its issues on a normal basis. Poetry and fiction retained
more of their democratic, social origins than at present, and many, many thousands of Americans—a
higher proportion of the population than now writes
letters to the editor—wrote and submitted poetry to
their newspapers about everyday, personal, and national concerns. Nor did "literature," now predominantly coded to mean more or less hermetic writing
for the appreciation of an elite audience, carry the social prestige arising from class-based practice. Instead, turn of the century American literature, in its
wide range of forms, was still in the process of being
transformed from a democratically practiced craft to
a socially privileged "art." The imaginative literature
printed in the *Appeal* reflects that democracy of forms
as well as a democratic access to publications far
greater than today's. The *Appeal*'s poetry and fiction
is political, sometimes in its expression of overt so-

cialist theory, at other times in its communication of
social justice, liberty, democracy, equality, and the
value of fulfilled human life. Capitalism had sorely
problematicized all of those values, in conception no
less than in practice, and the *Appeal* sought to give
them authentic meaning, not further affirm their
shrinkage by literary strategies of containment.

The bases for the *Appeal*'s selection of imaginative literature were several. The paper's audience was
variedly literate. Many of its readers, whether native
born or recent immigrants, had little formal education,
and the latter were only recently acquainted with English. Much of the literature, like the *Appeal* itself, had
to be made plain and accessible if it were to be understood. Additionally, the *Appeal* was an agitational paper with a broad national circulation, not a literary or
cultural journal with a restricted readership. Rather
than defined regionally, ethnically, or by content, the
Appeal's literary selections were national and sometimes international in their diversity. The *Appeal*'s aim
of building a mass base for socialism, its belief that
socialism would be achieved by people working on
many levels, widened the scope of its literary selection as well. The *Appeal* had no fully articulated body
of aesthetic principles, no theory, for example, of literature as an imaginative, complexly mediated form of
ideology. However, the editorial selections reveal that

Wayland, Warren, and, to a lesser extent, Haldeman-Julius recognized that capitalist relations are transmitted by literature, not only in overt content but also by language, literary strategies, and conventions. Aware that neither poetry nor fiction was a politically neutral practice, all of the paper's editors chose literature that sought to change consciousness and extend the boundaries of human possibility.

Although that literature took many forms, some forms never appeared. Absent was "art for art's sake," self-conscious writing estranged from common experience, and absent as well was literature proposing individual solutions to collective problems. Also missing was poetry and fiction focusing on the lives and concerns of America's ruling elite; in its place stood literature legitimizing and celebrating working class life. *Appeal* authors, some well known, others anonymous to literary history, both used and abused literary forms. The *Appeal* sought writers who avoided personifications of Truth and Justice, writers who gave unexpected life to rhymed couplets, but not every poem did and many were printed because they were expressly in earnest. Stereotyped conventions appear as well, not so much because their authors were "bad" poets, but because they had neither the access to formal education nor the familiarity with varied literary traditions to recognize the limitations of clichéd conceptions. However, standard forms and conventions bound readers in community and do not detract from the provocative subversion of those same conventions present elsewhere in the *Appeal*'s literary selections. In the paper's final years of publication, Haldeman-Julius's esthetic judgment came to be dominated by an elitist canon of taste, but neither Wayland nor Warren ever set out to ape high culture or to exclude diverse literary forms from the *Appeal*. From varied traditional forms to reworked literary strategies and conventions, the *Appeal*'s pages offer a rich selection of poetry and prose.

Much of the poetry in the *Appeal* is politically occasional. A characteristic occasion for political verse arose, for example, when George F. Baer, president of the Philadelphia and Reading Railroad, answered a letter requesting that he make a small concession to striking miners. "The rights and interests of the laboring man will be protected and cared for," Baer replied, "not by the labor agitators, but by the Christian men to whom God in his infinite wisdom has given the control of the property interests of the country." Baer's notion of Christian stewardship, if not divine right, struck an anonymous poet as blasphemous on several levels and the *Appeal* received, in part:

> God, knowing what is best,
> Has chosen Me to answer yea and nay,
> And if I crush, or if I kill,
> It is the Lord that shows the way.
> Therefore, beware, ye sacrilegious hordes,
> In striking down my hands, ye strike the Lord's;
> I represent His wishes and His will!

The secular meaning of Christian faith has often been a battleground in America, and the political implications of Christianity were particularly controversial at the beginning of the twentieth century. While the *Appeal* was socialist in outlook and policy, Christian and quasi-Christian ethics were so widely absorbed by the general population that they appear frequently in the paper's columns. Wilbur D. Nesbit's "The Judgment of Dives" is representative of many poems that confronted capitalist relations with Christian standards of justice. The greater a person's monetary success, Nesbit's poem concludes, the harder the eternal lesson of searching in a boundless heaven for those who were the source of that wealth. Heaven, in divine arithmetic, was a hell for capitalists.

Traditional Christian hymns, their melodies retained, had their words and politics adapted for new economic realities as well. Passive religious counsel to bear up in a world of tribulation, to look to heaven for consolation, was transformed by the advice that, hardly eternal, capitalism was a set of temporary historical relations susceptible to change. The answer to human suffering was to be found in human, not divine, agency. Not so apparent, but at least as powerful, was another effect of reworking religious hymns. By retaining the traditional meters, forms, and internal dynamics of the hymns themselves, empathy and continuity with a people's experience were preserved at the same time political answers were substituted for religious conservatism.

Unpretentious simplicity appears often in the *Appeal*'s verse. Few issues of contemporary importance are not taken on with impressive ease in Edward Blair's insistently transparent farming allegory, "A Rooster's Philosophy": class structure, employer-employee relations, "overproduction" and unemployment, Social Darwinism, false consciousness, gender construction, conservative Christianity, private philanthropy, and industrial morality. Among the most interesting of these because even indirect discussion of male sexuality appears so infrequently in the *Appeal*, is Blair's commentary on male gender. Only in illusion is the poem's human speaker an independent farmer, one of "God's [and Jefferson's] noble men." He, like the poem's other working men deprived of their manhood by an emasculating capitalism, is a "hen"—or chicken, as the same lore currently survives in the vernacular. Many millions of working men, as the *Appeal* often noted over its years of publication, were economically forced to leave their wives and families in search of work or to forego married life altogether. Other men, dependent upon a factory or a farm owner for an uneven survival at a time when dominant culture gender ideology identified a non-working wife as a badge of male success, found their social and sexual identity compromised by their inability to adequately support a family. Blair's identification of men as "hens" reflects an important but submerged male concern. Rarely explored overtly at the turn of the century, socialist injunctions to "be a man" carried both political and sexual desire for wholeness.

Some verse in the *Appeal*, such as "The Lost Game" by Charlotte Perkins Stetson (Gilman), is intellectually dense and powered by conceptual theory. Stetson's vision is one of ever-developing monopoly capitalism, a roulette game dominated by red blood, black sin, and human wreckage. The game is rigged and the odds impossibly bad; power and money are too strong ever to lose no matter how well the weaker players perform. "The Lost Game" contains the same sense of explosive crisis found in such novels as

Ignatius Donnelly's *Caesar's Column*, Jack London's *The Iron Heel*, and in J. A. Mitchell's *The Silent War*, excerpted in the *Appeal*. Class war had menacing, even cataclysmic, implications as the twentieth century began, and Stetson's poem captures that ominous threat more effectively than any other in the *Appeal*. In imagery, in its provocative open ending, and in its deliberate refusal to dissipate either meaning or the urgency of American conditions, "The Lost Game" rejects both moderation and evasion as closures.

The fiction printed in the *Appeal* shares many of the same characteristics of its poetry. Again, while varied fictional forms appear, others do not. Melodramatic conventions nearly ubiquitous in the popular novels of the period are very rarely adapted for political purposes in the *Appeal*. A passive, lovesick woman, whose seducer is morally educated as a prelude to marriage was not a convention, for example, the paper's editors found very promising. Unionization as a symbol for working-class victory over the owning class is not present in the *Appeal*'s fiction, nor is class cooperation through common understanding. Capitalism's structural contradictions, the *Appeal* believed, were hardly problems that better communication between workers and owners or status-quo unionism could solve. Utopian fiction by Edward Bellamy and William Dean Howells (*A Traveler from Altruria*) appear, as do political fables such as Fred Warren's "The Downfall of the Railroad King," but modernist, experimental prose forms are absent. Historically, capitalism's social contradictions, radically disturbed relations, and disordering of understanding arose when literary realism still held effective formal hegemony. American novelists did not respond to social fracture with modernist strategies such as multiple point of view, temporal shifts, and disordered sensibility until after the *Appeal* had ceased publication. Consequently, realistic conventions of omniscient, trustworthy narration, chronological ordering of plot, and verisimilitude held sway not only in American fiction during the first two decades of the twentieth century but in the *Appeal* as well. However, while *Appeal* fiction writers adopt those conventions, they challenge other orthodoxies fundamental to late-nineteenth-century realistic fiction. The process of adoption and rejection produces a self-conscious form of critical realism that is the dominant type of imaginative prose in the *Appeal*.

The *Appeal's* realism, a mode that problematicizes certain standard conventions, arose both as a political and literary response to the normative realistic novel. For all its richness, the American realistic novel is predominantly a record of political evasion. As witnessed by the nearly uniform delegitimization of characters with radical politics and radical movements, by characters turned inward onto themselves and a very few others for human satisfaction, the realistic novel's politics are accomodationist and ultimately conservative. Its fictional world is ahistorically static and eternalized. With astonishingly few exceptions (when one regards the fates of so many of the novels' major characters), neither authors nor their approved characters conceive of or believe in the possibility of structurally altering the social reality that presses so hard upon them. With hope and common work for structural change absent, political acquiescence and incomprehension reign. Individual solutions are repetitively proposed for what are simply not individual problems. Female characters in particular are given little or no option to oppressive gender roles; almost uniformly their longing for egalitarian relations and opportunity in the male-dominated public sphere is met by various forms of punishment. Exceptional practice aside, the realistic novel is bottlenecked in shape, its conclusions far too narrow for the issues they seek to contain. Powerful, varied desires for happiness, for human fulfillment, are regularly shrunken into four conventional closures: marriage, a shift in material fortune, estranged resignation, and death. All are cosmetic reconciliations of the social conditions the characters confront.

As their selections make clear, *Appeal* editors reacted to conventional realism with an awareness of its political limitations. Certain of the normative values and conventions had to be subverted if passivity and the status quo were not to be fictionally confirmed. However, neither *Appeal* editors not its creative prose

writers believed that socialist theory had to be overtly present in fiction. Understanding that all writing is teleologically productive of human change (in consciousness more than in action), *Appeal* editors chose prose that sought to educate readers, in Oliver Twist's phrase, to want "more." Social reality is neither avoided nor individually transcended in this fiction; hope, pain, and desire are not funneled into marriage, money, or resignation. The *Appeal's* fiction insists that trivializing answers are not solutions for meaningful human life.

Appeal fiction affirms socialist values both in its use and in its deliberate alteration of conventional strategies. Humor, the daily events of life, vernacular speech, and dialect, for example, all contribute to Ernest Poole's "Filling Up the Band." However, nonstandard English, commonly used at the turn of the century to stereotype characters by class and national origin, carries no condescension or nativist connotations in the story. "Filling Up the Band" unifies personal friendship with ethnic and political brotherhood and fuses political conversion dynamics with a socially powerful metaphor of music. Meaning emerges from the story's interior and reveals itself without reliance on socialist doctrine. "Filling Up the Band" authenticates better than explanation the socialist re-creation of musical and fictional forms.

Stephen Crane's "An Ominous Baby" symbolically renders American political conditions with the explosive potential they contained at the turn of the century. Crane's "children's story" seeks to reveal how far class division extends, how animosity between classes develops, and what can come of both—revolutionary action and expropriation. Crane's boy from the slums, wishing to share an expensive toy owned by a child of wealth, is moved to take it for himself when sharing is refused and private ownership is asserted as a justification for greed. Nowhere does Crane delegitimize the working class boy's action. No option exists to deprivation but to seize the expensive toy. The seizure that occurs is an act of liberation; the struggle between the boys is a battle for natural justice. Crane had the obvious choice of "resolving" political conflict in mutual harmony, the choice of fictively delineating an illusory, non-social level of humanness that would conclude his story and simultaneously alleviate his reader's tension. Crane chose not to do so. False reconciliation can deny social consequences, but it can hardly make them disappear.

The same refusal to conciliate is evident in May Beals, a writer whose poverty prompted the *Appeal* to establish a literary and political support fund. "In the Bowels of the Earth" is modeled on the conventions of the popular romance. In realigning popular formula, however, Beals subverts and reveals its conservative elements. The hard-working, poor-but-honest young man does not win his lover's hand in marriage. Love does not conquer class-determined poverty and certainly does not "conquer all." Instead of counseling upward mobility to a capitalist sphere (and access to the health care necessary to keep children alive), Beals argues that becoming a capitalist entails a personal corruption so great as to preclude any authentic form of love. Reversed as well is the romance heroine, passive to political conditions incomprehensible to her feminine mind. Beals's character Grace is the decisive one of the lovers. To prevent her intelligence and decisiveness from being taken as unfeminine, however, she is unable to marry precisely because of her maternal nature. "One-half of the children born to working people die before they are five years old," she states. "Half of them die, but none of them live." No marriage closure occurs: the story simply stops. Contained in the "ending," however, as in Dickens's "I want some more," is the impulse for a different, fulfilling life, one that is not closed, in actuality or in literary convention, by tranquilizing evasions.

In *The Eighteenth Brumaire of Louis Bonaparte*, Marx writes: "The social revolution of the nineteenth century cannot draw its poetry from the past, but only from the future." For Marx, the present contains the cancelled remnants of the past, both the dead weight and the unfulfilled potential for what could have been. In the present also are the many possibilities of what can be in the future. For the *Appeal* as well, the responsibility of the writer was to transform (in art) the present into liberating possibility. Dependence on dead-weighted routine, on false closures, and political evasions eter-

nalized the status quo. Eternalization steals the future from the present and silently steals from characters (and many readers) the human capacity to change the structural conditions shrinking their lives. However, programmatic "socialist" solutions could not succeed much better. Mediated by many intentions, some known and others obscure, art confronts enough necessity without adding programmatic limits that preclude the discovery and communication of possibility. Better instead, as the *Appeal* sought, to create and reflect a world as humanly empowered as possible, a world in which unalienated creation is part of everyday democratic experience. Nowhere else can skill and craft and art, like human life, succeed as well.

"A Rooster's Philosophy," a complex allegory cast in farming terms, typifies many of the deceptively simple poems published in the Appeal. *Edward Blair wrote from Cadmus, Kansas.*

A Rooster's Philosophy

ED. BLAIR

What an odd, unusual sight
Was presented here last night!
In the henhouse sat a cock
Of the kind called Plymouth Rock—
Nice, big, fat old rooster, he
Was as proud as he could be,
Perched upon the topmost round—
WHILE THE REST WERE ON THE
  GROUND!

"What's the row out here?" I said;
"Time you chickens were all in bed.
Get upon these perches, here,
Or you'll get no sleep, I fear."

"Cuck-cuck-oo," the rooster said;
From his perch up overhead,
"Guess I know what we're about:
SLEEPIN' THERE WILL MAKE 'EM STOUT.

Toughens up their muscles so
They won't freeze when cold winds blow.
I'm trustee for all this crowd;
What they need will be allowed.
Those are COMMON chickens there,
AND ARE USED TO SCANTY FARE!"

"But," said I, "are you aware
That the other poles are bare?
Why is it you don't allow
Them to roost there, anyhow?"

"Why 'tis plain as it can be—
ALL THESE POLES BELONG TO ME!"

"But when worms are easy found
They don't sleep then on the ground,
For each worm they bring to me
Gives them one night's lodging free!
When they bring me three or four
Then I let 'em roost still more;
And for bringing half a cup
THEY CAN ROOST STILL HIGHER UP!"

"But," said I, "it seems to me
You're as selfish as can be."
(I am glad I ain't a hen,
But one of God's noble men.)
If a chicken, as are these,
I would never sit and freeze
Just because I could not find
Worms enough to suit your mind.
I would take possession, there,
Of the roosts—all that are bare."

"Cuck-cuck-oo! Old man, what's that?
You are talking through your hat!
We have laws for just such hens,
AND WE PUT 'EM IN THE PENS!"

"Take your hat off and sit down
By that hen there on the ground,
And I'll prove to you I'm right,
Or I'll leave this roost tonight.
Guess you haven't yet surmised
That we're getting civilized.

Laws that rule God's noble men
Ought to be good for a hen!

"Right here in this very town
Empty houses stand all 'round,
And in tents and on bare ground
Thousands daily can be found;
Poorly clad, both young and old,
No protection from the cold.
What's the reason? Not a cent
Have they got to pay the rent!

"And if you would dare entice
These poor folks to take advice
Such as you gave to these hens,
It would put you in the pen!"

Then he winked one eye at me,
And remarked: "Sir, don't you see
I'm a great philanthropist?
(Though I'm selfish, you insist)
Once an old hen—now she's dead—
Almost got a broken head;
Couldn't scratch so couldn't pay,
Said she would some other day
When the others—now don't stare—
Raised one half, I called it square!

"I am spending much to school
Pullets in the Golden Rule;
Teach 'em if they're prompt to pay
They will have a perch some day
Higher still than this of mine,
Where the living will be fine.
Where no scratching needs be done,
But the whole time spent in fun!
Then there's other chicks that grow
In the regions where no snow
Ever comes to freeze their feet,
Where they're free from cold and sleet:
These must be taught labor, too,
And to keep a very few
Of the best on perches high
Where they'll be all nice and dry,
And we teach these black Lang-shans
Doctrines same as taught by man,

For rewards we promise these,
Ice cold lunch 'neath shady trees!

"Now, old man, go back to bed,
And remember what I've said;
And next time clean up your cellars
Of your Plymouth Rockefellers,
'Fore you meddle with a hen
THAT'S CONTENTED LIKE YOU MEN!"

March 13, 1897

Known primarily for The Red Badge of Courage *and shorter
fiction such as "The Open Boat," Stephen Crane died all too
soon at twenty-nine. "An Ominous Baby" appeared first in the*
Arena, *a Boston monthly devoted to reform and literary realism with which the* Appeal *exchanged articles for publication.*

An Ominous Baby

STEPHEN CRANE

A baby was wandering in a strange country.
He was a tattered child with a frowsled
wealth of yellow hair. His dress was soiled with
the marks of many conflicts like the chain-skirt of a
warrior. His sun-tanned knees shone above wrinkled stockings. From a gaping shoe there appeared an array of tiny toes.

He was toddling along an avenue between
rows of stolid brown houses. He went slowly,
with a look of absorbed interest on his small,
flushed face. His blue eyes stared curiously. Carriages went with a musical rumble over the
smooth asphalt. A man with a crysanthemum was
going up the steps. Two nursery maids chatted as
they walked slowly, while their charges hob-
nobbed amiably between perambulators. A truck
wagon roared thunderously in the distance.

The child from the poor district made way
along the brown street filled with dull gray
shadows. High up, near the roofs, glancing sun
rays changed cornices to blazing gold and silvered

the frosts of windows. The wandering baby
stopped and stared at the two children laughing
and playing in their carriages among the heaps of
rugs and cushions. He braced his legs apart in an
attitude of earnest attention. His lower jaw fell
and disclosed his small, even teeth. As they moved
on, he followed the carriages with awe in his face
as if contemplating a pageant. Once one of the
babies, with twittering laughter, shook a gorgeous rattle at him. He smiled jovially in return.

Finally a nursery maid ceased conversation
and, turning, made a gesture of annoyance.

"Go 'way little boy," she said to him. "Go 'way,
you're all dirty."

He gazed at her with infant tranquility for a
moment and then went slowly off, dragging behind him a bit of rope he had acquired in another
street. He continued to investigate the new
scenes. The people and houses struck him with interest as would flowers and trees. Passengers had
to avoid the small absorbed figure in the middle of
the sidewalk. They glanced at the intent baby face
covered with scratches and dust as with the scars
and powder smoke.

After a time, the wanderer discovered upon the
pavement a pretty child in fine clothes playing
with a toy. It was a tiny fire engine painted bril-
liantly in crimson and gold. The wheels rattled as
its small owner dragged it uproariously about by
means of a string. The babe with his bit of rope
trailing behind him paused and regarded the child
and the toy. For a long while he remained motion-
less, save for his eyes, which followed all movements of the glittering thing.

The owner paid no attention to the spectator,
but continued his joyous imitations of phases of
the career of a fire engine. His gleeful baby laugh
rang against the calm fronts of the houses. After a
little, the wandering baby began quietly to sidle
nearer. His bit of rope now forgotten, dropped at
his feet. He removed his eyes from the toy and
glanced expectantly at the other child.

"Say," he breathed softly.

The owner of the toy was running down the

walk at top speed. His tongue was clanking like a bell and his legs were galloping. An iron post on the corner was all ablaze. He did not look around at the coaxing call from the small, tattered figure on the curb.

The wandering baby approached still nearer and, presently, spoke again. "Say," he murmured, "le' me play wif it?"

The other child interrupted some shrill tootings. He bended his head and spoke disdainfully over his shoulder.

"No," he said.

The wanderer retreated to the curb. He failed to notice the bit of rope, once treasured. His eyes followed as before the winding course of the engine, and his tender mouth twitched.

"Say," he ventured at last, "is dat yours?"

"Say," said the other, tilting his round chin. He drew his property suddenly behind him as if it were menaced. "Yes," he repeated, "it's mine."

"Well, le' me play with it?" said the wandering baby, with a trembling note of desire in his voice.

"No," cried the pretty child, with determined lips. "It's mine! My mamma buyed it."

"Well, tan't I play wif it?" His voice was a sob. He stretched forth little, covetous hands.

"No," the pretty child continued to repeat. "No, it's mine."

"Well, I want to play wif it," wailed the other. A sudden fierce frown mantled his baby face. He clenched his thin hands and advanced with a formidable gesture. He looked some wee battler in a war.

"It's mine! It's mine," cried the pretty child, his voice in the treble of outraged rights.

"I want it," roared the wanderer.

"It's mine! It's mine!"

"I want it!"

"It's mine!"

The pretty child retreated to the fence, and there paused at bay. He protected his property with outstretched arms. The small vandal made a charge. There was a short scuffle at the fence. Each grasped the string of the toy and tugged. Their faces were wrinkled with baby rage, the verge of tears.

Finally, the child in tatters gave a supreme tug and wrenched the string from the other's hands. He set off rapidly down the street, bearing the toy in his arms. He was weeping with the air of a wronged one who has at last succeeded in achieving his rights. The other baby was squalling lustily. He seemed quite helpless. He wrung his chubby hands and wailed.

After the small barbarian had got some distance away, he paused and regarded his booty. His little form curved with pride. A soft, gleeful smile loomed through the storm of tears. With great care, he prepared the toy for traveling. He stopped a moment on the corner and gazed at the pretty child whose small figure was quivering with sobs. As the latter began to show signs of beginning pursuit, the little vandal turned and vanished down a dark side street as into a swallowing cavern.

March 19, 1898

Poet, nationally famous lecturer for the Bellamyite Nationalist movement, feminist, and socialist, Charlotte Perkins Stetson (later Gilman) remains best known for Women and Economics, Herland, *and "The Yellow Wallpaper."*

The Lost Game

CHARLOTTE PERKINS STETSON

Came the big children to the little ones,
   And unto them full pleasantly did say,
"Lo! we have spread for you a merry game,
And ye shall all be winners at the same.
    Come now and play!"

Great is the game they enter in,—
   Rouge et Noir on a giant scale,—
Red with blood and black with sin,
Where many must lose and few may win,

And the players never fail!

Said the strong children to the weaker ones,
    "See, ye are many, and we are but few!
The mass of all the counters ye divide,
But few remain to share upon our side.
        Play—as we do!"

Strange is the game they enter in,—
    Rouge et Noir on a field of pain!
And the silver white and the yellow gold
Pile and pile in the victor's hold,
    While the many play in vain!

Said the weak children to the stronger ones,
    "See now, howe'er it fall, we lose our share!
And play we well or ill we always lose;
While ye gain always more than ye can use.
        Bethink ye—is it fair?"

Strange is the game they enter in,—
    Rouge et Noir, and the bank is strong!
Play they well or play they wide
The gold is still on the banker's side,
    And the game endureth long.

Said the strong children, each aside to each,
    "The game is slow—our gains are all too
        small!
Play we together now, 'gainst them apart;
So shall these dull ones lose it from the start,
        And we shall gain it all!"

Strange is the game that now they win,—
    Rouge et Noir with a new design!
What can the many players do
Whose wits are weak and counters few
    When the Power and the Gold combine?

Said the weak children to the stronger ones,
    "We care not for the game!
For play as we may our chance is small,
And play as ye may ye have it all.
        The end's the same!"

Strange is the game the world doth play,—
    Rouge et Noir with the counters gold,
Red with blood and black with sin;

Few and fewer are they that win
    As the ages pass untold.

Said the strong children to the weaker ones,
    "Ye lose in laziness! ye lose in sleep!
Play faster now and make the counters spin!
Play well, as we, and ye in time shall win!
        Play fast! Play deep!"

Strange is the game of Rouge et Noir,—
    Never a point have the little ones won.
The winners are strong and flushed with gain,
The losers are weak with want and pain,
    And still the game goes on.

But those rich players grew so very few,
    So many grew the poor ones, that one day
They rose from that table, side by side,
Calm, countless, terrible—they rose and cried
In one great voice that shook the heavens wide
    "WE WILL NOT PLAY!"

Where is the game of Rouge et Noir?
    Where is the wealth of yesterday?
What availeth the power ye tell,
And the skill in the game ye play so well
    If the players will not play?

August 6, 1898

Daily reality often produced politically occasional verse, such as W. H. Piper's poem on the influence of the cash nexus in American life. Like many men and women who sent verse and letters to the Appeal, *Piper is unknown today.*

Corpse Was Sent Home C.O.D.

W. H. PIPER

MILITIAMAN WALKER, WHO WAS
KILLED IN A WRECK,
SENT TO ST. LOUIS.

Corporal George M. Walker, Jr., a member of
Company D, first Missouri volunteers, who was

killed in the wreck near Chickamauga last week, was buried in Bethnia cemetery today. Rev. John H. Matthews of Centenary Methodist church, of which Walker was a member, officiated, and only the parents and close friends were present.

A sad part of the affair was the sending of Walker's remains C.O.D. Before his parents, who are not by any means wealthy, could have the body removed from the station, they were obliged to get an undertaking firm to pay the express charges of $30.—(St. Louis paper, May 24th.)

To arms, to arms, ye patriots,
This country grand and free
Will furnish everything you need—
But strictly C.O.D.

Though born to nature's heritage,
The ruling powers that be
Just let you live on sufferance
And strictly C.O.D.

When entering this world's portals,
The doctor sure will be
In legal full attendance,
But strictly C.O.D.

Unless possessed of hoarded wealth,
Still hungry you must be,
Though grocer, butcher, all may help—
But strictly C.O.D.

And if to Hymen's altar, you
Fulfill your destiny,
The legal job may be well done—
But strictly C.O.D.

And, if in glorious battle,
Your life should offered be,
Your body will be sent home sure—
But strictly C.O.D.

June 11, 1898

Rewording popular hymns to make them conform to contemporary American conditions was a common practice in the radical movement.

God Is Marching On

J. W. NICHOL

I have seen the guilty prosper and the wicked win
  renown,
I have seen the rich oppressor crush the poor man
  deeply down,
I have seen the widow tremble at a heartless land-
  lord's frown—
  But our God is marching on.
Chorus—Glory, glory, etc., etc.

I have seen the healthy fading for the lack of food
  and care,
And the city toiler sicken for the want of rest and
  air;

I have seen the gorgeous follies of the pampered
  millionaire—
  But our God is marching on.

I have heard the sound of weeping where the children cry for bread
And seen the parents creeping, cold and supper-
  less, to bed,
But a time is coming, brothers, when the poorest
  shall be fed—
  For our God is marching on.

Oh, luxury is pleasant for the few who feel its spell,
But sloth and wanton wastefulness are paths that
  lead to hell,
And the reign of right is coming which shall all
  these ills dispel—
  For our God is marching on.

Yes, the time is surely coming for all things chaste
  and choice,

When the fields shall bloom like gardens and the
toiler's heart rejoice,
And women, men and children, too, shall sing
with heart and voice,
"Our God is marching on."

July 2, 1898

A considerable body of poetry in the Appeal legitimates and
celebrates work and working-class life. "The Perfume of Labor" makes the effects of capitalism's class division power-
fully felt.

The Perfume of Labor

Hungry Unknam

I am weary of the people who so despise their
bodies,
That the smell of perspiration makes them hold
their dainty nose,
Who cover up their defects with the gaudiest of
shoddies,
Perfumed with fetid animals or with extracts from
the rose.
With me the sweetest memory of all my years of
thinking,
Is riding on my father's back at close of summer's
day:
A boy of only four short years his stories gladly
drinking,
While his honest perspiration smelled of labor all
the way.

Smelled of labor—oh, my father! Shall you for
this be despised?
And the memories that haunt me—shall I turn
from them with shame?
The memories of that body in honest sweat baptized,
On which I rode in triumph home, because my
feet were lame;
And, to the music of the bull-frogs in the duck
pond singing,

I fell asleep upon his shoulder, with my small arms
clasping tight
Around that dear old loving neck, with love
song's cadence ringing
Upon my little, listless ears, grown dormant for
the night.

Still to me there is no flavor with as rich and rare
perfume,
As that which fills my memory from days of long
ago:
God gave no man a fragrance sweeter than the
flowers that bloom,
Before work was called dishonor—is it now considered so?
Sleeping on my father's shoulder, as we passed beneath the trees,
While he sang those dear old ditties in a voice so
sweetly mild;
With the boughs above us bending in the summer's balmy breeze,
Was ever smell of heaven sweeter to a weary child?

April 15, 1899

"The Downfall of the Railroad King," written in the late 1890s,
was Fred Warren's first piece of fiction. This parable drew
Wayland's attention to his future editor.

The Downfall of the Railway King

or How the Citizens of Boytown Busted the Trust
Fred D. Warren

"Hi! Tommy, come ride on my steam car,"
cried young Bill Short, as his boon companion
passed the garden gate. Tom came over and in-
spected the "steam car." It consisted of a platform
about three by five feet, mounted on the running
gear of an abandoned hand car. A track made of
old scantlings, boards, etc., was carefully laid out
for a distance of a hundred feet or so.

"Ain't it a daisy?" said Bill, as he viewed his work with admiration. "Get on, and I'll give you a free ride." Tom mounted the car and Bill started the thing going by pushing it along.

"Golly, but that's nice!" exclaimed Tom, as the end of the journey was reached. "Lemme ride back?"

"All right," said Bill, "if you buy a ticket."

"Eh? a ticket? How much?" inquired Tom in surprise.

"What's you got?" shrewdly asked Bill, with the air of a financier. Tom emptied his pockets and took an inventory. It disclosed the usual assortment of articles. Bill look the collection over with a critical eye, and said: "That will buy four tickets."

After considerable haggling the trade was made. By this time rumors of the new railroad project had spread throughout the village, and boys of all sizes and descriptions appeared on the scene. Bill was soon doing a land office business. His exchequer disclosed the fact that he was getting wealthy. Soon he became weary of pushing the car, and decided to hire a couple of boys to do the propelling act. This he did, and soon the improvised train was going at a merry clip. Bill found this much more to his liking, and he made just as much "money" as before.

In a few days Bill had every marble, every pin, every ball and ball-bat in town, besides a miscellaneous assortment of kittens, dogs, cats, etc. But, notwithstanding he distributed his favors in the way of labor to the different boys, there was a falling off in business. He couldn't understand it. The boys were there and wanted to ride, the train was ready to start, and there were plenty of willing hands to do the pushing. Finally he hit upon the plan of offering reduced rates. This stimulated business a little, but after a short spurt the business fell off again.

"I've heard dad talk about panics; maybe we're havin' one. Still, I've got plenty."

Bill, who was a shrewd financier, set about to relieve the distress. Bill had noticed that the "legal tender" which he paid to the boys to push the car,

flowed back into his hands rapidly and easily.

"Now, I'll just have these boys do a lot of things for me, and get some more money in circulation, then my business will be good again."

So accordingly, Bill made it known that he wanted laborers to build a depot. The applications for places were numerous. He selected his gang, and then made it known that he would buy boxes, boards, nails, etc. Soon the back yard of Bill's parents was the scene of active industry. Boxes, boards and fence palings were surreptitiously hooked and brought to the scene, and exchanged by the boys for the very articles they had given for tickets for Bill's railroad.

It was a busy scene, and activity in every department was stimulated. The railroad assumed operations on a larger scale, and the depot was rapidly nearing completion. The work was finished, but the minature town had plenty of funds, and the railroad still ran lively. In a few days, however, the railroad business dropped off, and came to a standstill. Bill took an inventory, and found that he had accumulated a large amount of wealth, besides having his buildings up and paid for.

"Must be another panic," he soliloquized, as with hands deep in his pockets, he gazed out through the little window of his depot at the anxious looking faces of the boys without. "I guess I'll have to do something to stimulate business again."

His fertile brain conceived numerous ways to giving employment to the boys who were anxious to ride. The yard was cleaned, and the fences and trees were whitewashed, the garden was weeded, for all of which he paid liberally, knowing full well the "money" would come back. Business was good for awhile, but was followed by the usual stagnation when the money was gone.

This time there was muttering among the boys. Tom, the first passenger, appeared to be unusually demonstrative. He saw that Bill was accumulating all the wealth of Boytown without the least effort on his part, and he began to cast about in his own mind for a means to circumvent the youthful railroad magnate. He first concluded to build a road of his own, but he abandoned the idea, for he realized that the boys would have nothing with which to buy a ride.

At last he conceived an idea. He called a meeting in Jimmy Simpson's barn, just across the alley from Bill's railroad project. Bill viewed the meeting with some misgivings. He did not altogether like it. He sent his bosom friend and lieutenant, Skinny Jones, over to report the progress of the meeting.

Tom called the meeting to order, and commenced:

"Now, feller citizens, it won't be any use for me to explain the situation. Youse know it already. We fellers want to ride, but we ain't got nuthin' to ride with, notwithstandin' the fact we've worked hard. Of course, there air times when we've plenty of marbles, pins, chalk and sich, but as Bill's got it all, we can only get it when he has something for us to do, and then we'uns go an' spend it with him over again, and he soon has the money and the product of our labor." At this point he was interrupted by thunderous applause.

"Now, feller citizens, I have a plan that I think'll work, whereby we can have all the rides we want."

"What is it?" shouted half a dozen eager voices.

"It's this way; we'll build a road of our own."

"Can't be did!" shouted a voice in the rear.

"Oh, yes, we can," replied the speaker. "We'll issue a notice to all the boys of this 'ere town and tell them that if they wants ter help they can have all the rides they want."

Contributions of material, etc., were called for, and by evening an assortment of wheels, boards and timbers were gathered together. In a few days the Boytown Co-operative Railway was well under way. Little slips of paper were prepared, on which were scrawled the number of hours each boy labored. When the road was completed, lots were cast to see who would be the first passengers. After that, the boys pushed and rode in turn.

Bill, the capitalist, was non-plussed. As he

looked across the way and noticed the business the other road was doing, he became envious. He viewed with alarm his now rusty car.

"I'll go over and see the blamed thing," he said to himself, as he closed the door of his little depot, and went out. He was greeted cordially by his former passengers, who took pleasure and delight in explaining to him just how the thing operated.

"I see that," replied Bill, "but where does the profit come in—who's makin' any money outen it?"

"There ain't any profit, an' no one's makin' any money. We're all ridin' and pushin', an' every feller gets about six rides to one push. When we'se workin' on your road we had to push twice to get enough to ride once. Oh, I tell yer, it's a great scheme."

"Believe I'll ride," said Bill, as he stepped upon the car. He tendered the conductor some of the collateral that was good on his road, but that functionary refused it disdainfully.

"Dat don't go on dis line. If dats' all you've got, you'll have to get off and walk. See?"

"Well, that's all I've got. How'm I to get what you fellers have got?" he anxiously inquired.

"Get off an' push de car, an' den you can ride on dis line. Labor talks here."

August 17, 1901

No version of Christian stewardship—a "divine right" doctrine that God had given control of the United States to capitalists to do with as they chose—was better known at the turn of the century than George F. Baer's. The author of "Mr. Baer Explains" preferred to remain anonymous.

Geo. F. Baer

Wilkesbarre, Penn., Aug. 20:   W. F. Clark, a photographer of this city, recently addressed a letter to President Baer, of the Philadelphia & Reading railroad company, appealing to him as a Christian to settle the miners' strike. The writer said that if Christ was taken more into our business affairs there would be less trouble in the world, and that if Mr. Baer granted the strikers a slight concession they would gladly return to work, and Baer would have the blessing of God and the respect of the nation.

BAER'S REPLY WAS:

"I see you are evidently biased in your religious views in favor of the right of the working man to control a business in which he has no other interest than to secure fair wages for the work he does. I beg of you not to be discouraged. The rights and interests of the laboring man will be protected and cared for, not by the labor agitators, but by the Christian men to whom God in his infinite wisdom has given the control of the property interests of the country. Pray earnestly that the right may triumph, always remembering that the Lord God Omnipotent still reigns, and that His reign is one of law and order, and not of violence and crime."

September 6, 1902

MR. BAER EXPLAINS

I.

God reigns on high;
From there in His infinite wisdom He
Is guiding and inspiring Me.
The power I hold God gave Me. I
Am sent to drive, to crush, to stand
With warning and uplifted hand,
Waving the clamorous throngs
Back to the slavery they would shun!
What of the stories of their wrongs?
Their sacrilegious cries
Offend the Powers in the skies!
'Tis the Lord God's will that is being done!
Through Me He gives, through Me He takes;
I am the blossom and the fruit;
Through Me He bends, through Me He breaks.
I am His agent absolute!

II.

By right divine
I let Starvation's fangs sink deep
Within the vitals of men's children.
Mine is the voice they must obey. I keep
A holy order locked within My breast.
God, knowing what is best,
Has chosen Me to answer yea and nay,
And if I crush, or if I kill,
It is the Lord that shows the way.
Therefore, beware, ye sacrilegious hordes,
In striking down my hands, ye strike the Lord's;
I represent His wishes and His will!
Through Me He gives, through Me He takes;
I am the blossom and the fruit;
Through Me He bends, through Me He breaks,
I am His agent absolute.

January 3, 1903

Josephine Conger's poetry appeared often in the Appeal during the period when she edited the paper's Woman's Department.

Alone

JOSEPHINE CONGER

It is hard to live when nobody cares.
It is hard to believe in the very prayers
    We say at night. It is hard to toil
      And face the crush of the world's turmoil
Alone. It is hard to stand upon your feet
Straight and proud, without the sweet
    Approval of one who knows.
    It is hard to live at all, when woes
Seem to spring from the seed we've sown—
As they do when we work our fields alone.

November 21, 1903

May Beals Hoffpauir worked as a Socialist party organizer among fieldworkers in Louisiana and coal miners in Tennes-

see. She wrote for and edited Red Flag, *a left cultural publication in Louisiana during 1907–8.* The Rebel at Large *is a collection of her fiction and non-fiction.*

In the Bowels of the Earth

MAY BEALS

It was the first time the new doctor's wife had been inside of a mine. Her staccato shrieks of laughter and somewhat effusive exclamations came back to them from the end of the passage, where a little party of young people—the *elite* of the mining camp—surrounded one of the electric machines that do the work of many men.

They sat in the empty car that had brought the party through the mine, their absence unnoticed by the crowd around the machine.

"If you are going away tonight," he had said, "you shall at least give me these few minutes. You shall tell me why you are going."

He could see her very dimly by the flickering light from the lamps in the caps of the miners who were running the machine. Something in her face kept him silent, waiting for her reply.

"I am going," she said, at last, "because I think I ought to go." He leaned forward from his place on the opposite edge of the car, trying in the dim light to find in her face the key to her words.

"I don't understand," he said. "Why do you say 'ought'? Nobody else needs you as I do—and you love me."

His voice was not pleading—only puzzled and hurt. She drew a quick breath and turned her face away from his sorrowful scrutiny.

"If I had not happened to come over tonight," he said, "you would have gone without letting me know that you were going—without giving me a chance to tell you how much I want you to stay—though you know that without telling."

He paused, but the girl did not answer.

"It doesn't seem quite fair," he said, trying to speak very gently, "after all we've planned—after you'd promised—"

"Don't," she said, "I will tell you. I meant to write after I left and tell you. It wouldn't be so hard."

Her hands were clasped in her lap. He took them in his and felt how tensely the fingers were locked together. They did not relax in his grasp.

"You know I love you," she began, half whispering. "I always loved you. When I was little and you taught me to play boys' games and thrashed those who said I was 'only a girl.' We have been such jolly chums, and I thought it would last forever. I still think I will love you always—I know I will, Jack, but I must leave you."

"Why?"

"Because if I stay here I will marry you."

"You have promised to marry me."

"Yes, but you wouldn't hold me to that promise, Jack, now that I see we *oughtn't* to marry."

"Oughtn't? Why oughtn't we?" the boy cried, impatiently. "You've no parents to forbid it, and your sister only objects because I'm a miner. Is that your reason, too?" he asked suddenly, "because I am a miner? But, no, I can't think that of you, little chum."

"It—is—because you are a miner." She spoke slowly and very low.

He drew back, astonished, hurt, disgusted; but a flash of green light from the electric machine showed him the girl's white face and his hands closed over hers again.

"Why should that worry you so, little chum?" He moved closer to her. "I'll quit being a miner if you say so."

"That wouldn't make any difference," she said wearily. "You would still be poor."

He did not answer; perhaps he could not. Presently the girl went on: "She has been reminding me of that ever since she found out I cared for you. At first it was 'How would you like to live in those miners' shanties with only one new hat a year?' And I laughed at her. What are houses and hats compared with you? She would say: 'He dresses well enough now, but after you are married he won't care anything about decent clothes, and couldn't afford them, anyway.' I told her I would marry you if I knew you would always wear blue overalls. She kept on; you know she is very persistent. She said everything she could to dissuade me, but I only laughed."

The green light from the end of the passage showed the girl's face now and then as she talked. You would have thought there had never been any laughter in that little white face.

"You remember, Jack, when little Tommy Johnson was sick so long, and they couldn't take him to the hospital—they couldn't afford it. They had only the company doctor and he finally performed the operation alone. It was the only chance—" she shuddered. "I was there when he died, and his mother's cry, 'It was poverty that killed him—Poverty murdered my baby!'—oh, Jack, it was horrible. And my sister said to me when she heard about it, 'Poor people never can take care of their children as they ought.' And I was angry with her—unreasonably angry—and she saw her advantage and followed it up.

"Whenever a child is sick or ragged or hungry looking, she says to me: 'Poor people oughtn't to have children.' Whenever a man dies or is killed in the mines and leaves his wife with a little, helpless family that she can't possibly take good care of, my sister looks at me pityingly and says: 'What else can girls expect when they rush headlong into marriage without thinking of the future?' Whenever a child dies—and, oh, Jack, they die so often—she reminds me that one-half the children born to working people die before they are five years old."

The girl's voice choked and stopped. There came a fresh outburst of exclamations and giggles from the party at the end of the passage.

"That is why I am going away," she said. "Because I never can marry you, Jack."

He was crouching at her feet in the empty car, clinging to her hands as a drowning man might cling.

"I hadn't thought of that," he said. "My God!"

There was a moment's silence. The green flash

came and went, showing to each the face of the other.

"Maybe you can forget me," she whispered. It was the only comfort she could offer him.

"Forget you?" He raised his head. "No, I won't forget you. I won't let you leave me. This is madness, Grace. You are mine. You shall not let such a little thing separate us."

"*Little*?" She turned on him as a mother might turn on one that menaced her child. "It is *not* a little thing."

He bowed his head on her knee.

"I might have known," he said. "I oughtn't to have thought of you in this way. I might have known that you couldn't stoop to such as me. Why should you sacrifice yourself—"

"Don't, Jack," she said. "It wouldn't be a sacrifice if I had only myself to consider. You know I'm not afraid of poverty for myself. Tell me you understand."

"I understand," he groaned; "little chum, I understand."

After a long while he spoke again.

"If I should work and save and push and grab and become successful—a capitalist—would that make any difference?"

"No," she said. "Business men are such soulless things. I don't want you to try. I could not love a money-making machine."

She spoke bitterly—half mechanically. She had thought it all over so many times and had found no way of escape.

"Half of them die," she said, "but none of them live. It is not life—this sordid struggle of each against all. The struggle that dulls man's intellect and kills his soul, and makes him worse than the beasts of the field. It is not life."

January 14, 1905

John Ames Mitchell was a caricaturist and founding editor of Life, *which in its early form was a humorous and satirical mag-*

azine. Other novels by Mitchell include Amos Judd *and* The Pines of Glory.

The Silent War

J. A. MITCHELL
CHAPTER VIII

Fame is no moral teacher.

The man who robs a bank is more likely to see his portrait in the paper than he who watches by the bedside of a dying friend. Anecdotes of ladies with a shocking past are better travelers than purer tales. When Florence Nightingale is long forgotten the name of Catherine de Medici will echo through the halls of fame. And as the movements of a burglar are of more popular interest and divert a larger audience than the movements of a trained nurse, so the triumph of a gambler excites a wider interest than the duller doings of the agriculturist.

And fame had come to Billy Chapman and his playmates in "The Game." Their names were often in the mouths of other citizens; their portraits were familiar to the public. Billy Chapman himself, designed by nature for a different career, still felt the prickings of a surviving conscience.

Had he been reared under different conditions—less affluent and less conventional—he would have been a "crank"; that is, he would have been guided oftener by his own convictions, allowing his moral courage a freer chance to develop. Incidentally he would have enjoyed a closer acquaintance with the Golden Rule. He realized that he had suffered a civic deterioration. Nevertheless, in the furtherance of financial schemes it was continually expedient to "fix" a legislature, to "see" a judge, to ignore the statutes and to put occasional rivals out of business. And all for the excitement and the triumphs of "The Game."

But to him, the sort of glory that came with all this, while enjoyed by his fellow magnates, was not wholly welcome. He well knew that an unjust proportion of the nation's treasure was flowing to favored pockets; that these stupendous fortunes were captured, not earned; that in this game between rich and poor the dice were loaded. He and his class were fully aware that this dazzling, golden flood was unwilling tribute, and that mutterings were clearly heard. But from the shorn lamb there is little to fear. The law, when a captive in golden chains, has no terror for its owners.

So, during the next day, with certain remarks of Ellis Tucker fresh in his mind, Billy reflected—when business allowed. Toward the end of the afternoon, two lawyers and a mining engineer left his private office after a lengthy interview. There had been much talk and reading of documents pertaining to an enterprise in which the prospective profits were enormous. But the enterprise itself promised no unusual risk or excitement, and the interview—for Billy—had been a trifle tiresome.

As the door closed on the mining engineer, who was the last to disappear, Billy look at his watch.

Five minutes of four.

He glanced through the window, up over the opposite skyscraper, and studied a fragment of dull, December sky. Snowflakes, beginnings of a heavy storm, tumbled leisurely toward the street beneath. Recalling nothing of importance that needed his personal attention, he decided to go to the riding club. He needed a little exercise. As this decision was made, Whittaker, his private secretary, entered from the outer office and presented a card. . . .

Turning to the card in his hand he read:

MR. EDWARD FOWLER

"Who is it?" he asked.

"A gentleman who says you made an appointment with him—on a personal matter."

Billy frowned in an effort to remember.

"Well—show him in."

. . . .

Mr. Fowler removed his hat, placed it on a

neighboring chair and drew his own chair nearer the open table which Billy used as a desk. Taking a few papers from a pocket, he said with an agreeable—and what seemed an habitual—smile:

"Mr. Chapman, the object of my visit I will state in the fewest words, as I know how valuable your moments are."

Upon the table he laid a typewritten list of about a hundred names.

"That is a list of American millionaires, most of whom you know."

Billy took up the paper. Mr. Fowler waited in silence until the list was scanned. It was alphabetically arranged, and among them Billy read his own name. Many were personal friends. It seemed a list of the richest men in the country. Against half a dozen of the names were little black crosses. Raising his eyes to his visitor's face, he said:

"Well?"

Mr. Fowler's clean-cut mouth was large and rather flexible. As his lips parted with a smile to reply, Billy was inwardly startled. He felt a tingling up his spine and through the roots of his hair, for several of Mr. Fowler's teeth were of gold. He remembered Payson's words, "the man with the teeth of gold is the angel of death."

To conceal a slight tremor of his fingers—coming more from anger than from fear—he laid the paper upon the desk.

"That is a list of men," said Mr. Fowler, "whom we are asking to contribute to the People's League. Perhaps you have heard of it."

. . . .

Billy raised his chin and looked his visitor calmly in the eye. The look was defiant. Mr. Fowler's smile abated, but without completely vanishing.

"My errand is a disagreeable one, Mr. Chapman. Nothing could be more so. But I have no choice in the matter."

"Don't waste words. State your business."

"My mission is to ask you to subscribe two hundred thousand dollars to the People's League. Most of the men on that list have already given."

"And if I decline?"

"Against your name is placed a cross."

Billy glanced mechanically at the crosses. His heart beat faster at the discovery that four of the names with the small black crosses were those of Waldo Greene, David Armstrong, John B. Stockton and George Payson. The other two were wealthy men of other cities whose unexplained death within a fortnight had surprised—and startled—the community. Leaning back in the chair he regarded his visitor in silence.

"Perhaps you are also the assassin who has the pleasure of dispatching us."

Mr. Fowler's smile diminished, but his amiable manner remained.

"No, sir. With that I have nothing to do. I merely explain the purpose of the subscription and see that the case is fairly stated and clearly understood."

"I congratulate you on your line of business, Mr. Fowler. It pays you well, I have no doubt."

"Your sarcasm is misplaced, Mr. Chapman. We sincerely believe we are averting a revolution—a popular uprising that would probably result in mob violence, the shedding of blood and the looting of homes."

"Assassination, then, is not violence."

"These deaths by assassination are not compulsory. They are optional. If a wealthy gentleman prefers death to relinquishing a small fraction of his fortune, the choice is his own."

"Really! Well, Mr. Fowler, I take the assassination. This interview is closed."

And Billy directed a finger toward an electric button on his desk. But Mr. Fowler extended a hand in protest.

"One moment. For your own sake, Mr. Chapman, and that of your family, allow me a few words."

Billy did not withdraw his hand, but allowed his finger to remain upon the button. "Make it short."

"I will. If you decline to subscribe, you know the result. The only six men who have already refused are those with crosses against their names. You know what has become of them. It merely means that your wife or son will give the money. Your death will be a useless sacrifice."

"Excuse me. Not entirely useless. There is a principle represented. A few lives are not thrown away if they help defeat your kind of work."

"That would not be the result, Mr. Chapman. It cannot be defeated. The whole working population is behind it. We are the many against the few. Besides, the rich men who refuse are less than one in ten. The actual proportion so far is six out of seventy."

"How much money, then, has your league acquired?"

"About eleven millions of dollars—so far."

Billy tightened his lips, withdrew his hand from the electric button and drummed with his fingers upon an arm of his chair.

"The working people of this country, Mr. Chapman, are on the ragged edge of revolt. You rich men, here in the East, have no conception of the bitterness—the deep resentment—at the conditions that result in this unequal distribution of wealth. Those who work the hardest get the least."

"If you can believe that American workmen are worse off than those of other countries, you can believe anything."

"That is not the question. In a country like this, there is plenty for all; plenty of food, clothing, space and fuel, more than enough for everybody. Why should a few have not only the best of it all, but a thousand times more than they can use, while all the others, those who work the hardest, live in attics and cellars, eat the meanest food and never enough? And all in a land of plenty. You will admit there is something radically wrong when a few are amassing fabulous fortunes, and many, however industrious, can barely live."

"All that is an ancient tale. Every community since history began has had its useless members, its agitators, its paupers and its loafers. I give nothing to your league."

Mr. Fowler smiled and nodded. "An ancient tale, perhaps, but with different actors. They are Americans this time, not peasants. They consider their republic in danger when they become servants of corporations that own the industries of the country and control the whole machinery of government. It is not merely a question of wages—of food, clothes and shelter. And even if it were, our country is the richest in the world, and incredibly prosperous. The American workman has awakened to all this, and demands a share in its prosperity. He doesn't get it, however hard he toils. That is his grievance. If the People's League can raise enough money we can achieve our object by peaceful means. If you give this money you are giving to a cause upheld honestly and seriously by a vast majority of your fellow citizens. And I beg you to believe, Mr. Chapman, that I would not be visiting you today upon this repugnant errand—as a highwayman—unless I believed in the cause."

"Every cause, however false, has had firm believers," and Billy looked at his watch as if to end the interview. But his visitor went on, more earnestly:

"I sincerely hope you will change your mind, Mr. Chapman. You fail to realize the extent of this uprising. The People's League represents millions of men of various classes, all determined upon a change. And they are order-loving citizens."

"And anarchists."

"Not one—at least to our knowledge. They and their tribe are not admitted. The People's League, so far as we can make it, consists of law-abiding voters."

Billy indulged in a faint smile. "Law abiding is good. I see you are a humorist."

Mr. Fowler also smiled. "Nothing could be more humorous than your use of our own money to defeat our own votes. We are merely meeting you capitalists on your own ground and with your own weapons. You hold us up with your trusts, your tariffs, your irresponsible and somewhat peculiar management of the people's savings. Is it not better that a dozen or more millionaires should quietly disappear, especially if they prefer death to parting with a fraction of their fortunes, than that mobs should rule?"

"Possibly, but I do not care to discuss my own assassination, however holy the cause."

Billy looked at his watch and straightened up. "We are both wasting time. I shall never give a dollar to a cause that achieves its ends by assassination."

"Just one word more, Mr. Chapman. You think our method brutal. We have no choice. The American magnate disregards the law, for he owns it. He has no fear of public opinion, for he owns the press. The only way of inducing him to take the slightest interest in our affairs is through fear of death. In that he resembles his poorer brothers. By that alone can we reach him. Our cause is good. We need a fraction of his money, just a small return of some of our own earnings. Hence the People's League."

"In securing laws to suit you, is it a part of your amiable system to assassinate the president of the United States, his cabinet and the leading members of congress?"

"No, sir. We mean to elect the next president, if votes and money can do it. With ten millions of voters, out of the fourteen millions, and seventy millions of dollars as a campaign fund, we feel some confidence in success. As for the United States senate,"—here Mr. Fowler's gold teeth were again in evidence, when he added with a generous smile, "they are easy fruit. Those gilded patriots bear the same relation to Wall Street as a yellow dog does to a butcher's cart."

"Your president, I suppose, will be some walking delegate; your congress the choicest spirits of the poor house, and your chief justices retired assassins."

Billy, as he spoke—and his manner of speech was impatient—pushed back his chair and stood up.

Mr. Fowler also stood up and replied, pleasantly: "At all events, our supreme court will agree to an income tax. Turn about is fair play. It seems an innocent plan to tax the millionaire for the ben-

efit of the workingman, instead of taxing the working man for the benefit of the millionaire."

"My decision is final. Good day, sir."

Mr. Fowler bowed, and as he took his hat from the neighboring desk the door opened and another man entered. The newcomer was George Payson.

[NOTE—An attempt had been made on Payson's life the night before, but he had escaped.]

CHAPTER IX

After a familiar nod to Billy his eyes encountered those of Mr. Fowler. Payson's figure stiffened. His chin rose a little higher. For an instant he surveyed the other man with half-closed eyes and elevated brows.

"So you are here?"

Mr. Fowler's only reply was a slight movement of the head. Payson added slowly and with obvious contempt:

"The usual errand, I suppose."

Again Mr. Fowler's only response was a silent and a barely perceptible acknowledgement. Payson looked toward Billy.

"The gentleman demands a check or your life?"

"That's the game."

"Well, Mr. Fowler, you certainly know your business, for you are still out of state's prison. It's a jolly trade you are in. Perhaps you were one of the gentlemen who knocked me into the river last night."

"No, sir, I was not."

"Ah? Then, perhaps, you were the enthusiastic patriot who threw the paving stones at me when I was trying to swim?"

"I was not there at all, Mr. Payson. I knew nothing about it."

"Knew nothing about it! Knew nothing about the fulfillment of your own threat?"

"I tell you, Mr. Payson, I have nothing to do with that end of the business."

"Of course not! Who could doubt the word of a gentleman in your calling!"

A flush moved swiftly over Mr. Fowler's face.

With compressed lips, he drew a hand across his chin. But he was resolved to keep his temper. Calmly, but in a harder voice, he said: "I am sorry you have such a poor opinion of me. But at least my pockets are not bulging with other people's money."

"Then," said Payson, "you are failing in your enterprise. But your hands are dripping with other people's blood."

"Perhaps you will admit, Mr. Fowler," said Billy, with exaggerated courtesy, "that there is something amusing in a gentleman of your calling being sensitive on a point of honor."

Mr. Fowler, with a gesture of suppressed anger, wheeled about and took three strides toward the door. Then, from a sudden change of purpose, halted, retraced his steps and again was standing in the center of the office. Planted solidly upon his feet, and standing erect, he moved his head slowly up and down to emphasize his words:

"You talk of honor! You who would be in prison but for buying your freedom with other people's money. Debauchers of law and justice, so hog-rich with plunder you cannot estimate your wealth. You have the impudence to talk of honor! Why, gentlemen, you are not in the same class with common thieves or with the man who steals for his family because he needs the money. You are a class by yourselves. You skim the cream from the whole continent. You hold the widow and orphan by the throat. You capture the savings of the poorest worker. And on what a scale! Never was there record of such unholy fortunes. Blind drunk with it—and still thirsty! So blind drunk that you can't see where you are going. So secure in your ownership of men and laws that you sneer at danger. Did rulers ever believe that a revolution was at hand? But the uprising is here—at your own homes—inside your doors. Even now you don't believe it."

In the fading light of the winter afternoon Mr. Fowler's tall figure seemed to grow taller still as he straightened up and said, in a tone yet more emphatic:

"When a man works ten hours a day to lay up

something for his family, it doesn't soothe him to know that his savings, if not stolen, are manipulated by his enemies to their own swinish enrichment."

"Enemies?" said Billy, gently.

"Yes, enemies. The war is now on. We may as well be frank. Enemies you are, not friends. Friends would not gorge themselves with the hard earnings of the poor. We know our savings yield you a thousand times more money in a day than we can earn by a life of labor. We know why some of our own productions are sold cheaper abroad than we can buy them ourselves in our own country. Oh, yes! Precious friends, you millionaires! You have the people well in hand—a lemon in a squeezer. You own the air, the earth and the mines beneath. Yes, and who pays for the coal strikes? Do you pay? You, the owners? Oh, no! You put up the price of your coal and tax the poor, the sick, shivering women in the tenements. We all pay the tax, until you are richer than before—already so gorged with money that your senses are besotted. What sort of groveling, patient, humble-minded things do you take us for—we, the American people?"

In silence Billy closed his eyes. Payson glowered and twirled his cane—but also in silence. For the crude force of the speaker commanded—and held—attention. Moreover, both men were impressed by the obvious sincerity of this messenger from the waking giant.

"We are tired of being fooled and fleeced—of getting a crumb after baking the loaf. We are tired of fattening financiers. For us, no more of this control of our savings by irresponsible gamblers. We want, and we propose to have the things for which our ancestors fought at Lexington. They threw off one set of kings and you have saddled us with another—and a damned sight worse. We don't ask our money back. You can keep it. But we do ask for the future a fraction of the profits on our own earnings. And, by God, we are going to have it! We are tired of the ditch. We have climbed the bank to have it out with you."

Billy sank lower in his chair, rested his chin in his fist, his eyes on the speaker's face.

Payson tapped a leg impatiently with his cane. "Well, I also am tired; tired of being murdered and then abused for it."

"Really!" And the speaker's manner revealed a fathomless contempt. "But you are not tired of buying half-grown paupers at the cheapest market. How many hundred children, Mr. Payson, are doing their day's work in your New Jersey factories? I have seen them—crawling to the shops in the early morning. There's no playtime for them. But you need the money! By God! I'd ask no hotter hell for you and your wife than to have your own children sold to the same job—with the same food and wages, the same work and the same hours."

Billy looked toward Payson, who made no reply.

With a gesture that included both of his listeners, Mr. Fowler raised his chin, set back his shoulders and seemed to add more inches yet to his stature.

"And when you combine politics with high finance, you millionaires—then heaven help the honest man. The present government is ideal—of the rich, for the rich and *by* the rich. It works to perfection. The laws are well enforced—against the poor. But we are tired of this feudal system where big thieves never go to jail. Later on we shall see some millionaires behind the bars."

January 19, 1907

Jack London's and Arthur George's awareness of the political nature of language anticipated by several decades an attention to language in American universities. The Socialist Intercollegiate Society, however, gave socialists access to students, not professors or administrators of learning.

The irrepressible Jack London and Comrade Arthur George, of Berkeley, Cal., as a committee on simplified language, have recommended that the following 300 words in the left-hand column be abolished in the interest of better living and a better society, and that conditions be established that will bring the 300 words in the right-hand column into more general and frequent use. Both plead guilty to the charge of trying to instigate Socialism, as the ulterior motive is plainly visible:

Simplified Language of Socialism

*Socialist Intercollegiate Society Takes a Hand
in the Reconstruction of Language in Conformity with
the Reconstructed Society that is About to be*

TO BE ABOLISHED.

We, the Simplified Language Committee of the Intercollegiate Socialist Society, recommend, after careful deliberation, that the following three hundred words, with

TO BE ENCOURAGED.

In order that the object of the committee may be better understood, we append an additional list of three hundred words, to represent the type of language that we de-their roots, derivatives and related forms, be as rapidly as possible retired to academic obscurity, or entirely abolished.

In order that this may be accomplished, we recommend that all habits, customs and practices that have caused their introduction in the language be, by every possible means, done away with, and that new laws, standards and methods be sought, that shall, by their logical operations, render the use of these words obsolete:

Adulteration, adultery, agitator, alien, alms, alimony, anarchy, animalism, aristocracy, army, arsenal, arson, artillery, assassin, avarice.

Bagnio, bankrupt, barbarian, bargain, bawdy, beastly, beggar, bestial, bet, bibulous, bigamy, blacklist, blackmail, bloodshed, bondage, boor, brandy, bribe, broker, brothel, brutality, burglar.

Cant, capitalist, charity (alms), cheat, contraband, convict(n), counterfeit, covet, crime, criminal, curse.

Damn, debauchery, debt, decadence, degeneracy, demagogue, detective, depravity, despair, despotism, destitution, devil, dictator, divorce, domestic(n), drudge, drunkard, dude, dupe, duplicity.

Effeminate, embezzler, employer, employe, ennui, envy, extravagance.

Faction, fake, fanatic, fiend, firm (n), foreigner, forger, fornication, fraud.

Garrison, gossip, graft (unlawful profit).

Haggle, handcuff, heathen, hell, heresy, homicide, hypocrisy.

sire to have preserved, and brought into more general usage, reflecting the growth of those laws, standards and methods of social activity which are indifferently known as democratic, republican or Socialist, replacing the anarchistic language and ideals that now prevail:

Ability, abundance, accomplish, accord, accrue, accumulate, achieve, acquire, activity, admiration, adorn, advance, affection, affluence, alacrity, alleviate, ambition, amity, ample, animation, anthropology, anticipation, appreciation, approbation, architecture, ardor, art, aspiration, assurance, astronomy, attainment.

Balance, bath, beauty, belief, beneficence, benevolence, best, better, brave, breeding, brisk, business, busy.

Candid, certain, capable, capital (productive property), cash, celebrity, champion, change, charity (affection, toleration), chastity, cheer, chemistry, chief, chivalry, choice, clever, comfort, commend, comparison, competition, conservatism, constancy, constructive, courtesy, creative, culture.

Decent, decorum, deference, democracy, devotion, dexterity, dignity, diligence, diversity, domestic (adj.), duty.

Earn, earnest, education, eminence, employment, emulation, encourage, endeavor, energy, engineering, enlightenment, equity, erudition, esteem, excellence, exchange, exertion, expert.

Faith, fame, family, federal, fidelity, foreman, freedom, free-will, friendship, fund.

Gain, genius, gentleman, genuine, geography, geology, geometry, graft (horticultural or surgical process), grandeur.

Harmony, health, heroism, home, homely (typical of home), honesty, honor.

Idiocy, idler, illicit, imbecile, immodesty, immorality, incest, indigence, indolence, inebriate, inhuman, iniquity, insanity, insolvency, insurance, insurrection, insurgent, intemperance, interest (usury), internecine, intrigue.

Jail.

King, knave.

Lackey, landlord, larceny, lawyer, laziness, lechery, lewd, laision, liar, libel, libertine, libidinous, licentious, lickspittle, livery, loafer, luck, lunacy, lust, lynch.

Machination, malcontent, malefactor, malevolence, malice, maniac, massacre, matricide, mayhem, meanness, melancholy, meretricious, military, minion, misanthrope, miscreant, miser, mob, monarch, monomania, monotony, morbid, mortgage, mutiny, murder.

Nefarious, nepotism, niggard.

Obscenity, oligarchy, oppression, ostentation, outcast, outlaw, outrage, overload.

Pander, paramour, parricide, partisan, paternalism, pauper, pawnshop, pawnbroker, peculate, peddler, penal, penitentiary, penury, perjury, perquisite, persecution, philanthropist, pimp, plutocrat, poacher, poll tax, polygamy, poorhouse, pornography, poverty, prejudice, prison, procurer, profanity, proletariat, prolicide, prostitute, prude.

Quack (a pretender in medicine).

Rake (libertine), rant, rape (criminal assault), rebel, regiment, revenge, renegade, ringleader, riot, robber, roue, ruffian, rum.

Sabre, saloon (a poison shop), sanguinary, satan, savage(n), scandal, scoundrel, sedition, seduce, selfish, sensual, serf, servant, servile, shiftless, shirk, shoddy, shoplifter, sin, sinecure, slander, slave, slum, smuggler, snob, soldier, spurious, squalor, starvation, strike (a labor mutiny), strumpet, suicide, superstition, sycophant, syphillis.

Idealism, improvement, incentive, independence, individuality, industry, innovation, integrity, intellect, intelligent, intercourse, interest, invention, income.

Justice.

Kindness, knowledge.

Labor, lady, law, leisure, liberty, library, lineage, literature, love, loyalty.

Machinery, manliness, mansion, marriage, mathematics, matrimony, melioration, melody, merchandise, merit, merry, method, ministry, modesty, money, monogamy, morality, music, mutual.

Navigation, navy, neighbor.

Order, organization, originality.

Palace, patriotism, pay, peace, philanthropy, philosophy, poetry, possession, praise, pride, privacy, probity, profit, progress, property, prosperity, protection, provident, pulchritude, purity.

Reason, rectitude, reliance, remuneration, repose, republic, residence, respect, responsibility, riches, right, robust, romance.

Sagacity, sale, saloon (a hall of art or entertainment), sanitation, sanity, sanguine, scholarship, science, sculpture, sedulous, seemly, self-help, self-control, self-interest, self-reliance, sensuous, sentiment, service, sincere, skill, sober, society, sociable, solidarity, song, soul, stately, statesman, statuary, statute, strength, strenuous, success, superb, superintend, superior, supreme, symmetry, sympathy, synarchy, system.

Tenant, tenement, termagent, terrorist, thief, time-server, tinsel, tip (a bribe), tipsy, toady, toper, tout, traitor, tramp (an outcast), traveler ("drummer"), treachery, treadmill, treason, trespass, trooper, turnkey, turpitude, tyrant.

Unlawful, unmanly, usury, uxoricide.

Vagabond, vagrancy, valet, vandal, venal, vengeance, villain.

Wager, wages, waif, war, whiskey, whore, working-class.

Tact, talent, teach, technology, techtonics, temperate, tenacity, tenderness, thoroughbred, thought, thrift, toll, tourist, trade, traffic, travel, treasure, triumph, truth.

Unity, university, upright, uplift.

Valiant, value, variety, veneration, venture, veriloquent, verve, veteran, vie, vigilance, vigor, virile, virtue, vim, vocation.

Wealth, wedlock, welfare, wholesome, wife, wit, womanly, work, worthy.

Zeal, zest.

March 30, 1907

Ohio native Wilbur D. Nesbit was a poet and feature writer for several major newspapers. His books include The Gentleman Ragman *and* Your Flag and My Flag.

The Judgment of Dives

WILBUR D. NESBIT

Out of the silent, skyless place he heard one call his name,
And boldly forth he stepped, and said: "I have but little blame;
My hands are clean of brother-blood, my tongue is clear of lies;
I pray you let me go that I may fare to Paradise."

Then came an angel who outflung a long and mighty scroll,
And cried: "This is the ledger page whereon is writ your soul;
This is the page both broad and long whereon is written fair
The burden which your own decree is that your soul must bear."

"Look down to earth," he said. "Look down to yonder swinging star—

Look down and see my monuments that scatter near and far;
The hospitals, the schools, the parks, the tributes to my fame—
And see how bravely over each is graven big my name."

"And that is all?" the angel cried. "But now I pray you tell
The way you got the gold you gave—how did you buy and sell?
Whence came the wealth you scattered north and south and west and east?
Tell on, ere yet your soul may from the Warders be released."

"They called it Opportunity," he said, and stammered then;
"I only know I held the grip upon my fellow men;
I only know I read the signs that they might never read
And with God-given wisdom I had all they held in need."

The angel smiled in pity then, the angel turned away;

The great shores of eternity were dull and dark
and gray.
And from a place he might not see a voice came
ringing clear:
"To cleanse your soul it is decreed that you must
enter here.

"That you must enter here and find the men from
whose hard toil
You filled your coffers when you made their
shrunken wage your spoil;
That you shall search through heaven's bounds
until in agelong whiles
You find the little children who at labor lost their
smiles.

"Come, find them all and pay them all—the children and the men;
Repay them one and one until each has his own
again,
And when you have from one and all received a
full release
Then may you walk in heaven's streets a soul that
knows of peace."

And heaven is a mighty place, and heaven has no
bound,
And he must go through endless day upon his
ceaseless round.
And pay, and pay, and pay, and pay in driblet and
in dole,
And through it all must think upon the volume of
the scroll.

So he goes on and has no time for song nor yet for
smile,
But murmurs: "I must find them all and pay them
for my guile.
And though throughout eternity in heaven must I
dwell
I know more than I ever knew what God has
meant by hell."

October 19, 1907

Socialist and founder of the Conservator, *a Marxist monthly published in Philadelphia from 1890 to 1919, Horace Traubel was also a biographer of Walt Whitman, a poet whose stylistic influence appears in "Debs."*

Debs

Horace Traubel

I see him now, the single man confronting the million men,
And I see him now, his forefinger raised, calling
upon the million for reasons,
And I see him now waiting, waiting with gentle
assauging eyes, silent, so silent,
And I see the million are unable to give the divine
reasons.
For the questioner, my brother standing there, is
asking for reasons.
Not the reasons of goods, not the reasons of ambition and reputation;
He knows all about these reasons, but they do not
satisfy him.
He stands there asking for reasons of equity—asking for reasons of right.
Asking for no reasons of enemies or owners—ask-
ing only for reasons of brothers.
It was no accident that brought the outcasts and
victims to my brother.
They came in their hunger and thirst, knowing he
would not turn them away.
They would not knock at the doors of the com-
fortable and the contented.
They came straight to him, invoking his measure-
less good will.
He refuses nobody; he has room enough for all;
they crowd him full.
Sunbeams are his swordblades; before them false-
hoods perish.
There is a fierce fire spread over the nations: my
brother is the answer to the fire.
There is a wrathful wind blowing across the seas:
My brother is the answer to the wind.

There is a black despair settling upon the people:
My brother is the answer to the despair.

There is a clank of slave chains growing clearer in
our ears: My brother is the answer to the
chains.

He comes in the fullness of evil times, and knocks
the cup from your hand.

November 21, 1908

---

*Socialist, Pulitzer Prize-winning novelist, settlement worker,
and World War I correspondent, Ernest Poole remains best
known for his 1915 novel,* The Harbor. *"Filling Up the Band" is
political allegory that simultaneously succeeds on the literal
level.*

Filling Up the Band

ERNEST POOLE

His name was Berger, but he didn't live in
Milwaukee. He lived in a city where Socialists as yet were only sprinkled here and there,
about one to every block. But by some chance it
happened that the one in his block lived right in
his room, a red hot little Scotchman, MacDougal
by his name.

He played the piccolo flute—the shrill one—
in a theater orchestra, where Berger played the big
bass horn. And somehow or other they became
chums. They lived in two tenement rooms. And
the Socialist talk of little MacDougal stung Berger
night and day.

"Damn!" he would cry. "How I hate mosqui-
toes! Vy can't you leave alone?" MacDougal had
red hair.

"Ain't it tough?" Berger would groan. "Ain't
it? You Socialist poys—shoost vun in a t'ousand,
und I am stuck mit shoost dot von! He lives right
in my ears! Schwarz de saloon keeper, ven he ain't
drunk, he says Socialism vill break up de home.
Vill it? You bett! I know shoost vot he means!"
Here he leaned back, lit his pipe, grew slowly

calm. "T'ank Gott," he added, in quieter tones,
"you can't do it. Dot damned Socialist party—it
vill never grow."

"Won't it?" asked MacDougal, with a cock-
sure fiendish grin. "Why not?"

"Because," said Berger placidly, "you poys ain't
got a band. Und mitout a band"—he blew smoke
expressively into the air.

"Ha! Now look here!" MacDougal began to
explain from beginning to end.

"Please! Please!" groaned Berger. All in vain.
The talk flowed on. At last in a spasm of pain and
rage he seized his horn and blew one shattering
blast, blew Marx into small atoms—up to the
clouds, brought the janitor up from the basement.

As the months went on, they compromised.
MacDougal hated sausages. Berger—was a
Dutchman. They cooked their own meals. They
now agreed to eat sausages twice a week, with Socialism for gravy. At all other times both were
sternly forbidden.

MacDougal saw his chance. He ate nothing, he
just talked. And whether from the force of his
words or the soothing influence of the repast, as
the weeks went by, Berger's ears and mind began
to open—till at last one night he even paused, fork
raised in his enormous hand, forgot to eat, and
stared at his chum.

"Yest," he said, at last. "It don't sound so bad."
There was another pause. Berger rose abruptly
and went over to the window, stood scowling
down into the tenement street. When he turned,
the scowl was still on his face. His chum watched
him in surprise.

"Wat's got into the Dutchman?" he wondered.

"Vunce," said Berger, speaking gruff and low,
"I had a poy. Not mine. I was his uncle. His father
vorked in a sweatshop. He died—lungs!—His
mudder vos a fighter. She said I vas too poor to
help. So she also vent in a sweatshop, und she
rented cheaper rooms—lungs again! Vot could I
do? I had fifty-two dollars saved alreatty. I got a
doctor. He said I ought to have five hundert. So
she died! Damn! How bad I felt!" His gruff voice

sank still lower: "I took dot poy und he vos mine. Did I like dot little ritzy? Did ve get to love each odder?—Yes—Vell. But he had dot sickness from his mudder—Vot could I do? Ve ought to have had five hundert." His voice grew suddenly harsh again:

"Now you show me how ve fix dot up—shoost dot—no speeches, no big books—shoost dot! Show me!"

MacDougal got to work. And Berger listened. But it looked too plain and simple.

"No," he said at last, "it sounds immense. But it ain't. It ain't real."

He had played his horn so many years in the theater, watching light operas night after night, that nothing seemed real any longer, least of all this. Too big. Too plain.

But little MacDougal was losing no chances. His nights, all except Sundays, were taken by his work. But now, as the autumn campaign drew on, he began to go out every afternoon late, at the hour when the streets were filled. He took Berger with him, he spoke on corners, spoke hard, and at first Berger was the only audience. But such an immense audience he made all by himself, and so earnest was the speaker, that passers-by soon stopped, a crowd gathered, listened—till a policeman shoved them on.

Berger listened hard. He knew this chum of his, through and through, knew how real he was. And now MacDougal's voice, his face, his eyes, the ideas he unfolded, in shrewd yarns, in ringing appeals, somehow it all seemed to fit together. One night he even told that yarn about the lungs, brief and plain. And though the Dutchman growled and forbad him ever to tell it again, that too fitted in. And he heard other speeches, saw other faces, eyes, heard stories by the dozen of men and women who were using every cent and hour they could squeeze out of their lives, just to push what they believed in. As he turned all this over and over in his mind, in the theater at night, glancing now at the painted chorus girls and again at the women in the two dollar seats close by,

somehow they didn't size up at all—not even the necks with diamonds. They seemed only showy puppets in an endless farce. And the tenement faces an eyes, the ringing words, the sacrifice all made as a matter of course, the never ending struggle to force those big ideas on and up at any cost—this seemed more and more the real part of living. Berger listened hard.

"Gott!" he cried one night at supper. A sudden thought had struck him. A mischievous ghost of a twinkle appeared in the corner of one huge eye. "I knew somet'ings vos wrong mit your scheme! I knew it!"

"Well?" asked his chum impatiently. "What is it now? Ain't it real?"

"Maybe. Maybe not. But shoost look here. If I vote your ticket, vot do I get for mein vote? Two dollars? Damn it—no! Not vun cent!"

MacDougal sprang from his seat and the words that he uttered are better omitted. It ended in a silence between them that lasted days and days. Only now and then did Berger chuckle softly. But he was so enormous and the chuckle was so small, that it passed completely unnoticed. Little MacDougal was mad.

So two silent weeks dragged by.

Again they sat at supper. It was a sparkling autumn night.

Suddenly from way up the street came the sound of a parade. Voices singing the Marseillaise. A band playing. What a band!

It came nearer. Both chums were at the window. Nearer! The voices louder, ever louder, by hundreds altogether shouting the old song. Higher rose the band. Two drums, three fifes, a clarionet, two horns that cracked.

"We have a band, a band at last!" MacDougal shouted. His face was red. He looked at his friend in keen suspense, as though he had been planning something.

"Mein Gott!" groaned Berger. "Vot a band!"

The next moment he was whirled around, and before he could even breathe or puff, his big bass horn was shoved into his arms.

"Come on! Berger!" cried his chum. "Come—get into line! You believe it, don't you? Ain't it real? Ain't it what we want to live for? Come on! Come on! Fill up the band!"

That was at seven o'clock. Four hours later, weary and worn, the pair came home. Under one of Berger's arms nestled the great shining horn; in the other hand was a can of beer. He sank into a chair, mopped his glistening brow.

"Damn," he said disgustedly. "Two dollars fine I get for dis—or maybe lose my job." He pulled out his application blank—already signed. "Two dollars more," he groaned, "for dot good vote I might have sold. Und vot a band! Mein Gott in Himmel, vot a band!"

He scowled and raised the can. There was a long cool gurgling sound.

"I tell you vot!" he cried. "Ve shoost grab dot band, you and me, ve fix it up alreatty! Fritzy Reiter—he can play! I'll get hold of Fritzy!"

December 12, 1908

Few British writers were as much admired at the Appeal *as Charles Dickens. "I want some more" expressed as succinctly as any statement the longing and socialist demand for a richer, fuller life.*

"I Want Some More"

Charles Dickens

The room in which the boys were fed, was a large stone hall, with a copper at one end; out of which the master, dressed in an apron for the purpose, and assisted by one or two women, ladled the gruel at meal times. Of this festive composition each boy had one porringer, and no more—except on occasions of great rejoicing, when he had two ounces and a quarter of bread beside. The bowls never wanted washing. The boys polished them with their spoons till they shone again; and when they had performed this operation (which never took very long, the spoons being nearly as long as the bowls) they would sit staring at the copper, with such eager eyes, as if they could have devoured the very bricks of which it was composed; employing themselves, meanwhile, in sucking their fingers most assiduously, with the view of catching up any stray splashes of gruel that might have been cast thereon. Boys have generally excellent appetites. Oliver Twist and his companions suffered the tortures of slow starvation for three months; at last they got so voracious and wild with hunger, that one boy, who was tall for his age, and hadn't been used to that sort of thing (for his father had kept a small cook-shop) hinted darkly to his companions, that unless he had another basin of gruel *per diem*, he was afraid he might some night happen to eat the boy who slept next to him, who happened to be a weakly youth of tender age. He had a wild, hungry eye; and they implicitly believed him. A council was held; lots were cast who should walk up to the master after supper that evening, and ask for more; and it fell to Oliver Twist.

This evening arrived; the boys took their places. The master, in his cook's uniform, stationed himself at the copper; his pauper assistants ranged themselves behind him; the gruel was served out; and a long grace was said over the short commons. The gruel disappeared; the boys whispered to each other, and winked at Oliver; while his next neighbors nudged him. Child as he was, he was desperate with hunger, and reckless with misery. He rose from the table, and advancing to the master, basin and spoon in hand, said somewhat alarmed at his own temerity:

"Please, sir, I want some more."

The master was a fat, healthy man; but he turned very pale. He gazed in stupefied astonishment on the small rebel for some seconds, and then clung for support to the copper. The assistants were paralyzed with wonder; the boys with fear.

"What!" said the master at length, in a faint voice.

"Please, sir," replied Oliver, "I want some more."

The master aimed a blow at Oliver's head with the ladle; pinioned him in his arms; and shrieked aloud for the beadle.

The board were sitting in solemn conclave, when Mr. Bumble rushed into the room in great excitement, and addressing the gentleman in the high chair, said:

"Mr. Limbkins, I beg your pardon, sir! Oliver Twist has asked for more!"

There was a general start. Horror was depicted on every countenance.

"For more," said Mr. Limbkins.

"Compose yourself, Bumble, and answer me distinctly. Do I understand that he asked for more, after he had eaten the supper allotted by the dietary?"

"He did, sir," replied Bumble.

"That boy will be hung," said the gentleman in the white waistcoat. "I know that boy will be hung."

Nobody controverted the prophetic gentleman's opinion. An animated discussion took place. Oliver was ordered into instant confinement; and a bill was next morning pasted on the outside of the gate, offering a reward of five pounds to anybody who would take Oliver Twist off the hands of the parish. In other words, five pounds and Oliver Twist were offered to any man or woman who wanted an apprentice to any trade, business, or calling.

"I never was more convinced of anything in my life," said the gentleman in the white waistcoat, as he knocked at the gate and read the bill the next morning. "I never was more convinced of anything in my life, than I am that that boy will come to be hung."

November 18, 1916

Written in the turmoil and economic depression following the Napoleonic Wars, Shelley's "Men of England" urged a proletarian revolution. "Men of England" remains a hymn of the British labor movement.

To the Men of England

PERCY BYSSHE SHELLEY

Men of England, wherefore plough
For the lords who lay ye low?
Wherefore weave with toil and care,
The rich robes your tyrants wear?

Wherefore feed, and clothe, and save,
From the cradle to the grave,
Those ungrateful drones who would
Drain your sweat—nay, drink your blood!

Wherefore, Bees of England, forge

Many a weapon, chain, and scourge,
That these stingless drones may spoil
The forced produce of your toil?

Have ye leisure, comfort, calm,
Shelter, food, love's gentle balm?
Or what is it ye buy so dear
With your pain and with your fear?

The seed ye sow, another reaps;
The wealth ye find, another keeps;
The robes ye weave, another wears;
The arms ye forge, another bears.

Sow seed—but let no tyrant reap;
Find wealth—let no imposter heap;
Weave robes—let not the idle wear;
Forge arms—in your defense to bear.

March 10, 1917

Art and Socialism

EMANUEL HALDEMAN-JULIUS

Among the many beautiful things said by that ardent and vigorous spirit, William Morris, who was so strong in body and in mind, is the memorable sentence: "I do not want art for a few, anymore than education for a few, or freedom for a few." Morris, who was an artist of life as well as of poetry and prose, knew that the material necessities of existence, although so important when they cannot be produced in sufficient abundance, are but the foundation for the higher life. Once the material question was settled life would become beautiful for all, not to the restricted few.

Once upon a time it was the fashion to accuse Socialists of being a crassly material sort, interested only in the matter of food, wages and shelter. Such an accusation was, of course, adding insult to injury. How do you expect a man to go wild over a great symphony when his stomach is empty? How do you expect a woman to dissolve in ecstasies over a thrilling story, when she's wondering where her family's next meal is coming from? The emphasis upon the material factors of life is necessary, and will be so until the problem of production and distribution upon an equitable basis is solved. The most beautiful palace must have a foundation in rock and dirt beneath the soil. The most beautiful life needs bread and butter and shelter to sustain the ardors of its spirit. But once that foundation is socially assured, then indeed will the vision of Morris come true. There will be art for everybody, education for everybody, and freedom for all. And it will be a different art—more social in structure, more deeply human in purpose, and yet more eternally artistic in style.

The average worker, it is true, cannot afford to give much time to art. And because he is so absorbed in the elementary task of making both ends meet, he sometimes gets to look upon art as a diversion of the rich, totally unrelated to him and his life. That is a false attitude. Life is something more than merely making a living. Making a living is merely the pedestal on which to place the statue, the foundation upon which to rear the palace. And as soon as the toiler's elementary problem of making a living is solved, he should adopt the view that art is as much his as anyone else's—in fact, more. For the basis of all enduring art is life itself, and who better than he and his knows that life? Art belongs to the rich no more than the country itself. In its highest form it is essentially human in its makeup. Because of its having been up to a recent time a luxury, it has often become what we call "highbrow" in nature. A closer approach to the world of the toilers will do art, as well as economics, a great service.

And where does Socialism come in? It's very simple. By assuring to able-bodied and willing labor the necessary elements of life, it will release a new world of Labor's energies for art and science, thus not only refuting the old accusation of Socialism's crass materialism, but in addition making art, for the first time in the world's history, a truly social inspiration—an "art for everybody."

November 16, 1918

What's It to You?

LUKE NORTH

What is it to you
That children starve in a land of plenty,
That girls are driven to the street for food and
　shelter,
And idle men tramp unused acres,

And broken lives strew every pathway—
What is it to You?

Not only the rich are guilty
Of the pauperism that degrades humanity.
But You, and all who assent,
Who do less than the most you can do
To stay it. Your hands are red
With the blood of discouraged, starved
Women, children, and men—your own kin.
The guilt is Yours, especially who, knowing
The cause of pauperism,
Do less than you might do to stay it.

What is it to you that children starve,
Women whore, men steal or beg or tramp
Merely for bread—in a land of Wondrous
    Plenty—
What is it to You?

January 29, 1921

SEVEN

World War I

This is how one pictures the angel of history. His face is turned toward the past. Where we perceive a chain of events, he sees one single catastrophe which keeps piling wreckage upon wreckage and hurls it in front of his feet. The angel would like to stay, awaken the dead, and make whole what has been smashed. But a storm is blowing from Paradise; it has got caught in his wings with such violence that the angel can no longer close them. This storm irresistibly propels him into the future to which his back is turned, while the pile of debris before him grows skyward.—Walter Benjamin, *Theses on the Philosophy of History*

World War I began with a suddenness few anticipated. When Austria-Hungary declared war on Serbia on July 28, 1914, first Germany, then Russia, France, and England entered the conflict within a matter of days. American socialists were in agreement on the fundamental causes of the world war: since the appropriation of surplus value by an owning class prohibited working people from buying back the goods and services they produced, capitalist nations were critically dependent on foreign consumption of the "overproduction" that could not be domestically absorbed. Radicals saw no mystery in the structural necessity for capitalist economies to expand and battle for foreign markets. After urging that

hostilities be ended through peaceful negotiations, American socialists campaigned to prevent the United States from entering World War I. When the United States became a combatant in the spring of 1917, the Socialist party stood virtually alone in formal opposition to the war. The *Appeal to Reason* similarly condemned World War I and American participation in the conflict, but then succumbed to political pressure and supported Woodrow Wilson and the allied war effort. After the armistice, the *Appeal* editorially returned to its initial stance. The war declared at home on American radicalism left the Socialist party with hundreds of its 1500 locals destroyed, with much of its energy absorbed in a defensive struggle against indictments charged under new loyalty laws, and left the party so delegitimized in the dominant culture that it was unable to regain its influence in American life. The *Appeal* survived until 1922 but, like the Socialist party, never recovered from the effects of World War I.

In 1914 the socialist analysis of the world war was coherent and, in fundamental respects, no different from that of sophisticated capitalist interests. Socialist William English Walling identified "militarism, social unrest, international grudges, and pseudo patriotism" as contributing factors, but he argued that, ultimately, the national economic interests of capitalist countries dictated competition and even war for foreign trade.[1] Walling's analysis showed how forbidding the task would be of preventing America from entering World War I. The precipitous depression of 1893–98 had created a broad consensus of agreement in American capitalism: since the economic and political welfare of the new industrial and financial order depended upon the development and control of foreign markets, a necessarily expansionist United States had too much at stake to remain isolated.

The confidence that accompanied American capital's growing economic and political dominance made imperialist sentiment overtly visible in turn-of-the-century America. "American factories are making more than the American people can use; American soil is producing more than they can consume," Senator Albert J. Beveridge of Indiana concluded in 1897. "Fate has written our policy for us; the trade of the world must and shall be ours."[2] Before the Hawaiian islands were annexed, ending their status as an independent republic, Henry Cabot Lodge observed: "We have a record of conquest, colonialization and expansion unequalled by any people in the nineteenth century. We are not to be curbed now."[3] The Philippines, Guam, and Puerto Rico were annexed; military invasions and occupations of Central American and Latin American countries followed; and an expansionist Open Door Policy was formulated that would dominate American foreign policy for the next fifty years. "Since trade ignores national boundaries and the manufacturer insists on having the world as a market," Woodrow Wilson wrote in 1907, "the flag of his nation must follow him, and the doors of the nations which are closed must be battered down." "Concessions obtained by financiers must be safeguarded by ministers of state, even if the sovereignty of unwilling nations be outraged in the process."[4] In 1914 Secretary of State William Jennings Bryan explained that the official policy of the Wilson administration was to "open the doors of all the weaker countries to an invasion of American capital and enterprise."[5] To speak of American foreign policy as imperial during the years of the *Appeal*'s publication, as political policy in the service of economic necessity, is to be accurate but also is to understate histori-

cal reality. American diplomacy and military threat succeeded more often than they failed during the period from 1898 to 1924, but the United States still launched twenty-four military interventions in countries such as Mexico, Nicaragua, and the Soviet Union to preserve and extend its growing commercial empire.

To American radicals aware of the economic mainspring in political life, the outbreak and human slaughter of World War I demonstrated conclusively that the capitalist classes in Europe were unfit to direct the affairs of nations or to safeguard the lives and security of millions of citizens. Capitalism produced war or the defeat of international competition by other means. During the summer and fall of 1914, American socialists urged President Woodrow Wilson's administration to initiate negotiations between the belligerent nations, and they urged foreign socialist support for American mediation of the war. Socialists developed a comprehensive peace program that included no indemnities, no forcible transfers of territory, and a precursor to the League of Nations, an International Federation with authority to mediate international disputes and prevent the outbreak of future wars. Expressed in the *Appeal to Reason*'s slogan, "Starve the War and Feed America," was the additional hope that, by depriving the warring nations of foodstuffs and critical war matériel, the deadly conflict could be halted and domestic food shortages, created by export to the allies, could also be halted. Instead, more powerful interests intervened.

As socialists, other radicals, and a number of Progressive organizations joined in efforts to stop the ghastly bloodshed—ten million died on the battlefield, twenty million more died from the hunger, disease, and destruction created by the war—expansionist forces in America regarded the war in Europe with imperial design and an outright directness that has since receded from public view. "The extremity of Europe is America's opportunity," wrote the Chicago *Tribune* on August 5, 1914. War orders pulled the United States out of the recession of 1913–14. Merchandizing the war were subservient politicians, the Navy League, the jingo press, and other proponents of preparedness. "Wars are not fought for glory," the Philadelphia *Public Ledger* editorialized: "Trade, in some aspect, figures directly or remotely as a cause in every modern conflict, and the present war is no exception."[6] The Washington *Herald* decoded the rhetoric of preparedness to mean staying out of the war only until America's commercial rivals, Germany and England, were seriously weakened. "Let us . . . blast a path to world leadership as soon as an opportunity presents itself."[7] World War I was that opportunity. The close of 1915 found the United States beginning to assume the position of world dominance that befitted a country changing from a debtor nation to, in 1917, the dominant creditor nation in the world. War, Randolph Bourne and many other radicals concluded, was the price that insured the health of the new American state.

Until the latter part of 1917, after the United States had entered the war, the *Appeal to Reason* was consistent in its opposition to World War I. The *Appeal* issued antimilitarist, antijingo editions, opposed conscription, warned readers repeatedly against preparedness, and explained the war as the gravest contemporary example of the human destruction created by capitalism. The *Appeal* condemned the increasing permeation of American life by militarism, and condemned as well the deflection of domestic grievances onto a foreign enemy. Militarism was critically important because American capitalism, unlike an envisioned socialist America, depended upon foreign markets for its life. Capitalism could be forced to capitulate and the way opened to socialism, the *Appeal* believed, if the state were shorn of the military power that guaranteed access to those markets and perpetuated its rule over America. When the left-leaning Socialist party met in St. Louis a day after the United States had declared war on the Central Powers, the *Appeal* agreed with the convention's majority resolution that condemned the war, opposed American participation in it, and called upon working people internationally to refuse to support the carnage produced by competing capitalist nations. However, the repressive consequences of America's entry into World War I, together with the contradictory politics of the *Appeal*'s new owners and editors, Emanuel Haldeman-Julius and Louis Kopelin, soon led the paper into support of Woodrow Wilson and the allies.

The *Appeal*'s first direct encounter with the war at home, the Espionage Act passed two months after the United States declared war, occurred when its June 30, 1917 issue was refused use of the United States mails. The *Appeal* had anticipated that repression would arrive with America's participation in World War I, that constitutional guarantees of free speech, free press, and free assembly would be sacrificed to military expediency, but the reality of suppression was far different from expectation. The *Appeal*'s editors were faced with a choice: the paper would either have to support the war or, like other radical publications, be shut down. A third possibility, editorial silence, was only a temporary option at best: neither the *Appeal*'s tradition of refusing to equivocate nor the paper's readership would permit the war to be ignored. The decision to support the allied war effort—even to create a *New Appeal* to symbolize a break from past policy and political commitment—came as a consequence of many factors: America's entry into the war, the apparent impossibility of a separate peace, humanitarian war aims proposed by Woodrow Wilson, division among socialists over the war, and the reverberating effects of J. A. Wayland's suicide five years earlier.

Wayland, in the years before his death, had sought but not found an answer to the problem of ownership and control of the *Appeal*. While private ownership was transparently wrong, Wayland was unable to find a satisfactory alternative and maintained his ownership of the paper as an informal trust for the socialist movement. Safe in his own and Fred Warren's hands, upon Wayland's death and Warren's resignation, ownership of the *Appeal* fell to Wayland's sons, Jon and Walter. Dwarfed by their father, Jon had no interest in the paper and Walter had little political understanding or capacity for radical newspaper work. Louis Kopelin was hired as managing editor and, tentatively at first, the Wayland brothers decided to sell the *Appeal*. Negotiating for its purchase in 1917 (and quite possibly at least a year earlier) were

Kopelin and Emanuel Haldeman-Julius. Wayland's suicide and the resulting departure of Warren and Debs in 1913 opened ownership and control of the *Appeal*'s politics to two men without a deep commitment to socialism, men who were finally more interested in the *Appeal* as a financial proposition than as an instrument for radical social change. They were also men, as the deteriorating quality of the paper demonstrated, who were mediocre writers and editors.

With the interlocked goals of acquiring the *Appeal* and making it survive government censorship, Kopelin and Haldeman-Julius set about, as much unconsciously as not, finding reasons to support the war. The task was easiest for Haldeman-Julius: never fully committed to socialism, he had voted for Woodrow Wilson in 1916 and had announced himself certain in February, 1917, that an American declaration of war would destroy an antiwar *Appeal*. For Kopelin the process was more difficult. On April 28, 1917, Kopelin had editorialized that "the *Appeal* can not and will not lend its support" to the war. "We have no assurance that the Entente Allies will content themselves with 'imposing' a free government upon the people of Germany (if such a thing were possible) and stop at that. The facts of history are that conquerors always reap the spoils of war. And no matter what the intentions of the United States may be, we feel that its allies would remake the map of Europe and of the world if Germany were defeated. . . ." Kopelin had to find a convincing political basis for supporting President Wilson and the war. On December 4, 1917, Wilson's reformulation of humanitarian war aims meshed well enough with such Socialist principles as no forcible annexations, no punitive indemnities, self-development and self-determination of nations, disarmament, and a League of Nations, that Kopelin found what he sought. He cabled his support to Wilson and discussed with Haldeman-Julius publishing a *New Appeal*, one that would support Wilson and the war. The first issue appeared on December 22, 1917. Three months later, after a number of false alarms, Kopelin and Haldeman-Julius were definitively informed by the Wayland brothers that the *Appeal* was theirs to buy.

The apostasy of America's most influential radical paper was welcomed by a small but disproportionately visible group of prowar socialists. Their principal institution was the Social Democratic League. Formally organized in Minneapolis in September, 1917, but headquartered in Girard the next year as a measure of the *New Appeal*'s influence, the League's membership was an amalgam of ex-Socialist party members and liberals. Specifically formed to support Wilson and the Allied war effort, the Social Democratic League was regarded by Haldeman-Julius and others as a rival and potential successor to the Socialist party. However, despite a spirited but unsuccessful membership drive mounted by the *New Appeal*, Morris Hillquit's description of the League as "an organization of leaders without followers" proved accurate. Before its early death, the League was able to do little more than send a delegation of prowar socialists—the newly enlisted Louis Kopelin among them— to Europe to seek to convince foreign labor and socialist movements that their American counterparts supported the war. Without much concern for accuracy, the Loyal Socialist Commission selectively reported American labor support in press releases and public meetings in England, France, and Italy.

When the *Appeal* repudiated the Socialist party's antiwar resolution, the paper was left with no other option in the American political spectrum than Wilsonian liberalism. Wilson's Fourteen Points were attractive as a basis for peace because, as the *Christian Science Monitor* and other papers editorialized, in important respects they were consistent with socialist proposals for a just settlement of the war. The *New Appeal* was not content, however, merely to support Wilson's international war aims. Haldeman-Julius argued that Wilson's wartime nationalization of the railroads, telephone, and telegraph, together with his proposal to tax profits meaningfully, represented nothing less than America's transition to socialism. Kopelin went so far as to claim that "the capitalists in no respect control the present administration of the United States government."[8] Meanwhile, threatened by domestic repression and the loss of mailing privileges, the *New Appeal* failed to fully report the wide-

Appeal to Reason, August 15, 1914.

spread arrests of socialists, IWW members, and other radicals. One sign of how readers of the *Appeal* responded to the paper's failures and compromised politics is found in its diminished readership. However, a letter to Haldeman-Julius from Adolf Germer, National Secretary of the Socialist party, was more explicit. "The one time 'Fighting Appeal,' " Germer wrote, "has become the disguised vassal of the Wall Street Gang."[9]

Only after the armistice of November 11, 1918, did the *New Appeal* begin to restore its socialist focus. The federal government's prosecution of Debs, Kate Richards O'Hare, some 2000 additional radicals, and

Wilson's later failures at the Paris Peace Conference were too obvious to be ignored and too clear to be misinterpreted. Wilson extracted a few modest concessions from Clemenceau, Lloyd George, and Orlando, but they only mitigated in minor degree a settlement so punitive in its terms as almost to seem calculated, some ten years later, to allow Hitler to exploit its effects. Wilson had created widespread hope, in Europe as well as in America, for a peace that would endure. However, when he sat down at table with Allied leaders and carved up the German Empire—Shantung to Japan, German colonies in Africa to England, Northern Africa and the Saar Valley to

France, parts of Asia Minor and Mediterranean islands to Italy and Greece, enormous monetary reparation owing to the Allies as well—the hope that Wilson had engendered was replaced by disillusionment and anger. The Versailles Treaty neither saved the world for democracy nor reflected a new humanitarian order. Only by enlisting the aid of European Socialist parties could Wilson, increasingly isolated in America, have mobilized the public support necessary to defeat the vindictive settlement terms secretly agreed to by the Allies. But with the Bolshevik Revolution bulking large on the political horizon, and fearful of the socialist potential in Europe, Wilson capitulated on his Fourteen Points and ratified the familiar terms of international capitalism.

On March 1, 1919, the *Appeal to Reason* reappeared on the paper's masthead. The restoration of the paper's original name signaled a hope that both the *New Appeal* and its contradictory politics were past. A week later the *Appeal* announced a program of general amnesty for political prisoners, prevention of the railroads, telephone, and telegraph from being returned to private ownership, and broad publicity for the activities of the socialist governments in the Soviet Union and Germany. In only the first of these goals was the *Appeal* able to achieve even mixed success. World War I had proven to be a convincing pretext: the *Appeal*, like other vital radical organizations and institutions, was effectively destroyed during World War I and its repressive aftermath.

On December 14, 1917, Gene Debs had written to Louis Kopelin to condemn the *Appeal*'s prowar apostasy and endorsement of the Social Democratic League. "You will not have long to live," Debs had predicted, "to see that the *Appeal* has committed suicide."[10] Since an antiwar *Appeal* would never have survived the Wilson administration's suppression of political dissent, the paper's only option would have been to close down voluntarily for the duration of the war and then begin publication again at the war's conclusion. Even so, however, it is difficult to believe that an *Appeal to Reason*, in its authentic form, could have succeeded in a nation in which radicalism was delegitimized. The defeat of the insurgent labor and political movements upon which the *Appeal* significantly depended, together with the disillusionment and emptiness permeating large elements of American life in the 1920s, left too much political space for an isolated counter-institution such as the *Appeal* to fill. The Socialist party, which before World War I represented the principal hope for a different form of social and economic relations in the United States, was so fractured after the war that it was unable to nominate a Socialist for President in 1924. The challenge mounted against American capitalism by socialism and the *Appeal* had been turned back.

The Appeal's *"Starve the War and Feed America" campaign reflected a major effort on the part of radicals to halt the bloodshed of World War I and prevent the United States from entering the war as a participant.*

An Open Letter to President Wilson

The *Appeal to Reason*, speaking for one and a half million workers who are Socialists, and for many more millions of workers who have not yet voted the Socialist ticket, respectfully represents to you that the crops of 1914 are under the normal, in spite of doctored reports to the contrary, and that to permit these crops to be sent out of the country at this time is to feed and prolong the war in Europe and at the same time starve thousands of the working class in America.

The *Appeal* represents to you that four million workers in America are now out of employment, in spite of the special control of credit given to the capitalists of America, in spite of the authorized raise in railroad rates, in spite of every encouragement for the revival of business. The coming winter for the working class of America will doubtless prove more trying than any winter has ever been in our history.

In view of these things—and it is well that you

Appeal to Reason, June 13, 1914.

listen to the cry of the workers who produce all the wealth of the country, instead of to the controllers of industry who fail to revive industry in spite of every favor granted them—we call upon you to *prohibit the shipment of all food from the United States until the war is ended*. This will starve the war and at the same time provide food for the hungry here. And inasmuch as the capitalists have failed to fulfill their implied contract of employing the people, we call upon you and congress *to find for them employment in needed public work*. And that there may be money for the work, without obligating the country to the capitalists who have so signally failed in this crisis, *we demand of you and of congress that the deposits in the postal savings banks be used in this crisis for employing the idle*, instead of being turned over to the private banks for them to use in making profits at the expense of the workers.

This is the demand of the workers of the country. You have given the capitalists control of the credit. You have given the capitalists subsidy in the guise of insurance and monetary aid. You have given the capitalists money and ships to bear wasters of wealth from Europe—and they won't come. You have given the capitalists soldiers to defend the jobs they control against the workers who have no jobs. The workers have the votes. They have received absolutely no consideration from you or your party. *They now demand these things and demand them at once.*

September 12, 1914

Resting on the principles of peaceful cooperation, international solidarity, and the end of surplus value appropriation by the capitalist classes, the socialist analysis of war was convincing to millions of people in America and abroad.

Strange How the Few Rule the Great Mass

One of the strange things of life, as that English historian and philosopher, Hume, has said, is the ease with which the few have always governed the many. It has always been the few who governed, always the few who dictated how the many should live, always the few who monopolized the good things of life. Half the world is today engaged in a bloody war, the results of which stagger the imagination; millions are facing one another with guns; millions are killing one another. The many are doing the fighting because the few ordered them to fight. The few have always issued the orders, the many have always obeyed. Always it will be so under a system that allows one man's loss to be converted into another man's gain, as long as men are allowed to exploit other men's labor, as long as the skill, the energy, the brains and the genius of the world is used for the making of profits instead of for the making of a better world in which to live. Socialism is the only remedy. And Socialism is only possible through the education

Must He Ever Continue to Scourge the Earth?

Appeal to Reason, August 22, 1914.

of the exploited many. When a majority of the people of the world understand Socialism then a majority of people will rule and not before.

January 2, 1915

War Is Murder Any Way You Scheme It Out

"Not a Man, not a dollar for war!" This is the only true position of real Socialists and sincere advocates of peace. War is murder—legalized only by the capitalist governments of the world. No one can stand for war in any way and at the same time claim that he belongs to the ranks of Socialism. A great deal of rot is being written in various publications demanding concessions from militarism. Some are willing to pose as Socialists and sincere advocates of peace and at the same time stand for small armies and small navies. If a small army or a small navy is right a big army and a big navy is right. The principle back of them is the same. Once we recognize the right of arming some men to shoot down other men either in this country or abroad we endorse the principle of militarism. And this is the very thing that has led up to the European war. Let the Socialists of America stand uncompromisingly against war and militarism. It is not for the revolutionary party of the working class to trim and compromise. Let such parties as the Progressive party containing as prominent leaders at the same time, Theodore Roosevelt, the arch militarist of America, and Jane Addams and Raymond Robbins, organizers of peace conferences, do the trimming.

Let the Socialists of America stand by their colors. Let our party be the only party that stands against all wars and against everything that is in-

tended to murder and maim human beings. Let our cry be clear and strong. Let us be at the head of the procession. Finally, let us remember the wise words of Benjamin Franklin, *"There never was a good war nor a bad peace."*

February 27, 1915

When I Shall Fight

Eugene V. Debs

Since my characterization of the soldier in the Jingo edition I have been asked if I was opposed to all war and if I would refuse to be a soldier and to fight under any circumstances, and to make my answer through the *Appeal to Reason.* No, I am not opposed to all war, nor am I opposed to fighting under all circumstances, and any declaration to the contrary would disqualify me as a revolutionist. When I say I am opposed to war I mean ruling class war, for the ruling class is the only class that makes war. It matters not to me whether this war be offensive or defensive, or what other lying excuse may be invented for it, I am opposed to it, and I would be shot for treason before I would enter such a war.

If I were in congress I would be shot before I would vote a dollar for such a war.

Capitalists wars for capitalist conquest and capitalist plunder must be fought by the capitalists themselves so far as I am concerned, and upon that question there can be no compromise and no misunderstanding as to my position.

I have no country to fight for; my country is the earth; I am a citizen of the world.

I would not violate my principles for God,

Appeal to Reason,
December 4, 1915.

CENSORED

By the Postmaster General

Here is "A Good Soldier," by Jack London, which has aroused the militarists of this nation to the extent that Postmaster General Burleson has barred from the mails envelopes containing this article. The APPEAL TO REASON was threatened with a "fraud order" if it persisted in sending envelopes through the mails containing London's article. The Postmaster General did not even give the APPEAL a chance in the courts. He said: "Either stop circulating 'A Good Soldier' on envelopes or we will close up your doors by refusing to deliver a single piece of mail to you." So in "Free America" the APPEAL has been forced by a War Censor to take this means to circulate Jack London's criticism of the soldier profession:

❖ ❖ ❖ ❖ ❖

A Good Soldier

BY JACK LONDON

Young man, the lowest aim in your life is to be a good soldier. The good soldier never tries to distinguish right from wrong. He never thinks; never reasons; he only obeys. If he is ordered to fire on his fellow citizens, on his friends, on his neighbors, on his relatives, he obeys without hesitation. If he is ordered to fire down a crowded street when the poor are clamoring for bread, he obeys, and sees the gray hairs of age stained with red and the life-tide gushing from the breasts of women, feeling neither remorse nor sympathy. If he is ordered off as one of a firing squad to execute a hero or benefactor, he fires without hesitation, though he knows the bullet will pierce the noblest heart that ever beat in human breast.

A good soldier is a blind, heartless, soulless, murderous machine. He is not a man. He is not even a brute, for brutes only kill in self-defense. All that is human in him, all that is divine in him, all that constitutes the man, has been sworn away when he took the enlistment oath. His mind, conscience, aye, his very soul, are in the keeping of his officer.

No man can fall lower than a soldier—it is a depth beneath which we cannot go.

[If you want to know more about Socialism or how to join the Socialist party, write to the Appeal to Reason, Girard, Kan. The Appeal to Reason is a weekly paper and costs 50 cents a year.]

---

much less for a crazy kaiser, a savage czar, a degenerate king, or a gang of pot-bellied parasites.

But while I have not a drop of blood to shed for the oppressors of the working class and the robbers of the poor, the thieves and looters, the brigands and murderers whose debauched misrule is the crime of the ages, I have a heart-full to shed for their victims when it shall be needed in the war for their liberation.

I am not a capitalist soldier; I am a proletarian revolutionist. I do not belong to the regular army of the plutocracy, but to the irregular army of the people. I refuse to obey any command to fight from the ruling class, but I will not wait to be commanded to fight for the working class.

I am opposed to every war but one; I am for that war with heart and soul, and that is the world-wide war of social revolution. In that war I am prepared to fight in any way the ruling class may make necessary, even to the barricades.

There is where I stand and where I believe the Socialist party stands, or ought to stand, on the question of war.

September 11, 1915

The Appeal's *response to the Marine Hymn was an effective piece of subversion.*

Jingoism in Verse

An advertising poster bearing the name of the U.S. Marine Recruiting Station, Syracuse, N.Y., has printed on it the following pretty patriotic poem:

"From the Halls of Montezuma,
    To the shores of Tripoli,
We fight our country's battles
    On the land and on the sea;
Admiration of the nation,
    We are the finest ever seen,
And we glory in the title
    Of United States Marine."

"Our flag's unfurled to every breeze
    From dawn to setting sun,
We have fought in every clime and place
    Where we could take a gun;

In the snow of far-off northern lands
    And in sunny tropic scenes,
You will find us always on the job,
    The United States Marines."

This would be an excellent poem for the jingoes to circulate along with the rest of their "national defense" propaganda. Not a word about defending the United States; not a word about defending our own shores from actual attack. Instead "our country's" battles are fought "from the Halls of Montezuma to the shores of Tripoli." "We have fought in every clime and place where we could take a gun"—and incidentally, where our patriotic capitalists could make a profit. "In the snow of far-off northern lands and in sunny tropic scenes" the gallant United States marines have been defending the country and now we want a bigger army and navy in order to quell the Esquimaux and make Mexico submit to being swindled by the capitalistic clique of our own dear U.S.A.

September 18, 1915

Federal censorship occurred even before the United States entered World War I. The Appeal *was able to circumvent that censorship for only a brief period. Short pieces by Socialist party member Jack London appeared often in the* Appeal.

Burleson Bars from U.S. Mails Jack London's "A Good Soldier"

APPEAL ARMY WILL OUT-GENERAL P. O. CZAR BY DISTRIBUTING MILLIONS OF COPIES OF CENSORED ARTICLE IN LEAFLET FORM

It seems that every postmaster general must have his own lesson taught him by the *Appeal* Army. Not one profits from his predecessor. That alone explains why Postmaster General Burleson has been foolish enough to start a rumpus over Jack London's "A Good Soldier" printed by the *Appeal* and circulated by the *Appeal* Army.

Burleson, of course, has the power to act as war censor of this country. No one can deny that back of him stands the government and all that it means. Of course, the government was placed in the hands of these autocrats by the unthinking working men of this country—but that's another story. We can't correct this mistake now. We will have to wait until the next election. Perhaps the workers will then realize what fools they were in turning over the government to hypocritical exponents of "The New Freedom."

But one thing the *Appeal* Army can do right now that will act as a boomerang to Czar Burleson and his satellites. AND THAT IS TO CIRCULATE JACK LONDON'S "A GOOD SOLDIER" IN LEAFLET FORM.

Burleson's ukase applies only to the printing of that revolutionary statement on the back of an envelope. The same article can be legally mailed inside of an envelope and surely can be distributed from door to door in your community. Here is where the *Appeal* Army can take advantage of the advertising given to this masterpiece of Jack London and distribute it by the millions.

The *Appeal* has just published Jack London's "A Good Soldier," as its January leaflet, with an appropriate introduction in which the story of Burleson's attempt at suppression is told. You can do no greater service to the cause of peace as well as of free speech than to order a large number of these leaflets and have them distributed among your friends and neighbors.

The leaflet is sold by the *Appeal* for 50 cents a single thousand and 40 cents a thousand in lots of 2,000 or more. These prices include postage. Those wanting to distribute 5,000 copies or more and pay their own expressage, can get them at the rate of 25 cents a thousand.

Send your order at once and take advantage of this extraordinary opportunity to strike a powerful blow at the postal autocrats and military maniacs.

"A GOOD SOLDIER"—By Jack London "Young man, the lowest aim in your life is to be a good soldier. The good soldier never tries to distinguish right from wrong. He never thinks; never reasons; he only obeys. If he is ordered to fire on his fellow citizens, on his friends, on his neighbors, on his relatives, he obeys without hesitation. If he is ordered to fire down a crowded street when the poor are clamoring for bread, he obeys, and sees the gray hairs of age stained with red and the life tide gushing from the breasts of women, feeling neither remorse nor sympathy. If he is ordered off as one of a firing squad to execute a hero or a benefactor, he fires without hesitation, though he knows the bullet will pierce the noblest heart that ever beat in human breast.

"A good soldier is a blind, heartless, soulless, murderous machine. He is not a man. He is not even a brute, for brutes only kill in self-defense. All that is human in him, all that is divine in him, all that constitutes the man, has been sworn away when he took the enlistment roll. His mind, conscience, aye, his very soul, are in the keeping of his officer.

"No man can fall lower than a soldier—it is a depth beneath which we cannot go."

November 27, 1915

The political sophistication and honesty of many mainstream American newspapers at the beginning of the twentieth century remains a dramatic contrast to present-day media analysis. The Appeal's willingness to reprint stories and editorials gave them broad dispersion.

"National Defense Is Just So Much Hypocritical Balderdash"

THE TRUTH OF IT
Leading editorial in the *Washington* (D.C.) *Herald* of December 11, 1915.

Twenty-five years ago Great Britain lifted a controlling voice in the council chamber of the nations. Today, after many years of careful preparation, a young, vigorous and rapidly growing empire is challenging her supremacy. Britain has many allies in the struggle because her power has nearly always been enlisted, sincerely if not always intelligently, on the side of freedom and justice. Germany, on the other hand, has few friends because her power has always spelled the rigorous exploitation of everything German and the destruction of everything that does not bear the hallmark of kultur. Therefore, she has been able to rally to her side only Austria, that inner sanctuary of the divine rights of kings and nobles; Bulgaria, betrayed by a Hohenzollern king, and Turkey, a nation whose name has stunk in the nostrils of civilization for six hundred years.

Colonel Roosevelt believes that when the war broke out we should have taken our stand in the ranks of the Allies. Morally he is right. Politically he is right only on the theory that the destinies of the Anglo-Saxon nations are inseparable, a theory that rightly or wrongly but quite naturally the majority of Americans who have hardly any trace of the Anglo-Saxon about them have repudiated. The struggle, however it may have commenced, is one between Britain and Germany for the leadership of the pack, Britain fighting to keep what she has, Germany to get what she believes is her right. That leadership, which in the hands of English statesmen has been anything but aggressive or irksome, the other nations of Europe do not dispute. One day Russia may dispute it, but the time is not yet ripe. What then of the United States?

We shall dispute this leadership either with Britain or Germany as the case may be when the opportunity presents itself. That is why we have kept out of the struggle. It is to our advantage that our potential rivals shall weaken each other as much as possible. This is what all of our apostles of preparedness have in their hearts and all the talk that our post-prandial orators and statesmen put forth about our objects being purely defensive and our having no interests in the eastern hemisphere, and

Where Comment Is Unnecessary

[There is no need to waste space in commenting upon this brazen and cold blooded letter from an American manufacturer of war munitions to fellow capitalists seeking profitable investments. When you get through reading the photographic copy reproduced below you will make your own comment. The Appeal has the original copy of this letter in its vault:]

MOTSINGER DEVICE MANUFACTURING CO.

HOMER N. MOTSINGER
PRESIDENT

L. A. CASEY
SEC'Y & TREAS.

AUTO-SPARKER

TELEPHONE, BELL AND LOCAL
PRIVATE EXCHANGE 1123
CABLE ADDRESS
"AUTO-SPARKER"

LaFAYETTE, INDIANA, U. S. A.

October 1, 1915.

Fabulous
War Profits!

$493,000,000 in a few short months!

A new crop of American Millionaires!

Read the amazing truth of how foresighted American business men are profiting from Europe's necessity. The enclosed report from the Chicago Tribune tells the whole story.

How can _you_ get in on these tremendous profits? How can _you_ secure your share of the gold that is coming to us from Europe? How can _you_ participate in the wonderful prosperity movement that has made the American dollar the money standard of the world?

Listen!

The Motsinger Device Manufacturing Company has a machine tool equipment that can turn out 4,000 to 5,000 shrapnel fuses a week. These fuses are in _great_ demand. Almost any price within reason will be paid to the company that can actually make delivery. _We can._

An order of this size would mean additional business of $ 10,000 to $ 15,000 a week-- with a generous margin of profit. It would mean net earnings at the rate of more than 40% on our entire capitalization.

There is little doubt that the overwhelming disasters recently suffered by the Russian armies were due to just one cause--lack of ammunition. A realization of this fact has intensely stimulated the demand for munitions. It has raised the prices the Allies are willing to pay.

All this we had foreseen. So now, instead of being loaded up with work at low prices, we are in a position to take orders at the high prices which now prevail. So tremendously profitable are these orders that we do not see how we can avoid taking them. But we will not sacrifice our regular production of carburetors, auto sparkers, magnetos, etc. This will go on just the same. The war order business will be additional--"velvet," if you will pardon the slang.

Sincerely yours,

L. a. Casey
Secretary-Treasurer.

LAC./PB.

Appeal to Reason, November 27, 1915.

If They Keep on They Will Have War

Appeal to Reason, September 25, 1915.

so on, IS JUST SO MUCH HYPOCRITI-CAL BALDERDASH. We desire to be a great nation and to have our "place in the sun" which is just a synonym for "bossing the show" and though we are not so truculent or so objectionable about it our aspirations in this respect are not a whit different from those that Germany has published broadcast to the world.

In living up to these aspirations we are acting naturally, legitimately and sanely, and therefore it is ridiculous to be dishonest about it and to attempt to conceal ambitions which we are rather scared of because we do not fully understand that they are inevitable.

At the present moment the American people is struggling between two conflicting emotions. We do not want Germany to win because we are op-

posed mentally and morally to her philosophy and politics. We do not want Britain to win on the other hand because if she does it means good-bye to our immediate chances of lifting a considerable, much less a dominant, voice in the affairs of the world's democracies. If we had been a little franker in stating this to be our position—and it is one that history, evolution, ethnography or what you will must account for and not a thing of our immediate choosing—our apparent surly neutrality would not have lost us the esteem of our neighbors. Selfishness—and all nations are and must be selfish—may not be admirable but it is not a sign of weakness. At the close of the present struggle we shall be in a position, in all respects but arms and the will to arm, to control the destinies of the terrestrial globe. On the other hand the European nations, impoverished financially and with their resources of "cannon food" materially depleted, will not only be armed to the teeth, but will have the immense reserves of spiritual vigor that war always begets. We shall look to them very much as a fat white caterpillar does to a party of hungry ants.

We must arm—if the poison engendered when "wealth accumulates and men decay" has not eaten so deeply into our system that we are no longer capable of arming, and arm well and lastingly. No semi-political outburst of enthusiasm that produces nothing but an extra pair of dreadnoughts and a world of sound and fury is going to suffice. The struggle from which we will not be permitted to stand aside may not and probably will not come for fifty years. But it will come, and fifty years is little time in which to prepare for it.

But above all let us not undertake this thing and imagine fondly that the other nations will accept our pacific protestations or will not realize exactly what we are about. Recently Lord Rosebery deprecated the proposed enlargement of our navy and stated that it simply meant a continuation of the burden of armaments since Britain would never consent to lose or to lessen the margin of her maritime supremacy. We regret that that is true, but are unable to oblige Lord Rosebery. He no doubt thinks that the so-called Anglo-Saxon races should exhibit some kind of give-and-take or harmony in this matter. To that we reply simply that we are not an Anglo-Saxon race as the English understand the term and the sooner they realize it the better for them though perhaps the worse for us. We have fought with Great Britain before. We shall exhibit no blushing reluctance to do so again. Then why not be frank about it?

There are many Americans who will deny the views here expressed. Let them realize that they are in a rapidly dwindling minority. Great Britain and the United States going hand in hand to lead the world into a warless era is only a beautiful dream. Bombs and dollars are the only things that count today. We have plenty of the one. Let us lay in a good supply of the other and blast a path to

world leadership as soon as an opportunity presents itself.

December 25, 1915

Comparatively free from patriotic rhetoric and mystification, federal support of capitalist policy was much more overt seventy years ago than it is at present. It was not at all uncommon at the turn of the century for government agencies to compute the monetary value added by labor to the final value of production. Frederick Monroe served as the Appeal's Washington, D.C., correspondent.

Official of Government Admits Big Capitalists Seek to Conquer World

FREDERICK MONROE

Washington, D.C.—"*Our success in foreign trade in the future is vitally necessary to us.*" Thus, in one sentence, a government official, high in the councils of the administration, clinches the contention which Socialism has made for years that commercial competition between nations is the cause of wars, and that the preparedness agitation which now confronts the country is merely a reflex of the necessity which the capitalists of the country are under of seizing and holding foreign markets after the present war. A big army and a big navy for the protection and fostering of foreign commerce—this is the proposal which is facing the nation today.

And the *reasons* back of it have been confessed in so many words by Dr. Edward Ewing Pratt, chief of the bureau of foreign and domestic commerce of the department of commerce. Speaking at the annual banquet of the National Paper and Pulp Association, held Thursday night, February 17, in New York City, Dr. Pratt, whose duty it is to foster the commerce and commercial interests of the masters of industry in this country, said:

"*I for one believe that the United States is entering upon a new period in her economic history. There was a*

time when the United States consisted of a few struggling colonies on the Atlantic coast. She gradually expanded into a great agricultural nation, and of late
we have developed industrially and our manufacturers have become important. Now we are entering upon a period of international commerce
when the United States will take her position at
the head of the commercial nations of the world."

How can a nation take her place at the head of the
commercial nations of the world unless she has the
armed force to back up her "place"? Foreign commerce must be protected. A heavy investment in
overseas traffic must be insured by a big navy and a
big army ready to "protect the interests of Americans" whenever and wherever they are "attacked."
This is the doctrine laid down by the administration. American cargoes must not be attacked. We
must protect "American lives and property" in
Mexico. Everywhere the cry goes up that we must
"protect" something. "National defense" is the
catchword used to fool the people into granting
great armaments, but not national defense, but
"national offense" is the purpose for which such
armaments are created. That is why Mr. Garrison
resigned as Secretary of War, because the national
guard—the state militia—cannot under the constitution of the United States be sent *outside the
borders of the United States*. Mr. Garrison said a
force of that kind is no good—what he wants is a
federal force at all times under the orders of the
war department and capable of *being sent anywhere
overseas*.

To those who think that there is no impending
conflict over the clash of commercial interests, listen again to Mr. Pratt. In another part of the same
speech, he says:

"It is sometimes urged that the hatred engendered
by war will soon pass away; that each country will
seek the cheapest market, irrespective of nationality. In an unorganized market this would be
true. But Europe is not unorganized. Legislation,
taxation, organized public sentiment will be the
means of continuing for decades, and even gener-

ations, the *commercial struggle* which will grow out
of the *armed conflict*. The United States, innocent
by-stander, can not expect altogether favorable
treatment at the hands of either group. *We must realize that not only our foreign markets which we had
before the war and which we have established since the
beginning of the war, but our home market, will be the
object of commercial attack.*"

Socialists have maintained that a manufacturing
nation *must* develop foreign markets if it is to continue to live. This is so because under the capitalist
system of industry, the wages paid to the workers
can never be equal to the value of the product. The
difference between wages paid and wages *earned*
goes to the capitalist in the form of profit. Thus,
the United States census figures for 1909 show that
in 268,000 factories engaged in manufacture, the
6,600,000 wage earners in these factories added
$1,290 apiece for this production! Not on your
life! They received exactly $518 apiece, on the aver-
age. Where did the other $772 go? It went to the
employers and landowners. This is the *surplus
value* which is appropriated by the capitalist employer. The harder the workers work the more *surplus value* they pile up for the employer.

Now it's a simple mathematical proposition to
find out if a worker who gets $518 is able to buy
back from the capitalists goods whose value is
$1,290 and *which he himself produced*. Suppose all
the 6,600,000 workers who worked in the
268,000 factories in 1909 had at the end of the year
tried to buy back with their total wages all the
products they had produced in these factories?
Isn't it obvious they couldn't do it? *What becomes
of this surplus value?* Some of it is used up by the
capitalists themselves. Much of it is wasted. But
the larger part of the product is neither used nor
wasted by the capitalists, *but must be sold—to somebody—in order that the capitalist may get his profit*.
The product is offered for sale to the public. *And
about 70 per cent of the entire public consists of wage
earners—workers*. Therefore, the problem is presented of *selling back to the workers what the workers*

have produced at a price much more than double what these workers have received in wages.

Obviously, it can't be done. *And this is the reason for foreign markets.* Listen to Dr. Pratt again:

"But the crux of the whole matter lies in our foreign trade. The war has indicated that our domestic prosperity is vitally linked up with the prosperity of our foreign trade. We found what to many of us was astounding, and to some unthinkable, that a small segment of our total business, very small when compared to the vast amount of our total trade, held the key to our prosperity. Our success in foreign trade in the future is vitally necessary to us."

No more candid confession of the truth of the Socialist contention was ever uttered by anybody than this confession that "success in foreign trade in the future is *vitally* necessary to us." Dr. Pratt has admitted the Socialist contention completely.

But, if foreign markets are *"vitally necessary to us,"* they must be equally *"vitally necessary"* to every other commercial nation in the world. They must be vitally necessary to Great Britain, to Germany, to France, to Austria, to Italy, to Russia, and to the other nations of Europe, which manufacture a *surplus* which their workers are not allowed to consume. And when all these nations face each other, *each with a surplus in its hand,* what is to happen? *Exactly what has happened—the European war. The European war is being fought for a place in the sun.*

That means the right to exploit certain foreign markets, the right to "develop" certain colonies, the right to make vast investments in underdeveloped portions of the world. *This results in commercial rivalry and antagonism, in secret treaties and agreements, in the necessity for preserving a "balance of power" in other words, in all the kinds of "preparedness" which our own capitalist class is now so frantically advocating. . . .*

March 6, 1916

Accounts from the battlefields in Europe strengthened the *Appeal's* resolve to oppose World War I and strengthened the opposition of many of its readers as well.

Lives Wasted Like So Many Grains of Sand

The effort to take Verdun has been titanic. A huge, powerful human machine has been hurled against a group of forts. This is the manner in which civilized human beings settle their differences. Flesh and blood stops to argue with steel and shell. Shrapnel always wins. Reports have it that the slaughter before the forts at Verdun has been simply ghastly. Human life is considered as important as a grain of sand. In the Paris *Matin* we find the following description of the awful scenes by a soldier who participated in the terrible battle:

Battalions advanced upon us in close ranks, twenty men abreast. Shrapnel from our 75's and our heavy artillery rained on them. It was blood-curdling. We could see great gaps being made. It was as if a man had been passing through the German ranks with a scythe steadily mowing them down.

Each time the shells exploded arms and legs flew high in the air. We were so near one another that odds and ends of amputated limbs fell almost on the top of us. In one small section of two sections—a mere nothing—they fell by hundreds and hundreds. Finally we made our way back up towards Maucourt. Our quick-firing guns, posted only five meters apart, belched forth, and we were confronted with the sight of corpses standing upright in bunches.

These pawns of aristocrats are dying by the thousand, and yet the rulers refuse to say what they are fighting for and what the terms of peace may be. Militarism has crazed the rulers, and the innocent victims of royal and capitalistic tyranny can do nothing but let their blood be shed in a stupid, senseless struggle.

As Socialists we must fight this demon, this diabolical fiend. We must continue our war on war.

April 1, 1916

Neither advertising nor public relations was a well-developed enterprise before World War I; consequently, clumsy federal efforts were susceptible to easy ridicule.

The United States government has suddenly turned agitator. We refer to a poster which a reader has been kind enough to send us. After looking over this invitation to join the navy (which we cannot accept), we wonder if the reactionary dodos are going to let the authorities expose social conditions so unmercifully. The poster uses the deadly parallel. Eleven reasons are marshalled to prove why civil life is grim and joyless. Here is Uncle Sam's indictment of capitalist society:

1. Jobs uncertain; strikes, lay-offs, sickness.

2. Promotion and advancement uncertain and slow.

3. Favoritism and partiality frequently shown.

4. Pay small and limited while learning a trade.

5. Same old, monotonous, tiresome grind every day.

6. Stuffy, gloomy, uninteresting working place.

7. When sick your pay stops and doctor's bill starts.

8. If disabled or injured you receive little or no pay.

9. If you die your family gets only what you have saved from your small wages.

10. Little clear money; nearly all your pay goes for living expenses.

11. Old age, sickness, little money saved, your job goes to a younger and more active man.

Who can deny that Uncle Sam's charges against the wage system are based on facts? We know, in reality, that this poster describes too accurately the workers who patronize the Cafe de Hash.

While the toilers are in want, the capitalists revel in Carthaginian ease. The bleak, gloomy Reaper who "gathers them in" finds the victims of capitalism easy prey because of hunger and privation. Capitalism is as harsh and cruel as Rome's marching legions. The system lets the useless capitalists walk rosy pathways, while the useful creators of wealth must travel aisles of gloom.

We refuse to be calm in the face of such injustices. We shall fight this rotten, despicable chaos until the last vestige of monopoly shall have been destroyed. We shall give up the struggle only when the people who make the wealth shall be the owners of the means of production and distribution.

April 15, 1916

Son of Swedish immigrants, Carl Sandburg began working at thirteen and remains best known as a poet and a biographer of Abraham Lincoln. Sandburg never lost his sympathy and rootedness with common people. "Buttons," reprinted often in the radical press, reflects both Sandburg's stylistic experimentation and his horror at human destruction.

Buttons

CARL SANDBURG

I have been watching the war maps
    slammed up for advertising in
    front of the newspaper office.
Buttons—red and yellow buttons—blue
    and black buttons—are shoved
    back and forth across the map.

A laughing young man, sunny with
    freckles,
Climbs a ladder, yells a joke to some-
    body in the crowd,

And then fixes a yellow button one inch
    west
And follows the yellow button with a
    black button one inch west.

(Ten thousand men and boys twist on
    their bodies in a red soak along a
    river edge,
Gasping of wounds, calling for water,
    some rattling death in their
    throats.)
Who by Christ would guess what it cost
    to move two buttons one inch on
    the war map here in front of the
    newspaper office where the freckle-
    faced young man is laughing to
    us?

July 5, 1916

As James St. Claire writes, those killed on the battlefield were not the only victims of World War I. Misery and desolation stalked Europe and, to a lesser extent, America.

The
Shambles

JAMES ST. CLAIRE

'Twas twilight and down a pathway
    Strewn with bleached and crumbling bones,
To a stream once crimson with battle-blood
    The War God stalked, alone.

Silent he gazed, and pondered
    At the havoc wrought by his hand—
At the ruined homes and the whitening bones
    And the misery in the land.

Gloating he turned, and startled, saw,
    A woman in sack-cloth dressed,
Resting hard by 'gainst a blasted tree—
    A babe clasped to her breast.

Tall of stature and sallow of face—
    Wasted of limb and hollow eyed
She crouched, and hungrily scanned the skies,
    For a vision of Him who a hero died.

Quoth the War God, "Behold my work;
    'Twas a goodly number here
That paid the price with hope and life
    Laid on a rocky bier."

Answered the woman, "Yea, my lord—
    Their debts are settled—their flesh is clay.
'Tis I who pay at this sad reckoning—
    'Tis I who pay—'tis I who yet must pay."

October 28, 1916

Meeting in emergency convention a day after the United States entered World War I, the large majority of Socialist party delegates endorsed the following condemnation of the war. Two minority resolutions were also filed, but the majority report was supported by Socialist party members by a nearly ten to one vote and became official party policy.

Reactionary Plans of American Militarists Must Be Thwarted, Declares Socialist Party Convention in Condemning the War

1. The Socialist party of the United States, in the present grave crisis, solemnly reaffirms its allegiance to the principle of internationalism and working class solidarity the world over, and proclaims its unalterable opposition to the war just declared by the government of the United States.

Modern wars as a rule have been caused by the commercial and financial rivalry and intrigues of the capitalist interests in the different countries.

Whether they have been frankly waged as wars of aggression or have been hypocritically represented as wars of "defense," they have always been made by the classes and fought by the masses. Wars bring wealth and power to the ruling classes, and suffering, death and demoralization to the workers.

They breed a sinister spirit of passion, unreason, race hatred and false patriotism. They obscure the struggles of the workers for life, liberty and social justice. They tend to sever the vital bonds of solidarity between them and their brothers in other countries, to destroy their organizations and to curtail their civic and political rights and liberties.

2. The Socialist party of the United States is unalterably opposed to the system of exploitation and class rule which is upheld and strengthened by military power and sham national patriotism. We, therefore, call upon the workers of all countries to refuse support to their governments in their wars. The wars of the contending national groups of capitalists are not the concern of the workers. The only struggle which would justify the workers in taking up arms is the great struggle of the working class of the world to free itself from economic exploitation and political oppression; and we particularly warn the workers against the snare and delusion of so-called defensive warfare. As against the false doctrine of national patriotism we uphold the ideal of international working class solidarity. In support of capitalism, we will not willingly give a single life or a single dollar; in support of the struggle of the workers for freedom we pledge our all.

3. The mad orgy of death and destruction which is now convulsing unfortunate Europe was caused by the conflict of capitalist interests in the European countries.

In each of these countries, the workers were oppressed and exploited. They produced enormous wealth but the bulk of it was withheld from them by the owners of the industries. The workers were thus deprived of the means to repurchase the wealth, which they themselves had created.

The capitalist class of each country was forced to look for foreign markets to dispose of the accumulated "surplus" wealth. The huge profits made by the capitalists could no longer be profitably reinvested in their own countries, hence, they were driven to look for foreign fields of investment. The geographical boundaries of each modern capitalist country thus became too narrow for the industrial and commercial operations of its capitalist class.

The efforts of the capitalists of all leading nations were therefore centered upon the domination of the world markets. Imperialism became the dominant note in the politics of Europe. The acquisition of colonial possessions and the extension of spheres of commercial and political influence became the object of diplomatic intrigues and the cause of constant clashes between nations.

The acute competition between the capitalist powers of the earth, their jealousies and distrusts of one another and the fear of the rising power of the working class forced each of them to arm to the teeth. This led to the mad rivalry of armament, which, years before the outbreak of the present war, had turned the leading countries of Europe into armed camps with standing armies of many millions, drilled and equipped for war in times of "peace."

Capitalism, imperialism and militarism had thus laid the foundation of an inevitable general conflict in Europe. The ghastly war in Europe was not caused by an accidental event, nor by the policy or institutions of any single nation. It was the logical outcome of the competitive capitalist system.

The six million men of all countries and races who have been ruthlessly slain in the first thirty months of this war, the millions of others who have been crippled and maimed, the vast treasures of wealth that have been destroyed, the untold misery and sufferings of Europe, have not been sacrifices exacted in a struggle for principles or ideals, but wanton offerings upon the altar of private profit.

The forces of capitalism which have led to the war in Europe are even more hideously transparent in the war recently provoked by the ruling class of this country.

When Belgium was invaded, the government enjoined upon the people of this country, the duty of remaining neutral, thus clearly demonstrating that the "dictates of humanity," and the fate of small nations and of democratic institutions were matters that did not concern it. But when our enormous war traffic was seriously threatened, our government calls upon us to rally to the "defense of democracy and civilization."

Our entrance into the European war was instigated by the predatory capitalists in the United States who boast of the enormous profit of seven billion dollars from the manufacture and sale of munitions and war supplies and from the exportation of American food stuffs and other necessaries. They are also deeply interested in the continuance of war and the success of the allied arms through their huge loans to the governments of the allied powers and through other commercial ties. It is the same interests which strive for imperialistic domination of the Western Hemisphere.

The war of the United States against Germany cannot be justified even on the plea that it is a war in defense of American rights or American "honor." Ruthless as the unrestricted submarine war policy of the German government was and is, it is not an invasion of the rights of the American people as such, but only an interference with the opportunity of certain groups of American capitalists to coin cold profits out of the blood and sufferings of our fellowmen in the warring countries of Europe.

It is not a war against the militarist regime of the Central Powers. Militarism can never be abolished by militarism.

It is not a war to advance the cause of democracy in Europe. Democracy can never be imposed upon any country by a foreign power by force of arms.

It is cant and hypocrisy to say that the war is not directed against the German people, but against the Imperial Government of Germany. If we send an armed force to the battle fields of Europe, its cannon will mow down the masses of the German people and not the Imperial German Government.

Our entrance into the European conflict at this time will serve only to multiply the horrors of the war, to increase the toll of death and destruction and to prolong the fiendish slaughter. It will bring death, suffering and destitution to the people of the United States and particularly to the working class. It will give the powers of reaction in this country the pretext for an attempt to throttle our rights and to crush our democratic institutions, and to fasten upon this country a permanent militarism.

The working class of the United States have no quarrel with the working class of Germany or of any other country. The people of the United States have no quarrel with the people of Germany or of any other country. The American people did not want and do not want this war. They have not been consulted about the war and have had no part in declaring war. They have been plunged into this war by the trickery and treachery of the ruling class of the country through its representatives in the National Administration and National Congress, its demagogic agitators, its subsidized press, and other servile instruments of public expression.

We brand the declaration of war by our government as a crime against the people of the United States and against the nations of the world.

In all modern history there has been no war more unjustifiable than the war in which we are about to engage.

No greater dishonor has ever been forced upon a people than that which the capitalist class is forcing upon this nation against its will.

In harmony with these principles, the Socialist Party emphatically rejects the proposal that in time of war the workers should suspend their struggle for better conditions. On the contrary, the acute situation created by war calls for an even more vigorous prosecution of the class struggle, and we recommend to the workers and pledge ourselves to the following course of action:

1. Continuous, active, and public opposition to the war, through demonstrations, mass petitions, and all other means within our power.

2. Unyielding opposition to all proposed legislation for military or industrial conscription. Should such conscription be forced upon the people, we pledge ourselves to continuous efforts for the repeal of such laws and to the support of all mass movements in opposition to conscription. We pledge ourselves to fight with all our strength against any attempt to raise money for the payment of war expenses by taxing the necessaries of life or issuing bonds which will put the burden upon future generations. We demand that the capitalist class which is responsible for the war pay its cost. Let those who kindle the fire furnish the fuel.

3. Vigorous resistance to all reactionary measures, such as censorship of press and mails, restriction of the rights of free speech, assemblage and organization, or compulsory arbitration and limitation of the right to strike.

4. Consistent propaganda against military training and militaristic teaching in the public schools.

5. Extension of the campaign of education among the workers to organize them into strong, class-conscious, and closely unified political and industrial organizations, to enable them by concerted and harmonious mass action to shorten this war and to establish lasting peace.

6. Widespread educational propaganda to enlighten the masses as to the true relation between capitalism and war, and to rouse and organize them for action, not only against present war evils, but for the prevention of future wars and for the destruction of the causes of war.

7. To protect the masses of the American people from the pressing danger of starvation which the war in Europe has brought upon them, and which the entry of the United States has already accentuated, we demand—

(a) The restriction of food exports so long as the present shortage continues, the fixing of maximum prices, and whatever measures may be necessary to prevent the food speculators from holding back the supplies now in their hands;

(b) The socialization and democratic management of the great industries concerned with the production, transportation, storage, and the marketing of food and other necessaries of life;

(c) The socialization and democratic management of all land and other natural resources now held out of use for monopolistic or speculative profit.

These measures are presented as means of protecting the workers against the evil results of the present war. The danger of recurrence of war will exist as long as the capitalist system of industry remains in existence. The end of war will come with the establishment of socialized industry and industrial democracy the world over. The Socialist party calls upon all the workers to join it in its struggle to reach this goal, and thus bring into the world a new society in which peace, fraternity, and human brotherhood will be the dominant ideals.

1. We recommend that the convention instruct our elected representatives in Congress, in the State Legislatures, and in local bodies, to vote against all proposed appropriations or loans for military, naval, and other war purposes.

2. We recommend that this convention instruct the National Executive Committee to extend and improve the propaganda among women, because they as housewives and as mothers are now particularly ready to accept our message.

3. We recommend that the convention instruct the National Executive Committee to initiate an organized movement of Socialists, organized workers, and other anti-war forces for concerted action along the lines of this program.

April 21, 1917

A number of well-known socialist writers and intellectuals such as Allan Benson, Charles Edward Russell, William English Walling, and John Spargo left the Socialist party soon after the party formally opposed World War I and America's participation in it. Initially, however, the Appeal held its ground.

Stand United!

Last week's first page of the *Appeal* was devoted to the three reports presented by the dissenting members of the Committee on War and Militarism to the Emergency National Socialist Convention at St. Louis. The majority report and [Leonard] Boudin's minority report condemned militarism in general and the German-American war in particular. John Spargo's minority report may be said to have been a semi-endorsement of the war between this country and Germany. We printed the three reports so that our readers may fully acquaint themselves with all possible views on this momentous question.

The *Appeal*'s position is, of course, known to our readers. As a consistent and militant opponent of militarism, the *Appeal* has fought this war from the beginning and to the very last. Even though the controlled press has lashed Congress and the administration into declaring war against Germany the *Appeal* can not and will not lend its support to this conflict. The *Appeal* is not disloyal to the government of the United States. The *Appeal* has no sympathies for the ruling class of Germany or of any other country. In the best sense the *Appeal* is pro-American and consequently pro-humanity.

We feel convinced that the present war is the inevitable result of the determination of American capitalists to carry on business as usual in spite of the military operations abroad. From the very beginning we called attention to this threatening disaster. We urged the administration to stop the war traffic. We pleaded with Congress to suspend our foreign commerce until the war was ended. However, the exploiting classes are more powerful and influential than the champions of the common people. Through their political power and through their control of the press, our war traffic was permitted to continue and develop. War was therefore the logical outcome. And war we now have.

It is true that many Socialists sympathize with the cause of the Entente Allies because they believe that these nations are fighting the battle of democracy against autocracy. Still others believe that it would be disastrous for the people of this country to have Germany win the war—hence they believe that we should support, in a measure, the government in successfully prosecuting the war. Prominent Socialists like Benson, Russell, Walling, Spargo and others, take this position. The *Appeal*, however, cannot support this view because we fear the consequences of any endorsement given to the militarists. We have no assurance that the Entente Allies will content themselves with "imposing" a free government upon the people of Germany (if such a thing were possible) and stop at that. The facts of history are that conquerors always reap the spoils of war. And no matter what the intentions of the United States may be, we feel that its allies would remake the map of Europe and of the world if Germany were defeated. . . .

April 28, 1917

Appeal's Issue of June 30 Is Barred from the Mails

Delivery Was Practically Completed When Authorities Found It to Be In Conflict With Espionage Act Signed June 15— Order Does Not Affect Future Issues of *Appeal* Provided They Do Not Violate New Law

Our subscribers—numbering in the hundreds of thousands and in every part of the country—were undoubtedly amazed when they read in the capitalist press a few days ago that the *Appeal to Reason* had been excluded from the mails by the authorities at Washington. So were we amazed— especially since we had information to the contrary. But after reflection we realized that it was just what we could expect of our beloved contemporaries. Having been informed by the Washington authorities that a single issue was found to be nonmailable under the new Espionage Law, the capitalist newspapers distorted this fact into a story of the complete suppression of the *Appeal to Reason.* Undoubtedly the wish was father to the thought. The following from the Kansas City *Star* of July 7 is a typical example:

BAR THE *APPEAL TO REASON*

The Mails Closed to the Kansas Socialist Weekly

Washington, July 7: The mails have been barred to the numerous publications for opposition to the war since

the Espionage Act was approved June 15, it was learned today. The latest stop order was issued yesterday against the Appeal to Reason, *Socialist weekly of Girard, Kans.*

Among the other publications, one or more issues of which have been barred by the Postoffice Department, are Tom Watson's Jeffersonian, *Georgia; the* Four Lights, *organ of the Women's Peace Party of New York; the* American Socialist, *Chicago; the* Blast, *Alexander Berkman's Anarchist periodical, and* Mother Earth, *Emma Goldman's mouthpiece.*

. . . .

It is a pretty sad state of affairs that permits the limitation of the freedom of the press by the Washington postoffice authorities. It is still a worse state of affairs when every postmaster and letter carrier in the United States can under this Espionage Act delay the delivery of printed matter which to him may appear as being illegal. Surely under such conditions censorship by one person would be preferable. At least then matter "passed by the censor" would reach its destination without delay.

That the Socialist and radical press do not intend to lie down and have their rights abrogated without making the best fight possible is shown by the following account of the action of the Socialist Party National Executive Committee, as reported in the New York *Call*:

Chicago, July 6: An appeal to President Wilson and Postmaster General Burleson against the suppression of a free press in the United States is to be made immediately, growing out of the plans made here today by the Socialist party's national executive committee.

Aroused to action by the holding up of the liberty edition, June 30, of the American Socialist, *and the suppression or holding up of various issues of the So-*cialist News, *Cleveland;* Michigan Socialist, *Detroit;* Rebel, *Halletsville, Tex.;* Social Revolution, *St. Louis, Mo., and* St. Louis Labor, *the national executive committee decided to protest to Washington immediately.*

A committee consisting of Clarence Darrow and Seymour Stedman, Chicago; Frank P. Walsh, Kansas

City, Mo., and Morris Hillquit, New York City, will proceed to Washington next week to protest against the suppressions that have already taken place and try to prevent similar suppressions in the future.

If it is impossible to secure any satisfaction through the president or the postmaster general, an appeal will be made to the courts as a last resort. Darrow and Stedman attended the meeting of the national executive committee of which Hillquit is a member, and the entire matter was discussed at length.

It seems incredible that any effort would be made to suppress or limit the freedom of press in America. No one disputes the right of the government to prohibit the publication of military or naval information that might be useful to the enemy. But what justification is there for the persecution of American citizens or publications who strive in their way to bring the international carnage to an early end? Even in Germany the discussion of peace is freely admitted. And in those countries where the rights of free press do not exist censorship is not invoked against entire issues or the existence of publications. Articles may be deleted by censors but indiscriminate suppressions are rare.

July 14, 1917

Notice to Our Readers

We have been advised by the post office department that the following are unmailable in any form under the Espionage Act approved June 15, 1917:

"A Good Soldier," generally accredited to Jack London.

"A Pledge," by George R. Kirkpatrick.

Buttons with the inscription, "Not a Man, Not a Dollar for War."

July 14, 1917

"The Voices of Humanity That Are in the Air" traces the Appeal's departure from socialist principles. Masked by these political rationalizations, however, are not only Louis Kopelin's and Emanuel Haldeman-Julius's desire to buy the Appeal but their recognition that the paper would have to continue publication if their indebtedness to the Wayland family was to be repaid.

President Wilson Has Heard "the Voices of Humanity That Are in the Air" and Declares in Favor of Democratic Settlement of War

To the Readers of the *Appeal*:

President Wilson has heard "the voices of humanity that are in the air." The cry of the plain people of every nation that "the war shall not end in vindictive action of any kind" has brought forth a full and frank answer. The democratic formula, "No annexations; no contributions; no punitive indemnities," has been espoused by the President of the United States.

Readers of the *Appeal* since the war began are well aware of the importance of President Wilson's splendid contribution to the early and just ending of the international conflict. Until our President delivered his address to Congress last week the democratic slogan of "No annexations; no contributions, no punitive indemnities," was practically sounded by the Socialists and liberals alone while the reactionary elements condemned this slogan as being tainted with pro-Germanism. Now we have the chief executive of the richest and strongest member of the Allies proclaiming in unmistakable tones that this "just idea" should be "brought under the patronage of its real friends."

After our entrance into the world war the *Appeal* realized that it would be foolish and unworthy of us to attempt to obstruct the war. Once in, the United States could not in honor and in fact withdraw. A separate peace was out of the question. In spite of the charges of the reactionaries no rational Socialist or liberal could entertain such a step. We therefore devoted our efforts to the fostering of public sentiment that would unite the common people of all countries, including the people of Germany and Austria-Hungary, against the military group of Prussia that more than any other single factor was responsible for the international carnage, and thus hasten the end of the war.

As a newspaper devoted to the interests of the working people in field and factory we felt that the first step to bring about unity among the Allies and dissension in the Teutonic countries was to convince the working people that the Allies had no selfish or greedy motive in waging war against their enemies. On May 12 we declared:

"The reason the Socialist of Germany and Austria-Hungary are fighting for their governments is because they feel convinced that their enemies lust for conquest and indemnities."

And in the *Appeal* of May 26 we said:

"The way to show the German people that we are their friends is by renouncing aggressive intentions upon their territory and resources. Russia has already told the Allies that it will not fight for annexation and indemnity for anybody. The United States has publicly declared that it does not want land and money for itself. However, it has not definitely stated that it will not fight for the remaking of the map of Europe and the imposing of heavy indemnities upon the German people for the benefit of other nations. It now remains our great and urgent duty to influence our government to publicly renounce any intention to fight for annexation and indemnity for any nation."

That our campaign to secure a statement of the aims of the war was prompted mainly by an intense desire to unite the liberal forces of the world in a moral offensive against the autocratic Prussian rulers is shown by the following extract from our issue of June 30:

"Not only will a clear and definite statement from our government based on the aims of the war bring unity and understanding in the allied countries but it will bring dissension and antagonism in the Teutonic countries."

It is true that the substance of a democratic peace was advocated by the President in his Senate address last January—while we were still a neutral nation. On the other hand the addresses and notes of President Wilson subsequent to our participation in the world conflict were principally devoted to the military aspects of the war. Not until the President's excellent reply to the Pope's peace proposal could the liberals make use of an official declaration against what might be called an imperialist settlement of the war. In that reply the President revealed that he was still in the ranks of the world's liberals. "Punitive damages, the dismemberment of empires, the establishment of selfish and exclusive leagues," were roundly denounced by President Wilson as being no basis for an enduring or just peace.

. . . .

Not being bound by any dogmas or formulas the *Appeal* is fortunately in a position to recognize the truth no matter where it shines. We are interested in the substance, not the phrases. We are not so narrow as to believe that only certain elements organized in a certain way or labeled in a certain manner are the sole devotees of peace and democracy. All the world longs for these essentials to life and liberty. No one has a patent method to attain them. Whoever advances the cause of democracy and peace heartily deserves our undivided support as long as he is engaged in that laudable pursuit.

In leading our moral support to the prosecution of the war we are enabled not only to help bring about an early and just peace but we are also enabled to battle for the things that are dear to our hearts—democracy in government and industry. The world war has done more to stimulate the socialization of industry than a century of propaganda. A new era is dawning. The exigencies of war are dethroning all the sacred gods of capitalism. Government ownership and operation of the principal industries is now in sight. What we have been fighting for a score of years is now coming to pass. We can greatly accelerate these tremendous changes and have them permanently benefit the masses if we adjust ourselves to new conditions and take advantage of our opportunities.

Strange as it may seem a destructive war is bringing constructive social effort in America. The *Appeal to Reason* has for years carried on a propaganda of negation against private ownership of industries socially necessary. We have exposed, criticised and denounced. That we have done this job well will be attested by our enemies as well as by our friends. But things are different today. We are living in a time when society is ready to listen to the argument of efficiency and economy for the common good. That there is a readiness and willingness on the part of men and women of all political faiths to join in the work of socialization and democratization is shown in the recent successful convention of the Public Ownership League of America at Chicago, which we so fully reported last week.

Hereafter we shall make a *New Appeal*. The *New Appeal* will be to the national unity and social consciousness for the establishing of fundamental democracy in political, industrial and international relations. The *New Appeal* will be constructive, positive, educational. All hail the *New Appeal*!

December 15, 1917

Haldeman-Julius avoided conscription and remained in Girard to edit the Appeal, but Louis Kopelin enlisted. As a "prowar socialist" given propaganda duties, he had the job of trying to sway American and international opinion in favor of the Allies' war effort. Kopelin's short series of "War Letters," written from Europe as well as the United States, were all printed in the New Appeal.

War Letters of an American Socialist No. 2

Louis Kopelin

To My Comrades in Europe:

I presume that the Socialists and laboring people of the Allied and neutral countries are mainly interested in knowing whether official Washington speaks the minds and hearts of the Socialists and laboring people of this country. In your countries, governments have been known to gauge wrongly the wishes of their peoples. Naturally you wonder how a peaceful and progressive nation such as the United States would voluntarily enter the world conflict and carry out the far-reaching program of military participation it has set out for itself. This question interests you doubtless because it deeply concerns the relation of the Socialists and working people of your countries towards the war. You have unquestionably been told by agents of the Central Powers that our government will not carry out its program because it has not the working people with it. This is told to you in order that you may be discouraged as to the possibilities of a victory for the cause of democracy.

Our people favor the war. Organized labor favors the war. The majority of the American Socialists favor the war. All the liberal and progressive organizations favor the war. It is true we have a few pacifists and objectors. But they are so few that they are negligible.

From the very beginning organized labor came out frankly and fully in behalf of America and the Allies. In fact our trade unions through their accredited representatives took this stand a month before the formal declaration of war against Germany. In our country the American Federation of Labor and the railway brotherhoods constitute approximately 95 percent of the organized workers. We have a few thousand organized workers who are extremists— on the order of your pre-war syndicalists. Although the latter are senselessly featured in the sensational press they are so few in number that no attention need be paid to them.

As to the Socialists a few words of explanation are necessary. You are probably aware that compared to European countries the Socialist party of America has always been a weak organization. But you have probably not been aware that the unaffiliated Socialists and sympathizers in this country number nearly two million. Due to poor leadership the Socialist party began to decline shortly after the 1912 presidential election. Regardless of changing administrations and conditions these dogmatic and domineering leaders persisted in tactics that failed to produce results. The party vote and party membership have since steadily declined. In 1916 the Socialist party lost nearly 400,000 votes and about half of its dues paying membership. At the same time the people were turning to socialistic ideas much more readily than they have at any time in the history of the movement. This is illustrated by the fact that Socialist papers devoted to propaganda have been thriving and increasing their circulation while Socialist papers devoted to the party organization lost circulation and in many cases suspended.

When the crisis between America and Germany was reached the Socialist party leaders no longer represented the wishes and desires of the great rank and file. A convention was held at St. Louis consisting mainly of party officials which adopted a rabid anti-war manifesto. Thousands of members resigned and among them were some of the most prominent workers in the movement. Daily we read and hear of groups and individuals leaving the Socialist party or declaring their allegiance to America's cause regardless of the party's official position. At this writing a movement is under way to reverse the party's position and failing in this to organize a new party.

The New Appeal, formerly the *Appeal to Reason*, is in itself the best proof of the sentiment of American Socialism towards the war. Previous to our repudiation of the St. Louis platform our paper was losing readers by the thousand. And since that repudiation *The New Appeal* has been forging steadily forward. It is a known fact that the Socialist party and its official organ are today heavily in debt and their influence constantly dwindling.

The American Socialists overwhelmingly favor the position taken by the Inter-Allied Socialist Conference recently held at London. As you know the principles of the Inter-Allied manifesto are very similar to the ones enunciated by the Presi-

dent of our country. Thus our Socialists are in hearty accord with the precepts of true internationalism as expressed by the Inter-Allied Socialist Conference and the principles of true Americanism as stated by President Wilson.

Next week I shall write you about the hearty cooperation given by our workers in the various war industries and the splendid recognition of their service by the government.

Fraternally yours,
Louis Kopelin
May 25, 1918

Truth, it has often been observed, is one of the first casualties of war. The American Socialist party was not "a foreign branch of the Socialist Democratic party of Germany" or a vehicle of "pro-German propaganda," nor did, as Kopelin claimed, "the majority of American Socialists favor the war." The Appeal's temporary support of the American and Allied war effort is a paradigmatic example of all that can be believed when the pressure to believe is stronger than truth.

Loyal American Socialists Send Mission to Europe With Message of Encouragement to War-Worn Toilers

EMANUEL HALDEMAN-JULIUS

Labor's language is international. We speak different tongues, but yet we understand one another because we are actuated by the same motives, by the same desires, by the same conditions. We who toil in America know what is in the mind and heart of the worker in England, in France, in Italy.

We well realize that the old International is dead. It died when the German Socialists sanctioned the rape of Belgium back in August, 1914. But there can be a new International—an international of the workers of democratic nations—and we can begin building now.

We in America have a serious work before us.

We must get ready to create a fighting force that will end for all time the rule of the Hohenzollerns. We must end Kaiserism. At the same time we must cement our ranks—we workers of the Allied countries must stand together, understand one another so thoroughly that the poison of German propaganda cannot separate us and thereby work harm to the winning of the war.

As things stand, there is need for quick action. We must tell the workers of the Allied countries to be patient, to stand firm until we get over there. And recognizing this as a great immediate need the loyal Socialists of America have decided to send a mission to England, France and Italy to deliver this important message. Such a mission is now on its way. As you read these lines it has just pulled out of an Atlantic Port, submarines or no submarines.

This mission, which is to take messages of cheer and encouragement from the loyal Socialists of the United States to the Socialists of democratic Europe, consists of the following:

Chairman, A. M. Simons; secretary, Private Louis Kopelin; Alexander Howatt, Frank Bohn and John Spargo. These men will be joined in Europe by Charles Edward Russell and George D. Herron.

These men are individually and collectively fitted to do their work. Private Kopelin will write voluminously—and his reports will be of great interest. Mr. Simons is a gifted speaker, as are Spargo and Bohn. Howatt is a son of the working class—he is a man who speaks the language of the toilers. They understand him as he understands them. He will do much good work in England among the miners. In all, here is a Socialist delegation that is as able as it is loyal.

This Mission has the approval and sanction of President Wilson and Secretary Lansing. It is however a Socialist Mission, and not a government Mission. It is supported in no way by government funds, as we shall show. These men are labor's ambassadors, and labor will pay the costs.

In arranging the details of this Mission the facts were placed before the Secretary of State Lansing in a letter signed by William English Walling, Henry L. Slobodin and J. I. Sheppard. The statement gives the reasons why the Mission is needed and just who stand behind it. The letter follows:

"Washington, D.C., June 12, 1918
"Honorable Robert Lansing, Secretary of State:
"The following facts are respectfully submitted for your consideration in connection with the Socialist Mission to England, France and Italy.

"The Socialist party of the United States was originally organized mainly by Germans and was always under German influence. In fact, it may be regarded as a foreign branch of the Socialist Democratic party of Germany. During this war it has become one of the main vehicles of pro-German propaganda in America. The great majority of American Socialists affiliated with the Socialist party were always and are more so now loyal to the country, but continue their affiliation with the Socialist party as a matter of habit. For that reason they are misrepresented by German control of the Socialist party, and were not heretofore represented by any organized movement. It is the object of the Socialist Democratic League and the *New Appeal*, a Socialist newspaper published at Girard, Kans., and having the largest circulation of any Socialist newspaper in the world, to organize a delegation of loyal Socialists to be sent to England, France and Italy, there to voice the true attitude of the loyal Socialists of America in this war. The necessity for it is obvious, and as has been said by an observer of recent events in France, almost desperate.

"Pro-German and pacifist propaganda in France and Italy has succeeded in spreading there the idea that the revolutionary American workmen are opposed to the American war aims, and to the further prosecution of the war. They are now using the Hillquit vote in New York, and the Berger vote in Wisconsin, cast largely by Germans, for this purpose. This pro-German propaganda goes to the extent of representing the American government as not being seriously and sincerely in this war for the defeat of Germany, but is prepared at any moment to negotiate an inconclusive peace.

"The task of the Socialist Mission will be to present to the Socialists of England, France and Italy the war aims of the American government, particularly as set forth by President Wilson in his address of January 8, 1918, as the war aims of all loyal American Socialists. The Socialist Mission will further advocate that these war aims be accepted by the European Socialists as a minimum peace program. It will be the particular object of this Socialist Mission to strengthen the determination of English, French and Italian Socialists to oppose and combat German autocracy not alone on the battle field, but also in its peace drives, calculated to bring about a German peace. . . ."

June 22, 1918

A little-known socialist journalist from Michigan until his columns for the Appeal gave him a national reputation, Allan Benson was a member of the inner-party conservative faction and Socialist party candidate for president in 1916. "Why Benson Resigned" reflects both his own and the conservative faction's view of the divisiveness in the Socialist party caused by World War I.

Why Benson Resigned

ALLAN L. BENSON

I herewith present my resignation from the Socialist party to take effect at once. I do so with profound regret. I believe in democracy as applied both to government and to industry. But I do not believe in the attitude taken by the party toward the war in what has come to be known as the "St. Louis resolution." I do not believe in pledging the party to acts of violence. Nor do I regard the belligerents as equally guilty. I know, for instance, that Belgium is not guilty at all and that Germany is guilty of all. I know the government of the United States wages war for neither money nor land, while the government of Germany covets both money and land. I know that Germany, any moment she will accept it, can get a just peace, and I feel that until she will accept a just peace she should be compelled to accept war.

Believing that nothing worse could happen to the world than to be placed under the heel of German imperialism, I sever my relations with a party that nationally places the belligerents upon a parity and, in the state of Wisconsin, recently demanded the withdrawal of the American army from Europe—a demand which, had it been granted, would have meant the speedy if not the instant collapse of the Allies.

Nevertheless I do not share the view of those who regard the Socialist party as "pro-German" if that term be deemed to indicate a state of mind which desires a German victory. I believe that the rank and file of the Socialist party, like the rank and file of all other American parties, is essentially American and therefore ardently desirous of the defeat of the Central Powers.

The Socialist party differs in this, that it has among its leaders an undue percentage of the foreign-born. What is mistaken for pro-Germanism in these men is non-Americanism. By reason of their foreign birth they cannot get the American point of view. All nations look alike to them, while to Americans no nation looks like America, however much they may sometimes criticize it.

These foreign-born leaders mislead the party, not because they desire to, but because they are incapable by reason of their birth of doing otherwise. They cannot feel what Americans feel. And they are assisted by an anarchistic, syndicalistic minority that the party, prior to the war, had always suppressed.

The last suppression of this faction was the beginning of the party's downfall. When the party, by direct vote of its membership, overwhelmingly prohibited the practice of sabotage, the dues-paying membership was 125,000. Pursuing their policy of rule or ruin the syndicalists began work within the party either to capture it or destroy it.

By persistent wrangling and quarreling at party meetings they discouraged and disgusted enough Socialists to bring the party dues-paying membership down to 65,000, where it was at the opening of the 1916 campaign.

Moreover, the syndicalists have contaminated Socialist doctrine by foisting anarchist ideas upon the country as Socialist ideas.

A few men in the party who should have known better have accepted and proclaimed the false doctrine that since "a workingman can have no country" it is immaterial to him whether the country in which he lives, if it be at war, shall be defeated or not.

Such men seem quite unconscious of the fact that this is the doctrine of Proudhon and Bakunin, the anarchists, rather than that of Marx the Socialist.

Marx believed that workingmen everywhere had a very real interest in the success of the North in our Civil War, and upon at least one occasion wrote to Lincoln congratulating him upon what he was doing to bring such a victory about.

The present foreign-born leaders of the American Socialist party, if they had lived during the Civil War, would doubtless have censured Marx for congratulating Lincoln.

For these reasons I now take leave of the Socialist party a year after I ceased to agree with it. It seemed to me that having been at the head of the national ticket two years ago it was particularly my duty to be patient and see if the party would not right itself. It has not righted itself. I therefore resign as a protest against the foreign-born leadership that blindly believes a non-American policy can be made to appeal to many Americans.

July 6, 1918

With the hostilities ended and the Allies victorious over the Central Powers, the Appeal to Reason replaced the New Appeal on the masthead and the editors and staff attempted to return to the paper's prewar socialist principles. However, not only had the Appeal lost credibility but, more importantly, American radicalism was being suppressed and faced more prosecution in the future.

Why Wilson Fell Down

Louis Kopelin

President Wilson went to Europe, so the world believed, to use his power and influence for the attainment of a democratic peace. President Wilson is now returning to America after having signed his name and the honor of his country to reactionary and an imperialistic peace. Many will speculate as to the causes that prevailed over the American President to make the greatest diplomatic flop in the history of nations. Some will accuse him of having been insincere in the first place. Some will accuse him of being mentally inferior to the astute rulers and diplomats of our Allies. Some will say—but very few of them—that President Wilson accomplished as much as could be expected in a practical way.

In the opinion of the *Appeal to Reason*, President Wilson is the mental equal of the men that have surrounded him in Paris and he was not fooled or tricked into approving the treaty that has only one parallel in history—namely the treaty framed by the Congress of Vienna. Mr. Wilson probably had a great deal to do with the framing and the phrasing of the treaty and perhaps used his power and influence to compel some of the other representatives of the Allied nations to approve of the reactionary document.

Mr. Wilson, with all of his liberal phrases, believes in the capitalist system. He is opposed to Socialism. He fears the rule of the workers. To him nothing can be worse than the overthrow of the capitalist governments of Europe and the rearing in their places of Socialist or communist governments. Believing as he does in the sanctity of capitalism and the divinity of the established economic order, President Wilson soon realized after his arrival in Europe that a democratic peace meant social revolution. For let this be known. In England, France and Italy, the capitalist governments stood for a stern peace, which means in plain language, a reactionary peace. The leaders of the opposition, Socialists in every case, stood for a democratic peace and were recognized in their countries as the spokesmen of the Wilson program. When Wilson first visited those countries, he learned that to force his program through he would have to unite with the Socialists. This would have brought the realization of his program. It would have also discredited the capitalist governments and turned England, France and Italy into Socialist republics.

President Wilson therefore had the choice of a reactionary peace and capitalism or a democratic peace and Socialism. He made his choice. He joined hands with the heads of the capitalist governments of Europe in bringing about the very thing that he more eloquently than any other denounced, namely a peace of might.

We do not blame Mr. Wilson for being true to the economic order he espouses. We can understand how after his beautiful phrases he went over bag and baggage to Clemenceau, that finely developed type of capitalist imperialist. But we cannot understand, and we refuse to absolve him from blame, when he returns to America and tells us that the capitalist League of Nations—which is dominated by the big powers, which does not reduce armament, which does not abolish conscription, which does not oppose imperialism, which does not give every nation equal rights, and which does not have the slightest semblance to that league of free peoples the world desires—is a true and genuine league that will preserve the peace of the world. Neither can we credit Mr. Wilson with sincerity when he tells us that the peace that has been prepared in Paris is a democratic peace, when

he continues to insist that none of his "fourteen points" had been violated. The contrary is too plain. . . .

July 5, 1919

————————

Brief and unformed as John Gunn's "America's New Policy" is, his understanding of America's new role in the post–World War I world proved more prophetic than many other predictions of America's future.

America's New Policy

John W. Gunn

. . . The desire of American as well as of European interests is to more securely fasten the grip of international capitalism upon the world. In Europe there is the special desire to avert imminent revolution and to forcibly maintain the unjust and artificial arrangement of the Paris peace. In America there is desired a world political policy to correspond to the world economic policy upon which capital plans to embark. They wish, also, to sustain the heavily burdened financial fabric of the world by insuring the collection of the enormous war debts. These desires the League of Nations appears to admirably satisfy.

America has for some time past been growing away from her traditional policy of self-sufficient and isolated independence toward a policy of world-wide imperialism. This growth has heretofore been more economic than political, following the well-established law that economic change always precedes political change. The world war brought about a change in America's political policy, which was made to correspond with her economic policy. She suddenly jumped into an active place in world affairs. Her politicians began to really participate in world politics, even as her captains of industry had previously participated in world commerce, her bankers in world finance.

With the war over, with American energy fresh

and unimpaired, with American resources practically untouched, and with Europe economically and financially tottering on the verge of ruin, American capitalism sees its brightest chance for success in pushing its exploitation of world markets. Already it controls many new markets, and it will control the world's credit for many years to come. It is resolved to proceed more vigorously and extensively than ever with its already well-defined policy of world expansion. This is no secret. American capitalists and financiers have freely discussed their plans in the press. They have told of the wonderful opportunity to make America industrially and financially supreme; they have told of their purpose to organize more closely with a view to flooding foreign markets in the farthest corner of the world with American goods. American capitalist supremacy throughout the world is the present aim of Wall Street—an aim that is openly declared, as a matter of course.

What the people generally fail to see is the meaning and inevitable consequence of this world activity of American capitalists. What they fail to see is that it draws America irresistibly into world affairs, not along the safe path of humanitarian fraternity and social cooperation, but along the dangerous path of capitalist imperialism. America is to compete with the world, not cooperate with the world. Therein lies the danger. Capital is aware of the danger, if the people are not. Thus it welcomes the League of Nations as a political instrument that will guarantee its international ventures. It does not regard the League as an instrument of peace, even among the nations whose rulers were chiefly active in framing it. For its purposes, it is sufficient that the League sets the seal of solemn approval upon an American world political policy that corresponds conveniently to the world economic policy of American capital. It visibly destroys the old American tradition of isolation, and visibly creates a new tradition of intimate concern which will logically lead to interference in world affairs in behalf of American capital. It completes politically what capital had

already begun economically—the making of America a world power in all that the term implies of good and bad.

Whether the League of Nations is ratified by the American Senate or not (and it is almost certain that it will be), America is thrust by economic forces in the direction of this new policy and tradition. The only hope that it will not bring disaster to the American people lies in the adoption of Socialism within the next decade and the establishment of a true world-wide cooperation.

August 2, 1919

A well-known attorney, army veteran, and reformer from Portland, Oregon, Charles Erskine Scott Wood had been an early supporter of President Woodrow Wilson. Wood's support, however, evaporated upon Wilson's capitulation to the Allies' secret agreements and division of the postwar spoils at Versailles. Heavenly Discourse, a collection of Wood's World War I writings originally intended for the Masses, which was censored by the federal government, appeared in 1927.

Woodrow Wilson: Egoist

CHARLES ERSKINE SCOTT WOOD

Some still admire President Wilson, many rage against him, but none pities him; and of all living men, he is most to be pitied. He has fallen from the pedestal of his own time and from the pinnacle of history. There are failures which Time lifts up and glorifies, because, though they failed in accomplishment, they were true to their ideals; and there are failures which Time leaves crumbled where they fell. Woodrow Wilson clothed the ideals of the world in such perfect phrases that he became the hope of the world—of the world which is to be, as the promise of spring is from the world that has died. He robbed the war of its character as a contest between tigers for the carcass of the world, and he stated the war aims to be "world freedom," "world democracy," "self-determination of the lesser peoples," "a war to end war," "a peace without victory or vengeance." His words robbed our own entry into this trouble of every sordid motive and made us a Sir Galahad or Sir Percival, defender of Liberty and Democracy at home and the world over for its own sake; asking nothing for ourselves, we did not ask for all mankind. He purified the selfish and savage struggle between rival exploiting Powers by stating such war aims as the Allies themselves had never dreamed, and in phrases they were not capable of, but which, in their desperation, they recklessly accepted. How could he know that they only accepted noble ideals as the gambler accepts honesty, till he can safely repudiate it?

"Peace without victory," "No punitive imposition," "No quarrel with the common people but only with their imperial, military masters," "Self-determination for the weaker nations," "The acid test, the treatment of the Russian revolution," "No secret treaties to be recognized and hereafter no secret diplomacy, but open covenants openly arrived at," "A league of all the nations of the earth, conquered as well as conquerors," "The toil of the people not to be wasted in armies and armaments," "The freedom of the seas, the common highway of all nations."

The common people, whom the centuries have trampled, shouted and prayed. There was no tongue that did not utter "Wilson." Here at last was the new Dawn; justice for the burden-bearers of every land, Germans as well as French, Austrians as well as English, Polish, Czech, Slav, Jugo-Slav, Italians, Russians and the Chinese (whom we had persuaded into the war as our associates, on our guaranty to them of justice with peace;) Irish, Egyptian and the far distant Hindoo. All these fixed their hopeful eyes on Wilson, their savior, walking to them across the sea, and strong in the wealth, food and young men of the United States.

Here was the dictator of the new destiny, the prophet of the new day; standing on a peak, to which the eyes of the world were lifted up. It was a glorious sunrise, and the toilers of the earth, who had waited so long for the day, believed their deliverer was at hand. They ran about, kissing each other, and in many languages they cried out to each other, "Wilson, Wilson, Wilson." Streets were named for him, and songs, and places, and children. His every principle was accepted by the Allies, and on this stated creed the armistice was signed. The world war was over.

And then—instead of peace without victory, victory without peace; instead of no punitive indemnities, the conquered were bled white and mothers and babies were starved by the millions. Even Frenchmen and Englishmen protested. Instead of self-determination of the weaker peoples, China was betrayed and Shantung, with her forty millions of people, mines, railways and forests, delivered to the only surviving feudal, military, imperialism, Japan. To render Germany economically helpless forever, France practically annexed the Saar Valley, with its iron and coal. England takes all the German colonies south of the equator and acquires new territory in Africa equal to nearly half the United States. Japan, in addition to the Shantung province, takes all the German colonies north of the equator. Instead of the acid test being a sympathetic attitude towards the struggling revolutionists of Russia, a ruthless and baby-killing war is waged on Russia because, within her own borders, she is trying the greatest experiment in democracy since the French Revolution, and greater than that, because it is an attempt at industrial democracy, not political; it is an experiment in the real freedom of the worker; and just as England led the thrones of Europe in their attack on the French Revolution, so England leads the blockade and the attack on the industrial revolution of Russia. Instead of protesting against this interference in the internal affairs of Russia, this attack on the new democracy, we join in that attack; not by an expression of the people's will, not by an act of Congress, as by the Constitution required, but by the sole will of Woodrow Wilson. The United States again and again has declared,

BUSINESS

Plenty of Demand---But No Market

Appeal to Reason, October 15, 1921.

especially in our Civil War, that there must be no meddling by an outsider in the internal affairs of any people; but this unwritten part of our Constitution is forgotten and only by the imperial will of Woodrow Wilson, we join with imperial England and imperial Japan in an effort to strangle by blood and blockade the attempt of the working classes of Russia to work out their own destiny. When President Wilson returned to this country and took the stump in the interests of his treaty, he declared there should be no peace with Russian revolutionists while "I am President." Is not this the very echo of Louis XIV, "The State? I am the State!" Instead of the repudiation of secret treaties, every secret treaty was given force and effect in the treaty frame-up at Versailles. Secret treaties, too, made as a betrayal of ourselves and as the price between France and Great Britain, on the one side, and Japan and Italy, on the other, for their entering the war. Instead of open convenants openly arrived at, the whole treaty plot is behind closed doors and practically by four men. When the lid is lifted, every one of the fourteen points has evaporated. . . .

May 15, 1920

"The Red Feast" remains a grim epitaph for both those who died and those who returned from the Great War.

The Red Feast

RALPH CHAPLIN

Go fight, you fools. Tear up the earth with strife
   And spill each others' guts upon the field;
Serve unto death the men you served in life
   So that their wide dominions may not yield.

Stand by the flag—the lie that still allures;
   Lay down your lives for land you do not own,

And give unto a war that is not yours
   Your gory tithe of mangled flesh and bone.

But whether it be yours to fall or kill
   You must not pause to question why nor
     where.
You see the tiny crosses on the hill?
   It took all those to make one millionaire.

It was for him the seas of blood were shed,
   That fields were razed and cities lit the sky;

And now he comes to chortle o'er the dead—
  The condor Thing for whom the millions die!

The bugle screams, the cannons cease to roar.
  "Enough! enough! God give us peace again."
The rats, the maggots and the Lords of War
  Are fat to bursting from their meal of men.

So stagger back, you stupid dupes who've "won,"
  Back to your stricken towns to toil anew,
For there your dismal tasks are still undone
  And grim Starvation gropes again for you.

What matters now your flag, your race, the skill
  Of scattered legions—what has been the gain?
Once more beneath the lash you must distil
  Your lives to glut a glory wrought of pain.

In peace they starve you to your loathsome toil,
  In war they drive you to the teeth of Death;
And when your life-blood soaks into their soil
  They give you lies to choke your dying breath.

So will they smite your blind eyes till you see,
  And lash your naked backs until you know
That wasted blood can never set you free
  From fettered thraldom to the Common Foe.

Then you will find that "nation" is a name
  And boundaries are things that don't exist;
That Labor's bondage, worldwide, is the same,
  And ONE the enemy it must resist.

June 10, 1922

EIGHT

The War at Home

Men make their own history, but they do not make it just as they please. . . .—Karl Marx, *The Eighteenth Brumaire of Louis Bonaparte*

On September 5, 1917, federal agents descended upon IWW headquarters in Chicago and meeting halls throughout the United States, confiscated files, correspondence, literature, such office furniture as they did not destroy, and arrested everyone in sight. In June, 1918, Eugene V. Debs was arrested and charged under the Espionage Act for making an anti-war speech in Ohio. The following year, Weirton, West Virginia, citizens forced striking steel workers to kiss the American flag. In Indiana, a citizen shot and killed an immigrant who had shouted, "To hell with the United States." A jury freed the killer after deliberating for two minutes. In Centralia, Washington, a mob of American Legionnaires and other superpatriots attacking an IWW hall were met by gunfire that toppled three Legionnaires. That night a crowd took from jail Wesley Everest, a Wobbly and ex-soldier who had served abroad, castrated him, repeatedly hanged him, and emptied their guns in his mutilated body. In Watertown, Connecticut, a salesman casually remarked to a customer that Lenin was either "the brainiest" or "one of the brainiest" political leaders in the world. Whichever the comment, the salesman was sentenced to six months in prison for it. In 1919 twenty-four states prohibited the public display of red flags; eight more states followed suit the next year. The political aftereffects of World War I, together with the upsurge of American nativism, anti-intellectualism, and xenophobia, had reached full flood.[1] Cultivated and when necessary financed by a governing corporate and political elite, the suppression of domestic radicalism was under way.

World War I brought an opportunity not only to crush radicalism but to delegitimize it as unpatriotic and unAmerican for years to come. The principal tools of federal suppression were the Espionage Act, the Sedition Act, the Post Office Department under Albert S. Burleson, and a newly swollen legal and investigative apparatus encompassed by the Justice Department. Passed by Congress on June 15, 1917, the Espionage Act prohibited conveying "false reports or false statements with intent to interfere with the operation or success of the military or naval forces of the United States or to promote the success of its enemies . . . or attempt to cause insubordination, disloyalty, mutiny, or refusal of duty . . . or . . . willfully obstruct recruiting or enlistment service."[2] The day after passage, Postmaster General Burleson directed local postal officials, in a message which substantively misquoted the new legislation, to send him any "newspapers, etc.," which would "embarrass or hamper the Government in conducting the war."[3] If the Espionage Act did not cover every case, the 1918 Sedition Act, which made it a crime to "utter, print, write, or publish any disloyal, profane, scurrilous, or abusive language about the form of government of the United States," opened the way to stifle any criticism that remained.[4] Woodrow Wilson and crucial members of his administration were bent upon crushing the domestic left (witness, for example, Wilson's and Attorney General A. Mitchell Palmer's postwar support for a peacetime sedition law harsher than either the Espionage or the Sedition act), a goal that was not exclusively limited to radical dissent during World War I.

Until the Great War, the legitimacy of dissent and free speech were honored though sometimes problematical American traditions. The free expression of ideas was as much at the heart of an America which radicals supported as it was at the center of the new society they hoped to build. Once the Espionage Act was passed, however, Postmaster Burleson wasted little time enforcing it. By July 15, 1917, fifteen major radical publications, including the *Masses*, the *American Socialist*, the *International Socialist Review*, and the New York *Call* had been censored. More followed. Burleson interpreted the Espionage Act so as to permit any local postal official or mail carrier to declare a periodical unmailable. Burleson had decided (and the Supreme Court supported him) that once censored, a publication was no longer "continuous," and consequently no longer entitled to a second-class permit. Burleson declared that no paper or periodical could "say that this Government got in the war wrong, that it is in it for wrong purposes, or anything that will impugn the motives of the Government for going into the War."[5] As events proved, the repressive atmosphere in America during and after World War I—a time when sauerkraut became "liberty cabbage," when American towns named Berlin were quickly changed to Belleville, when smiling at police was a criminal offense—made anything less than absolute endorsement of the war grounds for intimidation and prosecution.

No radical organization suffered that prosecution and suppression quite as directly as the IWW; no other was singled out by Woodrow Wilson as "certainly . . . worthy of being suppressed."[6] With the perverse logic of the time, Socialists, whose party formally opposed the war, were prosecuted as individuals. Wobblies, however, whose national organization refused to take an official position on the war, were charged with "a vicious, treasonable, and criminal conspiracy" under the Espionage Act and found guilty because they were members of the IWW. Justice Department officials may have smiled at their sardonic twist of the IWW's famous slogan—"an injury to one is an injury to all" became "an antiwar statement by one is the criminal responsibility of all"—but Wobblies had to find their humor elsewhere. Subject to mass trials and the longest prison sentences, they would be the last of the wartime political prisoners to be released.

The federal offensive against American socialists occurred simultaneously with the suppression of the IWW. Socialist meeting halls and offices were raided, publications were banned, and both party leaders and members were arrested. Again, the primary federal device was the Espionage Act, a law used to jail domestic radicals but not a single spy. Several cases typified the remainder. Kate Richards O'Hare was indicted for an antiwar speech in North Dakota, kidnapped by patriots in Idaho, found guilty under provisions of the Espionage Act, and sentenced to five years in prison. Her first job in the penitentiary was sewing a private manufacturer's label on convict-made goods. In Kansas City, Socialist Rose Pastor Stokes corrected a garbled newspaper account in the *Kansas City Star* which had her supporting the war. "No government which is *for* the profiteers can also be *for* the people, and I am for the people, while the government is for the profiteers," she wrote.[7] Prosecuted and convicted for those sentiments, she was sentenced to ten years.

In Milwaukee the principal quarries were Victor Berger and the *Milwaukee Leader*. After serving first in the Wisconsin legislature, Berger had been elected in 1912 and 1914 to the United States House of Representatives. The socialist *Leader*, which Berger edited, was denied use of the mails in 1917 and he, together with other antiwar socialists, was found guilty under provisions of the Espionage Act in January, 1919. However, Berger continued to prove vexing to authorities when his antiwar politics led to his re-election to Congress in 1918. In Washington, amid cries of "traitor" and "Bolshevik," he was refused his seat, thereby necessitating a special election. When Berger won again, the House again had to vote to deny him his seat. Not until 1922, re-elected once more and having had his conviction overturned on a technicality, was Berger permitted to join a less Red-Scared Congress.

The most significant federal prosecution of a single American radical was that of Eugene Debs. No one was more associated with American socialism than Debs. In 1918 no one not already in prison felt the effects of political repression more keenly than Debs; his empathy with others was authentic. In June, 1918, he journeyed to Canton, Ohio, to speak in Nimisilla Park. Looking into an audience of supporters and secret service agents, then across the park to the jail where antiwar socialists Alfred Wagenknecht and Charles Ruthenberg had been hanging by their wrists for two days until they managed to get word out, Debs began to speak: "The master class has always declared the wars: the subject class has always fought the battles. The master class has had all to gain and nothing to lose, while the subject class has had nothing to gain and all to lose—especially their lives." Debs reaffirmed his support for imprisoned radicals, for the IWW, for all those fighting for "a change from slavery to freedom and from despotism to democracy, as wide as the world."[8] He was arrested on June 30 for violating the Espionage Act.

At his trial in September, Debs addressed the jury himself and made it clear that he felt no guilt and had nothing to repudiate. "Congress shall make no law," Debs quoted, "abridging the freedom of speech, or of the press; or the right of the people peaceably to assemble, and to petition the government for a redress of grievances."[9] If the Espionage Act does not negate the First Amendment, he said, "then certainly I am un-able to read or understand the English language." Debs was found guilty and sentenced to ten years in prison.

In neither Debs's case nor in the trials of other antiwar dissenters did the government mount a serious attempt to establish a direct, causal relationship between antiwar or anticapitalist speech and acts provoked by them. Socialists and Wobblies were imprisoned for expressing their beliefs and political philosophy, repression the First Amendment was specifically enacted to prevent. Nor, unlike a libel suit, were radicals permitted to argue in court that their charges were true. Even the suggestion that the First Amendment was intended to be a constitutional protection during periods of political threat and controversy was regarded as a sign of disloyalty.

As Debs entered prison, the Red Scare was building to high hysteria. Neither before nor since has political repression so thoroughly dominated American life. When America entered World War I, war was simultaneously declared on dissent at home. Only momentarily did those two wars remain separate; incredulous radicals were almost immediately transformed into "German agents" paid by "German gold." Upon the Russian Revolution and the withdrawal from World War I of a previously capitalist Russian ally, antiwar dissenters were as quickly turned into "Bolsheviks." Some oddly discordant notes arose, but they were quickly brushed over. A conservative Senator from Ohio, Warren Harding, declared that "from the very beginning it was a lie to say that this was a war to make the world safe for democracy."[10] A few months later, in September, 1919, Woodrow Wilson announced in a speech in St. Louis that the "real reason that the war we have just finished took place was that Germany was afraid her commercial rivals were going to get the better of her."[11] The American left, of course, knew that those sentiments were still landing many less immune men and women in prison, but by the latter part of 1919 radicals had abandoned any attempt to make sense of contradictory capitalist discourse. American troops had already invaded the Soviet Union and attacked Bolshevik soldiers. "Yanks Drive on Reds," newspapers had headlined in February, 1919. Initially accepted as an indigenous insurgent movement, American socialism was, from World War I to the present, deliberately associated with a foreign enemy and delegitimized as traitorous. The Cold War began in 1918, not in the aftermath of World War II.

American capital, in its various agencies, moved quickly to cement the associations between domestic radicalism and unAmericanism. Employer associations and superpatriotic organizations carried the battle into every area of life their ample funds afforded. Superpatriotic groups circulated millions of antiradical pamphlets, press releases, patriotic exercises for school children, pamphlets for workers' pay envelopes, names of newspapers and periodicals for loyal Americans to boycott, and approved lists of patriotic speakers for colleges and fraternal groups. In Boston, when the city police modestly sought to affiliate with the AFL in 1919, they were deluged with cries of "radical," "Bolshevist," and "soviet." "Lenin and Trotsky are on their way," the *Wall Street Journal* warned. "BOSTON STRIKE CAUSES GRAVE WASHINGTON FEAR—Senators Think Effort to Sovietize the Government Is Started," another newspaper headlined.[12] The 1919 steel strike, a response to a 69-hour work week and subsistence wages in an inflationary postwar economy (the 1913 dollar was worth 45¢ in 1919), was cast as another attempt at "Bolshevizing industry." "STAND BY AMERICA," "BEWARE THE AGITATOR WHO MAKES LABOR A CATSPAW FOR BOLSHEVISM," instructed the steel trust through its Pittsburgh newspapers.[13] After the *New York Times* and other papers had written that the race riots in Washington, D.C., and Chicago during the summer of 1919 had been inspired by Bolsheviks and overseen by Lenin personally, virtually anything seemed credible to an America driven to political hysteria.

At the Justice Department, activity was not limited to prosecution under the Espionage and Sedition Acts. Wilson's first Attorney General, Thomas W. Gregory, began cultivating citizen informers throughout the United States during the summer of 1917. "Several hundred thousand private citizens," Gregory acknowledged, were "keeping an eye on disloyal individuals and making reports of disloyal utterances, and seeing that the people of the country are not deceived."[14] His successor in March, 1919, A. Mitchell Palmer, was an obsessive figure with an antiradical mission that dwarfed even his desire for the Presidency. Palmer saw Reds everywhere he looked. "The blaze of revolution," he declared, is "sweeping over every American institution of law and order . . . eating its way into the homes of the American workman, its sharp tongues of revolutionary heat . . . licking at the altars of the churches, leaping into the belfry of the school bell, crawling into the sacred corners of American homes, seeking to replace marriage vows with libertine laws, burning up the foundation of society."[15] When several anarchists responded to two years of domestic spying and political repression by planting bombs in April and June, 1919, in Washington, D.C., a piece of reality confirmed hysterical fantasy. Yet another piece fell into place when left factions splintered from the Socialist party and formed the Communist and Communist Labor parties in September. Federal and state governments, superpatriotic groups, and nearly all American newspapers responded with increased intensity.

The effort not merely to criminalize radicalism but to identify it as foreign to America had resulted in the October, 1918, passage of an immigration bill that permitted deportation of any alien who advocated anarchism, syndicalism, violent revolution, or who belonged to an organization that did. Deportation, interpreted by the Justice Department as an administrative matter, was an attractive method to deal with the radical menace because it required little in the way of constitutional protections—neither judge nor jury, for example. In the summer of 1919, Attorney General Palmer requested and received from Congress special funding for a General Intelligence, or antiradical, division. Appointed by Palmer as its chief, a then little-known J. Edgar Hoover was soon at work assembling 260,000 files on radical organizations and suspicious men and women. The first arrests occurred on November 7, 1919, when federal agents raided Union of Russian Workers' halls in twelve cities. State and local officials immediately followed by arresting several hundred additional aliens. On December 21, 1919, the *Buford* sailed from Ellis Island, past the Statue of Liberty to Finland, with 249 deportees. The majority of those deported were Russian Workers members; most of the remainder were anarchists, a group which included Emma Goldman and Alexander Berkman.

Palmer and Hoover were planning larger raids and moving their agents into positions of authority in radical organizations even as the *Buford* sailed. Again the primary targets were anarchists and the new Communist and Communist Labor parties. After undercover agents were directed by Hoover to call meetings on January 2, 1920, Justice Department raids in 23 states netted some 5,000 radicals and non-radicals, Communists and non-Communists, aliens as well as native-born citizens, and another 1,000 in the next few weeks.

The unprecedented scale of the Palmer raids— America had never seen anything resembling 6,000 mass political arrests—strained credulity and finally served to crystallize response. Information about the arrests emerged, and the conclusion became unavoidable that Palmer and Hoover had trampled on substantial parts of the constitution. An influential counter-elite was provoked, primarily by Roger Baldwin and the American Civil Liberties Union, to condemn the legal abuses of the raids and, within limits, condemn the raids themselves. With radicalism no longer defensible, the counterattack was focused exclusively on civil liberties.

The ACLU first formed a coalition with a Progressive organization, the National Popular Government League, to testify successfully against a variety of sedition bills under consideration by Congress. At the same time, as the public was made aware of the Palmer raids' illegalities both by the *Appeal* and increasingly by the mainstream press, general approval of the Palmer raids began to sour. In May, 1920, twelve lawyers with impeccable Progressive credentials, all of whom had supported the war, Felix Frankfurter, Frank Walsh, Roscoe Pound, and Zechariah Chafee, Jr., among them, signed a lengthy statement condemning the treatment of those arrested and charged with

fundamental constitutional violations. An equally respected group of political centrists and conservatives, led by ex–Republican presidential candidate Charles Evans Hughes, publicly condemned the New York legislature's exclusion of legally elected members of the Socialist party and the effective disfranchisement of thousands of voters. In Coyler et al. vs. Skeffington, Judge George W. Anderson ruled that since the "Government owns and operates some part of the Communist Party," party membership could not be automatic grounds for deportation. Sophisticated corporate spokesmen became critical of the Palmer raids as well. "Now that the immigrant seemed docile again," John Higham writes, "his bosses recalled his economic value."[16]Attorney General Palmer battled back for a time, but when he apocalyptically warned of a nonexistent revolt to be touched off on May Day, 1920, and then failed to receive the Democratic nomination for President, both his influence and that of the superpatriotic organizations began to fall away. The cessation of Red Scare excesses was also helped by the return to "normalcy" of Warren Harding's new administration. When Attorney General Palmer left office the Justice Department and Immigration Bureau had deported 505 aliens and had scheduled 1,119 for future deportation. In 1921, 446 aliens were deported, but thereafter the number dropped significantly. Will H. Hays, Burleson's successor as Postmaster General, repudiated Burleson's policies and restored second-class mailing privileges to proscribed periodicals.

The hysterical excess of the Red Scare drew to a close, but its effects and antiradicalism itself lingered on to be manipulated almost at will. Antiunion forces during the 1920s successfully sold the open shop as the American Plan. Many states instituted loyalty oaths for teachers. State bar associations supported censorship of textbooks and expurgation of any material that "tended to lessen the greatness of the nation and its leaders." The AFL was permitted to survive because of its agreement with fundamental capitalists assumptions, but union membership still fell by over one million in 1923. Membership in the Communist and Communist Labor parties fell from fifty to sixty thousand in 1919 to approximately ten thousand in 1920. Socialist party membership, over 109,000 in 1919, dropped to 13,484 in 1921. With radical organizations effectively destroyed and radicalism itself criminalized in the dominant culture, American capitalism, victorious in the war abroad, won the war at home as well.

The *Appeal* survived World War I in a weaker condition than it had been in for some twenty years. Inconsistency and accommodation to the war cost the paper not only many of its subscribers but its reputation as an uncompromising advocate of socialism. A political climate hostile to radicalism took a heavy toll as well. Still, the *Appeal* might have survived the aftermath of the war had Haldeman-Julius, editor during Kopelin's war duty and in total control of editorial policy by January, 1921, been fitted for serious political and cultural journalism. Instead, Haldeman-Julius had come to regard the *Appeal* and its socialist traditions as burdens to get rid of. However, before the *Appeal* dissolved into an expression of its new owner's idiosyncratic ideas and prejudices, it mounted a final campaign to free America's imprisoned radicals.

The *Appeal's* campaign meshed with similar efforts initiated by the ACLU, the Socialist party, and an AFL ambivalent about helping imprisoned Wobblies. The *Appeal*, by virtue of its still significant readership, was a potent force in the movement. Haldeman-Julius centered his attention on Debs, while Upton Sinclair and staff writer John Gunn extended the coverage to include IWW prisoners and Red Scare outrages. By 1920 the amnesty campaign for political prisoners began to prove a significant embarrassment for the Wilson administration. Of all the countries engaged in World War I, only the United States had refused to free its war-time dissenters.

Seeking to defuse the amnesty campaign, Woodrow Wilson commuted the sentences of Kate Richards O'Hare and a limited number of other political prisoners, but public pressure did not diminish. The ACLU picketed both the Democratic and Republican conventions. Richards O'Hare and others, in articles, speeches, and rallies, refused to permit the amnesty question to recede from view. The sixty-five year old

Debs, more than any other prisoner, became an increasingly visible symbol of the suppression of radicalism and, as the renamed *Appeal to Reason* now argued, of the ghastly results of the war for economic supremacy. In November, 1920, aided by only the most rudimentary electoral activity of a shattered Socialist party, Debs received over 900,000 votes for the Presidency. Nevertheless, he remained in an Atlanta prison. Wilson had vowed never to free the "traitor" Debs and not even the recommendation of the majority of Wilson's cabinet provoked Debs's release.

As pressure for amnesty continued, the *Appeal* and the Socialist party mounted a petition and letter campaign that resulted in over a million signatures for Debs's release. A variety of Progressive and labor organizations, their members totalling some three million, appealed as well. Soon after President Warren Harding took office, Attorney General Harry Daugherty acceded to political pressure and recommended that Debs be freed. "No action would be taken in [the case] were it not for the enormous mass of communications received in his behalf," he wrote Harding.[17] Debs was freed with twenty-three other wartime dissenters on Christmas Day, 1921. The remaining political prisoners were later released by Harding and, after his death, by Calvin Coolidge. A substantial part of the credit for the victory belonged to the *Appeal*.

The *Appeal* was within a year of dissolution as Debs left prison. Haldeman-Julius, Kopelin, and everyone at the paper sought to make the *Appeal* express the concerns and realities of a postwar America, but they were unsuccessful. The great years of the *Appeal to Reason*, its struggles and victories, the socialist movement which it articulated and so significantly helped to build, were behind it. The *Appeal* lingered on and then, in November, 1922, it disappeared from sight.

On September 12, 1918, Gene Debs was convicted of violating the Espionage Act for a speech delivered at Canton, Ohio, on June 16. He called no witnesses on his behalf, and he did not deny the factuality of the charge. Before being sen-

Statement to the Court

Your honor, years ago I recognized my kinship with all living beings, and I made up my mind that I was not one bit better than the meanest of earth. I said then, I say now, that while there is a lower class, I am in it, while there is a criminal element, I am of it, while there is a soul in prison, I am not free.

I listened to all that was said in this court in support and justification of this law, but my mind remains unchanged. I look upon it as a despotic enactment in flagrant conflict with democratic principles and with the spirit of free institutions.

I have no fault to find with this court or with the trial. Everything in connection with this case has been conducted upon a dignified plane, and in a respectful and decent spirit. . . .

Your honor, I have stated in this court that I am opposed to the social system in which we live; that I believe in a change—but by perfectly peaceable and orderly means.

Let me call your attention to the fact this morning that in this system 5 per cent of our people own and control two-thirds of our wealth; 65 per cent of the people, embracing the working class who produce all wealth, have but 5 per cent to show for it.

Standing here this morning, I recall my boyhood. At fourteen, I went to work in the railroad shops; at sixteen, I was firing a freight engine on a railroad. I remember all the hardships, all the privations, of that earlier day, and from that time until now, my heart has been with the working class. I could have been in Congress long ago. I have preferred to go to prison.

In the struggle—the unceasing struggle—between the toilers and producers and their exploiters, I have tried, as best I might, to serve those among whom I was born, and with whom I expect to share my lot to the end of my days.

I am thinking this morning of the men in the mills and factories; I am thinking of the women who, for a paltry wage, are compelled to work out their lives; of the little children who, in this system, are robbed of their childhood, and in their early, tender years, are seized in the remorseless grasp of Mammon, and forced in the industrial dungeons, there to feed the machines while they themselves are being starved body and soul. I can see them dwarfed, diseased, stunted—their little lives broken, because in this high noon of our twentieth century civilization money is still so much more important than human life. Gold is god and rules the affairs of men. The little girls, and there are a million of them in this country—this the most favored land beneath the bending skies, a land in which we have vast areas of rich and fertile soil, material resources in inexhaustible abundance, the most marvelous productive machinery on earth, millions of eager workers ready to apply their labor to that machinery to produce an abundance for every man, woman and child—and if there are still many millions of our people who are the victims of poverty, whose lives are a ceaseless struggle all the way from youth to age, until at last death comes to their rescue and stills the aching heart, and lulls the victims to dreamless sleep, it is not the fault of the Almighty, it can't be charged to nature; it is due entirely to an outgrown social system that ought to be abolished not only in the interest of the working class, but in the interest of a higher humanity.

When I think of these little children—the girls that are in the textile mills of all description in the east, in the cotton factories of the south—when I think of them at work in a vitiated atmosphere, when I think of them at work when they ought to be at play or at school, when I think that when they do grow up, if they live long enough to approach the marriage state, they are unfit for it. Their nerves are worn out, their tissue is exhausted, their vitality is spent. They have been fed

Eugene Victor Debs.
Courtesy Pittsburgh State
University.

to industry. Their offspring are born tired. That is why there are so many failures in modern life.

Your honor, the 5 per cent of the people that I have made reference to constitute that element that absolutely rules our country. They privately own all our necessities. They wear no crowns; they wield no sceptres; they sit upon no thrones; and yet they are our economic masters and political rulers.

I believe, your honor, in common with all Socialists, that this nation ought to own and control its industries. I believe, as all Socialists do, that all things that are jointly needed and used ought to be jointly owned—that industry, the basis of life,

instead of being the private property of the few and operated for their enrichment, ought to be the common property of all, democratically administered in the interest of all.

John D. Rockefeller has today an income of sixty million dollars a year, five million dollars a month, two hundred thousand dollars a day. He does not produce a penny of it. I make no attack on Mr. Rockefeller personally. I do not in the least dislike him. If he were in need and it were in my power to serve him, I should serve him as gladly as I would any other human being. I have no quarrel with Mr. Rockefeller personally, nor with any other capitalist. I am simply opposing a social order in which it is possible for one man who does absolutely nothing that is useful to amass a fortune of hundreds of millions of dollars, while millions of men and women who work all the days of their lives secure barely enough for an existence.

This order of things cannot always endure. I have registered my protest against it. I recognize the feebleness of my effort, but fortunately, I am not alone. There are multiplied thousands of others who, like myself, have come to realize that before we may truly enjoy the blessings of civilized life, we must reorganize society upon a mutual and cooperative basis; and to this end we have organized a great economic and political movement that spreads over the face of all the earth.

There are today upwards of sixty millions of Socialists, loyal, devoted, adherents to this cause, regardless of nationality, race, creed, color or sex. They are all making common cause. They are all spreading the propaganda of the new social order. They are waiting, watching and working through all the weary hours of the day and the night. They are still in the minority. They have learned how to be patient and to abide their time. They feel—they know, indeed—that the time is coming, in spite of all opposition, all persecution, when this emancipating gospel will spread among all the peoples, and when this minority will become the triumphant majority and, sweeping into power, inaugurate the greatest change in history.

In that day we will have the universal commonwealth . . . the harmonious cooperation of every nation with every other nation on earth.

Your honor, in a local paper yesterday there was some editorial exultation about my prospective imprisonment. I do not resent it in the least. I can understand it perfectly. In the same paper there appears an editorial that has in it a hint of the wrong to which I have been trying to call attention. (Reading)

"A Senator of the United States receives a salary of $7,500—$45,000 for the six years for which he is elected. One of the candidates for Senator from a state adjoining Ohio is reported to have spent through his committee $150,000 to secure the nomination. For advertising he spent $35,000, for printing $30,000, for traveling expenses, $10,000 and the rest in ways known to political managers.

"The theory is that public office is as open to a poor man as to a rich man. One may easily imagine, however, how slight a chance one of ordinary resources would have in a contest against this man who was willing to spend more than three times his six years' salary merely to secure a nomination. Were these conditions to hold in every state, the Senate would soon become again what it was once held to be—a rich man's club.

"Campaign expenses have been the subject of much restrictive legislation in recent years, but it has not always reached the mark. The authors of primary reform have accomplished some of the things they set out to do, but they have not yet taken the bank roll out of politics."

They will never take it out of politics, they never can take it out of politics, in this system.

Your honor, I wish to make acknowledgment of my thanks to the counsel for the defense. They have not only defended me with exceptional legal ability, but with a personal attachment and devotion of which I am deeply sensible, and which I can never forget.

Your honor, I ask no mercy and I plead for no immunity. I realize that finally the right must prevail. I never more clearly comprehended than now the great struggle between the powers of greed on the one hand and upon the other the rising hosts of freedom.

I can see the dawn of a better day for humanity. The people are awakening. In due course of time they will come to their own.

When the mariner, sailing over tropic seas, looks for relief from his weary watch, he turns his eyes toward the southern cross, burning luridly above the tempest-vexed ocean. As the midnight approaches, the southern cross begins to bend, and the whirling worlds change their places, and with starry finger-points the Almighty marks the passage of time on the dial of the universe, and though no bell may beat the glad tidings, the look-out knows that the midnight is passing—that relief and rest are close at hand.

Let the people take heart and hope everywhere, for the cross is bending, the midnight is passing, and joy cometh with the morning.

> "He's true to God who's true to man;
>   wherever wrong is done,
> To the humblest and the weakest, 'neath
>   the all-beholding sun.
> That wrong is also done to us, and they
>   are slaves most base,
> Whose love of right is for themselves
>   and not for all their race."

Your honor, I thank you, and I thank all of this court for their courtesy and their kindness, which I shall remember always.

January 11, 1919

The National Civil Liberties Bureau (which changed its name to the American Civil Liberties Union in January, 1920) was the source for the charge that some fifteen hundred political prisoners had been arrested or imprisoned for antiwar activity. When that charge was officially denied, the NCLB issued the following response.

Deny Attorney General's Statement Regarding Number of War Prisoners

In a published statement the Attorney General intimates that the current estimate that there are 1,500 political prisoners in the United States is the result of either frenzied imagination or deliberate intent to deceive the public.

We accept full responsibility for the estimate in question and wish to reassert our belief in its moderation and accuracy. The Attorney General evidently does not regard a person who is under indictment or is out on bail pending appeal as a

political prisoner. His view is that liberty on bail is the same thing as liberty without the threat of prison. Such an assertion needs no comment. Nor does the Attorney General include conscientious objectors. The following table shows how our estimate has been derived and we challenge the Attorney General to show that it is inaccurate in any substantial particular. The figures for prosecution under the Espionage Act are taken from the report of the Attorney General for the year ending June 30, 1918, and are the most recent published officially. We have repeatedly requested more recent figures but our requests have been refused.

Conscientious objectors now in prison 375
Convictions under the Espionage Act 363
Prosecutions under the Espionage Act
    pending 496
Convictions, Chicago I.W.W. case 98
Convictions, Sacramento I.W.W. case 46
I.W.W. under indictment at Wichita, Kans.,
    Omaha, Neb., and Spokane, Wash. 94

1,472

Moreover the figures for the Espionage Act prosecutions given above refer to prosecutions and not to individual defenders. In many cases there are more than one defendant. It should also be noted that the foregoing estimate does not include any of the 8,326 persons who had by June 30, 1918, been convicted of violation of the Selective Draft Law, for the reason that sentences in these cases were generally short.

Mr. Palmer's further statement that "there are no men in prison because of the expression of their views on social, economic, or political questions" is only legalistically correct. The Espionage Act, especially in its original form, was not very honest. It did not in clear words make views criminal; it purported to punish only the doing of various things, such as obstruction of the recruiting service. But almost invariably the evidence consisted principally, if not solely, in expressions of views. It was not for visible acts or results, but for possi-

Eugene V. Debs, federal convict no. 9653, Socialist candidate for President in 1920. Courtesy Western Historical Collections, University of Colorado.

SOCIALIST PARTY
FOR PRESIDENT

EUGENE VICTOR DEBS

bilities supposedly latent in opinions, that people were punished.

April 26, 1919

Helen Keller joined the Massachusetts Socialist party in 1909; from 1910 through the early 1920s she spoke and wrote for socialist, feminist, and working-class causes. Her 1913 collection of essays, Out of the Dark, *has recently been supplemented by* Helen Keller, Her Socialist Years: Writings and Speeches, *edited by Philip Foner.*

Helen Keller Sends Her Greetings to Gene Debs

Forest Hills, N. Y., March 11, 1919
To Eugene V. Debs

Dear Comrade—Of course, the Supreme Court has sustained the decision of the lower court in your case. To my mind, the decision has added another laurel to your wreath of victories. Once more you are going to prison for upholding the liberties of the people.

I write because my heart cries out, it will not be still. I write because I want you to know that I should be proud if the Supreme Court convicted me of abhorring war, and doing all in my power to oppose it. When I think of the millions who have suffered in all the wicked wars of the past, I am shaken with the anguish of a great impatience. I want to fling myself against all brute powers that destroy the life, and break the spirit of man.

In the persecution of our comrades there is one satisfaction. Every trial of men like you, every sentence against them tears away the veil that hides the face of the enemy. The discussion and agitation that follow the trials define more sharply the positions that must be taken before all men can live together in peace, happiness and security.

We were driven into the war for liberty, democracy and humanity. Behold, what is happening all over the world today! Oh, where is the swift vengeance of Jehovah, that it does not fall upon the hosts of those who are marshalling machine-guns against hunger-stricken peoples? It is the complacency of madness to call such acts "preserving law and order." What oceans of blood and tears are shed in their name! I have come to loathe traditions and institutions that take away the rights of the poor and protect the wicked against judgment.

The wise fools who sit in the high places of justice fail to see that in revolutionary times like the present vital issues are settled, not by statutes, decrees and authorities, but in spite of them. Like the Girondins of France they imagine that force can check the onrush of revolution. Thus they sow the wind, and unto them shall be the harvest of the whirl-wind.

Your dear comrade! I have long loved you because you are an apostle of brotherhood and freedom. For years I have thought of you as a dauntless explorer going toward the dawn, and, like a humble adventurer, I have followed in the trail of your footsteps. From time to time the greetings that have come back to me from you have made me very happy, and now I reach out my hand and clasp yours through prison bars.

With heartfelt greetings, and with a firm faith that the cause for which you are now martyred shall be all the stronger because of your sacrifice and devotion, I am,

Yours for the Revolution—may it come swiftly, like a shaft sundering the dark!

Helen Keller
May 17, 1919

"An injury to one is an injury to all" was an explicit part of socialist belief before it became a motto publicly associated with the Industrial Workers of the World. In "America's Blind

America's Blind Staggers

JOHN W. GUNN

. . . An injury to an I.W.W. is an injury to all of us. It is an injury for the added and very forceful reason that, speaking in the most general way, all of us are working in the same great and vital cause—the cause of working class emancipation from the economic tyranny and social oppression of capitalism.

Among the industrial and political prisoners confined in the stout bastilles of free America there are of course many I.W.W.'s caught in the hysterical and indiscriminate wartime drive against agitators, against individuals of whatever belief or description whose social views and activities were squarely in conflict with the present capitalistic industrial order. The Espionage Act, originating ostensibly as a war measure, was really a political and industrial measure. It was so applied, if not so intended. This is why there are such significant numbers of I.W.W.'s and Socialists in jail in America, including men and women of the most widely varying attitudes toward the war.

In Wichita, Kans., a group of I.W.W. boys endured the filth and darkness of a medieval jail for two years. Only recently they have been transferred to other jails in the state owing to investigations showing the frightfully unsanitary conditions in the Wichita hell-hole. These boys, like the other I.W.W.'s, are industrial prisoners. That is to say, their crime is that of having spread the principles of industrial unionism on the job. They were mostly active in the oil fields of this state, seeking to organize their fellow workers. They were filled with a seditious desire for better wages and working conditions. They entertained pro-German dreams of working class solidarity and emancipation from our industrial autocracy. The oil industry, that glittering bonanza of the great American grafter, could not tolerate the treasonable I.W.W.'s, these plotters and promoters of that worst type of treason—treason to the industrial masters of America.

There is another angle to the situation in which the I.W.W.'s in Kansas find themselves. It's a sharp and difficult one, too. Political ambition is its name. Fred Robertson, the federal district attorney for Kansas, has his eye shrewdly squinted in the direction of the governor's chair. He passionately longs to warm that particular chair. And he is getting up steam by vindictively—and vociferously—prosecuting the I.W.W.'s. Every now and then he breaks into print to loudly reiterate his determination to rid Kansas of the I.W.W.'s.

His present victims are facing the third indictment against them, two former indictments having been quashed. These men are to be placed in jeopardy the third time for what is practically, if not technically, the same offense—notwithstanding the law that no man shall be placed twice in jeopardy for the same offense. These men have been in jail two years—notwithstanding the law that every man shall be given a fair and speedy trial.

Obviously the ruling, relentless determination is that these men shall be railroaded to prison—no matter how, nor upon what labored and tortuous pretext. They must be put away in prison solely because they are I.W.W.'s—only this and nothing more. I understand that these boys can secure their liberty if they renounce their allegiance to the I.W.W., and repent of their radical ways. But they will not. They prefer freedom of the mind to freedom of the body, a thing which Fred Robertson, government attorney, probably cannot understand.

The grand offensive against the I.W.W.'s was launched in the Chicago trial of last year, and included William D. Haywood, head of the organization, in its list of prisoners. The injustice of this trial has been condemned by a conservative captain in the army intelligence service, who thoroughly sifted the evidence against the I.W.W.'s in the course of his military duties. These men were charged with conspiracy in violation of the Espionage Act. And of course the federal authorities proved them guilty of having entered into a written or spoken agreement to violate the Espionage Act. It did nothing of the kind. That's what conspiracy means in plain English, and what it previously meant in plain law. But in the Chicago trial of the I.W.W.'s it was ruled that no such agreement need be proved. It was sufficient that these men were members of the same organization, and engaged in the same industrial activities, to convict them of conspiracy. That is to say, they weren't really convicted of conspiracy at all, but of being I.W.W.'s.

A number of these Chicago defendants were not even active in the I.W.W. at the time of their indictment. Vincent St. John, former secretary, had ceased active participation in the work of the organization several years before. It was necessary to bring into court letters he had officially written in 1914, in order to identify his signature. One defendant was employed in a munitions factory, trying to respectably amass a "stake." His chief offense seems to have been that he informed the court he was a "citizen of industry." This strange and no doubt eerie phrase must have profoundly affected the judge, for he gave the offender a sentence of twenty years. You see what one gets for being a "citizen of industry"—for being a worker instead of a shirker.

The most astonishing fact in the trial of these I.W.W.'s is that it included members of the organization who were honestly for the war. The case against one of the defendants was dismissed so that he might respond to his draft call. Understand that he was willing to respond to this call, and had duly complied with the law by registering. Yet there he was, in the dock, facing a foolish charge of conspiracy to oppose the war! Another I.W.W., who was among those convicted and sentenced to the federal prison at Leavenworth, Kans., was a supporter of the war and, although married, had registered and waived exemption!

Against the majority of these I.W.W.'s it could not be proved that they had written or spoken or acted against the war cause of America. Many of them believed in the war—were honestly convinced that German militarism ought to be put out of business. With the exception of a few, who had been guilty at most of indiscreetly foolish remarks, none of them was guilty of a thing save the more or less ardent advocacy of industrial unionism. No doubt the belief of many of them was against the war. But not even our wonderful Espionage Act could make a man a criminal simply because of his private belief, when that belief wasn't translated into action or propaganda intended to hinder the prosecution of the war. It couldn't—yet it did. However, it was their private belief that capitalism was wrong, not their private belief that the war was wrong, which put the I.W.W.'s in prison. Else why were pro-war members of the I.W.W. put in prison along with the rest?

It should be explained that the I.W.W., as an organization, took no position on the war. This is shown, if by nothing else, by the fact that throughout the war this organization remained solid and undivided. There was no split among the I.W.W.'s as there was among the Socialists. Among them were both pro-war and anti-war individuals. But the war was never an issue with the I.W.W.'s—not even with those who were opposed to it in belief. The industrial issue was paramount. The I.W.W.'s were chiefly and supremely interested in organizing the workers according to the principles of industrial unionism. They were primarily occupied with the struggle for industrial democracy right here at home. Thousands of I.W.W.'s went overseas to fight the military autocrats of the Central Empires. Those who didn't go to war, stayed at home to fight the industrial autocrats of America. But a fighter for democracy is not without honor save when he fights for democracy in his own country—so a number of the I.W.W.'s who didn't go to war, went to prison instead.

The final disposition of most of the I.W.W. cases is still to come. Some of them, like the I.W.W. boys in Kansas, have not yet been finally convicted. Others are awaiting appeal trials—among them the group confined in Leavenworth federal prison. Of the Leavenworth boys, whose sentences range all the way from a year and a day to twenty years, a few have secured temporary freedom under bail and a few others, serving sentences of a year and a day, have completed their terms. More than seventy I.W.W.'s still remain in Leavenworth. A desperate campaign is being made to raise funds for the legal defense of these industrial prisoners. Whether they will yet wring justice from our unfriendly courts, depends upon the funds that are forthcoming, and very greatly upon the extent to which working class opinion can be aroused to a clear, class-conscious realization of the enormous injustices that are being committed against these propagandists of the New Day in industry.

Back of the attacks upon the I.W.W.'s during the war, and the attacks upon them since the ending of the war, was and is the simple purpose to crush radical thought and propaganda. This purpose of course takes in the Socialists as well as the I.W.W.'s. It is beginning to include the erstwhile conservative labor unions, now that they are becoming sharply engaged in a genuine class struggle with the labor-hating employers.

This purpose is just now most conspicuously directed against the I.W.W.'s because they furnish the most convenient and easy victims for the propaganda of reactionary terrorism. Socialism has come to be too well understood—at least the more obvious canards against it no longer are effective as of old. The same is true of labor unionism. But among that somewhat mysterious, uncategoried mass, vaguely known as "the public," the I.W.W. is little understood. Its chief aim not being political, it has never conducted the political propaganda necessary to make its principles familiar to the people at large. Its name carried the most obscure and fearful implications.

Public opinion, in short, will stand for a good deal of persecution against the I.W.W.'s. Precedents of social tyranny can be established, with the excuse that they are necessary to deal with the I.W.W.'s. Despotic laws can be passed with the same handy excuse. A government espionage system, provided with new pitfalls for the feet of freedom, can be carried over into peace times, can be made into a permanent feature of our political and social system. The liberties of the people—their most previous and essential liberties—can be stolen from them one at a time, and they won't notice the theft until they wake up with rather painful suddenness some day and find them all gone. Then they will find that they have lost the right to protest. They will find that it is a crime to attack the capitalist system in America; that they will be thrown in jail, into the cells not already occupied by I.W.W.'s and Socialists, if they dare open their mouths to speak against their industrial masters.

This fate is already clearly foreshadowed by the various so-called "criminal syndicalist" laws that have been passed in every state where the politicians have had a chance to seize advantage of the present wave of reaction and terrorism. These "criminal syndicalist" laws are apparently aimed at the I.W.W.'s only; but they are actually used as clubs against any and all labor agitators. Socialists and simple union men have been arrested under the cover of these infamous laws. These laws may be used to suppress advocacy of the strike, advocacy of industrial unionism, advocacy of an industrial, as contrasted with a purely political form of government—and, in the state of Maine, against the advocacy of any change whatever in the form of government!

In the state of Alabama the right to strike has even been explicitly abolished by law, with a penalty of fine and imprisonment for its violation! In the state of Ohio, coal miners belonging to the United Mine Workers—not I.W.W.'s mind you—have been arrested under the "criminal syndicalist" law for the crime of striking! The state secretary of the Socialist party in California was arrested for circulating Socialist literature!

Don't you recognize the huge footprints of the Iron Heel? Can't you distinguish them from bird tracks? Mr. Conservative Labor Union Man, wherever you are, if you are by your silence or indifference helping our new social tyranny in its persecution of the I.W.W.'s—if you are helping by just that much, little as you may think it is—you are helping to prepare an identical fate for yourself. For the capitalist system, once it is aroused, makes no fine distinctions between the different forms of protest. It smashes all protest alike. You will live to bitterly regret your present supine role, when the Iron Heel tramps upon your toes—and takes them off!

To the hundreds of thousands of Socialists who read this, this only need be said: Be more active than ever in spreading these facts, and the grim tremendous warning that they sound, among your fellow workers who are not yet fully awake. Arouse them to the deadly habit-forming nature of the debauch of reaction, the orgy of terrorism, the wild and insane and terrible spree of social tyranny which is giving America the most hideous blind staggers!

November 8, 1919

Combating un-American propaganda in all its insidious forms was a difficult task. However, not only was Kansas City police chief W. W. Gordon on the job in 1920, but so were, by a conservative estimate, hundreds of thousands of officials and Red-Scared citizens.

Bolshevism in Ballrooms

Each day it seems that some new cunning trick of "red" propaganda is discovered and horrifically exposed to a breathlessly waiting world. And yet these tricks appear to be quite simple, after all. For instance, the very essence of naturalness and simplicity is revealed in the practice of spreading radical or "bolshevist" doctrines through the medium of social intercourse at dances, whose discovery is proclaimed by W. W. Gordon, chief of police of Kansas City, Kans. This strange phenomenon was discovered, we are told, when raids were recently made on dance halls frequented by foreigners. The Kansas City *Times* quotes Chief Gordon as saying:

"One of the informants who assisted in the raids told me the dance halls are nests for spreading the doctrines of Bolshevism.

"It is the general practice of women agitators, workers from the general headquarters of the red parties to frequent these dance halls. They dance with the young men of inflammable minds and disgruntled natures and all during the dances the conversation was not of the music nor the pleasures of the evening, but was of the red doctrine of destruction and of Bolshevism.

"There is the young Russian who worked hard at Morris & Co.'s packing plant. He met a beautiful woman of his race at one of these dance halls. She told him she was from Chicago. They danced, and all the turns, steps, hesitations and waltzes were tempered with volleys of red propaganda, spoken in low whispers into the ear of the young man. The woman was beautiful and her words were soft. Days later, the federal officials raided a group of Kansas side reds and the young Russian knew then the beautiful woman's meaning."

This form of revolutionary seduction makes the authorities tremble. This ingenious faculty of female "bolsheviks" of combining business with pleasure excites ill and disquieting forebodings. Much evil has been attributed to the dance and its adaptability to the leveling of the strongest wall of moral resistance to temptation has been impressed upon us for these many years. And now the revolution is being fomented through the fox-trot, the tango has become the tool of treason, the waltz has been subsidized by seditious wobblies, the ballroom, in short, has become bolshevised, and all orchestras may now be considered as overt acts.

What shall be done? There are difficulties that suggest themselves when the abolition of dancing is proposed. Conversation might be barred at all dances. But alas! such has been the progress of mental telepathy that seditious thoughts may be communicated without audible utterance! All beautiful women might be excluded from dances, with the confident result that ugly specimens of the female "bolshevik" would be hopeless as propagandists. But then the young men might quit attending the dances and assemble, with the unerring instinct of gallant youth, wherever the beautiful women were. So that wouldn't work. It's a stunner. We'll let Chief Gordon of Kansas City solve it.

March 20, 1920

Remembered best for The Jungle, *Upton Sinclair was America's most prolific radical author. Converted to socialism in 1902, he very nearly won the California governorship in 1934. Sinclair's "Imprisonment of Debs" captures some of Debs's own power, and it evokes the fear and intimidation present in America during the years of the Red Scare. Sinclair published novels and essays in the* Appeal *for nearly twenty years.*

Imprisonment of Debs Is Part of Conspiracy Against Your Liberty

UPTON SINCLAIR

. . . For a hundred years and more we Americans have allowed the process to continue whereby all our natural resources, the means of producing the material necessities of our lives, have become the property of a small master class. Today we are owned by that class, and all our comings and goings are controlled by it; the food that we eat, the clothes that we wear, the news that we read, the very thoughts that we think. I dare not go so far as to say that our government is controlled by it—because if I said that, they might suppress this paper, and send me to join Debs in Atlanta. But I presume that one may quote the President of the United States, and I therefore refer to his book— *The New Freedom*, in which you may read about the "Invisible Government" of America, and how it controls American public life.

It used to be content to control the wages we were paid for our labor, and the prices we paid for everything we bought. But the war has made it bold; the war has accustomed it to propaganda, the art of creating hysteria in the public mind. The war has accustomed it to suppression of opinion, the violation of all constitutional rights. Also, the war has taught it new possibilities of profiteering. The big trusts and the big financial interests are taking today five times as heavy a tribute from our labor as they took five years ago. They do not mean to give up this plunder; they do not mean to permit even the beginning of a movement of the people to end this system of exploitation. They are alert and thoroughly informed. They have their spies in every union and in every shop. They have practically all the sources of publicity and propaganda. They have their Chambers of Commerce and their Associated Manufacturers, with their war chests of millions upon millions of dollars. They have, of course, the machines of both political parties. They have an overwhelming majority of legislators in Congress, and in all states of the nation. They have some judges and some prosecuting attorneys and some sheriffs and chiefs of police—if I should tell you all the things they have, how many years in jail would it cost me? I hasten to fly back to the protecting shelter of Woodrow Wilson; they are the Invisible Government of America, and their purpose is to keep themselves the owners and masters of America, and to keep you what you are today, a wage slave, a tenant, a man without property—or with just enough property to fool you, to keep you from realizing your true state.

What are you going to do about it? Here is where I bring you back to Eugene Debs, as I promised to do! There is a saying of Debs which will some day be graven upon the monument to him which will stand in our national capital. The saying reads:

> "While there is a lower class, I am in it.
> "While there is a criminal element, I am of it.
> "While there is a soul in jail, I am not free."

It may be hard for you, a free and haughty one-hundred per cent American workman or farmer, to realize that you have any identity of interest with the Hunkie and the Dago and the Wop, and all the rest of the low-down, lousy foreigners, and the anarchists and communists and Bolsheviki who are being clubbed and jailed and deported to make the world safe for Democracy. But here is the plain fact, none the less: When the vilest and lousiest foreigner is deprived of his rights under the American constitution, you also are deprived of your rights, your government ceases to function, your country ceases to be the thing for which our forefathers fought and died. When any man or woman in America is deprived of the rights guaranteed by the constitution—of freedom of speech, of press and of assemblage—you also are deprived of those rights. When any man is punished for expressing any opinion, no matter how outrageous, no matter how dangerous, you too, are punished. You are not in jail with your body, the part of you which eats and sleeps and talks; but you are in jail with your spirit, the part of you which hopes and aspires and progresses toward new powers and new achievements; the community to which you belong is in jail, your ancestors who left you a free country and your posterity who look to you for their happiness and freedom. Your country is in jail, with all that it was of justice and righteousness, and all that it ever hoped to be. And I, speaking to you with the voice of Gene Debs as I promised to do, call upon you—not to set me free from my felon's cell in Atlanta, but to set yourselves free, your spirit and your hope and your ideals, your community and your country, your past traditions and your future hopes!

"Why was I, Eugene Debs, sent to a felon's cell? Because for 30 years I have been the friend of the poor and oppressed, and because in a time of crisis I spoke the truth when others were blinded or cowed. Why am I kept in a felon's cell—now when danger of war is past? Because it is known that if freed, I will go on speaking the truth, I will speak it more effectively than ever, I will be more dangerous to the predatory powers that tried to shut my voice. I am not in jail because of myself, but because of you—in order that you may not learn the truth I have to teach; in order that the fire of justice and freedom which is in my soul, shall not come into contact with your soul and enkindle it. So when you go out among your fellows, to agitate and educate and organize, to make your voice heard demanding freedom for me, it will be freedom for yourself that you are really winning. When you have won it for yourself, then, and only then, will I be happy; for I am the author of the saying:

> "'While there is a lower class, I am in it.
> "'While there is a criminal element, I am of it.
> "'While there is a soul in jail, I am not free.'"

May 22, 1920

The seventy-page report on Attorney General A. Mitchell Palmer's constitutional abuses by twelve nationally and internationally famous legal authorities was a significant step in diminishing Red Scare hysteria. The narrow focus of the report, however, is not solely attributable to the legal training of the writers. Public hysteria, created by corporations and by numerous government agencies, made caution advisable.

Palmer Violated Law and Constitution, Is Indictment of Twelve Leading Lawyers

Attorney General Palmer has most shamefully and persistently and deliberately violated the laws and the Constitution of the United States in his campaign of political persecution against men and women holding radical opinions, is the cool and detached opinion, based upon careful investigation, of twelve of the most prominent legal authorities in the country, who have just issued an extensive "Report Upon the Illegal Practices of the United States Department of Justice."

Palmer is also charged with having instigated meetings of radicals in order to provide a greater number of victims for his sensational nationwide "red" raids, and with employing that odious tool, the "agent provocateur," hitherto known only in such barbarously governed countries as Spain and Russia, to stir up revolutionary sentiment and activity that he might gain the credit of suppressing them.

Palmer is charged with using the machinery of the United States government to imprison and persecute workingmen upon the information and advice of private detectives and agents in the pay of the steel trust, coal companies and other private corporations.

Palmer is charged with wrongfully using his office as Attorney General of the United States, and with wrongfully using government funds, to send out from Washington to the press of the country tons of dishonest propaganda designed to foster bitter and ignorant prejudice against radicals, thus preparing a public atmosphere in which Palmer could pursue his vicious autocratic course unrestrained by any consideration of common decency.

These charges against Attorney General Palmer are generally alleged and sustained by specific instances in this 70-page report presented by twelve of the nation's greatest legal lights, men who condemn the Attorney General simply and solely because he has flagrantly flouted the laws and the Constitution of the United States.

The report of these twelve attorneys condemns the Department of Justice in the following language:

"For more than six months, we, the under-signed lawyers, whose sworn duty it is to uphold the Constitution and laws of the United States, have seen with growing apprehension the continued violation of that Constitution and breaking of those laws by the Department of Justice of the United States government.

"Under the guise of a campaign for the suppression of radical activities, the office of the Attorney General, acting by its local agents throughout the country, and giving express instructions from Washington, has committed illegal acts. Wholesale arrests both of aliens and citizens have been made without warrants or any process of law; men and women have been jailed and held incommunicado without access of friends or counsel; homes have been entered without search warrants and property seized and removed; other property has been wantonly destroyed; working men and working women suspected of radical views have been shamefully abused and maltreated. Agents of the Department of Justice have also constituted themselves a propaganda bureau, and sent to newspapers and magazines of this country quantities of material designed to excite public opinion against radicals, all at the expense of the government and outside the scope of the Attorney General's duties.

"We make no argument in favor of any radical doctrine as such, whether Socialist, communist or anarchist. No one of us belongs to any of these schools of thought, nor do we now raise any question as to the constitutional protection of free speech and a free press. We are concerned solely with bringing to the attention of the American people the utterly illegal acts which have been committed by those charged with the highest duty of enforcing the laws—acts which have caused widespread suffering and unrest, have struck at the foundation of American free institutions, and have brought the name of our country into disrepute.

"These acts may be grouped under the following heads:

"(1). Cruel and Unusual Punishment. The Eighth Amendment to the United States Constitution provides that 'excessive bail shall not be required nor excessive fines imposed nor cruel and unusual punishment inflicted.'

"Punishments of the utmost cruelty, and heretofore unthinkable in America, have become usual. Great numbers of persons arrested, both aliens and citizens, have been threatened, beaten with blackjacks, struck with fists, jailed under abominable conditions, or actually tortured.

"(2). Arrests Without Warrant. The Fourth Amendment to the Constitution provides that 'The right of people to be secure in their persons, houses, papers and effects, against unreasonable searches and seizures, shall not be violated, and no warrants shall issue but upon probable cause, supported by oath or affirmation, and particularly describing the place to be searched, and the person or things to be seized.'

"Many hundreds of citizens and aliens alike have been arrested in wholesale raids, without warrants or pretense of warrants. They have either been released, or have been detained in police stations or jails for indefinite lengths of time while warrants were being applied for. This practice of making raids and mass arrests without warrant has resulted directly from the instructions, both written and oral, issued by the Department of Justice at Washington.

"(3). Unreasonable Searches and Seizures. The Fourth Amendment has been quoted above.

"In countless cases the agents of the Department of Justice have entered the homes, offices, or gathering places of persons suspected of radical affiliations, and, without pretense of any search warrant, have seized and removed property belonging to them for use by the Department of Justice. In many of these raids property which could not be removed or was not useful to the department, was intentionally smashed and destroyed.

"(4). Provocative agents. We do not question the right of the Department of Justice to use its agents in the Bureau of Investigation to ascertain when the law is being violated, but the American people have never tolerated the use of undercover provocative agents or 'agents provocateurs,' such as have been familiar in old Russia or Spain. Such agents have been introduced by the Department of Justice into the radical movements, have reached positions of influence therein, have occupied themselves with informing upon or instigating acts which might be declared criminal, and at the express direction of Washington have brought about meetings of radicals in order to make possible wholesale arrests at such meetings.

"(5). Compelling Persons to Be Witnesses Against Themselves. The Fifth Amendment provides as follows: 'No person shall be compelled in any criminal case to be a witness against himself, nor to be deprived of life, liberty, or property, without due process of law.'

"It has been the practice of the Department of Justice and its agents after making illegal arrests without warrant, to question the accused person and to force admissions from him by terrorism, which admissions were subsequently to be used against him in deportation proceedings.

"(6). Propaganda by the Department of Justice. The functions of the Attorney General are to advise the government on questions of law, and to prosecute persons who have violated Federal statutes. For the Attorney General to go into the field of propaganda against radicals is a deliberate misuse of his office and deliberate squandering of funds entrusted to him by Congress.

"Since these illegal acts have been committed by the highest legal powers in the United States, there is no final appeal from them except to the conscience and condemnation of the American people. American institutions have not, in fact, been protected by the Attorney General's ruthless suppression. On the contrary, those institutions have been seriously undermined and revolutionary unrest has been vastly intensified. No organization of radicals acting through propaganda over the last six months could have created as much revolutionary sentiment in America as has been created by the acts of the Department of Justice itself.

"Even were one to admit that there existed any serious 'red menace' before the Attorney General started his 'unflinching war' against it, his campaign has been singularly fruitless. Out of the many thousands suspected by the Attorney General (he had already listed 60,000 by name and history on November 14, 1919, aliens and citizens), what do the figures show of net results? Prior to January 1, 1920, there were actually deported 263 persons. Since January 1, 1920, there have been actually deported eighteen persons. Since January 1 there have been ordered deported an additional 529 persons, and warrants for 1,547 have been cancelled by Assistant Secretary of Labor Louis F. Post. The Attorney General has, consequently, got rid of 810 alien suspects, which, on his own showing, leaves him at least 59,190 persons still to cope with.

"It has always been the proud boast of America that this is a government of laws and not of men. Our Constitution and laws have been based on the simple elements of human nature. Free men cannot be driven and repressed; they must be led. Free men respect justice and follow truth, but arbitrary power they will oppose until the end of time. There is no danger of revolution so great as that created by suppression, by ruthlessness, and by deliberate violation of the simple rules of American law and American decency.

"It is a fallacy to suppose that, anymore than in the past, any servant of the people can safely arrogate to himself unlimited authority. To proceed upon such a supposition is to deny the fundamental American theory of the consent of the governed. Here is no question of a vague and threatened menace, but a present assault upon the most sacred principles of our constitutional liberty."

That the Department of Justice instigated meetings of radicals and employed "agents provocateur" is shown by the secret instructions given out by Frank Burke, Assistant Director and Chief of the Bureau of Investigation of the De-

partment of Justice, immediately prior to the famous nation-wide raid of January 2, 1920. These instructions read, in part, as follows:

"As soon as the subjects are apprehended you should endeavor to obtain from them, if possible, admissions that they are members of either of these parties, together with any statement concerning their citizenship status.

"Immediately upon apprehending an alien he should be thoroughly searched. If found in groups in meeting rooms, they should be lined up against the wall, and there searched, particular attention being given to finding the membership book, in which connection the search of pockets will not be sufficient.

"I leave it to your own discretion as to the method by which you should gain access to such meeting places and residences.

"If possible you should arrange with your undercover informants to have meetings of the Communist party and the Communist Labor party held on the night set. I have been informed by some of the bureau officers that such arrangements will be made. This, of course, would facilitate the making of the arrests.

"Persons taken into custody will not be permitted to communicate with any outside person until after examination by this office and until permission is given by this office."

"Undercover informants" is the Americanism for "agents provocateur" whose business is not only to seek but to stir up trouble. And, says this report:

"Undercover informants employed by private detective agencies, which in turn are employed by the steel and coal companies, supply to those detective agencies, and through them, to the companies and the Department of Justice, information concerning members of labor organizations; that arrests are frequently made upon the unsupported statements of these undercover private informants, without a warrant; that the Department of Justice sends its investigator to go through the men arrested and ascertain if there are any extreme radicals among them, and then set the machinery of the Department of Labor in motion for their deportation. In other words, the steel and coal companies use the local and Federal governments to harass and get rid of troublesome workers."

The report includes numerous affidavits from all parts of the country setting forth the brutal, inhuman and illegal tactics of Department of Justice agents. One of the most damnable of these cases wherein the frightfulness of Palmerism was exhibited, and which is exposed in this report, was that of the ninety-seven men arrested in Bridgeport, Conn., in November and December, 1919, and kept in jail for five months, in what amounted to solitary confinement, where they were beaten, starved, suffocated, tortured and threatened with death in futile attempts to extort admissions that would enable the Department of Justice to successfully proceed with their persecution. Regarding this case, the report adds:

"Other persons who applied at Hartford jail were also arrested and confined with these prisoners. During the five months prisoners were allowed no reading matter and were kept in their cells except for occasional visits from Department of Justice agents, or hearings before Labor Department inspectors; were refused knowledge of charges against them, or knowledge of the amount of bail under which they were held; were allowed only from two to five minutes a day to wash their faces and hands at a sink outside their cells and five minutes once a month to wash their bodies in a tub; were given no exercise and fed with foul and insufficient food. In the jail were four punishment rooms, all alike, unventilated and utterly dark, size 4 feet 3 inches by 8 feet 10 inches, with solid concrete floor, no furniture of any kind, and placed over the pump room of the boiler, so that the temperature became unbearably high. A number of the supposed anarchist or Communist prisoners, probably 10 or 15, were confined in these rooms for periods of 36 to 60 hours. During their imprisonment in the suffocating heat, without air, they were given one glass of water and one slice of bread every 12 hours. Some of them, on being released had to be revived before they could be carried to their cells. One man who was in only 30 hours was unable to get to his cell unaided. These Hartford prisoners were practically buried alive for five months, being even denied the privilege of seeing their relatives, who made constant attempts to communicate with them. That there were no substantial charges against at least 10 of them is shown by the fact that after being held in $10,000 bail for two months and a half, these 10 were released without bail January 24. Of the men still held, at least a majority had no political views of any special nature, but are simply working men of Russian nationality speaking little or no English."

A raid on the Russian People's House in New York City, according to affidavits in this report, was marked by brutality and vandalism that one expects to find in the worst criminals but not in officers of the law. Clubs and blackjacks in the hands of the government raiders freely rained upon the heads of these innocent Russians, who were engaged in conducting an ordinary night study class when the raid occurred. All of the furniture was destroyed and the place totally wrecked in the most wanton manner. Several hundred prisoners were hauled to the Department of Justice headquarters in New York, put through the notorious "third degree," and then four-fifths of them turned loose because there was absolutely no evidence upon which to retain them in custody.

In an affidavit made by an alien, Alexander Bukowetsky, of Detroit, it is stated that he and ten others arrested on November 9, 1919, at a concert given by the Union of Russian Workers were kept in jail ten days without being permitted to see or communicate with any one; that then they were taken to the Department of Justice headquarters, where they were ordered to be taken back to the jail, being kept there until January 21, 1920. They were on the latter date taken to another prison, where there was no cell room, and they were forced to sleep on the floor for two months. Later they were sent to a prison at Fort Wayne, In., and still later to Pontiac prison.

In Pontiac prison the prisoners were robbed of all their money and personal belongings, and within a short time were taken to Fort Wayne again. Here Bukowetsy states that his wife and 12-year-old daughter and 4-year-old son called to see him. He was let out of his cell, but as he was on the point of greeting his family, a guard jumped in the way and dragged his wife and children out of the room. The guard struck Bukowetsky's wife, and when Bukowetsky protested he was himself beaten. When he called upon his fellow prisoners for help, an inspector of the prison fired among the prisoners, wounding one of them in the leg. After being robbed of what few belongings he had left, Bukowetsky was then taken to Wayne county jail. He declares the Department of Justice agents have offered him his freedom if he will agree to report to them at certain periods, but he refuses to accept his freedom upon any such ridiculously enslaving and humiliating, not to say entirely illegal, terms.

After reading this report we feel justified in branding Attorney General A. Mitchell Palmer as the biggest violater of the law in the United States.

Charges
of the Report
Wholesale arrest and imprisonment of men and women without warrants, or pretense of warrants and illegal searches and seizures, in violation of the Constitution.

Forgery by agents of the department to make cases against innocent persons caught in illegal raids.

Criminal thefts of money, watches, jewelry and other personal property from victims of raids by agents of the department.

Cruel and unusual punishments visited upon prisoners taken into custody with and without warrants, in violation of the Constitution.

Use of government funds in violation of law to spread newspaper propaganda favorable to campaign of repression, and to purchase "boiler plate" distributed free to country newspapers to create popular opinion favorable to acts of the department.

Compulsion of prisoners to be witnesses against themselves in violation of the Constitution.

Brutal and indecent treatment of women taken in raids.

Filthy conditions of confinement, and refusal to let prisoners communicate with friends or lawyers.

Signers
of the Report
Roscoe Pound, Dean of the Law School, Harvard University; Tyrrell Williams, St. Louis, Mo., Dean of the Law School, Washington University; Frank P. Walsh, New York City, former joint chairman, National War Labor Board; David Wallerstein, Philadelphia, member American Bar Association; Jackson H. Ralston, Washington, Umpire Italian-Venezuelan Claim Commission; Former Judge Alfred Niles, Baltimore, Md., professor at Maryland University Law School; Francis Fisher Kane, recently resigned United States District Attorney, Philadelphia, Pa.; Felix Frankfurter, Assistant to the Secretary of War and Assistant Secretary of Labor during the war, and now Professor of Law, Harvard University; Swinburne Hale, New York, former captain, Military Intelligence Division, General Staff, U.S. Army; Ernst Freund, Chicago, professor at Chicago University Law School; R. G. Brown, Memphis, Tenn.; Zechariah Chafee, Jr., Boston, professor at Harvard Law School.

June 19, 1920

The Socialist party's amnesty demands were formally presented to President Woodrow Wilson on June 5, 1920. In comparison with all other combatant countries in World War I, the United States government's refusal to grant amnesty reflected a singular lack of charity toward its wartime dissenters.

Amnesty Demand Presented to Wilson by Socialists

Hon. Woodrow Wilson, President of the United States

Sir: This Memorial is respectfully presented to urge that you grant immediate amnesty and pardon for all federal prisoners convicted not of acts of treason in the service of the enemy, but on the basis of political speeches and writings, or labor union activities.

The practice of prosecuting citizens for holding and expressing political views opposed to those of the administration in power, or for participating in working-class movements and struggles not favored by it, is deeply repugnant to the genius of democracy. When it is resorted to in times of war, it is invariably done upon the justification that the critical emergency of war-time conditions necessitates extraordinary measures. Hence it has been the invariable custom of all enlightened nations to grant amnesty to war opponents immediately upon the cessation of hostilities.

In accordance with this custom the government of Italy has issued a far-reaching decree of amnesty in the month of February, 1919, supplementing the same by an even more radical and thoroughgoing enactment in September of the same year. The government of Great Britain has granted full amnesty to persons in prison for political and military offenses in connection with the late war, on June 5, 1919.

The government of Belgium followed with a general amnesty decree on August 4, 1919, while the French Chamber of Deputies voted a similar decree on October 24, 1919.

The amnesty decrees of the Allied Powers include offenses such as "outraging the flag," "offenses committed through the medium of the press," "offenses committed in connection with public demonstrations and agitations consequent on political and economic causes," "offenses arising from conflicts of a political or economic character," "offenses in connection with meetings, strikes and demonstrations," and even "crimes and misdemeanors against the safety of the state."

Full amnesty has also been granted by the governments of the Central Powers and of Russia.

The United States is the only country which has not granted amnesty to its alleged war offenders. At this time, one year and a half after the cessation of hostilities, hundreds of American citizens are still in prison serving long sentences for alleged offenses of a purely political nature. In most cases, they have been tried at a time when the war sentiment was at its height, in an atmosphere of passion and prejudice. They would never have been convicted under normal circumstances.

To say that the United States is still at war is to reply to a demand for justice by an unworthy quibble and technicality. The United States is not waging war at this time, and has not been engaged in warfare for eighteen months. Further detention of so-called political war offenders cannot be seriously justified on the theory of wartime necessity, but assumes the character of vindictive persecution of political opponents.

The Socialist party has named as its candidate for President of the United States in the coming elections, Mr. Eugene V. Debs, a prisoner of the character above described. As a matter of justice and simple political fairness, we demand that he be immediately released and pardoned by virtue of a general amnesty, so that he may address himself to the American electorate on the same terms as his rival candidates of the other political parties.

Dated May 14, 1919

Respectfully submitted in behalf of the Socialist Party of the United States by

W. H. Henry   Seymour Stedman

Freda Hogan   George E. Roewer, Jr.,
                     Chairman Committee

Madge Patton Stepens, M.D.

June 19, 1920

Although written with Kate Richards O'Hare's customary passion, "Debs and Other Political Prisoners" is a tempered view of her own and others' prosecution during World War I and its aftermath. After her release from prison, Richards O'Hare temporarily served as a staff writer for the Appeal.

Debs and Other Political Prisoners Are Victims of War Profiteers, Says O'Hare

Mrs. Kate Richards O'Hare
Staff Writer, *Appeal to Reason*

Political prisoners have always been the torch bearers who have carried the light of truth into the dark places of despotism's realm and uncovered the inner workings of the existing system of exploiting human labor. The old slave master chopped off the heads of political offenders, the feudal lords boiled them in oil, kings and emperors exiled them, and older capitalist governments of Europe sent them to prison.

The United States is a youthful nation, callow and brash, arrogant and conceited in its sense of power and boastful of the fact that it could well afford to permit the expression of any shade of political opinion. Not until we entered the world war, a "war to end war" and to "make the world safe for democracy" did our ruling class feel it necessary to bring about the imprisonment of people for holding disturbing economic and political beliefs and

to place the term "political pris er" in our national vocabulary.

As an ex-political prisoner I really have no bitterness in my heart for the capitalist controlled Democratic administration who sent 'Gene Debs and me and hundreds more like us to prison. What else could they do? The Democratic party claimed, rightly no doubt, to be the most effective protector of the profit system, and we insisted on telling the people annoying facts as to how and why war is the greatest profit maker for the capitalist class known to man.

We Socialists knew the relation of profits to war and we insisted on telling the truth about it. We told it in season and out, we whispered it and bawled it from the housetops, we expounded it in "highbrow" literature and gave it "punch" for the common man in street corner slang. We talked war and profits, War and Profits, WAR AND PROFITS until the administration was compelled, in sheer self-defense to attempt to squelch us. First the administration violated the constitutional provision for free press and by the stroke of a pen destroyed the greater portion of the Socialist press. But we could still talk if we could not publish newspapers, and we did talk and talk and talk. And the best method the limited intelligence of the administration could devise for squelching talking Socialists was to send them to prison.

In my case it was frightful strain on the "brains of the administration" to find some plausible excuse for sending me to prison. With the best sleuthing the Department of Justice could do it was compelled to admit that I had violated no law; I was of American blood for many generations; my family had always been properly patriotic and had participated in every war the United States had ever waged; my public utterances and private life proved that I was not pro-German and was most emphatically pro-American; I was entirely "nice" and "respectable" and "ladylike" and I had managed to amble along to comfortable middle age with the same husband and children I started with. In fact I had but one vice—I did insist on telling the truth about war and profits. And war and profits was the one subject the Democratic administration dared not permit me to discuss. There were too many billions in war profits at stake to allow the common people to know the truth concerning them.

So many people have marveled that I should have traveled all over the country telling the truth, as I saw it, about war and profits unmolested, until I landed in a little, unknown town in the northwest, and there to have been "framed," arrested, tried, convicted and sent to prison. But there is really nothing marvelous about it, I was simply more dangerous to the capitalists, the war profiteers and the Democratic party in the northwest than in any other section of the United States.

Human jackals have always preyed upon their government and the common people under the blood-red mists of war. When logic and reason, culture and civilization are clutched in the mad embrace of war, profit and plunder, murder and mammon are freed from the restrictions that sane society imposes. Under the guise of patriotism profiteer and plunderer, servant of mammon and licensed murderer are permitted to commit any crime if they deck it with glory, acclaim it with shouts of patriotism and drape it in flaunting flags.

Out there in the great, rich northwest were the lumber kings who controlled the spruce needed by the government for the aeroplanes, the copper necessary for munitions, the shipbuilding interests who controlled the shipping needed to wage the war, and the grain speculators who hoped to, and did to a great extent, control the bread supply of the world. Interlocked with these were the railroad interests that control the transportation of both the means of life in peace and the means of death in war. These powerful capitalists knew that their servile lackeys were safely placed where they could serve best in the political administration of the government, the newspapers were safely subsidized, and the only danger that threatened their orgy of unrestricted and thievish war profits were the pestiferous Socialists, the I.W.W.s and the

Nonpartisan Leaguers who insisted on discussing war and profits.

The whole story of why I should have been one of the victims of the war profiteers in the northwest, and there were many more, is perfectly plain and some day all of the details will be known. The I.W.W. was the first organization of the workers to challenge the despotic and brutal reign of the lumber kings and the copper kings, and naturally they were both hated and feared by them. I never aligned myself with the I.W.W., but I did understand its members. I knew the wrongs these most terribly exploited workers suffered and I comprehended the aspirations they cherished. No doubt my greatest crime in the eyes of the lumber kings and the copper kings was that I not only understood, but I could make others understand also.

Just previous to the war came that great revolt of the farmers which gave birth to the Nonpartisan League with its political and economic program so dangerous to the capitalist interests of the Northwest. I think I was the very first person who ever tried to carry to the Eastern wage workers and the Southern cotton farmers the thrilling story of the uprising of the Northwestern farmers. In the spring of 1917 something happened that struck terror to the hearts of the industrial pirates of the Pacific Coast. The I.W.W. was swiftly organizing the underdogs of the industrial world into one big union, and the Nonpartisan League was organizing the plundered farmers both politically and economically. As the harvest time neared that summer the League farmers made terms with the wobblies to harvest their wheat, and as the harvest progressed it was demonstrated that the despised I.W.W.s were fulfilling their "gentlemen's" contract with the League farmers to the letter and proving themselves the most loyal and dependable employes of men who treated them as human beings. The principal weapon used by the capitalists against the I.W.W. was slander, the claim that they were criminal, vicious, lazy and unfit as workers and the experience of the League farmers branded this as absolutely untrue. Naturally this cooperation between the migratory workers and the organized farmers struck at the very foundation of the power of Northwestern plunderbund, and these profiteers were wise enough to know that if the exploited industrial workers and plundered farmers ever joined forces politically and economically their days of unrestricted plundering were over. The war was the golden opportunity of the profiteers and they had no intention of being balked in their widespread program of "patriotic" war profiteering. The only thing they feared was that the people who fight the wars and pay for them, the working class, should be told the truth of war and profits.

When I look back over that fateful trip that ended in my arrest, in the light of the recent disclosures of greed and graft and thievish profiteering on the part of the capitalist interests of the Northwest, the whole story unrolls a mighty epic of war between capital and labor. From St. Louis I traveled East and South and everywhere record breaking crowds heard me gladly. I delivered the now famous lecture in Washington, under the very nose of the administration, but it did not discover that I was "dangerous" until the war profiteers of the Northwest advised them of the fact. I turned Westward and it was the Democratic farmers who had voted for Wilson because "he kept us out of war" who flocked to my meetings.

At Phoenix, Ariz., ten thousand metal miners stood packed in one solid mass for more than four hours and demanded that I go on and on, long after my regular lecture was finished. All the way to the Pacific Coast it was the same. As I traveled up the Coast I talked to great crowds of farmers, wobblies, lumberjacks and miners. At that time the capitalist newspapers were filled with lurid tales of I.W.W. "outrages," and the wobblies were being charged with burning lumber mills and threshing machines, firing forests and oilfields, destroying wheat and terrorizing women and peaceful workingmen.

All the way from the Oklahoma oilfields to the California beetfields, from there to Oregon and Washington forests and later to the Montana and Dakota wheat country I followed the will-o'-th-wisp of "wobbly outrages," but I never overtook it. The "outrage" always happened—not in the place where I chanced to be—but just over the county or state line. But when I too traveled over the line the "outrage" was just beyond.

I can understand now, just how dangerous and obnoxious we were to the plunderbund, we political prisoners who have been and are "doing time" in Federal prisons for the alleged "obstruction of the war," but in reality for the "crime" of telling the truth about war and profits. There were the I.W.W. boys, the Nonpartisan Leaguers and we Socialists, a "dangerous" lot of "damned agitators" who insisted on dragging out to the light of day the real cause of war. No wonder we landed behind the bars! The marvel is that more of us did not achieve that distinction. But time has demonstrated that the "espionage law" was not a war measure directed against the German Imperial government, but a war measure in the war between capital and labor. It never caught one single German spy, but it did catch many hundred active leaders of the labor movement, and the political prisoners are in prison not because they made war on the government, but because they made war on war profiteering.

'Gene Debs is in prison at Atlanta because the Democratic administration and the war profiteers who control it dared not leave him free to discuss war and profits with the common people who fight the wars and pay the profits. Debs is argus eyed: his understanding of the economic causes of war is crystal clear and the simple but dynamic language illuminates the minds of men as a great searchlight cleaves the blackness of the night. 'Gene Debs was arrested, tried, convicted and is serving his prison sentence. 'Gene knows, and told fearlessly the truth about war and the profits on coal and iron and ammunition and the thieves and grafters and war profiteers were forced to demand his imprisonment or have the camouflage of "patriotism" torn from their business.

The political prisoners from Oklahoma and the South are there because they knew and told the truth about war profiteering in foodstuffs and cotton. Joe Coldwell is in Atlanta because he knew and told the truth about the war profits on shoes, woolen textiles, and munitions, and the truth about war and profits is the one thing the Democratic party and the capitalist class dare not face in this campaign.

The Democratic administration and the capitalist press have strained every nerve to convince the voters that the political prisoners were sent to prison because they were "dangerous" to the country and "disloyal" to the government, but events have proven this claim a lie. We were "dangerous" only to the profiteers and "disloyal" only to the war mongers who fatten on the profits of war. If, as the administration claims, these political prisoners were "dangerous" only in time of war (and they have never claimed that we were dangerous at any other time), why are they still in prison? The war has been over almost two years and all danger has long since passed. The Democratic administration has never claimed that 'Gene Debs was a "criminal" being punished for a "crime." It claimed that he was a fanatic, dangerous in war time because of his pacifist beliefs, but harmless in peace. Why then is 'Gene Debs still in prison?

Why are hundreds of other political prisoners still in prison for the expression of opinions declared by the administration to be dangerous in war time but perfectly legitimate in peace? The war is over; peace has come. Why are political prisoners still in prison?

Every intelligent voter knows the answer. No political prisoner went to prison because he was an enemy of the United States, but he was an enemy of the capitalist class. 'Gene Debs is not in prison because he refused to serve his country; he is there because he did serve his country so valiantly by serving the working class so loyally; the contest between the political prisoners and the administration is not a war between traitorous, disloyal individuals and the government; it is a war between capital and labor.

The political prisoners will not be freed by the Democratic administration unless unbearable pressure is brought to bear by the people, because—while the war between the Imperial German government and the United States is over the world wide political struggle between capital and labor is still waging, and no human being is so dangerous, is so much feared and hated by capital as the laborer who has faced a prison cell in the defense of human liberty. This nation is a tinderbox of heartsick, disillusioned, plundered people that a spark of truth might kindle into a flame of revolt against the capitalist system that has drenched the world in blood while it wallowed in the filthy muck of war profiteering. This is the day when mankind is demanding a reckoning from political rulers and industrial despots and we Socialists are dangerous to them.

We are dangerous because we teach the already demonstrated truth that the capitalist system has broken down under the weight of its own limitations, and that a newer and more efficient system of production and distribution must take its place. Private ownership of the collectively used means of life can no longer adequately feed, clothe, shelter, educate and protect the masses of mankind. The capitalist system has failed to sustain an advancing civilization and plunged the race back into the barbarianism of a world war. If mankind is to be fed, clothed, sheltered, educated and protected; if civilization is to advance, private monopoly of the means of life must go. The people must own collectively used machinery of production and distribution and operate it by democratic industrial management.

We Socialists are dangerous to the capitalist class because we pin our faith to education and give the lie to their claim that we teach "violent revolution" by our endless campaign for intelligent, peaceful political action.

We Socialists are dangerous to the capitalist class because we know that no "radical minority" can ever inaugurate Socialism by "violence" and we are patient to carry on the slow, but sure, process of education. We knew we must have an educated majority with us before we can hope to gain the political power to take over the political management of our government and we must not only have the votes of the majority but the hearts as well that our political victories may be lasting. We must win the brains of the masses as well as the hearts that we may have the trained technical management of industry within our ranks when the day comes that we must manage the industries of the nation for the good of the whole people.

We want our political prisoners freed. We need their fire-tested loyalty to the working class; we need their broader vision and deeper spirituality that is the result of their prison experiences to help us meet in calmness and without bitterness the trying days that are ahead. But we know that inside or outside prison walls the voices of the political prisoners are being heard and that stone walls and steel bars cannot shut them from their appointed task of bringing the world to Socialism.

July 24, 1920

Dramatic Meeting of Kate O'Hare and Eugene V. Debs in Prison

In a visit full of dramatic incidents, Kate Richards O'Hare visited Eugene V. Debs in the Federal penitentiary in Atlanta on July 2, to carry to him the love of Socialists everywhere.

In a special message to his comrades, Debs said that while he deplored the recent differences between Socialist leaders, the rank and file is solidly behind the Socialist party. "The Socialist party," he said in effect, "is the organization through which they will win their freedom."

Kate O'Hare was ushered into the prison; the two comrades met and embraced; Kate Richards O'Hare recently freed from the Federal prison and Eugene V. Debs in prison garb with nine years of

prison life before him, with both his hands still upon her shoulders, said, "How happy I am to see you free, Kate." And—

And then smilingly he added. "Have you got used to being out yet?"

They then sat down facing each other across the table. It was a sun-baked afternoon and the rays of the sun filtered through the steel bars of the visitors' room of the Atlanta Federal penitentiary and illumined the features of Debs. He smiled a smile of joy to see his old friend free once again.

"Your coming here is like a new sunlight to me. Tell me about your prison experiences," said Debs. She answered, "'Gene, I am not thinking of myself, but of the little Mollie Steimer who now occupies my cell at Jefferson City and of her appalling sentence of fifteen years. She is a nineteen-year-old little girl, smaller in stature than my Kathleen, whose sole crime is her love for the oppressed."

As Debs listened to Kate relate the dramatic tale of this little child, his glasses became tear-stained and his face showed the emotion of his heart. When Kate asked him, "How long can you stand this imprisonment, 'Gene?" He replied, "I could stay here indefinitely; forever if necessary, as long as the cause needs me."

Then 'Gene told her how a few copies of her prison letters had drifted into the Atlanta penitentiary. "You know, I think that tale of Dick playing the cornet for you outside the prison walls was one of the most dramatic tales I ever read in all literature." The moment was tense, and for a second silence reigned; and then Kate O'Hare, recalling her son's prison serenade, could hardly control her mother emotions.

Then Kate opened her leather card-case and showed Debs her family group picture which she had carried with her during the fourteen months of prison life. The sight of that picture had afforded her much consolation through the hours of dreaded prison silence and monotony.

"'Gene, I shall present this to you with my autograph." "This is very beautiful of you," said Debs, "and I shall treasure this photo all of my days," and smilingly he added, "I shall hand it down as an heirloom."

Then they discussed the things closest to their hearts, the work of freeing the hundreds of political prisoners and furthering the cause of the Socialist movement.

Kate said, "In my lecture tour across the country, I find a greater crystallized Socialist sentiment than ever before. Great changes are imminent, and we are about to reap what we have sown, and although I find differences of opinion among the so-called leaders of the movement, I find the rank and file united."

Then Debs added what was really his message to his comrades. "This is no time for division. The rank and file will speak as they have never spoken before. Although some of my most dear friends, who are in the different factions and parties, who I know to be absolutely sincere, will some day realize that they are mistaken in their tactics, and they will discover that the Socialist party is best adapted for emancipating the American working class."

Kate O'Hare was accompanied on this visit by Frank P. O'Hare, her husband, and Attorney S. M. Castleton of Atlanta.

The visit was about to come to an end, and Debs said:

"Tell the comrades that I am well and my spirit is finer than ever before."

"Any special message, 'Gene?" asked Kate O'Hare.

"You know what is in my heart, Kate," he replied. "Yours is the voice of the voiceless, and with you out of prison we know that the message will be carried on."

The guard rose and twirled his club, and said, "Time's up."

With affectionate but sad farewell they parted, and as Kate O'Hare and the other comrades and visitors left, the tall, bent figure of Eugene V. Debs was lost in the file of the prisoners going to their mess.

July 24, 1920

Very few political cases concluded as fortunately or as instructively as Charles Krieger's 1920 trial in Oklahoma.

Palmerism in Oklahoma

New light was thrown on the methods of the Department of Justice in an incident occurring in the trial of Charles Krieger, at Tulsa, Okla., last week. Krieger, a working man, was acquitted of the charge of conspiring to dynamite the home of J. Edgar Pew, an executive of a Standard Oil Company subsidiary.

The "incident" was the disclosure at the trial that the chief witness against Krieger, Hubert Vowels, had been granted a pardon by the Department for his testimony. Vowels had been confined to the federal prison at Leavenworth for robbing a postoffice. He alleged on the witness stand that he had blown up the house in cooperation with Krieger.

The American Civil Liberties Union was able to obtain a certified copy of Vowel's pardon, granted by the Department of Justice. This was forwarded to the attorneys for the defense, who produced it on the stand. It led to Vowel's breakdown, and his admission that he had falsely accused Krieger and that he had been granted the pardon for his testimony. Two other so-called "coworkers" of Krieger, John Hall and Walter Remson, brought from Leavenworth, stated they had had nothing to do with the explosion or with Krieger, and that they had been offered pardons to testify against him. The jury returned a verdict of not guilty after two hours' deliberation.

July 10, 1920

As Upton Sinclair comments, John L. Murphy's letter has "the accent of truth" in it. The novel that Sinclair mentions is Jimmie Higgins, published in 1919.

The White Terror at Work

Upton Sinclair

Recently I published a novel dealing with the activities of spies and secret agents of big business. Our gracious Postoffice Department does not permit me to mention the name of this novel, otherwise this contribution will be considered as an advertisement. But here is a letter which has just come to me, and which you might take to be a chapter out of the aforesaid unnameable novel. Read it, and see how very proud of your country it makes you. I do not know the writer of this letter, but the accent of truth is in every word of his story, and what I have learned of hundreds of other cases, makes me quite ready to believe what he tells. If you know any 100 per cent American patriots in your neighborhood, take them this letter and try to get them to read it.

"Leavenworth, Kans., Feb. 13, 1921

"Mr. Upton Sinclair, Pasadena, Cal.

"Dear Comrade:

"Below I am sending you the facts of my case.

"I was born in Boston, the boasted cradle of Liberty. I am a working man, not a leech. In 1918 while working at Olympia, Wash., I wrote a letter to Chris Luber at Sacramento, Cal. He was an I.W.W. He was in jail at the time of my writing. This I did not know at the time. In fact he had been in jail almost two months before I wrote my first letter. My letter was the ordinary kind exchanged among workers—working conditions, etc. This letter was not delivered to Luber. The Department of Justice got it. They answered it and forged Luber's name to it. This letter was indeed very bitter against the government. I thought my friend Luber had gone 'bugs.' How was I to know that the Department of Justice agent was writing it to me? They had his name forged to the letter, and I did not know he was in jail at the time. They wound up by asking me to 'Pull off' something violent, just anything would do.

"I will now make it clear how they played the game. Unknown to me at the time, fifty-five I.W.W. working men were in jail at Sacramento,

Cal., and they wanted to get evidence to convict them. This is one of the games they played to get said evidence. They were willing to pay any price, and they cared not how they got it. In the letter I wrote to this 'agent,' I refused to agree to commit a crime, and I roundly scored this 'agent,' thinking I was scoring my working friend, Luber, for his d____d foolishness. Letter after letter came. Bribes, and big ones, pleas, offers, etc. I denounced such doctrine again and again. In those letters I would agree to the declarations that we were being run over by military hysteria, and that men were using the war frenzy to stifle legitimate discussion. Then I would denounce the writer for his plan to cure such things. Now, get the infamy of this trick. The parts of the letters which spoke of 'military hysteria,' and such terms were photographed so as to leave every declaration of my own out entirely. Then I was arrested, taken to Sacramento, Cal., and thrown in jail. The letters this forger wrote were secured and destroyed. I then found out my friend had received no letters from me, and knew nothing about any letter writing to me, as he had been in jail since December 5, 1917, and my first letter written to him was January, 1918. I then knew the characters England was employing to destroy American citizens, but I did not fear trial as I knew my own letters would clear me. Every scheme imaginable was resorted to in order to force me to lie on the men in jail. I was wined and dined at first; I was offered freedom and a goodly sum, to say something. I knew nothing, and I refused to be a perjurer. Then they tried threats and abuse. I told them I would spend my life in jail with clean hands, and my flag flying nailed to the mast, before I would place upon my heart the slime of perjury, and blood, and tears of innocent, helpless workers, whom I did not know anything about, much less anything against. That ended it. They feared to release me after what I had found out. Imagine my feeling when the trial day came for those workers, to find I was indicted with them.

"Then, if you can further imagine, do so, when

Promoting Another Fake Prize Fight

MAP OF THE NEAR EAST NATURAL RESOURCES CONCESSIONS PROFITS

FRENCH CAPITAL AMERICAN CAPITAL ITALIAN CAPITAL ENGLISH JAP

The big bosses privately planning another fight

FINISH FIGHT
CHRISTIAN RELIGION
ALIAS "HOLY LIGHT CHAMPION OF "CIVILIZED" NATIONS
VERSUS →
THE MOSLEM RELIGION
ALIAS "DEFENDER OF THE FAITH" — "TERRIBLE TURK" &C. &C.
RULES OF FIGHT AS REVISED BY THE LEAGUE OF NATIONS

As it will be advertised

Appeal to Reason, October 28, 1922.

I tell you that three or four short extracts from my letters were presented from photographic copies, so as to identify my handwriting, and these extracts, admissions of what had been sent me, and true in every word, yet torn out of all connection; and I was convicted and sentenced to a five-year term for 'espionage.' Since coming here not a mark or blemish has been put against me. I never had a mark or stain against my life, and have always worked for my bread. Yet, when I asked for parole, I was denied at Washington, not here. Counterfeiters, postoffice burglars, white slavers, and the worst kind of degenerates ever found, have been paroled, but not me. I can see now that I made a mistake asking for parole. Parole is for those who are guilty of some of the above crimes, while my only crime is that I have an opinion. I am a conscientious pacific Socialist and an I.W.W., that is all. I never gave any man or woman or child a moment's grief in my life. I have lived clean and honest. And as nearly as I can find out, I am in prison because a Department of Justice agent committed forgery on a worker in jail, abused the government, lied to me, and then failed to get me to carry out the crimes they were willing to pay me for. Only I did not fall to their level. That is why I am serving five years. Before the great Arbitrator, whose knowledge can weigh all truth, I swear that I write the truth. This is America too! I am not alone in blackened and ruined men here who have been honest. Do what you can. With all confidence in your honesty to the cause we are fighting for, I am

"Yours for Industrial Freedom,

"(Signed):

"John L. Murphy, Reg. No. 13586

"Leavenworth, Kans. P. O. Box 7

"P.S. Excuse this letter as my eyes bother me a great deal since I came here. It is the best I can do.

"Put my Reg. No. 13586 on address, if you write and it will prevent all chance of mistakes. I am not the only Murphy that has the honor of being in here.

"Respectfully,

"(Signed) John L. Murphy"

March 12, 1921

Many, many poems were written about Gene Debs. Sara Bard Field's poem suggests why.

To Eugene Debs

SARA BARD FIELD

A thousand centuries to come smile back on you.
Already, Debs, they gravely carve your seat
High on the rocks of Time where the defiant few
Of all the ages meet
And hold high converse to the beat
Of the stern sea below, drowning the millions
    who
Have crucified their Christs, nor ever knew
The bleeding brow and feet.

No, Debs, I cannot think of you in prison,
Although I know they hold your body there.
But always, as when you shot to me a vision,
Bending above the crowd whose hungry stare
Made you compassionate, and yet so wise
In your compassion. Rarely to a man
Is given the sensitive heart that feels Love's pain,
    the eyes
That hold Love's tears, and Mind to make the Plan
By which Love may appear in something more
Than merely sops and pity for the Poor.

We are the lonely ones—we who confess
The Truth that jailed you, but have not been
    found
Worthy to suffer for it. All brave loveliness
Of human life has taken camping ground
In cells like yours
And all the cowards and complaisant bores,
The cruel, selfish, dull and ignorant mass,
Are left outside with us who have no prison pass.

I like to think that long before you paid
The price of prison for the right to love,
You seemed to us like Jesus, and you made
Many a tale from ancient Galilee

Rise from the printed page in warm reality:
"Of such as these are the Kingdom of Heaven—"
You know that scene well, Debs, when Christ was
    given
The little children whom he loved; and knew
Must build what only Innocence can do—

Well, once in Cleveland, when I heard you speak,
I sat upon the platform with my little son
Upon my lap, and when your speech was done
You turned and laid your big hand on his cheek
And said, "My friend, such lads as this
Must finish what we old folks have begun—"
The crowd was surging round you but a kiss
You reverently gave him—Debs, that little lad
Cherished till death the words that you had said
And loved to think your hand had touched his
    head.

June 4, 1921

Both born in Italy, both anarchists, and both executed in the Massachusetts electric chair, Nicola Sacco and Bartolomeo Vanzetti remain martyrs of the post–World War I Red Scare. Their execution on August 23, 1927, was marked by mass demonstrations in the United States, Europe, and South America. Eugene Lyons was one of many who wrote poems, novels, plays, or nonfictional accounts about the Sacco and Vanzetti case. Born in Russia, he served as a news correspondent in the Soviet Union from 1928 to 1934, as an editor of the American Mercury, and lived a long, politically active life.

"We Are Innocent!"

EUGENE LYONS

When the verdict was read the younger of the two men in the cage jumped to his feet and pointing an accusing finger at the judge and jury cried, "We are innocent! You kill two innocent men!" He stood erect, unbeaten. A year of imprisonment, seven weeks of grueling trial, the deliberate melodrama of the stage-setting did not succeed in destroying the essential man. A straight, sympathetic young labor agitator to whom the idea of murder could not be attached without doing violence to one's sense of reality.

His wife, who had borne her sorrows with a courage expressive of her confidence in the man's innocence and the court's justice, listened for a moment without comprehending. She had been in court throughout the whole trial, sometimes with the baby in her arms, and was thoroughly satisfied that by no stretch of logic could a verdict of guilty be returned on the evidence presented. Others who had sat through the trial, newspapermen, police officers, members of the Civil Liberties Union, individuals interested in the fight against the frame-up system, shared her confidence in an acquittal.

When the woman realized the facts she shrieked and rushed to her husband. They were separated and the hysterical wife was taken home. Nicola Sacco and his fellow-defendant, Bartolomeo Vanzetti, were led to jail to await their fates. Judge Webster Thayer had blenched during the pronouncement but gradually recovered composure. On November 1 he will be sufficiently composed, no doubt, to sentence the men to death, despite the flimsiness of the case against them.

The trial took place in Dedham, Mass., and lasted almost seven weeks. Some sixty witnesses were brought into court by District Attorney Katzman to establish the facts that on the afternoon of April 15, 1920, the paymaster and guard of a shoe factory were killed and robbed in South Braintree; and the allegation that Sacco and Vanzetti were among the bandits. Ninety-seven witnesses countered the state's testimony and established the alibis of the accused men. The weight of evidence was so overwhelmingly in the men's favor that the verdict came like a shock.

It was no ordinary murder trial. No more than the [Tom] Mooney trial or the Everett, Wash., [IWW] trial were ordinary. The class issue had been brought into the case from the first, and was not to be eliminated even when the prosecution for its own purposes decided to do so. Sacco and Vanzetti were leaders among the Italian workers in the shoe factories of New England; this one circumstance stood out above all others. They were "agitators," social heretics, the sort of people who, according to modern folk lore, were capable of horrible crimes, even if they hadn't committed this one.

As in the Mooney case, it resolved into a question of identity. And on that question the men were exonerated. The state "identification" had all the ear-marks of fraudulent testimony, a strange certitude about one or two damning details and infinite vagueness in regard to all others. In a few cases witnesses developed inexplicable rehabilitation of memory, after having denied the identification in preliminary hearings or in statements to the defense lawyers. Men and women brought into court by the prosecution itself, but carefully shielded from questions about identity, admitted under cross-examination that they had seen neither Sacco nor Vanzetti on the murder scene.

In most cases these witnesses had been in a better position to observe the bandits than those who "recognized" the defendants.

The defense witnesses, on the contrary, were consistent and unimpeachable. There was Frank Burke, lecturer, who happened to be on the spot, who was shot at by the fleeing bandits, who saw the guilty men closer than any other, and asserted positively that Sacco and Vanzetti were not among them. There was Mrs. Barbara Liscomb, an honest hard-working woman, upon whom the tragedy made such an impression that she "will remember always," but she is certain she did not see Sacco and Vanzetti. There were two dozen others.

At the hour of the crime Sacco was in the Italian consolate in Boston, getting passports for himself and his family. The clerk in office remembers the fact and has testified to it. Nine others testified to having seen him at places other than South Braintree. The alibi of Vanzetti was also ironbound; he was selling fish in Plymouth at the time.

Failing to make a case of it on the evidence, the prosecution sought to establish "consciousness of guilt." At the time the two men were arrested they lied about their movements of that evening. They had good cause to do so, in view of the circumstances that their friend Andrea Salsedo had been found dead mysteriously under the window at the Department of Justice in New York the day before, and further that all the questions put to them were about their radical beliefs. They had gone to collect "literature" as a precaution against an expected raid, and had no desire to get their friends into trouble by telling everything about their evening's movements. To explain their attitude it was necessary to confess to the jury that the defendants were radicals. The state knew it and left the task to the defense.

The one thing that approximates convincing testimony was the effort of the prosecution to prove that one of the bullets in the body of a victim had come from a gun belonging to Sacco. It brought experts into court to make its point. In the defense case, however, two other experts, both of high note, explained that the bullet might have come from any of several other guns.

The story is not quite told. The defense has received a new impetus since the day of the verdict. Many had withheld their cooperation in the ingenuous belief that Sacco and Vanzetti would be freed because there was no proof connecting them in any wise with the murder. Now they know better. They know that there is no such thing as the presumption of innocence when labor men are being tried. They know that the powers are ready to go to the limit to clear undesirables out of the way, whether they do it by electrocution for a crime of which the men are innocent or by permitting a mob to wreak an ignorant vengeance.

August 13, 1921

Eugene Debs's release from Atlanta prison on Christmas Day, 1921, was a cause for celebration for millions of American working people. This account was written by David Karsner, a staff writer for the socialist New York Call *and later a biographer of Debs.*

2,300 Convicts Roar Great Farewell as Debs Leaves

"Remember, boys," Debs said as he went to the warden's office Sunday morning (the morning of his release), "my address is just Eugene Debs, Terre Haute, Ind., and I'm your friend if you ever need me."

From the office he went to the warden's home, where he had breakfast with Warden Dyche and his brother, Theodore Debs. After the breakfast it was announced that Debs would once more be taken back to the jail. Instead he was smuggled out of the gates and hurried, together with his brother and one or two friends to the station. There Debs created his own surprise, taking the train for Washington, instead of the one for Terre Haute.

It was an enthusiastic Christmas party that gathered about him on the station platform. The joy of Theodore Debs was irrepressible. Sam'l Castleton, district attorney, made no attempt to conceal his feeling of pleasure. The news correspondents, almost all of whom Debs counts among his friends, caught the spirit of the occasion.

"I am going to Washington," Debs declared as he stood on the station platform here, his face turned away from home and the Christmas welcome awaiting him there, "to confer with Attorney General Daugherty regarding a condition of my release which I cannot now divulge." Then he added:

"It is a matter about which I am not at liberty to speak now," he told reporters at the Atlanta terminal.

"After that I am going to my wife in Terre Haute as fast as the train will take me."

No man in this country ever received such a farewell tribute as Debs got when the steel bars of the prison closed behind him.

At every barred window of the prison stood groups of convicts this Christmas Day, 2,300 men, and when the tall figure of Debs was seen to get into the warden's automobile there was a roar from the throats of these men that could be heard for blocks.

Moving-picture camera men and press photographers were admitted to the prison gate at the request of Debs himself, and for 10 minutes America's foremost citizen posed for pictures. During all of this time the prisoners behind the bars yelled and screamed their hail and farewell.

Debs repeatedly turned around and waved his hat to them as tears rolled down the furrows of his face. It was the most dramatic and tragic farewell any man could receive from those who love him, and these were convicts.

Then the run was made to the Southern Railroad Terminal in the warden's car, which was driven by "Lefty" Graves, a prisoner, who an hour before had taken Joseph M. Coldwell, Rhode Island Socialist, to the station. The sentence of Coldwell was ended with that of Debs, and he, too, received a roaring farewell from the imprisoned men who had been his companions since the fall of 1919. Coldwell waved his hat to the men in prison blue and to the regiment of reporters and photographers at the gate.

At the terminal of the Southern Railroad, Debs was met by his brother, Theodore, who had been sent ahead, and a crowd of local friends and reporters. An old station agent shoved his way through the throng and grabbed Debs by the arm.

"Let me shake the hand of a full grown man," said the railroader. At that moment Debs had his arms around the neck of "Lefty" Graves, the con-

vict, whose eyes were eloquent with tears.

"Old scout, you're a railroader," said Debs swinging his long arm back to get a firm grip on the man's hand. The railroader's face twitched and he tried to say something. Gene flung his arms around the man's neck and kissed him.

A reporter approached with a pertinent inquiry.

"I can't tell you why it is necessary for me to go to Washington," said Debs.

He said he was feeling "like a young goat on a tin roof" and full of fight.

"The second part of my life is just beginning," said Debs to friends who were now surrounding him. "You know I have just graduated from a college where I got full tuition, and I am better equipped now to continue my work than before I was admitted to college."

"What are your plans for the future, Mr. Debs?" asked a newspaperman.

"To give every drop of blood in my body to the cause that embraces the working class," Debs replied.

Reporters fired specific questions of every nature at Debs, who smiled and gave general answers to all of them.

The Christmas throngs at the station soon realized that Eugene Debs was among them. Mothers sent their children to shake his hand and Debs kissed them. Men in all walks of life came forward to greet and to wish him a Merry Christmas. The start was made for the train, which was due to leave at 12:30 p.m. Photographers pursued the party and Debs again posed for pictures. Just before he boarded the train Debs ran up ahead of the engine. The engineer was examining his locomotive, oil cup in hand.

"My name is Debs," said Gene, gripping the big palm of the engineer.

"No, go on! You're kidding."

"Yes, this is I," said Debs.

"By Jesus, you're the greatest man in the country," said the engineer. "I'll take care of you, all right."

The day coach was packed, and most of the passengers had taken their seats before Debs reached the station. Even now, most of the passengers on this train do not know that Debs is aboard.

Debs is clothed in a suit of mixed material given to him in the prison. An overcoat that is too short for his long frame and a soft black felt hat completes his outer attire.

"Tell the comrades that I greet them with my love and I salute them for the loyalty they have shown toward me while I have been in prison."

Debs took a day coach to Washington. The "excess" fare saved by avoiding a Pullman, he said, he will devote to the fund for the relief of the starving in Soviet Russia.

January 7, 1922

Ralph Chaplin's poems speak of the pain and loneliness of prison; they also tell about the conviction and courage of the men and women who dared to resist World War I.

Song of Separation

RALPH CHAPLIN

Two that I love must live alone,
    Far away.
All in the world I can call my own,
    Only they.
Mother and boy in the rocking chair,
Thinking of one who cannot be there,
Breathing a hope that is half a prayer;
    Night and day, night and day.

Here in my cell I must sit alone,
    clothed in grey.
Bars of iron and walls of stone
    Bid me stay.
What of the world with its pomp and
    show?
Baubles of nothing! This I know:
Deep in my heart I miss them so
    Night and day, night and day.

The Industrial Heretics

RALPH CHAPLIN

They say we are revolters—that we stirred
The workers of all nations to rebel—
And that we would not compromise with Hell,
But damned it with our every deed and word.
They feared us as we faced them undeterred
And gave us each a coffin of a cell
In this steel cave where living corpses dwell—
Hate-throttled here that we might not be heard.

We are those fools too stubborn-willed to bend
Our necks to Wrong and parley and discuss.
Today we face the awful test of fire—
The prison, gallows, cross—but in the end
Your sons will call your children after us
And name their dogs from men you now admire!

June 10, 1922

Notes

Chapter 1

1. John Dos Passos, *The 42nd Parallel* (New York: Signet, 1969), 79–80.

2. George Allan England, *The Story of the Appeal* (Fort Scott, Kans.: n.p., 1915), p. 22. England was hired by Fred Warren early in 1913 to write a history of the *Appeal*.

3. England, *Story of the Appeal*, 24; J. A. Wayland, *Leaves of Life* (Girard: *Appeal to Reason*, 1912), 23.

4. Howard H. Quint, *The Forging of American Socialism* (New York: Bobbs Merrill, 1964), 180. Quint's study of Wayland's *Coming Nation* and early *Appeal* years is a fine one.

5. Wayland, *Leaves of Life*, 28.

6. Elliott Shore, "Talkin' Socialism: Julius A. Wayland, Fred D. Warren and Radical Publishing, 1890–1914" (Ph.D. diss., Bryn Mawr College, 1984), 237.

7. Quint, *Forging of American Socialism*, 190.

8. See Shore, "Talkin' Socialism," 66–67. Shore gives too exclusive credit to Fred Warren for the *Appeal*'s responses to early twentieth-century realities, but my account benefits from his discussion.

9. *Coming Nation*, August 3, 1895, quoted in Shore, "Talkin' Socialism," 67.

10. *Appeal to Reason*, December 8, 1906.

11. England, *Story of the Appeal*, 36.

12. For the chiliastic interpretation of American socialism, see Daniel Bell, *Marxian Socialism in the United States* (Princeton: Princeton University Press, 1967), 5–7.

13. James R. Green, "The 'Salesmen-Soldiers' of the *Appeal* Army: A Profile of Rank-and-File Socialist Agitators," in *Socialism and the Cities*, ed. Bruce Stave (Port Washington, N.Y.: Kennikat, 1975), 33 and *passim*.

14. England, *Story of the Appeal*, 141.

15. *Appeal to Reason*, March 10, 1906.

16. For a fine, detailed account of the *Appeal* Army, see Green, "The 'Salesmen-Soldiers' of the *Appeal* Army."

17. *Appeal to Reason*, November 22, 1913.

18. Quoted in England, *Story of the Appeal*, 167.

19. *Appeal to Reason*, November 23, 1912.

20. *Haldeman-Julius Weekly*, November 11, 1922.

Chapter 2

1. *Webster's International Dictionary*, quoted in W. J. Ghent, comp., *The Appeal Almanac of Facts for 1915* (Girard, Kans.: *Appeal to Reason*, 1915), 33.

2. First Regular Message, quoted in *The Appeal Almanac*, 9, 136.

3. *Appeal to Reason*, September 2, 1916.

4. *Industrial Relations: Final Report and Testimony Submitted to Congress by the Commission on Industrial Relations, Created by the Act of August 23, 1912, 64th Cong., 1st Sess., Doc. 415* (Washington: GPO, 1916), I, 1, 33.

5. Joyce L. Kornbluh, ed. *Rebel Voices* (Ann Arbor: University of Michigan Press, 1969), 12–13.

6. Ira Kipnis, *The American Socialist Movement, 1897–1912* (New York: Columbia University Press, 1952), 192.

7. Mari Jo Buhle, *Women and American Socialism, 1870–1920* (Urbana: University of Illinois Press, 1981). Buhle's study is as rich conceptually and methodologically as it is rich in important conclusions.

8. David McLellan, ed. *Karl Marx: Selected Writings* (Oxford, England: Oxford University Press, 1977), 223.

9. "Women and the Industrial Revolution," *Appeal to Reason*, December 13, 1902.

10. *Appeal to Reason*, February 20, 1904.

11. *Appeal to Reason*, December 23, 1911.

12. Samuel P. Hayes, *The Response to Industrialism, 1885–1914* (Chicago: University of Chicago Press, 1957), 95.

13. Quoted in Thomas R. Brooks, *Toil and Trouble: A History of American Labor* (New York: Dell, 1964), 76.

14. Kipnis, *American Socialist Movement*, 278–79.

15. Ibid., 287.

16. Oakley C. Johnson, *Marxism in United States History Before the Russian Revolution* (New York: Humanities Press, 1974), 73–74.

17. David A. Shannon, *The Socialist Party of America* (Chicago: Quadrangle Books, 1955), 52.

18. Johnson, *Marxism in United States History,* 75. As an indication of the power of orthodox materialist theory, Debs saw no contradiction in adding: "We have nothing special to offer the Negro, and we cannot make separate appeals to all the races."

19. Johnson, *Marxism in United States History,* 83.

20. *Appeal to Reason*, September 12, 1903.

21. *Appeal to Reason*, July 23, 1921.

Chapter 3

1. *Industrial Relations: Final Report and Testimony*, I, 21. Even apart from the testimony taken by the Commission, this *Final Report* is a rich source of social and economic life for the period.

2. Thomas C. Cochran and William Miller, *The Age of Enterprise: A Social History of Industrial America* (New York: Harper, 1961), 190–94.

3. *Industrial Relations: Final Report and Testimony*, I, 33.

4. Matthew Josephson, *The Politicos, 1865–1896* (New York: Harcourt, Brace, 1938), 344, and William White, *Masks in a Pageant* (New York: Macmillan, 1928), 79. Quoted in Cochran and Miller, *The Age of Enterprise,* 163.

5. *Industrial Relations: Final Report and Testimony*, I, 59.

6. Ibid., 34.

7. Cochran and Miller, *Age of Enterprise,* 230.

8. *History of Labor in the United States*, III, 366, quoted in Cochran and Miller, *Age of Enterprise,* 231.

9. *Industrial Relations: Final Report and Testimony*, I, 43.

10. Ibid., 20–24. As for the amount necessary to support a family modestly in 1915, the *Final Report* observes: "In the highest paid occupations among wage earners, such as railroad engineers and conductors, glass blowers, certain steel-mill employees, and a few of the building trades, the income will range from $1,500 to $2,000 at best, ignoring a few exceptional men who are paid for personal qualities. Such an income means, under present-day conditions, a fair living for a family of moderate size, education of the children through high school, a small insurance policy, a bit put by for a rainy day—and nothing more. With unusual responsibilities or misfortunes, it is too little, and the pinch of necessity is keenly felt." *Final Report*, I, 30–31.

11. Ibid., 21.

12. "Revolution," in *London's Essays of Revolt*, ed. Leonard Abbott (New York: Vanguard Press, 1928), 114–15. Various sections from London's essay appeared in the *Appeal* over the years.

13. For a provocative discussion of the meaning and significance of class, see E. P. Thompson, "Eighteenth-Century English Society: Class Struggle Without Class," *Social History* 3 (May 1978), 146–50.

14. *Appeal to Reason*, January 27, 1917.

15. *Appeal to Reason*, July 3, 1909.

Chapter 4

1. Oscar Ameringer, *If You Don't Weaken: The Autobiography of Oscar Ameringer* (New York: Henry Holt, 1940), 257.

2. Richard Hofstadter, *The Age of Reform* (New York: Vintage, 1955), 25–27.

3. Henry Nash Smith, *Virgin Land: The American West as Symbol and Myth* (New York: Vintage, 1950), 228.

4. These figures are found in Fred A. Shannon, *The Farmer's Last Frontier: Agriculture, 1860–1897* (New York: Farrar & Rinehart, 1945), 51–55, 72. Noting that the total acreage obtained by the railroads could not be determined until 1938, Shannon (64–65) puts the final figure at 183,000,000. The *Appeal's* 200,000,000 acres reflected the best estimates available at the time. Many railroads did not comply with the terms of their charters and some of their acreage grants were canceled or reduced.

5. Ibid., 295, 298, 175–76.

6. Shannon, 78, 184; Lawrence Goodwyn, *Democratic Promise: The Populist Moment in America* (New York: Oxford University Press, 1976), 27. Goodwyn's superbly rendered examination of populism is a model of historical inquiry.

7. *Appeal to Reason*, January 28, 1899.

8. *Appeal to Reason*, August 13, 1904.

9. James R. Green, *Grass-Roots Socialism: Radical Movement in the Southwest, 1895–1943* (Baton Rouge: Louisiana State University Press, 1978), 128.

10. Ibid., 81; Shannon, *Socialist Party of America*, 35–36.

Chapter 5

1. Shannon, *Socialist Party of America*, 8. For a much more complete view of Socialist diversity, see Shannon, 8–61.

2. Ibid., 5.

3. James Weinstein, "The Problems of the Socialist Party," in *Failure of a Dream? Essays in the History of American Socialism*, eds. John H. M. Laslett and Seymour Martin Lipset (New York: Anchor Books, 1974), 313–15.

4. "The Socialist Vote in the 1917 Municipal Elections," *National Municipal Review* VI (March 1918); see also James Weinstein, *The Decline of Socialism in America, 1912–1925* (New York: Monthly Review Press, 1967), 119–76.

5. Quoted in Charles Stephenson, "A Gathering of Strangers? Mobility, Social Structure, and Political Participation in the Formation of Nineteenth-Century American Workingclass Culture," in *American Workingclass Culture: Explorations in American Labor and Social History*, ed. Milton Cantor (Connecticut: Greenwood Press, 1979), 36.

6. Ameringer, *If You Don't Weaken*, 267. No one interested in the early years of American socialism should fail to read Ameringer's autobiography.

7. *New Appeal*, January 11, 1919.

Chapter 7

1. Michael E. R. Bassett, "The Socialist Party of America, 1912–1919: Years of Decline" (Ph.D. diss., Duke University, 1964), 70.

2. William Appleman Williams, *The Tragedy of American Diplomacy* (New York: Dell, 1962), 17.

3. Ibid., 26.

4. Ibid., 66.

5. Ibid., 78–79.

6. *Philadelphia Public Ledger*, December 9, 1915.

7. *Washington Herald*, December 11, 1915.

8. *New Appeal*, May 18, 1918.

9. Andrew N. Cothran, "The Little Blue Book Man and the Big American Parade: A Biography of Emanuel Haldeman-Julius" (Ph.D. diss., University of Maryland, 1966), 90.

10. Nick Salvatore, *Eugene V. Debs: Citizen and Socialist* (Urbana: University of Illinois Press, 1982), 289.

Chapter 8

1. For a sophisticated discussion of these issues see Murray B. Levin, *Political Hysteria in America: The Dem-*ocratic Capacity for Repression (New York: Basic Books, 1971).

2. Robert K. Murray, *Red Scare: A Study in National Hysteria, 1919–1920* (St. Paul: University of Minnesota Press, 1955), 13–14.

3. Donald Johnson, *The Challenge to American Freedoms: World War I and the Rise of the American Civil Liberties Union* (Kentucky: University of Kentucky Press, 1963), 56–57. Burleson, for example, omitted "*willfully* obstruct recruiting or enlistment service" from his directive. Nor did the Espionage Act include "*embarrass . . . the Government in conducting the war.*"

4. Murray, *Red Scare*, 14.

5. Johnson, *Challenge to American Freedoms*, 61.

6. Ibid., 93.

7. Shannon, *Socialist Party of America*, 113.

8. Jean Y. Tussey, ed. *Eugene V. Debs Speaks* (New York: Pathfinder Press, 1970), 260, 275.

9. *New Appeal*, January 11, 1919.

10. Loren Baritz, ed. *The American Left: Radical Political Thought in the Twentieth Century* (New York: Basic Books, 1971), 125.

11. Johnson, *Challenge to American Freedoms*, 178.

12. Murray, *Red Scare*, 129–30.

13. Ibid., 143.

14. Johnson, *Challenge to American Freedoms*, 65.

15. Ibid., 119.

16. *Strangers in the Land: Patterns of American Nativism* (New York: Atheneum, 1968), 232. Quoted by Levin, 85–86.

17. Johnson, *Challenge to American Freedoms*, 184.

Index